FRENCH ART DECO

FRENCH ART DECO

JARED GOSS

THE METROPOLITAN MUSEUM OF ART, NEW YORK

Distributed by Yale University Press, New Haven

This publication is made possible by the Mary C. and James W. Fosburgh Publications Fund and the Samuel I. Newhouse Foundation, Inc.

Published by The Metropolitan Museum of Art, New York
Mark Polizzotti, Publisher and Editor in Chief
Gwen Roginsky, Associate Publisher and General Manager of Publications
Peter Antony, Chief Production Manager
Michael Sittenfeld, Managing Editor
Robert Weisberg, Senior Project Manager

Edited by Emily Radin Walter
Designed by Susan Marsh
Production by Sally Van Devanter
Bibliography and notes edited by Jean Wagner
Image acquisitions and permissions by Josephine Rodriguez-Massop
Translations from the French by Jane Marie Todd

Photographs of works in the collection of The Metropolitan Museum of Art are by Joseph Coscia Jr., The Photograph Studio, The Metropolitan Museum of Art.
Additional photography credits appear on page 270.

Typeset in Fournier, New Fournier, Neutraface, and Meta Pro
Printed on 150 gsm Galerie Art Volume
Separations by Trifolio Srl, Verona, Italy
Printed and bound by Trifolio Srl, Verona, Italy

JACKET ILLUSTRATION: Jean Dupas and Charles Champigneulle, *The Chariot of Poseidon* (detail), 1934 (no. 22)

The Metropolitan Museum of Art
1000 Fifth Avenue
New York, New York 10028
metmuseum.org

Distributed by
Yale University Press, New Haven
yalebooks.com/art

Library of Congress Cataloging-in-Publication Data
Goss, Jared.
 French art deco / Jared Goss.
   p. cm.
This publication is based on "Masterpieces of French Art Deco," an installation organized by Associate Curator Jared Goss, presented at the Museum from August 2009 through January 2011, in which more than 150 works demonstrated the range and depth of the Metropolitan's holdings.
 Includes bibliographical references and index.
ISBN 978-1-58839-525-2 (Metropolitan Museum of Art) — ISBN 978-0-300-20430-8 (Yale University Press) 1. Metropolitan Museum of Art (New York, N.Y.)—Catalogs. 2. Art deco—France—Catalogs. 3. Art—New York (State)—New York—Catalogs. I. Metropolitan Museum of Art (New York, N.Y.) II. Title.
N6848.5.A77M48 2014
709.44'0747471—dc23
                                        2014015621

CONTENTS

DIRECTOR'S FOREWORD

French Art Deco is one of the great strengths of the Metropolitan's modern design collection. The Museum has been actively collecting in this area since the 1920s, when works were acquired directly from their designers and makers in Paris. Over the past nine decades, the collection has grown—in great part thanks to the generosity of many donors—to form one of the finest such collections in any public institution. This publication is based on "Masterpieces of French Art Deco," an installation organized by Associate Curator Jared Goss, presented at the Museum from August 2009 through January 2011, in which more than 150 works demonstrated the range and depth of the Metropolitan's holdings.

For centuries, the combined mastery of craft and design—the product of strict guild training—brought international recognition and renown to French designers, especially those involved with the luxury trades. The shift to industrial production in the nineteenth century was widely perceived as resulting in lowered standards in both craftsmanship and design. A return to the earlier traditions as the most effective way to regain pre-eminence in the decorative arts was urged by the community of French Art Deco designers. By raising standards to former levels, French decorative arts would again be considered the best of their kind, and Paris would regain its past reputation as the style capital of the world.

Each object in this catalogue was conceived to stand apart, to be exceptional, and each must therefore be understood as a statement of connoisseurship, setting forth its validity as a work of art through the beauty of its form, the richness of its materials, and the elegance of its embellishment. Most of them remind us that it is not necessary to reject history or tradition in order to be contemporary, that indeed one of the most effective ways to be modern is to build on the solid foundation of what has come before. By looking to and learning from the past, French Art Deco designers were able to invent a style that addressed the present and informed the future, creating a new aesthetic suited to life in the modern world. A wholly original style, French Art Deco continues to resonate with and shape present-day taste much as it did in its own time.

Craftsmanship combined with artistry, and a strong connection to a national patrimony, are the characteristics that define French Art Deco. They are also characteristics that give these objects a very special place in an encyclopedic art museum. We are grateful to the Mary C. and James W. Fosburgh Publications Fund and the Samuel I. Newhouse Foundation, Inc., for their support in bringing this material to the public.

THOMAS P. CAMPBELL
Director
The Metropolitan Museum of Art

ACKNOWLEDGMENTS

"Masterpieces of French Art Deco," an installation on view at The Metropolitan Museum of Art from August 2009 through January 2011, presented the rare opportunity to mount a large-scale display of nearly 150 important works of Art Deco from the collection; most of the objects had not been seen by the public for many years. In organizing the installation, it became readily apparent to me that there was a great deal to be discovered about this material and much research to be done. And so I got to work. This book represents the fruit of that labor. It could not have been realized without the considerable contributions of many individuals, both within the Metropolitan Museum and without.

First and foremost, I thank the Museum's director, Thomas P. Campbell, for his support of this project from its inception. Similarly, I thank Gary Tinterow, formerly of the Metropolitan Museum and current Director of the Museum of Fine Arts, Houston, for his early championing of both the installation and this subsequent publication. His successor, Sheena Wagstaff, Leonard A. Lauder Chairman of the Department of Modern and Contemporary Art, graciously allowed the book to be seen through to completion.

Fundamental to the project has been the participation of photographer Joseph Coscia Jr. and the book's editor, Emily Radin Walter. Joe's innate understanding of the decorative arts enabled him to capture in his extraordinary images not only the beauty and materiality, but the very essence of the works. Words are almost unnecessary with such photographs as his. Emily, however, managed to brilliantly transform my awkwardly composed manuscript into something not only intelligible but fully equal to the gorgeous photographs. It was my great good fortune to have had the opportunity to work with both these individuals, whom I consider not only two of the most important contributors to the book but also my friends.

Numerous discoveries—in particular, new attributions for several works—were the result of indefatigable research conducted by Alison Charny, Elizabeth De Rosa, and Marilyn Friedman. Their contributions form the backbone of this book, and are all the more significant and deserving of thanks because all three gave of their time and effort freely, as volunteers. It is nearly impossible to express the extent of my gratitude to them. I also thank Terry Ryan, who was a key part of the research team in the early days of the project. Research would not have been possible without the vast resources of the Metropolitan's Thomas J. Watson Library. The entire library staff was of enormous help throughout the project; I especially appreciate the enthusiastic support and assistance of Ken Soehner and Holly Phillips. I am indebted to Barbara File in Archives, whose extensive knowledge of the institution's long and complicated history provided answers to innumerable questions that arose during the project, especially those concerning the Museum's history of collecting French Art Deco. The contributions of many Museum conservators and research scientists have proven crucial as well. In particular, I thank Drew Anderson, Mecka Baumeister, Nancy Britton, Federico Carò, Daniel Hausdorf, Jan Hempelmann, Kristine Kamiya, Rachel Mustalish, Lisa Pilosi, Sherman Fairchild Conservator in Charge of Objects Conservation, Kendra Roth, and Florica Zaharia. I also thank Melinda Watt, Giovanna Fiorino-Iannace, and their team in the Metropolitan's Antonio Ratti Textile Center. In the Museum's Photograph Studio, I thank Barbara Bridgers for her steadfast support, and am grateful for the technical expertise of Einar Brendalen and Thomas Ling.

The help of many within the Department of Modern and Contemporary Art has also been invaluable. Specifically, I thank Christel Hollevoet-Force for her assistance with making sense of the dense, florid, and often inscrutable prose of 1920s French

critics and writers. I thank Catherine Brodsky and Rebecca Tilghman for their proficient record keeping and expert administrative assistance. The departmental technicians — Tony Askin, Jeff Elliott, Sandie Peters, and Brooks Shaver — must be acknowledged for their unfailingly careful handling of artworks. Perhaps most important has been the involvement of Cynthia Iavarone, who managed to keep under control all the practical aspects of this project from start to finish, which she did with the effectiveness of a valued colleague but also the good humor and eternal patience of a longtime friend.

In great part, this book is the product of the Museum's Editorial Department. Above all, I thank Mark Polizzotti for his constant enthusiasm and encouragement in all stages of its development and realization. I thank Gwen Roginsky, Michael Sittenfeld, and Elizabeth Zechella for guiding me through the process in a timely and painless manner. Peter Antony and Sally Van Devanter are responsible for the sumptuousness and accuracy of the color and black-and-white reproductions, and to them I extend my heartfelt appreciation. I gratefully acknowledge the considerable contributions of Jean Wagner and Jude Calder for their meticulous work on the notes and bibliography. I appreciate the exhaustive sleuthing by Jane Tai and Josephine Rodriguez-Massop in obtaining rights and reproductions, and the most helpful translations of Jane Marie Todd. To Susan Marsh I am especially indebted, for her elegant and sympathetic design, which brings to life the very essence of French Art Deco.

Many individuals outside the Metropolitan Museum have contributed to the project as well, offering information, advice, translations, and expertise on numerous other fronts. Specifically, I thank R. Louis Bofferding, Michaela Lerch (of Baccarat), Holland Lynch, Rui Macieira, Hideki Maikuma, John A. Moore, Philip Reeser, and Terry Wendell (of Prelle et Cie).

I must also acknowledge the long encouragement of two revered mentors: Lee Hunt Miller and the late J. Stewart Johnson. Together, over many years, they supplied me with all the tools necessary for realizing not only this book but, more important, my full potential as a museum professional.

Finally, I dedicate this book to my beloved parents, Richard and Michèle Goss, without whose continued support on every level none of this would ever have happened.

JARED GOSS

ix

FRENCH ART DECO

FRENCH ART DECO: AN OVERVIEW

What is Art Deco? For some it is a bob-haired flapper in a short fringed dress, bedecked in jewels by Cartier; for others it is the powerful, syncopated forms of New York skyscrapers or the streamlined façades of Miami and Bombay; still others think of the stylish swank of 1930s Hollywood movies or the glamour of the great ocean liners. The early twentieth-century impulse to create "modern" design — objects and environments suited to life in a fast-paced industrialized world — was broad-ranging and international and led to the development of countless expressions, all of which today fall under the rubric of Art Deco.[1] But because this impulse touched everything from luxury goods to machinery, just how meaningful a term is it?

Art Deco is commonly referred to as a "style," a designation that suggests specific shared characteristics. The diversity of expression, however, precludes conceptual unity. More accurate, perhaps, would be "movement" or "idiom," both of which connote a general philosophy or point of view. To understand Art Deco as a style, one must instead look to a more focused and coherent expression. And nowhere did Art Deco emerge more coherently than in France.[2]

The *style moderne*, as it became known in France during its development in the 1910s and 1920s, reached its zenith at the great Exposition Internationale des Arts Décoratifs et Industriels Modernes, which was held in Paris in the summer of 1925. It is testament to the shared vision of the designers whose works were exhibited that the fair's name — albeit in abbreviated form — has since come both to define French design of the period and to be used as an umbrella label for the vast range of design and architecture created globally between the First and Second World Wars. Accordingly, France may be considered the symbolic — if not the actual — birthplace of the larger Art Deco movement.

Origins

The narrative of French Art Deco was firmly established by the time of the 1925 Paris Exposition, formed in large part by the designers, museum professionals, and academics who had helped shape the style itself. In books and newspaper and magazine articles, they defined Art Deco's characteristics and explained its philosophy, noting that it was distinct from manifestations of the movement in other countries by its embrace of its national past as the intellectual point of departure for creating something new. While designers elsewhere often rejected earlier aesthetics, materials, and manufacturing techniques, French designers sought innovation by embracing history. Specifically, the roots of French Art Deco are to be found in the ancien régime — the political and social system of France before the Revolution of 1789 — and its time-honored traditions of apprenticeship and guild training. During the eighteenth century, France established itself in the forefront of the luxury trades, producing furniture, porcelain, glass, metalwork, and textiles (not to mention clothing, perfume, wines, and cuisine) of unsurpassed refinement and elegance. Indeed, Paris became what could be considered the style capital of the Western world.

The French Revolution abolished the guilds, and by the end of the reign of Louis-Philippe in 1848, most guild-trained craftsmen had either died or stopped working. The decline of the artisan coincided with the rise of the Industrial Revolution, when handcraftsmanship was replaced to a great degree by machine

L. H. Boileau. Porte d'Orsay, Exposition Internationale des Arts Décoratifs et Industriels Modernes, Paris, 1925

production and work-for-hire industrial designers who generally had little expertise as craftsmen. The rise of the middle class, many of whom had no direct knowledge of handmade objects, also led to a lowering in the standards of connoisseurship. Because there was no point of reference, affordable machine-made objects were generally considered perfectly satisfactory.[3] Manufacturers began to reproduce old models using new technology rather than to develop new models that expressed innovative methods of production. A sense of decline prevailed.

Several events led to a reinvigoration of the decorative arts toward the end of the nineteenth century. The Union Centrale des Arts Décoratifs was founded in 1882, an amalgamation of the historical collections of the Société du Musée des Arts Décoratifs with the Union Centrale des Beaux-Arts Appliqués à l'Industrie, a focused research library and teaching institution. The École Royale Spéciale de Dessin (founded in 1765) was reorganized in 1877 as the École Nationale des Arts Décoratifs, a school that offered specialized classes in applied arts and design. And the newly founded Société d'Encouragement à l'Art et à l'Industrie in 1889 opened the École Boulle, which offered theoretical and practical training in furniture design.[4] These organizations would continue to operate throughout the Art Deco era, raising aesthetic awareness and technical expertise in the applied arts.

"Happily, the sap was not exhausted," wrote Léon Deshairs, curator of the library of the Musée des Arts Décoratifs, in 1925. "The spirit of research and invention reappeared between 1889 and 1900."[5] These were the years that saw the flowering of Art Nouveau. The name derives from the shop opened by Siegfried Bing in Paris in 1895 that sold works by the movement's best-known designers—glassmaker Émile Gallé, potter Auguste Delaherche, jeweler René Lalique, and furniture designers Georges de Feure and Eugène Gaillard among them. The decorative vocabulary of Art Nouveau is characterized by organic forms inspired by nature, frequently accentuated with asymmetrical curves and elaborate flourishes. Purportedly anti-historicist, the most prized works in this style were those that rejected specific references to the past. Few of Art Nouveau's highly imaginative designers, however, were themselves craftsmen, and their work was criticized for its art-for-art's-sake approach, which was more concerned with aesthetics than with function, materials, and technique: "These artists were artists, as is only proper, but artists exclusively. . . . Ignorant of the technical necessities that might have guided or held in check their imagination, they tackled materials without understanding their possibilities or their constraints and often mistreated them, coercing them into dangerous tours de force."[6] Regrettably, poor-quality mass production of Art Nouveau objects hastened the demise of this wonderfully original style after 1900.[7]

If the French design community was disillusioned by the commercial failure of Art Nouveau, it was all the more wary of advances being made in other countries, including Britain, Belgium, the Netherlands, Austria, and Germany.[8] German superiority was particularly intolerable in light of the humiliating defeat suffered by the French in the Franco-Prussian War of 1870–71, still fresh in memory. Once again, designers felt a sense of urgency to reestablish France as the international leader in the luxury trades, both as a matter of national pride and for their important contribution to the French economy. The question was, How?

Early Expressions

Designers argued that the best way for France to attain a dominant role on the world stage would be to learn from the mistakes of Art Nouveau, avoiding in particular its insistence on originality at any cost, on "art" at the expense of craftsmanship. Accordingly, they looked to the preindustrial past, when guild-trained artisans, with their combined mastery of conception and execution, set international standards for excellence in the applied arts. Because the last generation of artist-craftsmen lived during the reign of Louis-Philippe, many designers chose to relate their own work to that style, although some looked also to the earlier eras of Louis XV, Louis XVI, the Directoire, and the Empire. Indeed, the historical connection became central to their mission. Perhaps the first designer in France to articulate this approach was André Vera in his 1912 article "Le Nouveau Style." Published in *L'Art décoratif*, it set forth, as the philosophical underpinning of the future of design in the applied arts, respect for tradition as a key element of French Art Deco. Tradition, however, was not the only source of inspiration. So, too, were the exotic, avant-garde trends in the fine arts, and fashion.

The vogue for exoticism developed following the arrival in Paris of the Russian impresario Sergei Diaghilev and his dance troupe, the Ballets Russes, in 1909. The company's wildly atmospheric and outré productions gained instant popularity in Paris society and had a significant impact on French taste. Léon Bakst's design for *Schéhérezade* (1910), for example, featured lavish Orientalist sets and costumes. The unexpected color combinations, vivid patterns, and louche furnishings — billowing curtains, low-slung divans, piles of tasseled pillows — were immediately imitated in stylish interiors by Paris artist-decorators. The company's innovative presentation of a readily identifiable "brand image" through the stylistic unity of sets, costumes, and publicity posters would be adopted in the marketing of French Art Deco. At the same time, the government encouraged designers to take advantage of resources — raw materials and a skilled workforce — that could be imported from the French colonies in Asia and Africa. This led to experimentation with new materials (ivory, exotic woods), techniques (lacquering, ceramic glazes), and forms that evoked distant cultures and faraway places. Fascination with the exotic, with what was foreign to France, would culminate in the state-sponsored Exposition Coloniale Internationale, a vast display of French colonial culture held on the outskirts of Paris in 1931.

The period also saw a fairly wide acceptance by the consumer public of many of the aesthetics put forth by avant-garde painters and sculptors, especially as they were adapted by designers and applied to luxury objects. Fauvism, Cubism, and Orphism were among the many fine-arts movements that played an important role in the development of the Art Deco style. The clashing colors and patterns exemplified in the Fauvist paintings of Henri Matisse and André Derain of 1905–7 inspired designs for textiles and wallpapers, as well as for the decoration of such objects as painted ceramics. The abstracted shapes and geometric stylizations of Cubism, created by Pablo Picasso and Georges Braque in 1907–9, and its offshoot, Orphism, were adapted to structural forms and surface embellishments.

The growing relationship between the worlds of design and fashion became increasingly significant, each heedful of the benefits the other could provide.[9] Couturiers used decorators to create suitably stylish premises, while designers recognized

Armand-Albert Rateau. Interior of Lanvin shop, Paris, 1924

the profits to be gained in bringing their work to the awareness of a rich, chic clientele. The collaboration of these two professions was an expression of the understanding that fashion is not simply what people wear but rather a projection of personality, of desires and aspirations, the domestic environment being an important component of an elegant lifestyle. Some individuals, such as the couturier Paul Poiret, straddled both worlds, and were looked to as important tastemakers in a broader arena.

Parallel to the rise of the artist-craftsman in the first decades of the twentieth century was that of the ensemblier, another profession that had its roots in the French past. The ensemblier offered his client a full range of services, fabricating complete interiors that achieved a harmony of colors, textures, materials, and workmanship. His creations — conceived as total works of art — encompassed not only the traditional

É.-J. Ruhlmann. Showroom,
Établissements Ruhlmann et
Laurent, Paris, in *L'Illustration*,
June 1928

Süe et Mare. Dining room, Jane
Renouardt villa, Saint-Cloud,
1926, in *Mobilier et décoration*,
July 1927

É.-J. Ruhlmann. Room setting,
Salon d'Automne, 1913, in *Art et
décoration*, January 1914

components of interior design such as furniture and objects, carpets, textiles, and lighting, but often decorative architectural features, paintings, and sculpture as well, with the idea that such artistic expressions were integral to the aesthetic unity of a particular scheme. The American Frances Schaefer, writing in 1911, described this development:

> *While there are in France many designers and craft workers who occupy themselves with certain details of ornamentation, there are many artists and firms of artists and architects who undertake entire houses, both structurally and decoratively. In some modern houses of Paris the architectural plans, as well as the smallest hinges of their least conspicuous doors, have been designed by one master mind. This minute attention to detail, this attempt to tie together all the component parts of any building are as typically French as is their national love of beauty.* [10]

Ensembliers — among the best known were É.-J. Ruhlmann and La Compagnie des Arts Français, under the direction of Louis Süe and André Mare — both designed and made, or commissioned to be made, everything they needed in their pursuit of a desired effect. In this, they resembled the architect-decorators of the late eighteenth and early nineteenth centuries, such as Charles Percier (1764–1838) and Pierre Fontaine (1762–1853), who designed not only houses but everything that went into them, so that no single element would offend the eye because it was inconsistent with the whole. Ensembliers also looked to more contemporary models, such as the Wiener Werkstätte, a designers' cooperative under the direction of the Austrian architect-designer Josef Hoffmann (1870–1956). Founded on the principles of the British Arts and Crafts movement, the Wiener Werkstätte provided a wide range of well-designed, often handmade products for a sophisticated audience, supplying everything from an architectural framework to the smallest decorative accessory.

Because ensembliers were rarely craftsmen themselves, they assembled teams of artists and makers who could collectively realize their singular vision:

> *[French artist-craftsmen] do not fear to work together with some of the old guild spirit. The "individuality" of the Frenchman is something so distinct and so natural that he knows it will not suffer from coöperation with his fellow artists. In this way he gains a certain power of solidarity to protect himself from the copyist . . . and the opportunity to work with his peers in the development of an ensemble.* [11]

The way of the ensemblier was essentially a custom trade. His way of doing business was like that of the couturier, who designed clothes to be sold in small numbers and at high prices, a fact that É.-J. Ruhlmann recognized when he pointed out that "style doesn't come from the bottom. It appears in the house of the *grand couturier* and is taken up only later by the ready-to-wear trade." [12] This prescient observation would later be borne out when the large department stores — Au Printemps, Le Bon Marché, Les Galeries Lafayette, and Les Grands Magasins du Louvre — established design ateliers to create interiors and to offer decorating services to a less affluent clientele.

The Société des Artistes Décorateurs, a professional association for artist-craftsmen and ensembliers alike, was founded in 1900, marking the first official encouragement of new standards for French design and production through their annual exhibitions. [13] At the society's Salons, for which new displays were created each year, members displayed their most recent work in a full range of media, from individual objects to complete room settings, fostering interdisciplinary dialogue and an active exchange of ideas. Other important annual exhibitions included the Salon d'Automne, the Salon Nationale des Beaux-Arts, and the Salon des Artistes Français; these, however, were principally fine-arts displays, with sections for the applied arts on a smaller scale.

The First World War

The First World War had a devastating impact on every aspect of life in France. More than 1,300,000 French soldiers were killed in action. Like all other able-bodied Frenchmen, artists and designers were called to serve, whether at the front as infantry and officers or behind the lines as ambulance drivers and translators, or by providing other crucial support. Because most of the materials and resources used in the manufacture of

André Mare. Drawing of a cannon painted in camouflage, January 1916

decorative arts were reserved for meeting military needs, and with the inevitable reduction in demand, production came to a virtual halt.

One especially interesting development to emerge during the war years was that of camouflage. In 1915, under the direction of the French painter Lucien-Victor Guirand de Scévola, the French Army formed a special Department of Camouflage. De Scévola's camoufleurs included Jacques Villon, André Dunoyer de Segonzac, Charles Camoin, and André Mare—artists and designers who used their specialized skills to devise methods of disguising or concealing trenches, observation posts, vehicles, and weapons. One method involved painting patterns inspired by the fractured forms of Cubism. The designer André Mare kept extensive notebooks in which he recorded his experimental ideas, many of which would be adopted and used during the war (see above).

The Exposition Internationale des Arts Décoratifs et Industriels Modernes

After demobilization, the French design community quickly resumed its quest to create a national modern design vocabulary: "The experiments, tragically interrupted by the war, were resumed with feverish activity in 1919. People applied themselves to reacting against the false principle of art for art's sake."[14] Much of this activity was focused on the Exposition Internationale des Arts Décoratifs et Industriels Modernes, held in Paris in 1925. It was from the title of this exhibition that the term "Art Deco" derived.

In 1912, the French government—with the particular encouragement of the Société des Artistes Décorateurs—agreed to sponsor an international exhibition of contemporary decorative arts to promote the renewal of French preeminence in the design field. First planned to take place in 1915, the project was interrupted by the war. The government later resurrected the idea, and the fair finally materialized in 1925. More than twenty foreign countries were invited to participate. Prime sites were offered to France's four major wartime allies—Great Britain, Italy, Belgium, and the United States. The invitation to the United States was declined, "on the ground that American manufacturers and craftsmen had almost nothing to exhibit conceived in the modern spirit and in harmony with the spirit of the official specifications."[15] Germany was pointedly excluded from the fair. All told, however, the Paris Expo was effectively a vast French-sponsored trade fair.

The Exposition's fifty-five-acre site in the center of Paris stretched north to south across the Seine from the Grand Palais to the Invalides and east to west from the Place de la Concorde to the Pont de l'Alma. During its seven-month run, from April through October 1925, it attracted more than 16 million visitors. In addition to the preexisting Grand Palais, over 130 temporary pavilions, arcades, gardens, barges, and entrance gates were built; these were further subdivided into many hundreds of boutiques, stands, and displays. More than 15,000 exhibitors (both French and foreign) participated, and over 7,000 prizes were awarded by the official juries. Most of the foreign pavilions were situated along the right bank of the Seine near the Grand Palais, while the French pavilions were concentrated on the Left Bank, on the Esplanade des Invalides and along the river.

The French pavilions were organized by ensembliers, individual artist-craftsmen, manufacturers, and retailers, and represented geographic regions and professional associations. Foreign pavilions were understandably less ambitious, mainly exhibiting smaller displays. Among the most notable of the French pavilions were those of Süe et Mare, Lalique, Poiret, the Manufacture Nationale de Sèvres, and the major Paris

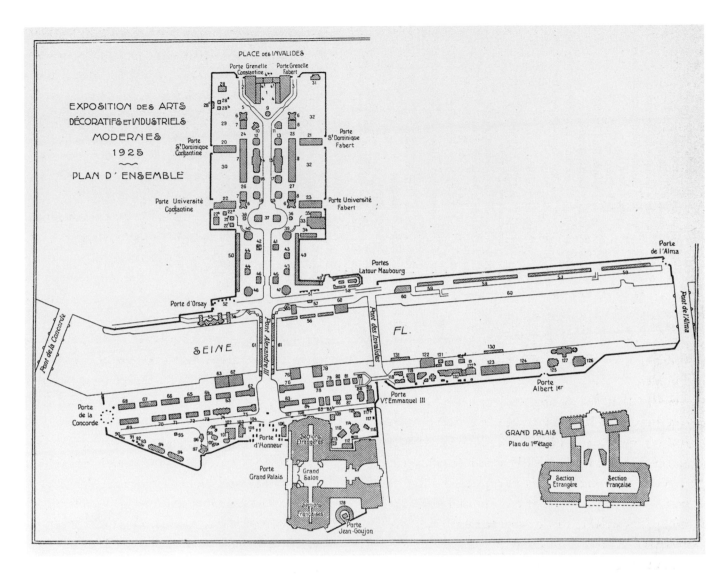

Plan of the Exposition Internationale
des Arts Décoratifs et Industriels
Modernes, Paris, 1925

Edgar Brandt, Henri Favier, and André
Ventre. Porte d'Honneur, Exposition
Internationale des Arts Décoratifs et
Industriels Modernes, Paris, 1925

department stores. Perhaps the most prominent pavilion (with the greatest number of participants) was that of the *Société des Artistes Décorateurs*: The *Ambassade Française* presented rooms for an idealized French Embassy, complete with both grand state reception rooms and more intimate private spaces for the ambassador's family; the decoration of each room was carried out by a different member of the *Société*.[16] The pavilion that best epitomized the Exposition was Ruhlmann's *Hôtel du Collectionneur*. Based on the model of an eighteenth-century hunting pavilion, it was designed (in collaboration with the architect Pierre Patout) to resemble a luxurious private modern house.

French design was the fair's main focus, with the works exhibited — everything from architecture and interior design to jewelry and perfumes — intended to proclaim French supremacy in the production of luxury goods. Everything was for sale (the Metropolitan Museum acquired several pieces at the Exposition; see nos. 12, 26, 38, and 65). The exhibits were officially divided into five categories: architecture; furnishings; dress; theatrical, street, and garden arts; and education. These were further divided into 37 classes, such as stonework, woodwork, metal, ceramics, glass, furniture, leather, and paper. Each class was overseen by a president, vice president(s), and jurors, who awarded the prizes.

The rules governing what could be exhibited were very specific. The primary requirement was that all works had to be thoroughly modern; no copying of historical styles would be permitted:

Works admitted to the Exposition must show new inspiration and real originality. They must be executed and presented by the artists, artisans and manufacturers who have created models and by editors who represent the modern decorative and industrial arts. Reproductions, imitations and counterfeits of ancient styles will be strictly prohibited.[17]

René Lalique. Dining room, Lalique Pavilion, Exposition Internationale des Arts Décoratifs et Industriels Modernes, Paris, 1925

Henri Rapin and Pierre Selmersheim. Grand salon, Ambassade Française, Exposition Internationale des Arts Décoratifs et Industriels Modernes, Paris, 1925

É.-J. Ruhlmann. Grand salon, Hôtel du Collectionneur, Exposition Internationale des Arts Décoratifs et Industriels Modernes, Paris, 1925

Nevertheless, despite these strictures, much of what was exhibited was firmly rooted in the traditions of the past. At the same time, the stylistic unity of the exhibits demonstrates that Art Deco was a mature style by 1925:

> The cause of decorative arts is won. Let us recall its origins. It set out as a reaction against routine and imitation, [an effort] to return the spirit of invention to its rightful place, to restore true tradition. . . . This goal has been achieved. A decorative art is under way that is modeled on life, that is in harmony with an architecture transformed by the progress of science and industry, and that, like dress, follows certain proprieties [mœurs]. The character of its output may vary depending on public taste and artistic talent. [But] the main objective has been achieved: It has a life of its own; it is no longer derivative.[18]

The official report of the United States government on the Exposition put it more succinctly:

> From all appearances the modern movement has been accepted to such a degree by the French people as to insure its continued place in modern production in France and to establish it as the important note of design for the immediate future.[19]

The French Art Deco Style

Two principal characteristics dominate French Art Deco: its simultaneous expression of both modernity and national historical precedent, and its alliance of art and craftsmanship. The first characteristic announces not only an object's suitability to life in the modern world but also its special French character through its link with the past:

> What are these elements of 20th century life that one should expect to find expressed in its decorative forms? First and foremost—directness, the bold approach to a task by the shortest, most efficient method. . . . There is always a certain beauty resulting from the methods of workmanship if they are true to materials used, and beauty is achieved through a perfection of form to function. . . .

> And yet, nothing new can be developed satisfactorily without a dependence upon the work, discoveries and experience of that which has gone before. In this respect, we find modern decoration with its roots deep in the old traditions. The créateurs, as those of other ages, have a complete knowledge of past forms and methods of workmanship, and are themselves masters of both design and craftsmanship. . . . [In them,] we find men who not only design, but can and do model and complete the object.[20]

The second characteristic demonstrates not only technical mastery—be it represented by an object made by hand or with machinery (makers certainly recognized that new materials and technology could provide improvements and refinements)—but also the aesthetic vision of the artist.

> Never [before] . . . has there been such an appreciation of the beauty of materials necessary for the construction of an object, or the simple beauty of the evidences of good workmanship. . . . This has resulted in new and surprising forms. Nor is this decoration a result of a superficial desire to produce something new and different. Instead, it has developed gradually, had its failures and successes, and its flowering has only been attained by the continued efforts and high ideals of artists devoted to their work.[21]

By their very nature, these two characteristics precluded industrial manufacture. Because limited or one-of-a-kind production was invariably costlier than mass production, it is clear that French Art Deco was unabashedly aimed at an affluent clientele. Such clients generally recognized and appreciated the qualities that rendered their purchases exquisite, exceptional, and as desirable as any masterpiece from the glorious past. Indeed, connoisseurship was fundamental to French Art Deco; it could with good reason be considered a third characteristic.

Early on, French Art Deco was divided into two camps: the traditionalists, whose work made reference to the past, and the modernists, whose work appeared to reject it. In many ways, however, the two were not so very different, since the traditionalists were not averse to introducing a certain aesthetic modernity and the modernists often used materials and techniques rooted in tradition.[22]

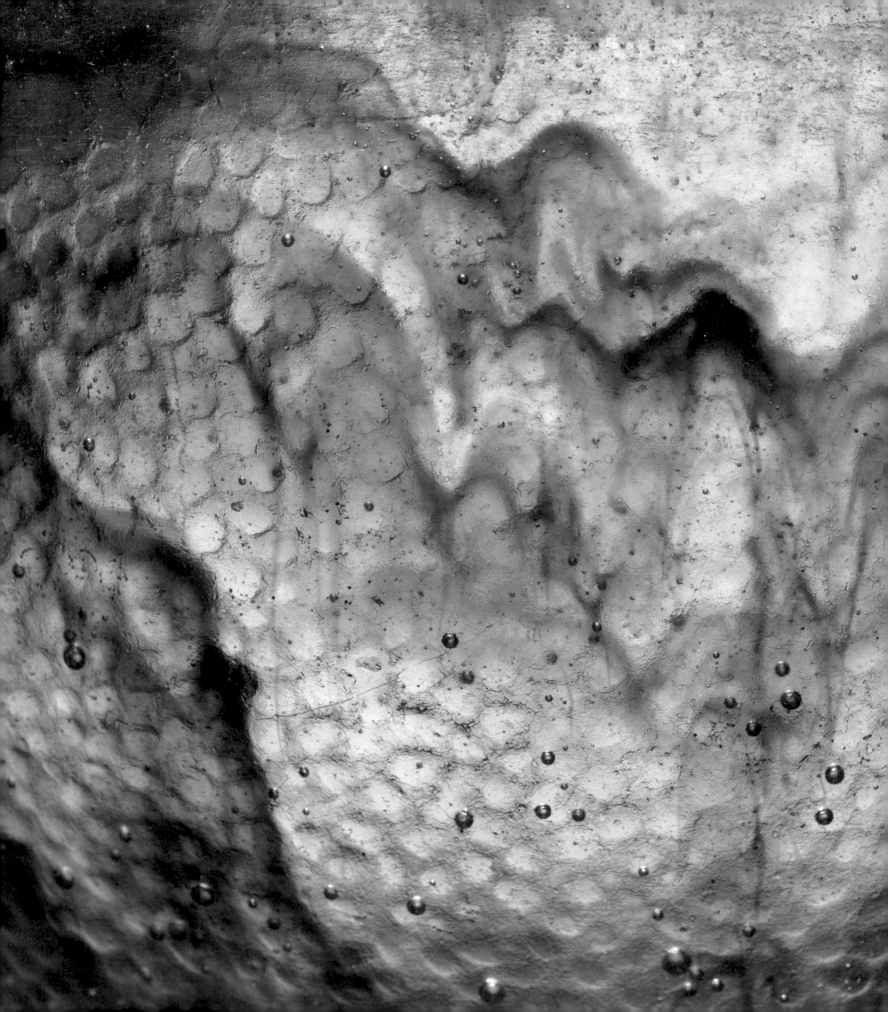

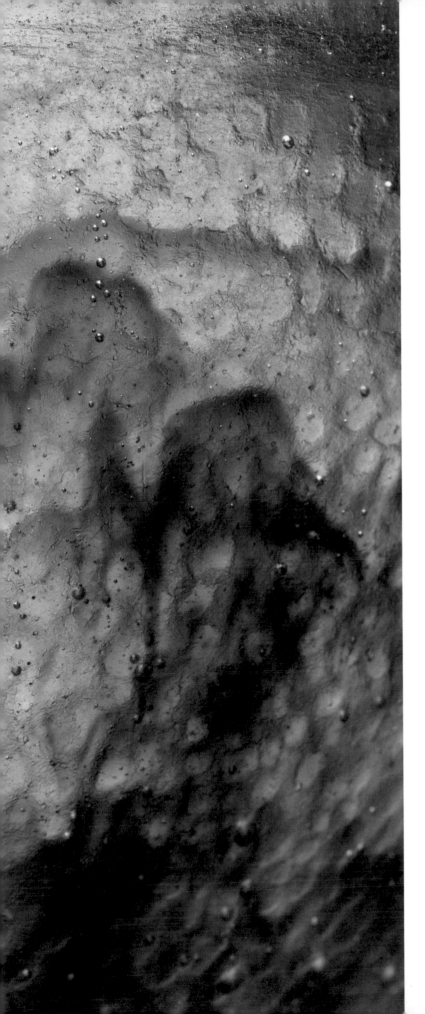

Paris in the 1920s and 1930s

The subject of modern design was addressed widely in print during the interwar years. Writers of articles in books, magazines, and newspapers introduced the new style and helped readers to understand it; many were themselves acknowledged experts in the field, and their contribution not only established the narrative of Art Deco but also identified its key players.[23] Journalists reviewed exhibitions, wrote profiles, and conducted interviews which were disseminated through magazines and trade journals that not infrequently supplied translations of their articles in multiple languages.[24] Art publishers presented deluxe folios of lavish pochoir-printed color plates, not only to show the vivid color schemes in favor at the time but, more important, to raise design to the level of fine art.[25] Further, many designers published their own treatises, which in essence served as polemics for the Art Deco style. Louis Süe and André Mare, for example, in *Architectures* (1921), contended that the basis of Art Deco was a synthesis of the fine and decorative arts, and Paul Iribe, in *Choix* (1930), argued for the production of luxury objects during the Depression years.

Although Art Deco flourished throughout France during the 1920s and 1930s — especially in major cities, such as Bordeaux and Lyons, or chic resorts like Deauville and Biarritz — the epicenter of the movement was without any doubt Paris, for it was in Paris that the majority of artist-craftsmen and ensembliers established their workshops and showrooms. Most of the furniture workshops were situated, as they had been for centuries, in the Faubourg Saint-Antoine, a neighborhood that was home to the École Boulle. Other ateliers, such as those for pottery and glassmaking, also tended to be located on the outskirts of the city, mainly because it was there that spaces large enough to accommodate such equipment as kilns and furnaces were to be found.

Paris also presented a vast array of commercial establishments where Art Deco was displayed and sold, mainly showrooms, galleries, and shops in the more fashionable city center on the Right Bank. Ensemblier showrooms, such as those of Ruhlmann (on the rue de Lisbonne), Süe et Mare (rue du Faubourg-Saint-Honoré), and Martine (rond-point des Champs-Élysées), not only were filled with individual pieces

Pierre Mourgue. Cover for *Art et industrie*, December 10, 1928

Léon Bénigni. Cover for *Art et industrie*, June 1930

Jean Colin. Cover for *Art et industrie*, July 1935

André Arbus. Cover for *Art et industrie*, April 1936

A L'OASIS
ou
LA VOUTE PNEUMATIQUE
ROBE DU SOIR, DE PAUL POIRET

for sale but presented fully furnished interiors that suggested the range of what the ensemblier could produce on commission. Many ensembliers displayed works by their fellow designers, both for aesthetic variety and for mutual promotion.

Each of the four big department stores established a specialized decorating department: La Maîtrise at Les Galeries Lafayette, Pomone at Le Bon Marché, Primavera at Au Printemps, and Studium Louvre at Les Grands Magasins du Louvre. Although some makers, such as Fouquet, Puiforcat, and Sèvres, opened their own salesrooms, many specialty shops, including Jean Luce, La Crémaillère, and Le Grand Dépôt, sold a wide range of glass, ceramics, linens, and other utilitarian and decorative goods. And independent art galleries—A. A. Hébrard, Barbazanges, Georges Bernheim, Bernheim-Jeune, Renaissance, Georges Rouard, and Arnold Seligmann—frequently presented exhibitions of applied arts.

Museums—the Musée des Arts Décoratifs and the Musée Galliera most prominently—mounted regular exhibitions devoted to the decorative arts. Often these were focused on specific genres and mediums: textiles, wallpapers, ceramics,

metalwork, or jewelry. Monographic exhibitions were rare, although the Lalique exhibition of 1933 and the Ruhlmann retrospective of 1934, both presented at the Musée des Arts Décoratifs, were important exceptions. It was not until 1937 that the first survey of French Art Deco, "Le Décor de la vie de 1900 à 1925," was held, at the Musée des Arts Décoratifs.

Of preeminent importance in the social and artistic life of Paris were the annual Salon exhibitions organized by professional organizations and artistic associations. The most important of these for the design community was the Salon of the Société des Artistes Décorateurs, mounted each spring. From 1901 until 1922—excluding the years 1915–18—a monthlong display was presented at the Musée des Arts Décoratifs. After 1922, longer exhibitions were held at the Grand Palais. Tens of thousands of visitors streamed through the galleries. The Salon practice of displaying complete room settings was adopted at a number of international exhibitions. Paris was also the site for three fairs that were especially significant: the 1925 Expo, the 1931 Exposition Coloniale Internationale, and the 1937 Exposition Internationale des Arts et Techniques dans la Vie Moderne.

The fashion houses of Paris—*maisons de couture*—and related businesses also offered lessons in modern design, as many of them were decorated by noted ensembliers—Armand-Albert Rateau (Lanvin), Jean Dunand (Mme Agnès), Martine and Edgar Brandt (Poiret), and Süe et Mare (Parfumerie d'Orsay), among others. French couturiers were very much in tune with the latest trends, and the public looked to them as tastemakers in general. Theaters and nightclubs as well as restaurants and bars were just as up-to-date. Day or night, it was nearly impossible to avoid Art Deco in Paris.

French Art Deco Abroad

French Art Deco was marketed to both domestic and foreign consumers. Many visitors to France had their first taste of the *style moderne* well before setting foot on soil—on the great French ocean liners. The French government, eager to promote its national products, recognized early on that the liners could serve as floating advertisements for the *arts de vivre*, and in 1912 drew up a contract with the Compagnie Générale Transatlantique (CGT)—known in English as the French Line—to build four passenger-mail ships over the next quarter-century for its most prestigious route, the North Atlantic. Three of the four were realized: the *Paris* (maiden voyage, 1921), the *Île de France* (1927), and the *Normandie* (1935). Production of the *Bretagne* was halted by the advent of the Second World War.

The CGT promoted its liners as bona fide representations of France, hoping to seduce their well-to-do passengers, who paid not so much for transportation as for atmosphere, with lavish décor, good food, and fine wine that suggested the height of Continental sophistication and, it was hoped, would inspire purchases upon arrival in France. With particular attention paid to first-class travelers (the most likely shoppers), the CGT hired the best French designers of the day to fit out the ships in the latest décors. In Paris, visitors could rely on readily available shopping guides to direct them to the showrooms, shops, and galleries owned by the very makers whose works they had admired on board. Two popular guides,

Pierrre Patout and Henri Pacon. First-class dining room, with light fixtures by Réne Lalique and carved and gilt bas-reliefs by Raymond Delamarre, SS *Normandie*, ca. 1935

Edgar Brandt. Grand staircase, SS *Paris*, ca. 1921

É.-J. Ruhlmann. Salle des Fêtes, Chamber of Commerce and Industry, Paris, 1927

Jules Hardouin Mansart and Charles Le Brun. Hall of Mirrors, Palace of Versailles, 1684

written for American visitors to Paris, were the sisters Louise and Thérèse Bonney's *Buying Antique and Modern Furniture in Paris* (1929) and Katharine Morrison Kahle's *Modern French Decoration* (1930).[26]

To further promote Art Deco, between 1910 and 1940 a considerable number of exhibitions and displays of French design were presented at museums and world's fairs in North and South America, Africa, and Asia, not to mention across Continental Europe.[27] Two of the most important were the American Association of Museums' 1926 exhibition "A Selected Collection of Objects from the International Exposition of Modern Decorative and Industrial Art at Paris 1925," in which nearly 400 representative works in a range of media were presented in nine American cities, and the Japanese Woodwork Association's 1928 "Exhibition of French Decorative Art," shown at the Tokyo Imperial Museum. Organized in cooperation with several French cultural institutions, the Tokyo exhibition presented room settings and displays by 28 prominent ensembliers and furniture makers, including Leleu, Rapin, Ruhlmann, and Süe et Mare.

Over time, French Art Deco was sold through an international network of art galleries, department stores, and decorators.[28] By the Second World War, collectors and clients could be found worldwide. Most of them were wealthy, although few

were members of established society or the aristocracy; rather, they tended to be newly rich industrialists, bankers, actors, and couturiers — in short, people of fashion. Many of their names still resonate today.

The Final Years

During the late 1920s, industrially produced furnishings — in particular, the spare, functional work of the Bauhaus school in Germany — began to capture the imagination of the international design world.[29] Most French designers, accustomed to luxury production, were reluctant to follow this trend, but a small number began to explore a new approach. In 1926, four designers and one design firm banded together to form Les Cinq; it was the first French group to actively challenge Art Deco. In 1929, they joined forces with like-minded designers to found the Union des Artistes Modernes (UAM), an organization that broke away from the Société des Artistes Décorateurs and promoted the forward-looking, radical ideals of modernist design in France.[30]

The worldwide economic crisis precipitated by the crash of the American stock market in 1929 dealt a blow to the luxury trades. In France a series of riots paved the way for the victory of the left-wing Popular Front in the 1936 elections, leading to sweeping social and economic reforms. With fewer clients in a position to buy or commission expensive furnishings, the 1930s saw fundamental changes in French design. Art Deco, having reached its apogee at the 1925 Paris Exposition, gradually waned, its decorative flourishes and emphasis on luxury increasingly irrelevant, especially in light of the deprivations of the Great Depression.[31]

At the same time, however, the geometric forms and plain, undecorated surfaces and industrial materials favored by the rising International Style modernists—specifically, Le Corbusier and the designers of the Bauhaus—proved too demanding; few consumers, for example, were willing to introduce the austerity exemplified by chrome-plated tubular steel furniture into their domestic environments. It was thus with a sense of relief that many high-end clients found refuge in the familiar language of classicism in the years before the Second World War. The decorative arts of the so-called Return to Order (the term derived from Jean Cocteau's 1926 book *Le Rappel à l'ordre*) relied on historical precedent even more than did works of the 1910s and 1920s. Unlike the early French Art Deco designers, who mined the aesthetic of the ancien régime for its sophistication, refinement, and charm, their counterparts a quarter century later looked to the glacial monumentality of the French past, creating historicist designs that projected, through their stately opulence, a sense of unassailable security and authoritative confidence in a period that was characterized by economic and social crisis (see the Salle des Fêtes and the Hall of Mirrors, page 19). A quality of almost desperate theatricality pervades the design of this era (see above), as though the designers and their clients were trying to escape the increasingly dismal reality of daily life.

In 1937, the French government sponsored the Exposition Internationale des Arts et Techniques dans la Vie Moderne. Less ambitious than the 1925 Paris Expo, the fair focused on the place of France in the modern world as reflected through her achievements in science and technology rather than in the arts and luxury trades. The 1937 Exposition in effect marked the end of the Art Deco era. It was not without significance that the same year saw the first retrospective exhibition devoted to Art Deco, "Le Décor de la vie de 1900 à 1925," presented at

Louis Süe. Salon d'Ambassade, Exposition Internationale des Arts et Techniques dans la Vie Moderne, Paris, 1937

the Musée des Arts Décoratifs. The nearly 1,500 works that were displayed established the roster of preeminent Art Deco designers. But with the outbreak of war in September 1939, an entire way of life was about to disappear.

Rediscovery

In the years following the Second World War, veterans with young families struggled to rebuild their lives. A pressing need for affordable housing and furnishings led to a boom in inexpensive design and mass production, and the elaborate households of the prewar years were replaced by homes characterized by informality and adaptability. By and large, the long-established approach to furnishings as expensive and permanent status objects disappeared. New materials and technologies—many developed during wartime—lowered production costs and

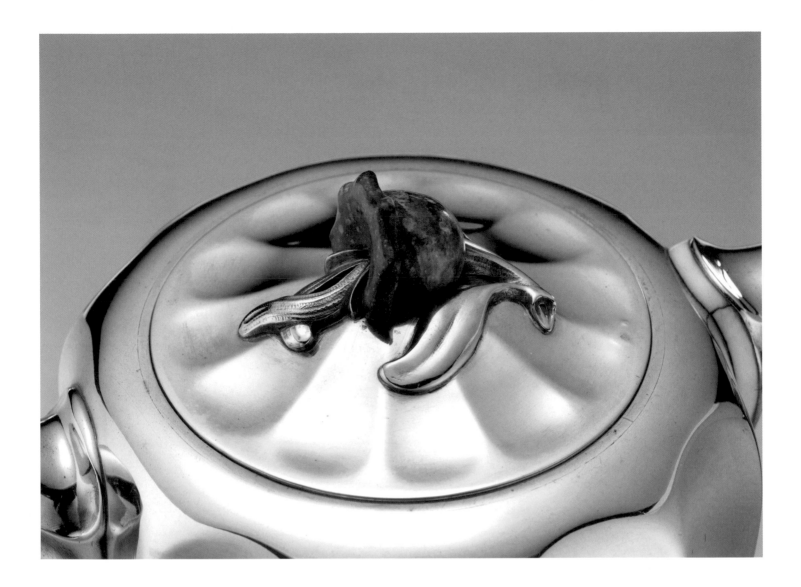

helped free design from tradition, which led to an aesthetic that was increasingly abstract and ascetic. Nevertheless, in the face of these developments, a dwindling number of upmarket French designers continued through the 1950s to ply their trade to a small circle of clients who still appreciated and could afford exquisite luxury goods.

Then in the mid-1960s, perhaps as a reaction against two decades of postwar austerity, a new generation rediscovered French Art Deco, regarding it with the increased objectivity that comes with time. Art Deco objects were again valued for their refined aesthetic and superb craftsmanship.[32] A new appreciation emerged not only among connoisseurs and collectors but among scholars and art historians, who began to explore the culture that produced the style. In 1966, the first postwar museum exhibition devoted to Art Deco was mounted at the Musée des Arts Décoratifs; the first in America was held in 1971 at the Minneapolis Institute of Arts.[33] It was at this time that the term "Art Deco" was first used.[34]

FRENCH ART DECO
IN THE METROPOLITAN MUSEUM OF ART

The Metropolitan Museum of Art began collecting French Art Deco in 1922; its pattern of acquisition parallels the broad pendulum swings in taste for the style that have occurred to the present day. The initial impetus came in the form of a monetary gift in 1922 from Edward C. Moore Jr.:

> *Provided that you deem it desirable, I would like to give the Museum the $10,000 enclosed with which to buy from time to time as opportunity offers, examples (of only the finest quality) of the modern decorative arts of America and Europe. If this gift is accepted by you for the above purpose, I hope to give to the Museum for the same purpose a like yearly sum until the total thus given by me shall amount to $50,000 or more.*[1]

The Museum accepted, stating that it "especially welcomes this gift which comes at a time when it has planned to give modern decorative art its proper relation to other forms of modern art by a special exhibition, to the success of which this gift will make an important contribution."[2]

The gift was received by Joseph Breck, assistant director and curator of decorative arts, who was responsible for European objects and furniture from antiquity to the present (a purview that—in his time—was said to account for a full third of the museum's holdings).[3] From that moment, Breck took an active interest in modern design. In 1922 he made his first purchases, 47 works in total—mainly French, Danish, and American ceramics, of which 18 were French. The following year, many of these works were already installed in the first of the Museum's galleries dedicated to modern decorative arts.

Breck's objective in forming and displaying a collection of modern decorative arts was "to show that at the present time

there are being made in different parts of the world beautiful things along strictly modern lines, which will fairly rival the work of early masters."[4] In the Museum's *Bulletin*, Breck explained:

> *During the nineteenth century . . . the decorative arts tumbled to a level so appallingly low that the heights have seemed discouragingly far away and difficult of ascent. But today, after a decade ripe with promise, there is every indication that we are to see in our time the triumph of a modern style, based on tradition but modified, as this perilous inheritance has always been modified in every great period of the past, to meet the new requirements of changed conditions of life.*[5]

Breck hoped that his installation would serve as an inspiration to contemporary American designers. Based on his purchases, it is clear that he was drawn to the French concept of innovation in the context of tradition. Although his taste might be considered conservative by today's standards, Breck nonetheless recognized such works as representing the finest achievements of his day.

Breck made three buying trips to Paris between 1923 and 1925, acquiring 77 French works that now form the basis of the Metropolitan's collection, including several pieces of furniture by ensembliers such as Ruhlmann and Süe et Mare.[6] On his final trip, in July 1925, he visited the Exposition Internationale des Arts Décoratifs et Industriels Modernes. He wrote immediately, on July 4, to the Metropolitan's president, Robert W. de Forest, encouraging him to do the same: "I hope you are going to have time to do the exhibition quite thoroughly. I feel it is worth the trouble." He urged de Forest to visit many of the pavilions, singling out Ruhlmann's Hôtel du Collectionneur as "one of the most interesting." He also cited the purchases that he had made on the Museum's behalf, and several days later appended to his letter: "Since writing the above I have made other purchases."[7] Upon his return to New York, Breck duly added his acquisitions to the Museum's design gallery.

The following February, the important traveling exhibition of works from the 1925 Paris Expo, organized by the American Association of Museums, was on display. It had an attendance of nearly 19,000 visitors. Breck noted in the Museum's *Bulletin*:

The exhibits will be entirely unfamiliar in style to the great majority who see them, and every student of the history of art knows that the unfamiliar meets at first with indifference, even with hostility. The most natural gesture in the world is to throw a stone at the stranger! But the stranger may be a delightful person when we come to know him better. The work in this exhibition has been admired by many whose taste commands respect. That is no reason why we should like the "modern style," but it does give food for thought.[8]

Edward C. Moore Jr. made his final donation of $10,000 in 1926: "I do hope that in using this last installment it may be possible to find more artist-craftsmen in the United States."[9] Accordingly, purchases of non-American decorative arts using this fund dropped off exponentially, although they did not stop entirely.

Breck died in 1933, of a heart attack, at the age of forty-eight. His successor, John Goldsmith Phillips, continued to use the Moore fund to purchase French Art Deco through the mid-1930s.[10] Although the fund generated enough interest to subsidize acquisitions until 1970, the purchases by Phillips would be the last of French Art Deco that the Museum would make until 1969. During that thirty-year period, the Museum acquired only about a dozen works—all as gifts (see nos. 2, 5, 11, 20, 36, 37, and 69).

In 1967, Henry Geldzahler was appointed curator of the recently created Department of Contemporary Art. While not a decorative arts specialist himself, Geldzahler had a personal interest in French Art Deco, and he was among the first museum professionals to revisit the subject. In a memorandum of February 1970 requesting funds for the purchase of French Art Deco objects, he pointed out to the Museum's director, Thomas H. Hoving:

The term Art Deco comes from the full name of the Exposition des Arts Decoratifs [sic] which in 1925, in Paris, revealed the style fully for the first time. It is, logically, the successor to Art Nouveau and is the most recent international movement in the decorative arts to have esthetic importance.[11]

Geldzahler added that over the previous two years he had seen galleries specializing in Art Deco open in Paris, London, and New York. He had also watched prices rise steadily. Specifically, he cited vases by Lalique which had sold two years earlier for $65 and that were now bringing $200.[12] Over the course of his ten years at the Metropolitan, Geldzahler made several important acquisitions that saw the collection of French Art Deco grow into one of the finest in any public institution.[13]

Since 1978, a succession of curators—including Penelope Hunter-Stiebel, R. Craig Miller, and J. Stewart Johnson—have continued to build the collection, and a number of focused exhibitions and installations—many drawn solely from the Museum's holdings—have been organized on French Art Deco themes.[14] The most recent of these, "Masterpieces of French Art Deco," which was on view from August 2009 through January 2011, formed the basis of this publication.

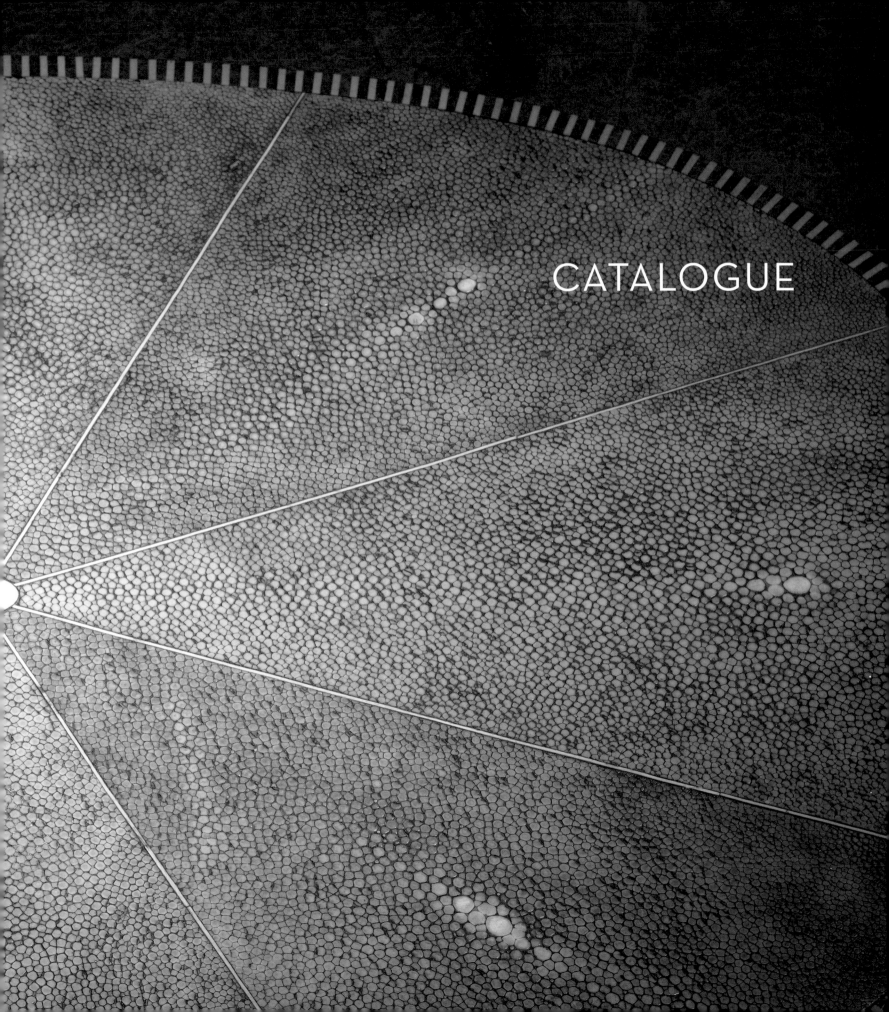

CATALOGUE

GABRIEL ARGY-ROUSSEAU

Meslay-le-Vidame 1885–1953 Paris

Pâte-de-verre—literally, "glass paste"—has its roots in ancient Egypt and imperial Rome. Historically used to imitate precious stones, the technique was lost for thousands of years until, in the late nineteenth century, it was revived by, among others, the French glassmaker Henri Cros. In the Art Deco era, two glassmakers specialized in the technique: Gabriel Argy-Rousseau and François-Émile Décorchemont (see pages 58–61).

Argy-Rousseau was born Joseph-Gabriel Rousseau to a family of farmers who lived near Chartres. Academic excellence led to a scholarship for secondary school, and in 1902 he entered the École Nationale de Céramique de Sèvres. One of Rousseau's schoolmates there was Jean Cros, the son of Henri Cros, whose atelier was in Sèvres and whose work in *pâte-de-verre* sparked the young Rousseau's interest in the technique.

After graduating in 1906 with a degree in engineering, Rousseau took a job at a research laboratory in Paris that made dental ceramics. He also rented a small studio where he experimented with *pâte-de-verre*, refining and developing his skills over several years. It was not until 1914 that he first showed his work, small-scale bowls and vases, at the Salon of the Société des Artistes Français. By then he had combined his surname with that of his wife, Maxianne Argyriades, whom he had married the previous year.

During the war, Argy-Rousseau served as an engineer for the Ministry of Defense and in that capacity received patents for a number of unusual inventions, including an electric torpedo launcher for automobiles. He continued his scientific experimentations after the war, in 1925 inventing an apparatus for single-exposure color photography; until that time, color images could be achieved only through multiple exposures. He also resumed working with *pâte-de-verre*, expanding the market by developing new uses for it, such as on lampshades and night-lights, which exploited the material's mottled translucency. He began participating in the annual Paris Salons. And soon his *pâte-de-verre* was seen regularly at galleries throughout Paris and in museum exhibitions.[1]

In 1921, Argy-Rousseau founded Les Pâtes-de-Verre d'Argy-Rousseau in partnership with Gaston Moser-Millot, the owner of a decorative arts gallery in Paris and a glassworks in Karlovy Vary, Bohemia. Moser-Millot financed the business while Argy-Rousseau served as artistic director, his designs produced by a small army of workers in a large shop at 9, rue du Simplon. By 1923 their products—which included vases and bowls, lamps and shades, perfume burners, chandeliers, jewelry, and statuettes—were being sold not only at Moser-Millot in Paris but, through a large distribution network of international agents, across Europe, in North Africa, and in both North and South America. They were also seen in international exhibitions, as well as at the Paris Salons, notably those of the Société des Artistes Décorateurs.

Pâte-de-verre had traditionally been made using molds that were destroyed during production, which meant that each piece required a new mold. Argy-Rousseau's principal contribution to the technique was the development of reusable molds that enabled serial production. During the 1920s, Argy-Rousseau relinquished the naturalism of Art Nouveau for the stylized abstractions of Art Deco. He expanded his aesthetic vocabulary to include figural motifs and vivid color contrasts, and he experimented with *pâte-de-cristal*, a more brilliant and more translucent *pâte-de-verre* made with lead crystal. At the 1925 Paris Exposition, he served as a juror and exhibited his work at the Grand Palais and at the Ambassade Française.

The worldwide economic crisis that began in 1929 forced Les Pâtes-de-Verre d'Argy-Rousseau to close in 1931. In his private atelier, Argy-Rousseau continued to make small objects, but for a dwindling clientele. Following a general shift in taste, his designs became increasingly simplified; massive and monochromatic, they incorporated abstract geometric decoration only sparingly, if at all. His work was exhibited, though less frequently over time.[2] It drew little public interest after the Second World War, and did not attract widespread appreciation again until the 1960s.

1 | *Eurythmics* Vase
1932; glass

This vase is from a series Argy-Rousseau made in 1932 and decorated with nude female figures rendered to create the effect of cameo. At least one other version, executed in shades of brown (private collection, Paris), is known.[1] Although figural cameos had been made since antiquity, here the women are up-to-date, sporting fashionably bobbed hairstyles and, on this vase, engaging in a thoroughly modern activity: eurythmics. Gymnastic exercises performed to music, eurythmics was developed about 1905 by the Swiss musician Émile Jaques-Dalcroze as a tool for music education. It was later adapted to dance, and popular interest in the technique led to its use as a motif in the decorative arts. Although this model was created in 1932, the year after Les Pâtes-de-Verre d'Argy-Rousseau closed, Argy-Rousseau probably produced several examples.

A range of decorative effects can be achieved in *pâte-de-verre*. It can be opaque or translucent, matte or polished, vividly hued or colorless, striated, occluded, bubbled, or cameo-like, and it can resemble hardstone or ceramic as well as traditional glass. First, glass is pulverized into a fine powder, which is mixed with water, binding agents, and other materials (such as kaolin, metal oxides, or lead) that determine the consistency, color, and opacity of the final product. The paste that results is then put into a mold and kiln-fired. The process is imprecise and the material fragile; with each firing there is as much a chance for failure as for success.

Pliny recounts that a Roman emperor had the potter who invented [pâte-de-verre] decapitated, so that his secret would disappear forever. . . . But in our time, long and patient labor was undertaken to find the formula and Argy-Rousseau's technique makes it possible to obtain the most varied forms, the most brilliant colors, and the sharpest reliefs in a diaphanous paste, where the play of light passes through infinite nuances, from the most delicate to the most intense. The pâte-de-verre technique is certainly the most artistic and the most personal of all techniques for working glass and crystal, since it allows the artist to easily render his idea complete.[2]

GEORGE BARBIER

Nantes 1882–1932 Paris

Writing in 1965, Metropolitan Museum curator Edith Standen noted that George Barbier had been "so completely forgotten that it has proved impossible to discover whether he is now alive or dead."[1] By then he had been dead for more than three decades; it would be another forty years before the first monograph devoted to his work would appear.[2] It is curious that someone so prolific—during his career he produced thousands of drawings, set and costume designs, and decorative-arts objects—could have fallen into such obscurity.

Barbier's graphic work, for which he is best known, reveals much about French taste in the Art Deco era and exquisitely encapsulates many of the varied impulses that informed it, especially in its earliest incarnation: the grace of classical antiquity, the elegance of the eighteenth century, the alluring exoticism of Asia and the Near East, the shocking spectacle of the Ballets Russes. Aspects of all these elements appear throughout his work, which perfectly reflects the spirit of the time.

Barbier took little interest in the more avant-garde trends of his day, preferring to draw inspiration from history than to break with the past for the sake of novelty. In so doing, he created an original body of work that was greatly admired. The novelist Francis de Miomandre, writing in 1914, described Barbier as

. . . one of the most celebrated artists of our time . . . and I venture to say that this success reassures us about our taste. So long as people continue to like that elegance of the imagination, that ornamental clarity, that precision of line, that sobriety of the arabesque, that intensity of color, which never sinks into excess; so long as people understand that a judicious assimilation of influences by a temperament that absorbs them and keeps them in balance attests much more surely to a real originality than the garish disorder and concerted derangement of someone seeking attention at all cost; so long as people continue to retain a fondness for the moderation, charm, and appeal of someone like George Barbier, we will be able to contemplate with serenity what some call the ravages of cubism, futurism, and every form of orphism.[3]

The son of a shopkeeper, Barbier was by 1902 enrolled at the École Régionale des Beaux-Arts in Nantes. While a student there, he had two particularly formative experiences: he copied paintings at the Musée des Beaux-Arts—he was especially taken by the work of the eighteenth-century master Antoine Watteau—and he made trips to England, where he encountered the graphic work of Aubrey Beardsley. Barbier became something of an Anglophile on these trips, which probably occurred between 1905 and 1908; as a result, before 1911 he often signed his work E.[dward] W.[illiam] Larry. When he resumed using his own name, he anglicized the spelling to "George."

In 1908, Barbier entered the École des Beaux-Arts in Paris, where he studied under the narrative painter Jean-Paul Laurens. Many of his fellow students would, like him, develop an interest in fashion illustration. The group, which included Jean Besnard, Bernard Boutet de Monvel, Pierre Brissaud, Paul Iribe, Georges Lepape, Charles Martin, and André Édouard Marty, was given the sobriquet "Knights of the Bracelet" by *Vogue* in 1914, a reference to the fact that each member wore a bracelet and, more broadly, to their dandyism and flamboyant manner of dress.[4]

At the Louvre, where he discovered the art of classical antiquity, Barbier was in particular drawn to the imagery on Etruscan and Greek vases and to

Egyptian sculpture. At the same time, like most of fashionable Paris, he was seduced by the extravagant productions of the Ballets Russes, which made its debut in 1909.[5]

These many interests came together in Barbier's first exhibition, at the Galerie Boutet de Monvel in 1911. The 92 drawings and paintings were organized into three sections—"Belles du Moment," "Danseuses," and "Ballets Russes"—and the accompanying catalogue was written by the poet Pierre Louÿs.[6] The exhibition established Barbier's reputation and instigated his career as an illustrator.[7] Over the next twenty years, Barbier produced an astonishing number of drawings for journals and magazines, including *La Gazette du bon ton*, *Le Journal des dames et des modes*, *Vogue*, *Femina*, *Harper's Bazaar*, *Comœdia illustré*, and *L'Illustration*.[8]

Barbier's drawing style was flat, graphic, and precise; invariably his figures were anatomically correct and other details were rendered with equal accuracy (he had an encyclopedic knowledge of costume and decorative arts history). Nevertheless, invention trumped realism: "He possessed the necessary knowledge and will to stylization," wrote the critic Marcel Valotaire in 1927, "a vivid imagination, and the taste for that magnificence in which the present-day audience loves to forget the harshness of its ordinary routine."[9] For Miomandre, a drawing by Barbier was "something infinitely elegant and rich, accurate yet stylized, which has an affinity with calligraphy and with ceramics, with the print and with watercolor, and which is full of charm."[10]

It is unclear how Barbier spent the war years; he may have served in an administrative post in the War Ministry. Upon his return to civilian life, he set up a fantastical Paris studio in Montparnasse at 31, rue Campagne-Première, where the Dada and Surrealist artist Man Ray also had a studio. The space was filled with antiques and furnishings from distant lands—Chinese porcelains and jades, Japanese prints, lacquer screens, animal skins, even a Venetian glass chandelier in the shape of a galleon—exotica that provided inspiration for drawings and ideas for objects. One such object was a jeweled aigrette made by Cartier in 1911. Barbier had met Louis Cartier the previous year, when the famous jeweler acquired some of his drawings. In 1914, Cartier commissioned a panther-themed invitation

from Barbier; it was the first appearance of what would become a signature motif for the company. Barbier continued to supply Cartier with designs into the late 1920s.[11]

During the 1910s, Barbier expanded his repertoire to include Murano glass, textiles, and wallpaper. For such clients as Cartier, the Compagnie Générale Transatlantique, Renault, and the American perfume maker Richard Hudnut, he made posters and publicity materials. In Hudnut's Paris shop on the rue de la Paix he painted dazzling mural panels. And perhaps inspired by the Ballets Russes, he designed sets and costumes, notably for Maurice Rostand's play *Casanova* (1918) and for the silent film *Monsieur Beaucaire* (1924), starring Rudolf Valentino. At the 1925 Paris Exposition, his illustrated books were displayed in the Grand Palais.

Barbier's output declined during the late 1920s, likely the result of the unspecified illness of which he died at the age of forty-nine.

One may say of M. George Barbier that he is drawn to any surface with the capacity to receive a decoration. He is a born decorator. And his extraordinarily prolific inventiveness allows him always to envision the possibility of more works, indefinitely.[12]

2 | Fan
1914; painted ivory, metal, silk, gilding

Barbier is best known for his fashion illustrations. Less well known are his decorative arts, such as this folding fan. The design of the fan was originally published in 1912, in *Le Journal des dames et des modes*, where it was credited to the Parisian couturiere Jeanne Paquin, "after G. Barbier."[1] In fact, the design had been made for Paquin the previous year, probably as a work-for-hire commission, appearing in a deluxe publicity album depicting fans and furs, *L'Éventail et la fourrure chez Paquin*.[2] Although this was the only fan by Barbier in the album, he may have designed others for Paquin, as noted by Francis de Miomandre in 1914:

He designed a series of fans for Mme Paquin—at last, these were not the never-ending copies of the eighteenth century!—even the most insignificant is exquisite.[3]

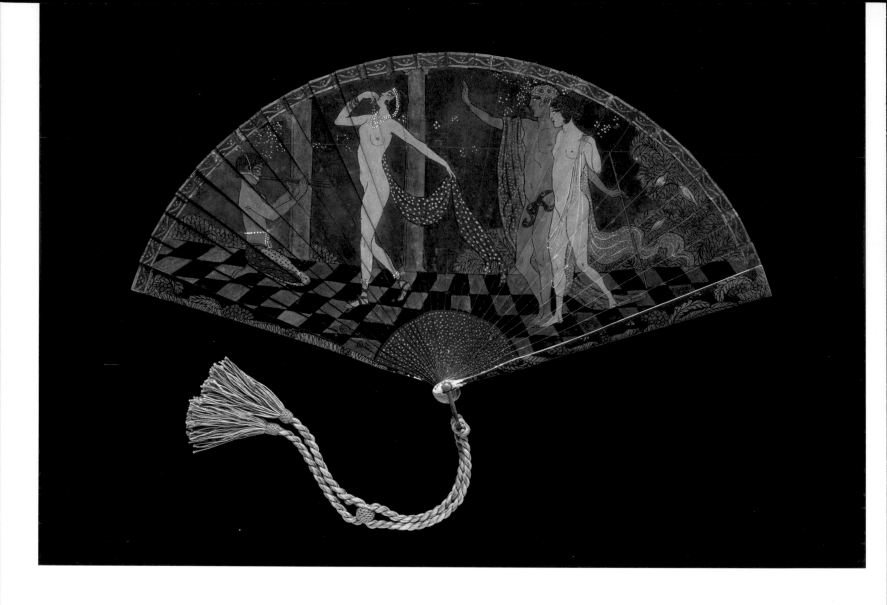

Etruscan frescoes, Tomb of the Triclinium, Necropolis of Monterozzi, Tarquinia, Italy, ca. 470 B.C. Tarquinia National Museum

Although the design was conceived in 1912, the fan is signed and dated 1914, suggesting that Barbier realized it later, probably on commission; it is unlikely that he made more than one.

The fan's ivory sticks are painted on the obverse with a scene of dancers and musicians in an architectural setting; the reverse and the end sticks are decorated with a pattern of flowers and fruit. Both sides have a deep blue-green ground and a rich red border embellished with gilded details. The sticks are secured with a metal D ring from which dangles the tasseled silk cord used to carry the fan.

While the imagery recalls the sets and costumes of the Ballets Russes, in 1914 Miomandre described a print that he saw in Barbier's studio which revealed the source not only for the design, but perhaps even Barbier's choice of métier:

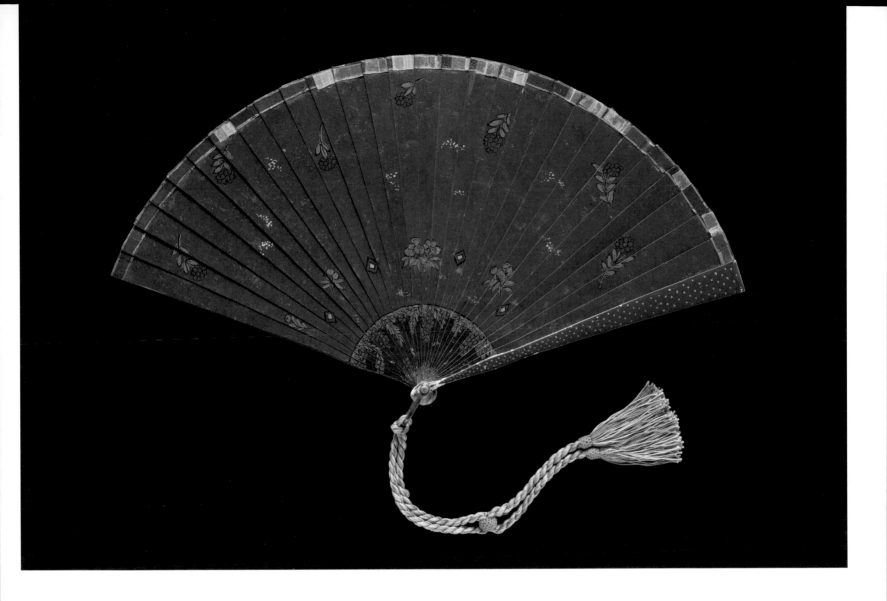

It may be of some interest to know what was, if not the origin of M. George Barbier's vocation, then at least the occasion on which he became clearly conscious of it: the sight of a reproduction of paintings in the Etruscan tomb of Corneto known as the Tomb of the Dancers. On the day he stood before that beautiful object, he felt something crystallize inside himself. Certainly he had always been attracted to Japanese prints, Persian miniatures, Greek vases, and even the mysterious drawings of Beardsley, but these did not make an impact strong enough to determine his creative impulse, such as the one the Tomb of the Dancers unleashed.[4]

The author refers to one of the many fifth-century B.C. Etruscan tombs in the Italian town of Corneto, today known as Tarquinia.[5] Barbier's design borrows directly from the ancient imagery, not only the style of drawing but also the composition. Both have heavily outlined figures and a palette of red, blue, green, and ochre, and Barbier follows the antique convention of rendering the males with darker skin tones than the females. The figures themselves — draped dancers and a piper — are inspired by those in the tomb paintings, specifically their lively poses, midstep with arms raised. Barbier's friezelike procession mimics that of the architectonic paintings, and the fan's checkerboard floor derives from similar patterns on many of the tomb ceilings. Like the paintings, the fan has a red border.

The fan was given to the Metropolitan in 1963 by Mrs. William Randolph Hearst as part of a collection of 136 fans, of which this was the only twentieth-century example.[6]

VALÉRY BIZOUARD

Dijon 1875–1945 Paris

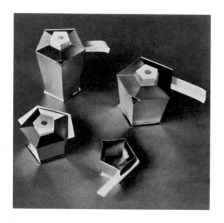

Valéry Bizouard, for Tétard Frères.
Silver and ivory tea service,
ca. 1930

Very little is known about Valéry Bizouard, artistic director during the 1920s and 1930s of Tétard Frères. Along with well-known firms such as Cardeilhac, Christofle, Keller Frères, Linzeler, and Puiforcat, Tétard Frères was one of the most prominent Paris silver manufacturers of the early twentieth century.[1] Bizouard seems to have been active by 1898 in Paris, where he worked for the silversmith Alphonse Debain, described by the curator and critic Henri Clouzot as "one of the first to have attempted to give new life to old forms."[2] By 1919 he had joined Tétard Frères, where he continued working until 1936. He may have worked concurrently for another Paris silversmith, Fouquet-Lapar, or at least retailed Tétard Frères designs through them.

Founded by Hugo Tétard in 1851, Tétard Frères specialized in tableware and enjoyed its most creative period between the two world wars under the artistic direction of Bizouard and Louis Tardy. Although Tétard Frères produced works conceived by several designers, Bizouard in particular created models that gave the firm a reputation for beautifully designed and meticulously executed works that demonstrated both an understanding of modern taste and a respect for the past.

In an article on Tétard Frères published in 1930, the designer-critic Georges Rémon wrote of the company's vision of silver in a contemporary idiom:

Modern silverwork is concerned above all with creating models for everyday use. It isn't about large sumptuous pieces, vitrine objects or museum-quality art that today compel our admiration. . . . It is the exquisite ingenuity used to invent new forms of ordinary silver in an effort to modernize table décor. . . . Utilitarian silver, as it develops ever more broadly, will adopt simple, judiciously conceived shapes in which unnecessary

ornament will be ruthlessly sacrificed or subordinated to form. . . . In [Tétard's] search for new patterns and pure harmonies, we will readily discover the care they have always shown for adorning the modern home with pieces that are clearly of our own time and whose forms reflect its spirit and style while still retaining . . . noble and subtle affinities with the finest productions of the past.[3]

Under the Tétard name, Bizouard participated in the annual Salons of the Société des Artistes Décorateurs, the Salon d'Automne, and the Salon des Tuileries. At the 1925 Paris Exposition, Tétard was represented at the Grand Palais. In New York, Tétard Frères silver was exhibited at B. Altman & Co. in 1928 and at the Fifty-Sixth Street Galleries in 1929. It was retailed through B. Altman and at Lord & Taylor in the 1920s and 1930s.[4]

3 | Flatware

1929–30; glass, silver gilt

a | Spoon

b | Fork

c | Knife

M. Valéry Bizouard is one of those who recognized, almost from the start of his brilliant career as an artist, the necessity of exercising the strictest economy in the choice of lines and the use of ornament. Pieces he designed twenty years ago seem to have been conceived yesterday. But his pursuit of sobriety has never led him to forget the great traditions of balance and taste from which the French genius intends to remain inseparable.[1]

Bizouard designed a number of flatware services for Tétard, of which this glass and silver-gilt set is

one of the most elegant. Almost certainly conceived as a dessert service, it demonstrates nothing if not economy of line and ornament. But any sobriety is offset by dazzling materials, the warm golden glow of the metal balanced by the cool refractions of the brilliant, faceted glass. The use of silver gilt, in addition to being an aesthetic choice, would have been a practical consideration as well, since gilding prevents tarnish even after exposure to acidic food such as fruit. As a dessert utensil, the solid glass knife does not require a sharp blade, and was probably intended to do little more than coax some tasty morsel of food onto the fork.

While Tétard certainly produced the metal components of the service, it is unclear who made the glass, although presumably it was done to Bizouard's specifications. The most likely candidate is Baccarat. It is known that the two firms collaborated.[2] Furthermore, around the time this service was made, Baccarat produced a very similar flatware service for the lavish Art Deco Manik Bagh Palace, commissioned by the Maharaja of Indore in 1930.[3]

EDGAR BRANDT

Paris 1880–1960 Geneva

Not only was Edgar Brandt the undisputed master of *ferronnerie* (ironworking) during the French Art Deco era, but indeed he is regarded as one of the most accomplished figures in the field. In 1924, Metropolitan Museum curator Joseph Breck wrote:

There can be no two opinions about the distinguished position which Edgar Brandt holds among contemporary craftsmen as a worker in metal. The beautifully designed and executed grilles, ramps, radiator- and fire-screens, lighting fixtures, and other pieces of wrought iron which come from the ateliers on the Boulevard Murat, Paris, have given to this artist an international reputation. . . .

Brandt uses all the resources of modern technical science in the handling of the metal, but never to the violation of the nature of the material employed. In this he follows the best traditions of the great periods of ironworking in the past; but within these conditions, his designs display creative ability of high order. His style is original, unmistakably personal.[1]

During the nineteenth century, the metal industry was dominated by cast iron, which was mass produced inexpensively and efficiently, employing molds and steam-operated stamping machines. However, what could be manufactured by such means was limited, both technically and artistically. With the twentieth century came a renewed interest in the traditional arts of France, including the ironwork of the eighteenth-century masters Jean Lamour and Jean Tijou. Newly founded organizations such as the Société des Artistes Décorateurs further encouraged a return to craftsmanship and a cross-disciplinary approach—for example, combining such diverse materials as glass or porcelain with metal—which fostered a unity of aesthetic expression within the broader field of the decorative arts. Perhaps as important, in 1903, Edmund Fauce, a French metalworker, invented a blowtorch that employed the highly flammable gas oxyacetylene to fuse metal parts together without solder. Using this torch—autogenous welding—saved craftsmen considerable time and effort, and allowed for greater artistic freedom than cast iron.

It was from this historical context that Edgar Brandt emerged.[2] He began working in metal at the age of fifteen, when he enrolled at the École Nationale Professionnelle, a technical school in Vierzon. In 1901 he moved to Paris, where he set up a studio in the upscale neighborhood of Auteuil. He was one of the first metalworkers to master autogenous welding. The oxyacetylene torch made his reputation, allowing him to realize tour-de-force flights of fantasy. From the beginning, Brandt displayed exceptional artistic invention and technical virtuosity. Private projects led quickly to important public commissions, and his business thrived before the outbreak of war in 1914.

Like many craftsmen who served in the war, Brandt brought specialized skills with him. Noting deficiencies in weapons and ammunition, he developed ideas for new mortars and artillery shells that not only were taken up by the military but prompted an interest in weaponry on Brandt's part that would remain with him and serve him financially throughout his life.

Returning to civilian life after the war, Brandt established a lucrative manufactory of armaments, which he sold to the French government. In 1919 he commissioned the architect Henri Favier to design a new building in Auteuil to house ateliers, administrative offices, and a showroom. Embellished with Brandt's fixed architectural metalwork and

filled with his domestic furnishings, the complex served as a real-life catalogue of his work. To meet the range and number of commissions that came his way, Brandt employed nearly 150 people, each of whom performed specialized tasks, from concept (drafting and model making) to production (forging, stamping, and patination). Nevertheless, every work was overseen by Brandt himself. Progressive and forward-looking, he was described in 1926 by the curator and critic Henri Clouzot:

Brandt, resolutely adopting mechanical tools: blow-pipe, steam-hammer, press and so on, turned his art into a great industry without depriving it of any esthetic qualities. . . . He spread designs of unprecedented freedom and vastness. He resolutely entered upon intense production such as fits our epoch of great building problems which afford iron endless opportunities.

At the same time, that new technique [autogenous welding] enabled him to make iron speak a new language.[3]

Brandt's career peaked in the 1920s, when he developed a distinct and dynamic personal style principally characterized by a rich density of stylized, finely detailed flower and plant motifs, sometimes offset with animal or human figures and areas of gilding. Architectural projects — especially

stylish entrances for many of the fashionable shops that opened in postwar Paris — were an important part of his production, as was lighting, especially the very popular lamps he made in collaboration with the glass manufacturer Daum. He also devised new forms for decorative metalwork, such as radiator covers. Radiators, which delivered steam heat (a technology developed during the second half of the nineteenth century), were a prominent feature in most new buildings of the Art Deco era, and Brandt, rather than concealing them, drew attention to them with elegantly designed covers.

He also continued to develop armaments for the French State. For this work, he was rewarded with important commissions, such as the holder for the eternal flame at the Tomb of the Unknown Soldier under the Arc de Triomphe (1923) and metalwork for the state-supported ocean liners the *Paris* (1920) and the *Île de France* (1927). Brandt was made a chevalier of the Légion d'Honneur in 1920 and an officer in 1926.

Brandt actively participated in the Paris Salons, and his displays garnered prizes and brought him international attention. At the 1922 Salon des Artistes Français, for example, he displayed his grille Les Cigognes d'Alsace (The Storks of Alsace). Gordon Selfridge, when he visited the exhibition, liked it so much he commissioned Brandt to adapt it

Edgar Brandt display, Salon d'Automne, 1923. The grille acquired by The Metropolitan Museum of Art is at left.

for the elevators of his famous London department store. Brandt's considerable contributions to the 1925 Paris Exposition were extravagantly praised:

Among the phalanx of original creators who secured the triumph of our national art in the great tournament of 1925, he stands one of the most representative and to be sure one of those who exhibited the most perfect and numerous works. With the principal gate in the Champs-Élysées, the doors of the national Monaco Pavilion, of the Pavilion of "the Intransigeant," of "the Renaissance," of the shop of the "Illustration" [three arts publications], doors and inner gates of the collector's [Ruhlmann] Pavilion, enclosure of the Court of Trades, chandeliers lamp-posts, screens of the embassy [the Ambassade Française] drawing-rooms, not to mention the master's own stand in the 7th class, Brandt was everywhere, and everywhere represented the original French modern art, poised, free from any odd affectation, with powerful plain lines, variegated in the extreme in new personal motives, displaying such rich decoration as had not been met with since the grand epoch of the XVIIIth century.[4]

It was a testament to Brandt's reputation that he was awarded the commission for the Porte d'Honneur (see page 11), the main entrance gate to the Exposition. Brandt's own display, created with the architect Henri Favier, presented a spectacular room setting, the centerpiece of which was his five-panel Oasis screen—considered his masterwork.[5]

In 1925, Brandt opened his own gallery in Paris at 27, boulevard Malesherbes, the Galerie Edgar Brandt. There, he showed not only his own work but also that of friends and firms with whom he had collaborated over the years—among them Decœur, Dunand, Lalique, Pompon, Puiforcat, Ruhlmann, and Süe et Mare. In addition to displays of decorative arts, he organized exhibitions of fine arts—painting and sculpture—to underscore the close relationship between the two disciplines. The gallery remained open until 1933.

The year 1925 also saw the opening of showrooms—called Ferrobrandt—in Hanover Square in London and at 247 Park Avenue in New York. Brandt's work was widely admired, especially in North America; it was seen in department store displays and museum exhibitions, and he received many important private and public commissions.[6] Brandt's contributions to architecture were acknowledged by the American Association of Architects, which made him an honorary member in 1929, an exceptional recognition for a foreigner. The worldwide financial crisis of 1929 curtailed much of Brandt's work abroad, although his business in France continued to grow in the early 1930s. In 1932 he opened a vast state-of-the-art factory in the Paris suburb of Châtillon-sous-Bagneux, where upward of 3,000 workers fabricated both decorative metalwork and armaments under the Brandt name. Among Brandt's most prestigious commissions of the 1930s were those for the Paris Exposition Coloniale Internationale (1931) and for the ocean liner *Normandie* (1935).[7] During the 1930s his work became simpler, airier, and almost calligraphically abstract.

The Châtillon factory was nationalized in 1936. Following the German occupation of Paris, in 1942 Brandt moved with his family to Switzerland. He returned to France after the war but did not reopen his studio, choosing rather to work on small projects until his death in 1960. After many mergers, the Brandt name lives on today as FagorBrandt, a manufacturer of household appliances.

4 | *Perse* Grille
ca. 1923; iron

This grille was first exhibited at the 1923 Salon d'Automne as part of a larger grouping presented in an alcove and prosaically titled *Quelques Ferronneries* (Some Ironworks).[1] The focal point was *L'Age d'Or* (The Golden Age), a monumental tripartite screen set into the alcove's rear wall; it was flanked by two nearly identical grilles with mirror images of the same pattern. The grille acquired by the Metropolitan Museum was installed at the alcove's left.[2] While a very similar grille by Brandt was published in 1925 as an "entrance door," none of these panels appear to have been conceived for this purpose.[3] Brandt later added the stabilizing feet to the Metropolitan's panel, allowing it to stand alone.

The 1926 catalogue of the American Association of Museums' traveling exhibition of selected works from the 1925 Paris Exposition describes Brandt as:

*. . . the outstanding genius of the modern French move-
ment. More than any other leader he combines apparently exhaustless talent for composition with mastery of
technique and a perfect sense of functional and decorative fitness. His creations are never bizarre, but they
compass the whole gamut of moods: light, delicate and
elegant . . . stately, rich and dignified . . . flowering
with wondrous fancy . . . sober, strong and even monumental . . . they are always perfectly fitted for the place
they fill. Rarely indeed has a designer compassed successfully such extraordinary variety in his work and
more rarely still without developing a mannerism.
Edgar Brandt has no manner except it be the manner
of almost faultless composition in each new production.
He creates one striking design and passes to another
equally novel before we have ceased to admire the first.*[4]

"Flowering with wondrous fancy" aptly describes
this magnificent grille. Its rich, free pattern creates
a sense of highly charged motion, like cogwheels
spinning in a complex piece of exquisite machinery.
The extremely fine detailing could have been made
only with the use of an oxyacetylene torch: the floral
motifs, made from hammered and chased cast-iron
discs embellished with hair-like iron slivers or bands
of cast-iron beads, are attached to rippling scalloped
bands of forged iron that suggest exotic foliage. While
the dense composition suggests the Persian miniature
garden painting evoked by its name, the decorative
patterning, geometric stylization, and apparent flat-
ness also bring to mind Japanese art, an aesthetic that
for Brandt held considerable fascination.

Brandt's patterning was widely imitated. Writing in 1929, the American journalist Walter Rendell
Storey noted that his floral motifs "achieved such
popularity that adaptations of it soon appeared in
damasks and other silk weaves. Wallpapers have
been developed in this pattern, as have also carpets."[5] Several of Brandt's motifs were adapted by
Cheney Brothers of New York for printed silk textiles, which were displayed at the Louvre in 1925.

RENÉ BUTHAUD

Saintes 1886–1986 Bordeaux

In 1930, critic Marcel Valotaire defined ceramics as

. . . an art with three aspects, one corresponding to the wish of the technician in the thrall of material perfection, the second to the temperament of the sculptor in love with form and relief, and the third and final, to the desire of the painter passionate for rich deep colors; ceramists could easily be classified on this tripartite scheme.[1]

Valotaire cited René Buthaud as one of the few ceramists of his day to have mastered all three aspects. Nevertheless, it was his skill in the last mentioned that singles him out; of his many contributions, his revival of surface decoration on ceramics must be seen as the most significant. Indeed, it was Buthaud's early training as a painter and engraver that first led him to ceramics as a decorator; only later did he become an accomplished technician and a "sculptor in love with form."

The son of a haberdasher, Buthaud expressed an early interest in painting, and reluctantly, in 1903, his father agreed that he could enter the École des Beaux-Arts in Bordeaux.[2] He served his apprenticeship with a Bordeaux engraver and developed a talent for copperplate engraving—"Had I wished, I could have earned my living that way"—but because the École des Beaux-Arts did not teach engraving, he opted to train as a painter.[3]

In 1907, Buthaud moved to Paris, where he enrolled at the École des Beaux-Arts and also attended design classes at the École des Arts Décoratifs. He first exhibited as a painter at the 1911 Salon of the Société des Artistes Français, where he was awarded the prestigious Attainville Prize. At the outbreak of the war, Buthaud was drafted into the Army but, due to an illness, was soon transferred to the auxiliary corps and spent the remaining

years of the war working as an engraver for the military. Returning to civilian life in Bordeaux, Buthaud learned the basic techniques of ceramics at a small pottery. He experimented using a small, wood-burning kiln that he built in his backyard, somewhat unexpectedly looking to traditional French faïence and stoneware for inspiration rather than to Japanese ceramics, as had been the practice among French potters for nearly half a century— "because I am French—European—and there are things I am better able to do than ape fantasies [*singeries*] that are not mine."[4] From the beginning, his preference was for simple forms decorated with figural motifs.

In 1919 and 1920, Buthaud submitted examples of his ceramic work to the Salon d'Automne and the Salon des Artistes Décorateurs. The award of the Prix Blumenthal, a grant given to young artists who had served in the war, allowed Buthaud to spend time at the Maison l'Hospier, a commercial pottery in Golfe-Juan, where he developed his technical skills.[5] In 1923, the Printemps department store hired Buthaud as director of its Primavera pottery workshop at Sainte-Radegonde. There, he oversaw the factory's production and its staff of nearly forty workers.

Following his wife's death in 1926, Buthaud returned to Bordeaux, where he set up a studio, this time with a coal-fired kiln, and began to develop his personal style, favoring bulbous forms with visually integrated figurative decoration.[6] He often used *céramique du grand feu* (closely related to stoneware, it is fired at a high temperature that fuses body and glaze) covered with *peau-de-serpent* (snakeskin) glaze. Made by adding feldspar and ground algae to the batch, the glaze after firing takes on its characteristic crackle. Of such work, the critic Guillaume

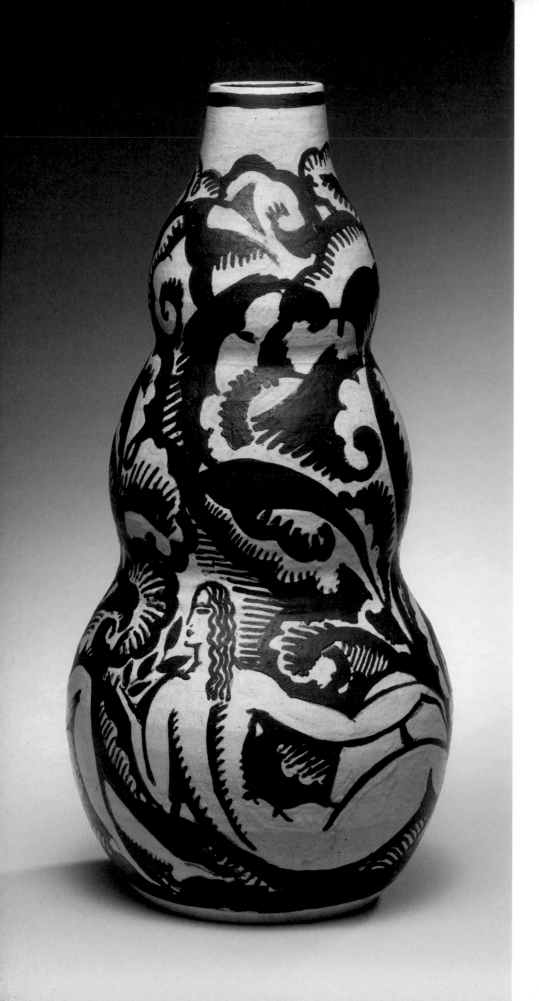

Janneau wrote that it revealed "not only the skill of a decorator but the sensibility of an artist."[7]

Throughout the 1920s and 1930s, Buthaud's work was seen at the Paris Salons and sold at galleries such as Druet and Georges Rouard.[8] He participated in the Paris Expositions of 1925 and 1937, exhibited widely in France and abroad, and, beginning in 1931, was a professor of art at the École des Beaux-Arts in Bordeaux.[9] In 1937, Buthaud was made a chevalier of the Légion d'Honneur. Highly productive throughout the postwar years, he died in 1986 at the age of one hundred.

5 | Three Vases

a | Vase, ca. 1923–24; glazed stoneware

b | Vase, ca. 1923–24; glazed stoneware

c | Vase, 1929; glazed stoneware

Buthaud's work exemplifies the increasing interaction between the fine and decorative arts in the early twentieth century. In this light, after citing Buthaud's training as a painter, writer Marcel Valotaire noted:

It is not surprising that although he greatly appreciated pure ceramics, he turned instead to decorated ceramics. In this context, René Buthaud readily invokes the example of the Greeks, the Persians, the Spanish Moors, and our own early French potters, whose undisputed masterpieces are excellent proof of the legitimacy of decoration.[1]

He continued by pointing out Buthaud's preference for stoneware,

. . . the material that allows the greatest possibility for painted decoration while retaining a robustness of form, of solidity. . . . [To it, he applies] resolutely modern decoration, geometric compositions, and, above all, nude figures, which he adapts to the curve of his vases.[2]

Buthaud rarely conceived his pots as utilitarian wares but rather as decorative works of art—canvases in the round; indeed, the crackle-glazed pieces are by nature decorative, since their surface is porous. His decoration invariably relates directly

to form. In his figural work, he generally followed his own convention: standing figures appear on tall or elongated forms; kneeling or partial figures on medium-size forms; and recumbent figures on low, squat forms. In general, he favored a limited palette, which customarily included at least one dark color.

These three vases perfectly illustrate Buthaud's distinctive style. The triple gourd–shaped vase (see page 40), dating from 1923–24, is probably the earliest of the three, and was likely made at the Primavera factory in Sainte-Radegonde. The bold black imagery has the graphic look of a woodblock, reflecting Buthaud's early career as a printer. The reclining figures, confined to the lowest register of the vase, and the stylized foliage are typical of his decorative vocabulary.

The abstractly decorated vase (at left) dates from about the same time and was also probably made at Sainte-Radegonde. Although Buthaud favored figural decoration, like many designers of his time he also experimented with abstraction. Cubism offered a fashionable new vocabulary that could be configured for decorative effect, though in the decorative arts generally — as opposed to painting — it carried no allusive content. Here, Buthaud uses a series of rhythmic stepped and curved contours to carry the eye around the cocoon-shaped body. The *peau-de-serpent* (snakeskin) glaze immediately establishes the work as by Buthaud. In a letter dated December 24, 1969, to Metropolitan Museum curator Henry Geldzahler, the dealer Lillian Nassau states that "the René Buthaud vase is one of the remaining 25 vases from his atelier which his wife sold directly to my buyer in France. I was lucky to get all 25."[3]

The third vase (opposite and page 44), dating from 1929, is perhaps the most characteristic, its bulbous form accentuated by the lolling nudes and swirling foliage wrapping around it. One figure is presented frontally, the other (on the opposite side) from the rear. The crackle of the *peau-de-serpent* glaze is here more subtle than on the earlier vase.

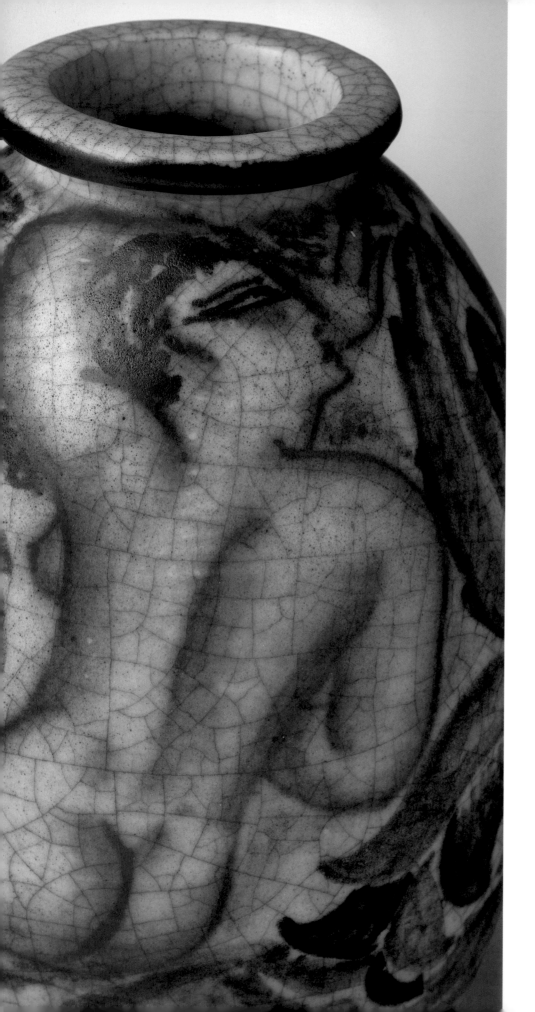

6 | Statuette
ca. 1935; glazed earthenware

Ceramic figurines have been made since man first fashioned objects from clay, appearing in virtually every era and in every culture of global history. The genre flourished in Europe between the two world wars, and it is not surprising that many French potters, including Buthaud, were drawn to it. Like many artists, Buthaud was also a collector. As a young man he acquired African art, but later became interested in eighteenth- and nineteenth-century ceramic figurines, notably those from provincial France, Scotland, and England. He owned a number of early nineteenth-century figurines made at the Staffordshire pottery. He was also intrigued by contemporary statuettes from Austria, probably produced for the Wiener Werkstätte, which he first encountered around 1925.

About 1927, with the encouragement of his dealer Georges Rouard, who was interested in the commercial potential of ceramic figurines, Buthaud began to make his own statuettes, which emulated those earlier models. He spent several years developing a series, employing tin-glazed earthenware—from which figurines had traditionally been made—rather than the stoneware or *ceramique du grand feu* (high-fired ceramic) he was best known for. He sent his first pieces to the Rouard gallery in December 1934. They sold well and met with favorable press:

[Buthaud's] early works, high-fired vases and cups decorated with feminine faces, are well known. Now he offers us a totally different aspect of his talent, bluish paste figurines heightened with shining enamels in bright colors. . . . This is all very agreeable. The colors are vivid, and the works create an overall impression of freshness and clarity, recalling the charming Scottish faïence of the nineteenth century. A gentleman will enjoy resting his eye on these lighthearted bits of gaiety.[1]

Buthaud continued to make such statuettes until the early 1960s, producing more than two hundred examples, many of which represent figures generically drawn from classical mythology, perhaps making reference to the figural pottery of ancient Greece and Rome (Buthaud had a thorough knowledge of early ceramics). This one, dating from about 1935, depicts a flute-playing youth with the horns of a faun. It remained in the artist's collection until he offered it to the Museum just before his one hundredth birthday.

7 | Study for an Athlete

ca. 1937; gouache, charcoal, graphite on paper (backed with fabric)

This large drawing—it is virtually life-size—depicts an athletic nude male figure posed in front of stylized drapery and a small flowering plant. A full-scale study for an image on one of four monumental urns at Lescure Stadium in Bordeaux, it typifies Buthaud's graphic style and is one of a series of drawings for these vases, which Buthaud kept in his own collection his entire life.

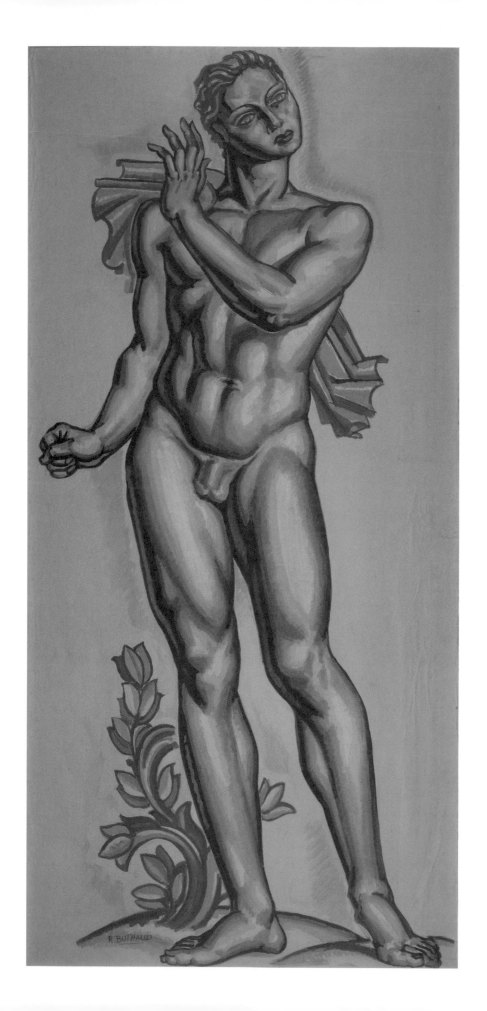

René Buthaud. Concrete urns with mosaic decoration,
Lescure Stadium, Bordeaux, 1936. Photograph, 2013

Adrien Marquet, mayor of Bordeaux from 1925 until 1944, was responsible for building the new stadium as part of an ambitious program of public works completed between 1930 and 1940.[1] Building began in 1933, and the stadium was inaugurated on June 12, 1938, with a World Cup soccer match.[2] Buthaud, by then one of Bordeaux's most celebrated citizens, was invited to design the four monumental urns that stand in the arena's forecourt. Each of the urns, which on their bases are over 12 feet high, is appropriately embellished with three images of heroic athletes, rendered in earthenware tile mosaic set onto cast concrete forms. The urns remain in place today.

ÉDOUARD CAZAUX

Cauneille 1889–1974 Cauneille

It is not surprising that Édouard Cazaux became a ceramist, having been born to a family of potters extending back many generations. His shared talent as a sculptor, however, sets him apart.[1] At the age of fourteen he went to work at a local ceramics factory and at eighteen moved to Paris, where he was drawn to the art pottery of nineteenth-century French masters Ernest Chaplet and Auguste Delaherche. In 1909 he met the sculptor Charles Despiau, whose encouragement was instrumental in developing his burgeoning interest in sculpture. Awarded a scholarship to the École des Beaux-Arts, Cazaux studied sculptural modeling while supporting himself by working in pottery workshops, namely those of Edmond Lachenal and Georges Garing. During the war he served in the ambulance corps, which took him, in 1916, to the town of Baccarat, home to the famous glass factory, which likely inspired his later interest in glassmaking.

When he returned to civilian life, Cazaux embarked on his double career as potter and sculptor.

He settled with his family in the town of La Varenne-Saint-Hilaire, a suburb of Paris, and began making pottery. Around 1925 he mastered the notoriously difficult process of firing red-copper glazes. In the early 1920s, he also received several important sculptural commissions from the French State, including memorials to the war dead in Biarritz, Saint-Vincent-de-Tyrosse, and Castets-des-Landes. Both his ceramics and his sculptures were exhibited concurrently at the Paris Salons.

Perhaps most notable about Cazaux's ceramic work was that—unlike that of his contemporaries—Cazaux himself carried out every step of the process. Critics were impressed. Clément Morro, writing in 1921, noted:

In the case of M. Cazaux, the craftsman is the equal of the artist: his pottery has the rare merit of being thrown, decorated, and fired by him personally, without the assistance of any collaborator. In this respect he has returned to a great tradition and, in these times of excessive specialization, this is significant.[2]

Also citing Cazaux, another critic wrote:

A masterpiece is more easily produced by one person working alone than by several. In a genre as refined as that of ceramics, in which every detail demands the artist's attention, [a misstep] in any phase of the long and difficult process of execution can destroy or completely distort the original idea.[3]

Cazaux's pottery was widely exhibited in France and on the international scene, and he had a strong presence at the 1925 Paris Exposition.[4] In the 1930s, architecturally scaled ceramic works—namely, fountains—were added to Cazaux's repertoire.

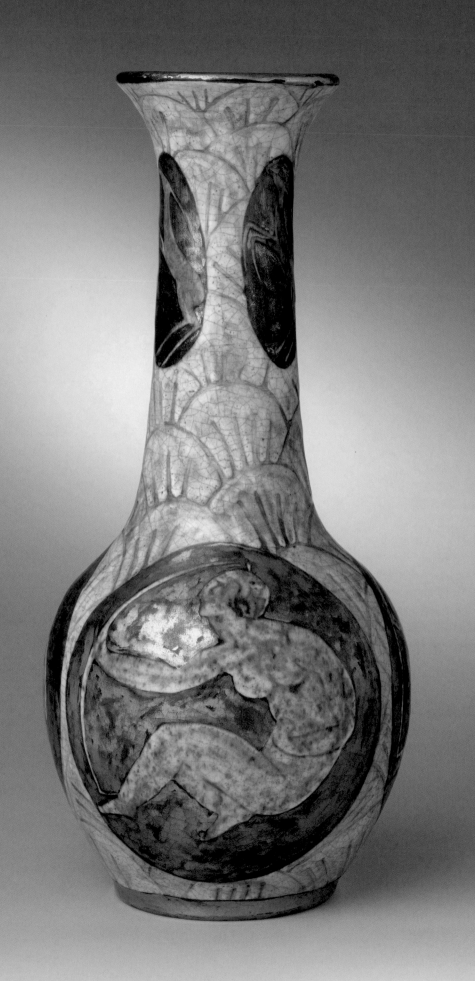

Ever expanding his field of endeavor, Cazaux in 1928 went to work at the renowned Cristalleries de Compiègne, a glassmaking factory.[5] As a designer of art glass, and until 1939, he made plaster models—many based on his ceramic forms—which were then used to create molds for glass vases. In 1933, Cazaux was elected a chevalier of the Légion d'Honneur. He continued working as both a potter and a sculptor until his death in 1974.

Cazaux's mastery of his métier, highly praised during the artist's lifetime, continues to impress. As early as 1922, a critic wrote: "Édouard Cazaux, as an artist and as a craftsman, is a master. I would be very surprised if people do not realize this before long."[6] They did, and indeed, we still do.

8 | Vase

ca. 1935; glazed earthenware

Cazaux's fascination with traditional Persian pottery is reflected in much of his own ceramic work and is exemplified by this glazed earthenware vase. Indeed, just about every aspect of this piece suggests a Middle Eastern precedent: the palette of blue, green, and gold; the metallic luster glaze; the long-necked bottle form; and the motif of archers and gazelles. Nevertheless, it is in no way a pastiche but rather the transformation of a traditional idiom. Monumental in scale and with a bold, simple profile, the body displays a frieze of three athletic female archers (with fashionably bobbed hair) set within gold-and-blue luster-glazed roundels. Around the neck are similar oval panels, with images of fleeing gazelles. The pale blue crackle-glaze fish-scale pattern suggests abstract foliage.

Of such work, the critic Clément Morro wrote: "His vases, very pure in form and agreeably decorative, display lines at once elegant and robust."[1] His assessment was echoed by C. de Cordis: "This excellent artist knows how to be fanciful without extravagance, plain without banality, reserved without affectation."[2]

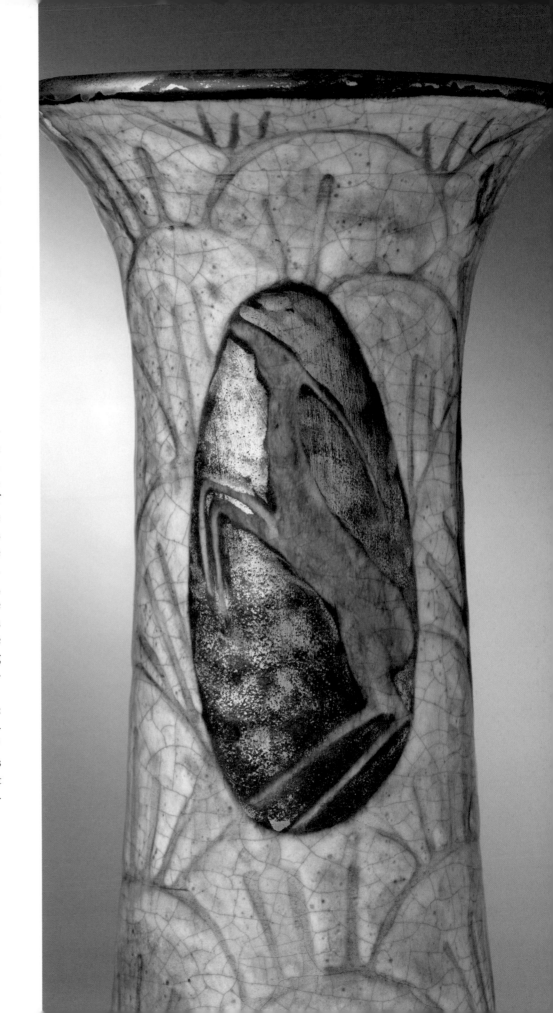

RENÉ CREVEL

Born Rouen (?); dates unknown

René Crevel. Study, Salon d'Automne, 1924

Almost nothing is known about the designer René Crevel, who is often confused with the well-known Surrealist writer of the same name. Life dates of 1900–1935 are frequently assigned to the designer, but in fact they are those of the writer, who was born and committed suicide in Paris. The Bénézit dictionary cites (without life dates) a painter-decorator René Crevel born in Rouen who could well be our man.[1] His career seems to have covered the period 1920 until 1940, based on his participation in the annual Salons of the Société des Artistes Décorateurs in 1921–23, 1925, 1927–30, 1934, 1936, and 1940.

Crevel the designer seems to have turned his hand to a wide range of projects. The earliest, which dates to about 1920, is a group of wallpapers designed for, among other manufacturers, C. H. H. Geffroy and, later, Nobilis. At the 1924 Salon d'Automne, he presented a complete room setting (a study), and

around the same time he designed a façade for a fishmonger's shop, published in 1925.[2] By 1930 he was also designing carpets, tapestries, and enameled objects. Throughout his career he also worked as a decorative painter; most notably, at the 1925 Paris Exposition he created murals for an antechamber designed by Paul Follot (see page 52) for the Ambassade Française.[3]

The year 1930 seems to have been a busy one for Crevel. As a designer for Les Ateliers d'Art Legédé, he created a line of table ceramics and linens, exhibited at the Paris gallery Le Grand Dépôt. He also contributed ceramics and glass—exactly what sort is unclear—to the French section of the Exposition Internationale in Liège, where he served as a juror for both utilitarian and art ceramics. At that fair he won a Grand Prix for his contribution to the category of art glass.

Between 1925 and 1934, Crevel supplied decorative designs to the Manufacture Nationale de Sèvres. It is possible that he found his way to the factory through Georges Lechevallier-Chevignard, director from 1920 until 1938. Established in 1740 under royal patronage, Sèvres—which continues to operate today—is the official French manufacturer of ceramics. Its output includes not only the porcelains for which it has been renowned for centuries but all aspects of the ceramic arts, including faïence and stoneware. By the early twentieth century, it was primarily producing expensive but conservative wares for the high-end market. Lechevallier-Chevignard was brought in with the mandate to update production to align with the tastes of the time and to meet the demands of its modern clients. To do so, he recruited outside talent, some with specific expertise in technical matters, others—artists, designers, and decorators—with no previous experience in ceramics, who advised on new product ideas. Crevel appears to have been one of these advisors, along with Raoul Dufy, René Lalique, François Pompon, É.-J. Ruhlmann, and many others.

Under Lechevallier-Chevignard's directorship, Sèvres expanded its repertoire, which up until then had comprised mainly costly table services and decorative pieces in porcelain or stoneware, to include faïence, terracotta, translucent porcelain, metal-inlaid ceramics, and ceramics suitable for outdoor and architectural use. Most of these products were introduced at the 1925 Paris Exposition, where the manufactory had its own pavilion on the Esplanade des Invalides, the epicenter of the fair. Designed by the architects Pierre Patout and André Ventre, the pavilion complex, two buildings flanking a central courtyard, served as a dramatic setting for everything produced at the Sèvres factory. Installations demonstrated how ceramics could be incorporated into a variety of interiors—a reception room, dining room, and bathroom among them. Noteworthy among the objects displayed was a series of translucent illuminated porcelain lighting fixtures conceived by the ensemblier Henri Rapin, who also designed porcelain blanks for Sèvres, including one decorated by Crevel (at right). The commercial success of these new products allowed Sèvres in 1927 to become, for the first time in its history, financially independent of the French State.[4]

9 | Lidded Vase

RENÉ CREVEL AND HENRI RAPIN
1926; glazed porcelain

Following his 1925 visit to the Paris Exposition, Metropolitan Museum curator Joseph Breck wrote: "I find the exhibition of . . . Sèvres [disappointing,] although it is interesting to note that this sedate institution has quite definitely climbed aboard the [modern] bandwagon."[1] Breck's somewhat lackluster assessment may explain why he never acquired any Art Deco works made by the manufactory. Indeed, it was not until 1987 that the Metropolitan acquired its first example—this vase.

Cocoon shaped and lidded, the vase rests on a domed foot. Its form is articulated by grey-glazed

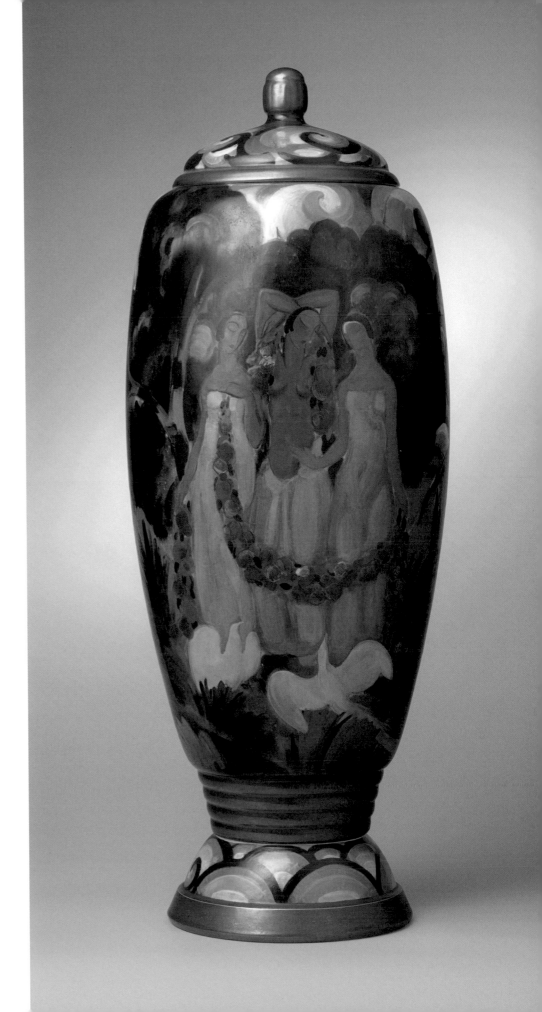

accents at the foot, the stepped waist, the rim of the lid, and the finial. The body is painted overall with a dense landscape in blues and greens with, on one face, a trio of flower-bedecked maidens and birds and, on the other, two nude male musicians. Crevel's decorative composition relates closely to the two murals he painted for Paul Follot's antechamber in the Ambassade Française at the 1925 Paris Exposition, both of which incorporated imagery of musicians, birds with outstretched wings, and dense foliage. The lush colors, coarse brushstrokes, and formal simplifications so characteristic of his style show the influence of Fauvism, a movement that, while it reached its zenith about 1905 to 1907, exerted its impact in the decorative arts through the 1920s. Crevel produced the master design, which was then painted onto the porcelain blank by Adrien-Auguste Leduc, who worked in the Sèvres workshops.

The blank was designed by Henri Rapin, probably around 1924–25, and assigned the Sèvres factory number 11. It was produced into the late 1930s, exclusively in hard-paste porcelain, a lustrous and durable material made at Sèvres beginning in the 1760s.[2] At least six other painted designs were offered for the model, and depending on the complexity of the painting, pieces sold for between 4,500 and 10,250 francs.[3] At least four other examples with this design were made, each with slight variations in the painting.[4]

Paul Follot. Antechamber, with mural by René Crevel, Ambassade Française, Exposition Internationale des Arts Décoratifs et Industriels Modernes, Paris, 1925

ÉMILE DECŒUR

Paris 1879–1953 Fontenay-aux-Roses

Emile Decœur stands at the head of French ceramists of today. He is still a young man but his untiring experiments, guided by superior intelligence and high artistic taste, have brought to the art of grand feu stoneware and porcelain a richness and refinement unattained before in modern times. The beauty of his subtle, unctuous glaze effects have revealed possibilities in the art of the ceramist that have never been rivalled, it is safe to say, since the high period of the old Chinese potters.[1]

These words introduced Decœur's work to the American public in 1926. Perhaps more telling yet is this assessment of Decœur from 1952, a moment when Art Deco was held in especially low regard:

French esteem of Emile Decœur is pointedly expressed in the word "Ceramiste"—a man who is no ordinary potter, but one who has searched beyond. He is at once an artist, who feels form in his mind; and has penetrated the many secrets of glazing and the materials belonging to that phase of potting. On the potter's wheel he brings dead clay to life and intuitively creates a clay being that in form is beauty itself. In glazing he handles a master wand. For genuine artistry Emile Decœur lives above his fellows.[2]

Since the 1920s, Decœur has been considered the most accomplished French ceramist of the Art Deco era. Orphaned at an early age, he apprenticed with the celebrated potter Edmond Lachenal in Châtillon-sous-Bagneux, a suburb of Paris, where he learned the fundamentals of ceramic making.[3] In the evenings, he studied art at the Conservatoire des Arts et Métiers and the Bibliothèque Forney in Paris. Although most of Decœur's initial work with Lachenal was in faïence, they later experimented with the more complicated techniques of stoneware.

Their cosigned works in this medium would garner a bronze medal at the Paris Exposition Universelle of 1900. Decœur first showed his own work at the 1901 Salon of the Société des Artistes Français, marking the beginning of his lifelong participation in the annual Salon exhibitions. In 1907 he opened his own studio in Fontenay-aux-Roses. Much of his work during this period was sculptural in conception (he made a small number of busts and figural statuettes, while his elaborately contoured vessels had twisting handles, rims, and other such details), and generally made from stoneware covered with complicated, multicolored, copper-reduction flambé glazes of Japanese inspiration. Following his discovery of traditional Chinese pottery, around 1910 he began to simplify both his forms (limiting himself mainly to vessels) and his glazes.

Decœur's work was also seen in galleries and at museum exhibitions and world's fairs.[4] His work was first exhibited at Georges Rouard in 1908; the gallery would represent him throughout his life. In 1907, Decœur met Atherton Curtis, a rich Brooklyn-born collector living in Paris who made his fortune in patents for medicine. Curtis became an ardent supporter and Decœur's most important private patron.

In 1909 Decœur settled with his wife, Augustine, in Fontenay-aux-Roses.[5] There, he developed specialized skills as a *céramiste* through tireless experimentation, grinding his own clay batch, hand throwing his pots, formulating his glazes, and firing pieces in kilns of his own design.

After serving in the war, in 1920 Decœur was elected vice president of the Salon of the Société des Artistes-Décorateurs. The same year, he was made a chevalier of the Légion d'Honneur, and in 1926, an officer. In 1922 he was given a solo exhibition at the Musée des Arts Décoratifs. His work was widely represented at the 1925 Paris Exposition, seen throughout the 1920s in international exhibitions, and sold through dealers abroad.[6] In New York, he showed at the Jacques Seligmann gallery, and in Buenos Aires at the Maison de l'Art Français.

By the late 1920s, Decœur had developed his distinctive, subtle style, which looked to ancient Chinese models for inspiration. His simple, minimally decorated pots were made from specially formulated clays covered with opaque, subtly colored slips and glazes, emphasizing materials and techniques as vehicles of artistry and meaning. In his work, wrote the critic René Chavance, one discovers

. . . a contained sensibility, the refined elegance of the poet. What dominates . . . is an irreducible integrity that allows for no trickery and finds satisfaction only knowingly. Each of his works is unique in the true sense of the word, and he dedicates himself entirely to them, with skill and honesty. Hence their austerity, but also the impression of fullness verging on perfection that one feels when one contemplates them.[7]

The critic Guillaume Janneau noted that Decœur never placed his virtuosity on display:

. . . the great simplicity of his decorations, the beauty he seeks in the distinctness of a hue, the purity of a his material, and the refinement of his workmanship are anything but ostentatious. His art scorns artifice and facile expression. He endeavors to achieve perfection.[8]

Decœur's reputation continued to grow in the 1930s. In 1939 he was hired as an artistic advisor by the Manufacture Nationale de Sèvres, an association that would continue until 1948. Decœur died in 1953 at his home in Fontenay-aux-Roses, where he had lived since 1909.

The art of Émile Decœur satisfies the profound need for completeness felt by men who reflect, who work, who know the price of honest toil. That spare, filtered, refined art, which has been called Racinian, and which, by its elevation and elegance, is worthy of the great poet, contains an important lesson: a lesson first in taste, and then in morality.[9]

10 | Jar and Two Vases

a | Jar, ca. 1925; glazed stoneware

b | Vase, ca. 1920; glazed stoneware

c | Vase, ca. 1922; glazed stoneware

In 1929, Metropolitan Museum curator Joseph Breck put on view several pieces of ceramic by Decœur. He described them in the Museum's *Bulletin*:

Of notable interest is a group . . . in stoneware by Emile Decœur that exemplify the masterly skill of this French ceramic artist in the production of simple, well-proportioned forms covered with glazes unobtrusive in color and exquisite in texture. . . . In technical perfection, purity of form, and charm of color, Decœur's work is wholly admirable.[1]

Decœur had by then a reputation as one of the most talented, sophisticated, and well-known French Art Deco studio potters. These three pieces epitomize the range of his subtle, elegant, and studied work. When asked by the critic W. B. Dalton, who visited Decœur's studio in 1952, whether he "relied on the ideas that come to mind while throwing on the wheel," Decœur replied that "no, his 'throwings' were planned, that before beginning a proportioned vision of the whole should be in mind, and that all parts should be mentally related." Dalton added, "There is no hit or miss about Decœur's ways. Everything is calculated carefully."[2]

The classic baluster form of the blue vase at center, for example, was calculated to show off the rich, complex glaze; the warm, deep indigo, which imitates the color of ancient Roman glass, also suggests the rich color of lapis lazuli. Decœur developed this glaze about 1919, using it on a number of his pots.

With the gourd-shaped vase at right, he employed an early Chinese technique, applying a pale grey glaze to a simple form, the surface of which he impressed with small tightly spaced squares. The pattern is enhanced by the pooling of glaze in the depressions, and the effect is one of cool modern abstraction tempered by ancient warmth and richness. Of such treatment, Dalton wrote: "Though glaze volume is characteristic in most of this potter's work, he uses cut surface decoration . . .

occasionally, diaper-like and restrained, as [if] it were an echo into a later century."[3]

The bold, simple shape of the low jar at left is typical of the Art Deco era. Its dark brown underglaze—visible on the interior, the lip, and the foot—is covered with a thick, creamy, faintly crackled overglaze, at once matte and luminous in its finish. "Decœur never dips or sprays any of his pieces," wrote Dalton. "All glazes are brushed on. . . . To glaze the inside of bowls or vases he pours and works the glaze carefully about over the entire area to insure good glaze quality."[4]

Living room, with Decœur vase at left center on bookcase, Mr. and Mrs. Charles Liebman residence, New York City, ca. 1926

11 | Vase

ca. 1925; glazed stoneware

The ancient Chinese were for Decœur the undisputed masters of the art of ceramics.[1] Throughout his career, he never ceased trying to understand their methods and to transform them into new and modern forms of expression. While the elegant lines and purposefully irregular celadon glaze of this vase clearly draw on Chinese precedent, it can be understood only as a loving and carefully considered homage to that tradition and never mistaken for anything but the work of Decœur. Such pieces moved critic W. B. Dalton to write in 1952 that "it was clear that Decœur had not halted on the threshold of Chinese achievement of the Sung Dynasty in all their outstanding excellences."[2]

Decœur was particularly fascinated by traditional Chinese celadon glazes, especially the tonal variations created by the buildup of the glaze in hollows and its diffusion in areas of relief. "'Glazes at rest,'" continued Dalton, "as the Chinese once described them, jade-like and enduring, have been the companions [Decœur] has sought through years of experiment while studying material and asking new uses of it." He could well have been describing this very piece in saying that Decœur's work "had all the reserve and unobtrusiveness of music in a minor key."

The vase was owned by Mr. and Mrs. Charles Liebman of New York. Aline Meyer Liebman was the sister of Florence Blumenthal, who established the prestigious Prix Blumenthal, a stipend awarded to young French artists who had served in the First World War. The Liebmans traveled frequently to France and on their trips made many acquisitions of modern fine and decorative arts. They acquired this vase about 1925 and placed it prominently atop a low bookcase in the living room of their New York apartment at 907 Fifth Avenue (see above).

FRANÇOIS-ÉMILE DÉCORCHEMONT

Conches-en-Ouche 1880–1971 Conches-en-Ouche

Referring to ongoing French efforts to renew the alliance between artistry and craftsmanship, in 1926 the critic René Chavance wrote:

In the incessant search [for new techniques] in which the beaux métiers [the craft industries] are today competing, the works that come closest to perfection are without a doubt those conceived and executed by the same artist.[1]

Chavance pointed to objects by François-Émile Décorchemont as exemplifying such works. For most of his career, Décorchemont worked exclusively in *pâte-de-verre*, an ancient technique closely related to ceramics that he, together with Gabriel Argy-Rousseau (see no. 1), was one of the few artist-craftsmen of his generation to master.

Ceramist? Glassmaker? It's not important. M. Décorchemont is an artist who, in using his own technique and a material that he himself created, has achieved effects whose refinement and completeness are a delight.[2]

Décorchemont was born to a family of artists.[3] His father, a sculptor, taught at the École Nationale des Arts Décoratifs in Paris. Raised during his early years in Normandy by his maternal grandparents, he moved to Paris at the age of twelve to be with his parents. In 1895 he entered the École Nationale des Arts Décoratifs. While initially Décorchemont considered becoming a potter, about 1902 he became fascinated by the related technique of *pâte-de-verre*, which he later claimed to have taught himself through trial and error. He was a quick study. Already in 1903 several pieces were exhibited at the Salon of the Société des Artistes Français. The following year, his work was acquired by the Musée

Adrien Dubouchée in Limoges, and in 1905 further examples were acquired by the Musée des Arts Décoratifs in Paris. His early production—made before 1913—consisted mainly of small-scale decorative bowls and vases with thin, opaque walls in soft, pale colors. Naturalistic motifs betrayed a lingering taste for the organic forms of Art Nouveau.

In 1907 Décorchemont returned to Conches, where he was born (the symbol of Conches was a conch shell; Décorchemont would later frame his signature stamp with this device). There, he built gas-powered furnaces specifically designed for *pâte-de-verre*, allowing him to experiment with the material. Most notably, he explored lost-wax casting and developed *pâte-de-cristal*, a more brilliant and luminous variant of *pâte-de-verre*. For the most part, he continued his production of small bowls and vases, which he embellished with defined areas of relief decoration: medallions, masks, or patterned friezes. Fragile and difficult to produce, his one-of-a-kind work was marketed as a costly yet exquisite decorative luxury.

During the war years, Décorchemont worked in the Secretariat of the War Ministry. In the 1920s, in step with the tastes of the time, Décorchemont's pieces became massive and simplified. The gleaming, mottled translucence of the *pâte-de-cristal* he increasingly favored—which often suggests minerals like jade, quartz, or agate—was ideally suited to his growing preference for straightforward vessel forms of a sort that, in ancient times, might have been carved from such precious hardstones: handled coupes, footed vases, flared urns. His decorative vocabulary became more concentrated on the language of classical antiquity, though he limited relief decoration mainly to the lips, handles, and feet of his vessels in order to focus greater attention on the

inherent beauty of the material through an emphasis on the veining, streaking, and bubbling of the colored glass.

Throughout his career, Décorchemont was unusually active in showing his work. In Paris, it was regularly displayed in the annual Salons, in museum exhibitions, and in numerous galleries, most notably Georges Rouard, which represented Décorchemont until it closed in 1966.[4] At the 1925 Paris Exposition, his pieces were shown in several locations.[5] In addition, there was considerable international interest in his *pâte-de-verre*, which was included in many museum exhibitions and by the late 1920s was being sold by dealers as far afield as Algeria and Argentina.[6]

The late 1920s were the busiest years of Décorchemont's career, but with the worldwide economic crisis of the 1930s, demand for his luxury goods declined and he turned to the production of stained-glass windows, which would occupy him for the remainder of his life. During his last years—following the rediscovery of his early pieces by collectors in the 1960s—Décorchemont briefly resumed working in *pâte-de-verre*. In 1926 he was made a chevalier of the Légion d'Honneur and in 1955 an officer.

12 | Bowl
1925; glass

What characterizes these pâtes-de-verre, what suffuses them with serenity and mystery, is a diffuse glow, a soft illumination that spreads from within, so that they seem composed of glimmering lights that never die.[1]

This extravagant glass bowl was purchased by Metropolitan Museum curator Joseph Breck from É.-J. Ruhlmann's pavilion, the Hôtel du Collectionneur, at the 1925 Paris Exposition, where it was displayed in the entrance hall with a group of works by other designers in glass and ceramics. Décorchemont conceived the model (to which he assigned the number 260) in 1925; thirteen examples in different colors were produced in 1925 and 1926.[2]

Highly sophisticated in conception, the bowl is one of Décorchemont's finest works. Although the form, with handles, probably derives from classical antiquity, in feeling the bowl also suggests an Asian influence. The green glass, for example, resembles jade, a material that holds meaning and significance in Asian cultures. (Décorchemont's glass was often compared to such natural substances, including amber, lapis lazuli, onyx, and marble.) Further, the meandering pattern created by the mottling of the glass evokes the ascending mountains of an ancient Chinese landscape. And richly veined, the glass has a pebbled surface, lending the bowl an archaic, rough-hewn character. The coiled snakes, discrete yet disturbing, are not so much contained within the bowl's handles as form them, skillfully exploiting the irregular tones of the glass to suggest the natural coloration of exotic serpents, perfectly camouflaged. The bowl is at once mesmerizing, terrifying, and exquisite. Form and motif coalesce to draw attention to the beauty of the material.

The critic Henri Clouzot could have been referring to this bowl when he said that Décorchemont's works "preserve the gleam, fluidity, and radiance that are the magic of glass. . . . Imprisoned within [his] translucent *pâtes-de-verre* is a muted light — the very soul of the material."[3]

13 | Bowl
1928; glass

This bowl exemplifies the simplified forms that Décorchemont favored in the late 1920s and early 1930s, when he abandoned the use of figural motifs. Stylized scrolling feet and a band of incised decoration around the body subtly enhance the decorative effect, which derives almost entirely from the rich and dense translucency of the material. The highly refractive glass, which seems to explode with color, suggests that it is probably *pâte-de-cristal*.

René Chavance described such works in 1926:

Massive and yet harmonious, at once solid and precious in their vigorous design, the works of M. Décorchemont have the sober beauty that derives from the unusual quality of the material and the rigorous balance of proportions. The colors — sometimes deep, sometimes subtle and shifting — fuse with the vitreous substance itself, creating mottled patterns or indefinable clouds within. The decoration, increasingly simple, serves only to enhance the rest.[1]

This model (assigned the number 357 by Décorchemont), produced in at least seven different colors, was first introduced at the 1928 Salon of the Société des Artistes Décorateurs.[2] This example was a gift to the Metropolitan Museum from Arthur M. Bullowa, a noted collector of Precolumbian art, in 1972. Accordingly, it marks an early instance of the renewed interest in French Art Deco which began only in the late 1960s.

MICHEL DUBOST

Lyons 1879–1952 Grasse

In 1928 the French writer Colette described the silk manufacturer François Ducharne as "the one who weaves the sun, the moon, and blue slashes of rain."[1] She might more accurately have directed these words at Michel Dubost, the principal designer at the Soieries F. Ducharne, for it was he who conceived the company's renowned silks, extraordinary not only for their artistry but also for the complexity and ingenuity of the techniques needed to make them. Ducharne opened his business in Lyons on January 1, 1920, at the beginning of a prosperous decade that saw tremendous growth in the silk industry both for household furnishings and — more important — for fashion.[2] The company, which was in operation until 1960, quickly became a preeminent manufacturer supplying high-quality silks for the luxury markets in Europe and America.[3] To be in close proximity to important couturiers and dressmakers, branch offices were opened in Paris in 1920 and New York in 1921. The year 1922 saw further expansion, with a showroom and a design studio in Paris (the factories remained in Lyons); Dubost was recruited to serve as director.[4]

Born in Lyons, Dubost was very much a *canut*, as the native silk workers of that city — long famous for its cloth industry — were traditionally known, and, as he displayed an early aptitude for art, it was almost inevitable that he ended up a textile designer.[5] At the age of fifteen, he entered the École des Beaux-Arts in Lyons, following a general arts curriculum; he also studied weaving. At eighteen, he secured an apprenticeship in a local design studio, and over the next thirteen years he worked as a freelance designer for a range of Lyons manufacturers, including the well-known firm Prelle (still in operation today). In 1910 he opened his own textile design studio.

Drafted into the Army at the outbreak of war, Dubost returned in 1917 to Lyons, where he taught at both the École des Beaux-Arts and the École Municipale de Tissage (Municipal Weaving School). Over the next several years, he became one of the most influential educators in his field, developing rigorous yet practical academic programs for a burgeoning generation of textile designers. A 1919 article from the trade journal *La Soierie de Lyon* summarized his two-part teaching methodology. The first was subdivided into four sequential classes: the scientific study of flowers; studies from life in both black-and-white and color; interpretation from life; and the principles of composition, which included harmonies, volumes, surfaces, and colors. The second offered an overview of the history of textiles and hands-on workshops in spinning, weaving, printing, and dyeing to provide context as well as experience in all steps of the manufacturing process.[6] Recognizing the close relationship between the weaving, fashion, and decorating industries, Dubost encouraged his students to consider the effects of a fabric's texture, weight, and pattern when draped on a moving body or in an interior. He believed textile designers and manufacturers should be aware of the latest trends and influences, and to that end he raised funds from the Silk Manufacturers' Syndicate for annual field trips to Paris with his students:

Once in the capital they visited the leading dressmakers, the most important converters [retailers], decorative studios etc. They were taken to the theatres, to the races and everywhere in town where manifestations of fashion are to be seen. In this way . . . they were able to see the practical use of all the fine fabrics which are manufactured in Lyons.[7]

In 1922, Dubost set off for Paris to head the Ducharne design studio, a position he held until 1933. With a staff of thirty designers, he oversaw the full range of the company's production. Following his own teachings, he developed relationships with the couturiers and retailers the firm supplied with fabrics in order to better know their tastes and to anticipate and meet their needs. Notable clients included the couturiers Hartnell, Poiret, Schiaparelli, Vionnet, and Worth.

Although he always favored natural motifs of the kind that had provided inspiration to textile designers for centuries—especially flowers and foliage—Dubost also shared his era's taste for geometric abstraction and the expression of motion. From the beginning, his textiles were highly praised not only for their beauty but for their technique. In 1927, curator-critic Henri Clouzot noted that Ducharne fabrics were "all of a suppleness which would permit their being drawn through a ring, but yet as gorgeous as the heavy brocades of Louis XIV," while in 1925 *Vogue* declared, "Youth is the essential quality of the Ducharne collection. . . . The mastery of conception and execution compels one's interest and attention. . . . Great beauty and simplicity of technique go hand in hand, a simplicity only achieved by great technical knowledge."[8] Dubost's textiles were displayed at the 1925 Paris Exposition and in an important silk exhibition organized by Clouzot at the Musée Galliera in 1927.

In 1933, Dubost left Ducharne to teach at a Paris atelier. He returned to Lyons in 1937, and the following year moved on to Grasse, where he spent the last fourteen years of his life, mainly occupied with painting.

14 | *L'Oiseau dans la lumière*
    ca. 1925; silk and metallic thread brocade

Around 1918, Michel Dubost befriended the curious and multitalented Édouard Monod-Herzen, librarian at the École Nationale des Arts Décoratifs in Paris. Monod-Herzen's interests were wide-ranging: he was an accomplished metalworker and printmaker, and a student of various sciences including psychology and morphology. His research in this last field led him to make detailed mathematical studies of natural forms, which resulted in diagrams that traced their schematic motion paths. Unable to find any practical use for these drawings, he sold a number of them to Dubost, who later adapted their overlaid, interlacing patterns for a series of dynamic textile designs made by the Soieries F. Ducharne. One of these was *L'Oiseau dans la lumière* (Bird in Light).

Arguably the most sophisticated and accomplished of Dubost's textiles, *L'Oiseau* was likely conceived as a decorative panel for an evening cloak or gown. It was first exhibited—flat—at the 1925 Paris Exposition, the centerpiece of the Ducharne display in the Grand Palais. As much as any other work displayed, it encapsulates the successful alliance of art and industry that the fair actively encouraged. The panel—together with its designer—was singled out in one of the many catalogues published at the time:

It is an expert and subtle, yet mathematical orchestration. . . . M. M[ichel] Dubost is its composer. He is not only the artist who composes its design, but also the [craftsman,] one versed in all aspects of its technique, who knows how to obtain the maximum effect from limited means, who understands how to realize mathematically the decoration he conceived so as to create the kind of textile that either has been requested of him or which he has proposed in order to meet the needs of a couturier.[1]

Ducharne specialized in fabrics that were at once technically complicated, aesthetically innovative, and expensive. In this case, metallic threads have been woven through the panel's sheer surface with varying degrees of opacity according to the composition. The bird-and-flower motif—a conventional and oft-recurring one in the history of textiles—is here treated in an avant-garde manner, the superimposed pattern of intersecting arcs and parabolas suggesting not only the rapid movement of a bird's feathered wings but also the changing play of light and shadow. Shimmering gold threads, offset by the black background, enhance the dazzling, luminous effect. Of such work by Dubost, Henri Clouzot wrote in 1931:

Contemplating one of these large panels . . . the uninitiated viewer admires only the harmony of colors and the lightness of the decoration, so beautifully incorporated in the fabric that it seems to have settled like a powder. . . . He cannot imagine what marvels of technique and ingenuity were deployed in the delicate process of creating it to obtain, through its combinations of weaves, the best result with the minimum of possible means.[2]

RAOUL DUFY

Le Havre 1877–1953 Forcalquier

Raoul Dufy's contributions to the decorative arts—textiles and ceramics in particular—are considerably less familiar than his painting and works on paper.[1] He began experimenting in this area when still a young artist embarking on his career, making textile designs probably as a means of financial support. But although his subsequent involvement with the decorative arts—specifically, his collaborations with established textile manufacturers—would provide a welcome and reliable source of income, such motivation can hardly explain his dedication to this form of creative expression.

The son of an accountant at a metallurgical company, Dufy was born and raised in the port city of Le Havre. He began working there, at the age of fourteen, for a coffee importer, a job that first exposed him to the exotic flora and fauna that arrived by boat daily from distant ports of call. Ships, sailors, and wistful daydreams of far-off places would become recurring themes in his work. He attended the École Municipale des Beaux-Arts in Le Havre and the École Nationale des Beaux-Arts in Paris, and began exhibiting his paintings at the annual Paris Salons in 1901. Keenly attuned to the work of his contemporaries, he was early on greatly influenced by the rich colorations of the Fauves, especially Henri Matisse. His style changed around 1908, when, under the influence of Cubism, his compositions became increasingly simplified and fractured and his expression more purposefully naïve. At the same time, he was drawn to woodcut printing, a medium not only well suited to the new aesthetic but which sparked his interest in printed textiles. In 1910 he produced his first design for the Lyons manufacturer Atuyer, Bianchini et Férier, based on illustrations he made for Guillaume Apollinaire's *Bestiaire ou Cortège d'Orphée* (1911).

In 1909 or 1910, Dufy met the flamboyant couturier Paul Poiret, an encounter that opened the way for new creative opportunities. Drawn to Dufy's colorful and vibrant paintings, Poiret hired him to paint decorative panels for his country house. Thus began a series of collaborative projects:

We had the same inclinations in decoration. His spontaneous and ardent genius had splashed with flowers the green panels of the doors of my dining room in the Pavillon du Butard. We dreamed of dazzling curtains, and gowns decorated à la Botticelli. Without counting the cost I gave Dufy, who was then making his beginnings in life, the means whereby to realise a few of his dreams.[2]

Over the next two years, Dufy designed a range of products for Poiret: letterheads, perfume labels, and party decorations. Renowned for his lavish entertaining, Poiret in 1911 organized the Thousand-and-Second Night, a gala held in the garden of his Paris town house. For the event Dufy, together with André Dunoyer de Segonzac, painted an awning that depicted Poiret as an enormous Buddha presiding grandiosely over his assembled guests.

Dufy also took a special interest in Poiret's newly established École Martine and its printed textiles (see no. 45), and in 1911 Poiret provided financial support for the Petite Usine, a "little factory," set up for Dufy so that he could experiment with textile printing. The project lasted only a matter of months, its demise paradoxically the result of its success:

We fixed up a printing workshop in a little place in the Avenue de Clichy, that I had specially hired. We discovered a chemist called Zifferlein, as tiresome as a bushel of fleas, but who knew from top to bottom all about colouring matters, lithographic inks, aniline dyes, fats and acids. . . . Dufy drew for me and cut on wood designs taken from his Bestiary. From them he created sumptuous stuffs, out of which I made dresses which have, I hope, never been destroyed. . . . After we had spent a great deal of money and much time in getting together our first materiel . . . and in carrying out our first trials, we saw one day the immense, looming silhouette of M. Bianchini, one of the proprietors of the great firm of Atuyer, Bianchini and Férrier [sic], who came to propose to Dufy that he should provide him with more worthy industrial facilities. Dufy was gentleman enough not to accept without informing me of the proposition which had been made to him, and I was enough of a grandee not to prevent him from furthering his career, although I was to suffer from his defection. . . . I liquidated the little factory in the Avenue du Clichy, and since, I have had the consolation of admiring, in the productions of the Maison Bianchini, all that was due to the collaboration of my friend. There were brocades and prints of utter beauty that one day will rank in the history of decorative art as high as the designs of Philippe de la Salle, or Oberkampf.[3]

Charles Bianchini immediately offered Dufy a three-year contract as a designer for his company. The war intervened before Atuyer, Bianchini et Férier could begin production of Dufy's designs, although he supplied the firm with design concepts during the war years, when he served as a volunteer driver.

In 1919, Dufy signed another contract with Bianchini-Férier (as the company was then known), designing, over nine years, a wide range of textiles including toiles, brocades, and damasks. He also produced tapestry cartoons for the Beauvais and Aubusson workshops, sets and costumes for the Opéra de Paris and the Comédie-Française, and a series of ceramics in collaboration with the Catalan potter Josep Llorens Artigas. From 1930 until 1933 he supplied textile patterns to the Onondaga Silk Company of New York, and in 1935 he was commissioned to design paving tiles for the swimming pool on the ocean liner Normandie (the project was never realized). He also carried out private and public commissions for decorative murals, including those for the Théâtre du Palais de Chaillot (1936) and the Paris zoo in the Jardin des Plantes (1937).

Dufy's design work was displayed at international gallery exhibitions and fairs throughout the 1920s and 1930s. In particular, the Galerie Bernheim-Jeune in Paris devoted several exhibitions to his textiles and ceramics. To the 1925 Paris Exposition he contributed a ceramic fountain (made with Llorens Artigas) and fourteen wall hangings specially woven for the Orgues, a fabulous barge built by Poiret both as a venue for displaying his fashions and as a site for concerts and dancing.[4] His vast mural La Fée Électricité (The Electricity Fairy) was displayed at the 1937 Paris Exposition. Dufy was made a chevalier of the Légion d'Honneur in 1926, an officer in 1938, and a commander in 1949.

15 | Four Textiles

Manufacturer: Bianchini-Férier

a | La Chasse, designed 1911; manufactured ca. 1920; printed linen

b | L'Afrique, designed 1912; manufactured ca. 1920; printed linen

c | Les Fruits, designed 1912; manufactured ca. 1920; printed linen

d | La Moisson, probably designed ca. 1912; manufactured ca. 1920; printed linen

Designer, retailer, and critic Paul T. Frankl described Dufy's printed linen textiles as

. . . [revealing] incomparable beauty of design and a profound understanding of the medium. Dufy studied his problems as subordinate to the process of hand-block printing. With characteristic probity Dufy made profound researches into the antique wood-block prints. His designs are characterized by boldness, but boldness based upon erudition. In the beautiful treatment of their given subjects, their strength is the fruit of his mastery of medium and knowledge of manufacturing processes. The artist has conceived them essentially as fabric designs. In this field Dufy has yielded graciously to limitations in order to surmount them.[1]

Dufy was hired as a textile designer by Bianchini-Férier in 1912, their collaboration described by curator and critic Henri Clouzot as "the most unusual and the most perfect example of cooperation between a decorator and a manufacturer."[2]

15a

15b

Clément Goyenèche. Salon
d'Été, with Dufy's *L'Afrique*
textile, Alpes-Maritimes pavilion,
Exposition Internationale des
Arts Décoratifs et Industriels
Modernes, Paris, 1925

its rustic driver, it plunges into the rows of grain. Then it reappears several inches above, going in the other direction. This little machine snaking across the immense field of cut hay creates a charming and original effect. The toile vibrates, it quivers. It is the most extraordinary jeu de fond [play of structure] I know.[4]

Many of Dufy's textile patterns relate closely to his art woodcuts. The process for making both was essentially the same, although the scale of the textile prints was larger and the image had to be continuously reproduced to create a repeat pattern; as many as four stamps of the woodblock were necessary for the ink to fully penetrate the fabric. While initially Dufy himself carved the blocks used to print the textiles (just as he had done for his art prints), this work was later turned over to a firm called Dournel, which closely followed his original designs.[5] To emphasize the spirit of the woodblock technique, Dufy initially restricted his textiles to black on a white ground, a minimal and unexpectedly severe palette for furnishing fabrics that intrigued at least one critic:

It is only because of the total artistry and the profound beauty of the black vegetal dye . . . that this negation of color can be brought successfully into the realm of household decoration. But why not! [These hangings,] which could seem funereal, take on the look of velvet and silk! And one would be harsh indeed not to allow that these textiles also reveal—at least to a small degree—a taste for the exceptional.[6]

Dufy later agreed that the textiles could be printed in a limited range of colors—brown, red, and blue—but only on a white ground.

The Metropolitan Museum purchased all four textiles in 1923; *L'Afrique* and *Les Fruits* were immediately placed on view in the gallery of modern decorative arts. At the 1925 Paris Exposition, decorator Clément Goyenèche selected *L'Afrique* as a furnishing fabric for his Salon d'Été setting in La Pergola, the Alpes-Maritimes pavilion.

Production of Dufy's designs, postponed by the war, did not begin until about 1920.[3] Their imagery evoked the monochromatic, bucolic scenes on the eighteenth-century fabric known as *toile-de-Jouy*, and because they were manufactured in the town of Tournon, they were called *toiles-de-Tournon*.

Clouzot favored one design in particular, *La Moisson* (The Harvest), where Dufy invigorated the pastoral motif with the fractured geometries of Cubism:

The machine beats down the rows of grain, dragged along by a little black horse, mowing the walls of wheat and disappearing into a pile of bundles so that it becomes nothing more than a spot in the confusion of straw. With

150

15d

16 | *Five Swimmers*

RAOUL DUFY AND JOSEP LLORENS ARTIGAS
1926; earthenware

Dufy began his collaboration with the Catalan potter Josep Llorens Artigas in 1923.[1] Together they produced approximately 170 ceramics, modeled by Llorens Artigas and painted by Dufy. They realized their first complete work, a monumental ceramic fountain for the pavilion of the magazine *La Renaissance*, at the 1925 Paris Exposition. The following year, their pots were displayed at the Galerie Bernheim-Jeune in an exhibition titled "New Ceramics of Raoul Dufy." Included in the display was a group of vases decorated with images of swimming figures; in all likelihood, the Metropolitan's vase was one in this series. They were described by one critic as "those large vases, on whose harmonious forms sirens and sea creatures play and wondrous plants flower, rendered in a material whose color is a source of joy in itself."[2] The contour of the Metropolitan's gently flared vase suggests a cresting wave, and the thick, shiny glaze and imprecisely rendered submerged swimmers convincingly approximate the optical effects of being underwater.[3]

Dufy and Llorens Artigas continued to make ceramics until the Second World War. Notable among them, a collaborative effort with a young Catalan architect, Nicolau Maria Rubió i Tudurí, was a series of charming architectonic planters they called *jardins de salon* (salon gardens), which were exhibited at the Galerie Bernheim-Jeune in 1927.

Raoul Dufy. Interior furnishings, with ceramic *jardin de salon* by Dufy, Llorens Artigas, and Rubió i Tudurí, 1929–30

JEAN DUNAND

Lancy, Switzerland, 1877–1942 Paris

Jean Dunand is among the best-known figures of French Art Deco. The volume of his output was prodigious and the range of his activity comprehensive: complete interiors, architectural panels, furniture, decorative and utilitarian objects for the home, paintings, sculptures, textiles, fashion, jewelry—virtually anything he could make, he did.[1] In 1926 he was described as a

. . . many sided artist-craftsman. First a worker in beaten and inlaid metal, he later learned the process of making Oriental lacquer and in recent years has produced in both these fields achievements that place him high among the leading creative craftsmen of the modern movement.[2]

Dunand first trained as a sculptor, at the École des Arts Industriels in Geneva, continuing his studies under Jean Dampt, who believed that craft was the essence of art and that to be an accomplished sculptor one must also be a craftsman. Accordingly, Dunand undertook an apprenticeship with a Geneva metalworker from whom he learned the traditional technique of dinanderie: making domestic wares from hammered copper and brass. In 1897 he moved to Paris, where he earned his living modeling and casting the winged horses on the Pont Alexandre III.

Active as a sculptor until 1907, Dunand around 1903 began to explore the potentially more lucrative field of decorative arts, particularly metalwork. From the start, he focused on dinanderie; labor-intensive and time-consuming to produce, dinanderie would nevertheless remain a staple of his career. "A visit to his workrooms is most interesting," wrote a critic in 1911. "Besides being an excellent lesson in honesty and patience, it teaches you that if you really wish to produce something worth while, there are no short cuts."[3]

Dunand's decorative vocabulary, initially dominated by organic forms and motifs from nature, mainly vegetal and floral in inspiration, became increasingly simplified and stylized over time. Around 1910, he came across traditional Japanese objects made of metal embellished with natural lacquer, in the Louvre, perhaps, or in one of the many Paris shops that sold works from Asia. The closely guarded secrets of working natural lacquer were still unknown in the West, although imitation lacquer varnishes had been produced in Europe since the seventeenth century. In 1912, Dunand met Seizo Sugawara, a Japanese lacquer artist living in Paris; each artist was interested in the other's work, and they agreed to exchange lessons in their respective specialties.[4] Not long after, Dunand began producing his own lacquer, experimenting with new, unorthodox ways of exploiting the age-old material.

Notwithstanding his Swiss citizenship, Dunand served in the French Army during the war, bringing his skills as a metalworker to the trenches. After a close friend lost an eye to flying shrapnel, he designed a special helmet with a detachable mesh visor to protect the eyes. Nearly three thousand visors were manufactured.[5] Following the war, Dunand was awarded the commission for the commemorative victory helmet presented in 1921 to Marshal Ferdinand Foch, commander in chief of the Allied Armies in 1921. The hammered steel helmet was given the form of a cockerel—symbol of France—wearing a gilded laurel wreath. Dunand became a naturalized French citizen in 1922.

Dunand's Paris premises, at 72, rue Hallé, eventually included a showroom, workshops for metalworking, lacquer, cabinetmaking, and model making, and a design studio. More than one hundred craftsmen and assistants were employed

there, including a number of Indo-Chinese lacquer specialists.

During the 1920s and 1930s, Dunand frequently worked in partnership with other designers and artists, many of whom were close friends. É.-J. Ruhlmann, Pierre Legrain, and Eugène Printz were among those with whom he collaborated on furniture, Dunand providing sophisticated and refined lacquer surfaces to their structural frames. Among the painters, sculptors, and illustrators who supplied pictorial programs for screens and decorative panels were George Barbier, Jean Goulden, Paul Jouve, Jean Lambert-Rucki, Gustav Miklos, and François-Louis Schmied.

Dunand's innovations with lacquer also found their way into the world of fashion. Noting that the silk rags he used to clean his lacquer brushes did not lose their suppleness after contact with the material, Dunand realized that lacquer could be applied to finished textiles to similar effect. Encouraged by his friend the milliner Madame Agnès, he began producing spray-lacquered silks, and eventually his designs were being lacquered onto garments by such renowned couturiers such as Vionnet, Worth, Boulanger, and Lanvin. Dunand also produced lacquered silk dresses under his own name. In 1925 the Fifth Avenue dress shop Franklin Simon & Co. advertised "original modernistic fashion by Jean Dunand—Paris," describing his work as "fresh, original, and strangely smart."[6] For Madame Agnès, he designed a complete line of lacquered accessories including jewelry, powder boxes, buckles, and hatpins. A lacquer portrait of Madame Agnès dominated her showroom, which was decorated and furnished entirely by Dunand in the hope that such exposure might lead to commissions from her wealthy, fashion-conscious customers. The residential interiors of Vionnet and Worth also incorporated Dunand commissions.

Dunand was an active participant in the Paris Salons, at which he invariably displayed a broad range of his work. His pieces were also seen at some of the most prominent Paris galleries—Georges Petit, Charpentier, Devambez, Malesherbes, and Georges Rouard—and he was an important contributor to the 1925 Paris Exposition, the 1931 Exposition Coloniale, and the 1937 Exposition Internationale.[7] Dunand was a regular presence at important international exhibitions, perhaps most notably during the 1920s and 1930s, when his work was prominently featured in several exhibitions held at American museums, galleries, and department stores.[8]

Throughout his career, Dunand carried out private and public commissions for an international clientele. He counted among his American patrons Mr. and Mrs. Solomon R. Guggenheim, Templeton Crocker, and Mr. and Mrs. Frederick Lewisohn. He supplied large-scale decorative panels for the *Île de France*, *L'Atlantique*, and the *Normandie*—the great ocean liners that were showcases for the best of contemporary French design. His work was covered extensively and with interest by the international press throughout his career, and examples were acquired during his lifetime by major museums, including The Metropolitan Museum of Art. Dunand was made a chevalier of the Légion d'Honneur in 1919, and in 1926, an officer. After his death, his studio remained open under the direction of his sons Bernard and Pierre.

Nothing was more important for Dunand than the integrity of the artist-craftsman:

[For me,] handcraftsmanship will always remain most moving, most pure. The most exciting discoveries, [such as] the particular (I was going to say "personal") curve of a vase or the harmony of colors in a decoration, often come from something unpredictable that happens suddenly in the course of making one's work: a sort of irregularity, surprising in nature. What a machine makes is too regular, too rigid, too perfectly geometrical. It is cold, without a soul. I refuse—and I suppose that I have the right—to "manufacture."[9]

17 | Cobras

ca. 1919; Bronze, gold

Dunand's training as a sculptor is evident in the skillful modeling of these cobras, while the confident handling of the metal demonstrates his abilities as a craftsman. Cast in bronze, the scales were then chased and highlighted with gilding. Dunand made a number of such sculptures in the late 1910s, in a progressive range of attitudes — coiled, hissing, rearing, advancing. Poised to strike, they present an especially menacing vision: metal transformed into the very idea of slithering, glistening, threatening reptiles.

Dunand was not the only artist of the period drawn to the serpent motif. Others who favored it include the ironworker Edgar Brandt, the glassmaker Émile Décorchemont (see no. 12), and the potter Maurice Gensoli. While the subject may seem odd for decorative ornaments, the sculptures represent not only the

ghoulish side of *animalier* art but the postwar taste for decadence that was celebrated and satirized especially well in the fashion press — most notably in the drawings of George Barbier, Umberto Brunelleschi, and Drian — and personified by the outré Marchesa Luisa Casati. The Italian-born Casati was a fixture of Parisian society during the interwar years. Her antics, which included appearing in public with her pet cheetahs, marmosets, and baby crocodile, were avidly covered in the international press. She notoriously carried her pet boa constrictor, Anaxagarus, to a party at the Paris hôtel of Count Étienne de Beaumont. With her Medusa-like appearance and scandalous reputation, Casati served as a muse to avant-garde and fashionable artists, not to mention many a budding Hollywood vamp.

These cobras are part of a group of important French Art Deco works acquired by curator Henry Geldzahler in 1970 from the Galerie Sonnabend in Paris.

18 | Five Vases

a | Vase, ca. 1920; copper, inlaid silver

b | Vase, ca. 1923; lacquered metal
   (probably steel), eggshell

c | Vase, ca. 1925; copper, plated gold

d | Vase, ca. 1920; brass, inlaid silver

e | Vase, ca. 1925; lacquered metal

Dunand first built his professional reputation as a dinandier, hand-beating copper, brass, and bronze vessels. Unlike much traditional dinanderie, however, which often retains telltale signs of craftsmanship such as visible hammer marks, Dunand's is distinguished by the ultra-refinement of its finish. The decoration on his earliest vessels, often chased or hammered in repoussé, was inspired by nature and the organic motifs of Art Nouveau. Dunand also explored the decorative surface effects of

contrasting metal inlays, oxidized patination, enameling, gilding, and — most famously — lacquering.[1] Over time, as a reflection of his progressively sophisticated vision, both his forms and his decoration became increasingly simplified and abstractly geometric. During the 1920s, he was especially fascinated by the sphere, making countless variations on the theme. Although he would also establish considerable renown as a lacquer artist, Dunand never abandoned his work as a dinandier, employing a large staff to meet the ever-increasing demand by collectors for his work in metal.

Most of Dunand's metalwork was decorative — objects intended to adorn the interior in the manner of small sculptures — rather than utilitarian (though he did make housewares such as lamps, tea and coffee services, and other small accessories). These vases make up a representative group, showing the range of his shapes, techniques, and materials. Collectively, they illustrate not only Dunand's mastery of the métier, but his particular skill in uniting form with decoration.

The triple-gourd-shaped vase at far left (18a) has a copper body; the faintly visible hammer marks are highlighted with inlaid silver. The tiny vase (18b) — its body probably of steel — is encrusted with eggshell in off-white, providing a satisfying contrast to the rich, natural tones of the brown-black lacquer. The cocoon-shaped vase in the center (18c) has a patinated copper body and stepped top; the gold-leaf decoration on the upper banding suggests the blades of some exotic grass. The ovoid form of the brass vase at right (18d) is beautifully echoed in the pattern of inlaid silver raindrops. Perhaps most sophisticated and evocative of the period is the red, black, and silver lacquered spherical vase (18e), whose form is accentuated by a dynamic, vividly colored composition of jagged points superimposed on curving bands, which circles the body in a manner that suggests the dissonance and syncopated rhythms of jazz.

19 | Three Lacquered Panels

a | *Panther*
JEAN DUNAND AND PAUL JOUVE
ca. 1924; lacquered wood, eggshell

b | *African Woman*
1928–30; lacquered wood, oxidized copper

c | *Juliette de Saint Cyr*
ca. 1925; lacquered wood, eggshell

Dunand was among the first Western craftsmen to learn the technique of working natural lacquer. Although he first used lacquer as a protective coating for his dinanderie wares, he soon experimented with it for other purposes, principally for decorative furnishings. In an effort to widen the market for lacquer products, however, over time he devised a variety of unorthodox uses for the material: for jewelry, textile decoration, and even as a medium for painting portraits.[1]

Lacquering is a laborious and time-consuming process but produces a luminous and extremely durable surface, resistant to water, heat, solvents, and bacteria.[2] Natural lacquer is the byproduct of the sap of various trees indigenous to parts of Asia. The harvested sap separates into layers of varied density and opacity. Because lacquering generally involves the application of multiple layers, the densest sap is used for undercoats while the finest is applied on top (traditionally using brushes made from human hair). Each coat must be allowed slowly to harden and is then polished before the next coat is applied. Color can be obtained by adding metal oxides or natural vegetable dyes to the translucent lacquer. White, however, is impossible to achieve. Asian lacquerers traditionally used eggshell as a means of introducing it, placing tiny particles of crushed eggshell into a layer of fresh lacquer, a task generally reserved for small-scale objects because of the painstaking nature of the work.

Dunand's skill with working lacquer brought him considerable renown. Demand for his pieces was such that he established specialized workshops and employed a small army of expert assistants, all of whom had emigrated from the French colonies in Asia, a fact noted by the American sisters Thérèse and Louise Bonney in their 1929 shopping guide to Paris:

19a

Among the decorators who have become famous for some particular development, the outstanding is probably Jean Dunand, with his work in lacquer. I have never asked him where he finds them, but there they are — a dozen or more quiet little Indo-Chinese, busy producing lacquer. In other ways, seemingly inexpressive, in this particular medium they tell strangely beautiful stories. On screens, wall panels, whole walls of rooms, tables, decorative objects, this hard-surfaced, shining medium is modern, completely modern, although its origin is far back in the past.[3]

Eggshell lacquer was a particular specialty of the Dunand workshops, and Dunand used it — unexpectedly — to cover the surfaces of large-scale pieces, including furniture. So successful did this novel aspect of his business become that Dunand, in order to obtain enough eggshells of suitable quality and color, had to take matters into his own hands:

Needing thousands of eggshells, because it is really what it seems — tiny pieces of shell bedded in lacquer, Dunand raises his own chickens, a variety furnishing

the whitest shells, and also leases the output of the neighborhood.[4]

Decorative lacquer panels form a large and significant part of Dunand's oeuvre. Combining the traditional European easel-painting format with a decidedly untraditional medium (and often with equally exotic iconography), they exemplify Dunand's efforts to find innovative uses for lacquer. Many decorative panels were made to his own designs; others were made in collaboration with artist friends. These three panels, essentially wall-hung pictures painted in lacquer, are at once reassuringly conventional and excitingly new, and suggest the range of Dunand's output in this genre.

The exoticism of the French colonies provided a rich source of inspiration for Dunand and is exemplified here by the panther — an especially popular motif in the Art Deco era — he made with the *animalier* artist Paul Jouve (19a). During his career Jouve addressed the subject repeatedly in drawing, painting, prints, sculpture, mosaic, and even tapestry. Here, the panther is modeled in low relief,

19b

19c

carved—probably by Jouve himself—directly into the panel and then lacquered by Dunand. At the time the Metropolitan Museum acquired the panel, curator Joseph Breck noted how skillfully "the effect of the spotted skin is . . . obtained in the lacquer," adding that "the background of tawny orange and green [in fact, more brown and yellow], interspersed with eggshell, is particularly effective in suggesting light breaking through a tangled underbrush."[5]

The seated African woman (19b) is another expression of colonial influence.[6] By adding copper powder to the natural lacquer, Dunand created the shimmering orange of her dress and turban and the cool verdigris of her jewelry. The figure sits against an expanse of glossy black lacquer. The floor is patterned with concentric circles, which blend at the right into a vertical strip of stylized foliage; this patterning is carved into the lacquer surface, revealing the different colors of the layers underneath. While the overall composition suggests a doorway giving onto a jungle landscape, the woman's languorous elegance transforms her from an ethnographic stereotype into a dignified modern woman.

Dunand used oil studies from life and photographs to compose his portraits. He would transfer an approved image to a wood panel, which he would then paint in colored lacquer. The portrait of Juliette de Saint Cyr (19c) represents especially well Dunand's efforts to broaden the market for lacquer products, serving as a sort of catalogue of his innovations. Not only were such lacquer portraits considered fashionably novel, but here Dunand depicts the sitter wearing an abstractly patterned spray-lacquered dress fabric and lacquered jewelry of the sort he made beginning in the mid-1920s.[7] The subject was one of the three daughters of the Turkish-born Morris Schinasi, who, together with his brother Solomon, manufactured several popular brands of cigarettes in New York. It is perhaps not surprising that, when the panel was restored in 1997, it was discovered that the lacquer had yellowed over time, probably the result of long exposure to cigarette smoke. Upon her marriage, Juliette Schinasi became the Marquise Raoul de Saint Cyr.

20 | *Fortissimo* and *Pianissimo* Screens

JEAN DUNAND AND SÉRAPHIN SOUDBININE
1925–26; lacquered wood, eggshell,
mother-of-pearl

This magnificent pair of three-paneled screens, made for the music room of the Port Washington, Long Island, residence of Mr. and Mrs. Solomon R. Guggenheim, represents a collaborative effort between Dunand and the Russian-born sculptor Séraphin Soudbinine. The bas-relief figures of angels and geometrically abstracted rocks, conceived and carved by Soudbinine, were first affixed to the panels with nails and wooden dowels and the screens in their entirety were then lacquered by Dunand to Soudbinine's specifications. The gold, both matte and glossy in finish, was layered on probably by a craftsman from Dunand's studio named Zuber, whose sole responsibility was the delicate application of gold leaf and powder to freshly lacquered surfaces. Tiny shards of eggshell and shimmering mother-of-pearl were embedded in the rich dark green surface to create the sumptuous and alluring effect.

The Italian Renaissance-style house in Port Washington was built in 1916 by Isaac Guggenheim and named, after his wife, Villa Carola.[1] After Isaac's

Music room, with Dunand–Soudbinine screens, Mr. and Mrs. Solomon R. Guggenheim residence, Port Washington, New York, ca. 1927

Fortissimo screen

Pianissimo screen

death in 1922, the house was acquired by his brother Solomon and Solomon's wife, Irene (née Rothschild). They moved into the house in 1924, renaming it Trillora Court (after their daughters Gertrude, Eleanor, and Barbara). Solomon Guggenheim had not yet developed his well-known interest in modern art, and the couple asked for decorating help from a young family friend, Rowland Burdon-Muller.[2] He recalled:

It happened that Mrs. Guggenheim, who was a friend of my mother, asked me to help her when they bought Trillora in 1924 as they did not want a decorator and she did not know what to do and liked our house in England. I was busy and had never done such work but she begged and begged me so that eventually I did it and it was most exhausting as it was a huge house but everything went in place and I never tried anything in the house in advance.[3]

He described the house as

. . . well built but abominably decorated in modern machine made furniture with every room a different period. I cleaned it up and eliminated much excess decoration in about 4 months. . . . It was all unbelievable, and was quite fun turning what looked like a brothel into a gentleman's residence.[4]

One of the main features of the house was the music room. As described in an article that appeared in *Town & Country* in 1927, Burdon-Muller, frustrated by various decorating predicaments, turned to Soudbinine:

The problem presented by the music room was that of converting what was practically an open passageway, divided from the other apartments and the corridors only by open arches, into a chamber; also to provide some means of using decoration. The position of the lighting fixtures precluded the use of pictures which might

have been employed to introduce a color contrast to the dark wood paneling. After considerable deliberation Mr. Burdon-Muller remembered Soudbinine, the Russian sculptor, skilled worker in woods and lacquers. Consultation resulted in the two screens and doors which serve the triple purpose of giving the room unique works of art, of eliminating glass doors, of concealing walls too consistently pierced with arches.[5]

Burdon-Muller himself recalled that the screens

. . . were my idea. . . . I ordered them in 1925 as far as I can remember and they took about 2 years to make. . . . The 2 screens and 2 doors cost $37,000 which . . . was no more than a second rate [painting by George] Romney and the screens and doors were more interesting and filled the need for decoration in the room.[6]

Soudbinine, as the principal artist, acted as an intermediary between the Guggenheims and Dunand, who in December 1925 was obliged to request $500 to cover the cost of the additional gold needed for the lavish gilding. He duly passed Dunand's request on to Burdon-Muller, explaining that "it is very difficult to calculate in advance how much gold will be needed for this work, since inevitably at least ⅓ will be lost—which is to say, embedded in the lacquer."[7]

The screens, which were among the very few works of contemporary art in the house, were displayed at the Reinhardt Galleries in April 1926. Soudbinine sailed to New York aboard the SS *Paris* to attend the opening. A review in *The New York Times* described the screens as "huge, with expanses of flat and modeled surfaces in heroic designs and rich smoldering color."[8]

Published as *Crescendo—The Battle of the Angels* and *Pianissimo* in *Town & Country* in 1927, the titles *Fortissimo* and *Pianissimo* were specified by Mrs. Guggenheim when she offered them to the Museum in 1950.[9]

21 | Bedroom Furniture and Wall Maquette made for Templeton Crocker

ca. 1927–28

a | Bed; lacquered wood

b | Easy Chair; lacquered wood, goatskin

c | Bench; lacquered wood, goatskin

d | Commode; lacquered wood, ivory

e | Side Chair; lacquered wood,
    replacement chamois

f | Bedside Table; lacquered wood, ivory

g | Table; lacquered wood

h | Wall Maquette; painted plywood

Although the great majority of Dunand's clients were French, one of his most important projects was realized in America. Two exhibitions of contemporary French art held in San Francisco in 1923 and 1924–25, to which Dunand contributed work, probably led to the commission to decorate several rooms in the San Francisco residence of Templeton Crocker (1884–1948), the millionaire grandson of the founder of the Union Pacific Railroad Company. Explorer, naturalist, author, and collector, Crocker was divorced in 1927 and needed a home suitable for a newly single man of means. The dazzling penthouse apartment he moved into, completed under the supervision of French decorator Jean-Michel Frank in 1929, featured a master bedroom, dining room, and breakfast room designed and executed by Dunand; other rooms were designed by Frank, Pierre Legrain, and Madame Lipska. A contemporary writer praised the novelty of the apartment:

Mr. Templeton Crocker has built the first large and luxurious apartment to be done completely in the modern manner in the United States. And it is, perhaps, one of the most beautiful apartments in the world. . . . Within, one surveys an interior as new to the world as the skyscrapers outside. . . . And although Frank and Dunand interpret the modern movement differently, the complete effect is harmonious, perhaps because there are no long vistas of merging rooms and no connecting archways. Each room is a separate entity.[1]

Top: Wall maquette (21h)

Bottom: Master bedroom, Templeton Crocker residence, San Francisco, California, as set up in a Paris photography studio, ca. 1927

The project was cited as a model by the sisters Thérèse and Louise Bonney in their book *Buying Antique and Modern Furniture in Paris*, published in 1929.[2] And ten years later, the well-known American decorator Ruby Ross Wood commented:

The Templeton Crocker apartment on the top of Russian Hill, the climax of San Francisco's thrills. Done ten years ago by Jean-Michel Frank of Paris, it is still the best modern decoration in America.[3]

After the lacquer wall panels and furniture were completed in his workshops, Dunand's three rooms were fully set up at a studio in Paris to be inspected and photographed, and then packed and shipped to California. In San Francisco, using the photographs as a guide, Frank supervised the installation and the furniture arrangement of the apartment.

The master bedroom had lacquer walls depicting a woodland scene executed in soft tones described as "frozen luminous greys, frosted silvers, varying greens, and warm red-browns."[4] Chamois curtains in three shades of grey hung at the windows, and the seating furniture was upholstered in goatskin and grey chamois. The sophisticated suite of furniture—lacquered in grey, black, and silver, with small ivory blocks that serve as drawer pulls—provided a foil to the patterned walls. The seven pieces

owned by the Metropolitan make up the entire suite save for the writing table with a lacquered wood frame and patinated metal top, currently in a private collection in New York.

The furniture's spackled surface is characteristic of *lacque arraché* ("pulled-up" lacquer), a deceptively simple looking technique in which a smooth top coat of lacquer (in this case, a slightly metallic grey made with the addition of aluminum powder) covers lower layers (here, black) that have been roughly applied using a spatula-like tool. Polishing the grey top surface reveals the raised peaks of the black lacquer below, creating a mottled yet smooth effect. The angled or beveled edges of some pieces are lacquered black or silver, giving the suite a bold, graphic, and decidedly modern look.

The refined abstraction of the furniture forms is atypical for Dunand, and it is possible that they were supplied by another designer, perhaps Pierre Legrain. The small table in particular illustrates the transformation of a utilitarian piece of furniture, using the fractured vocabulary of Cubism, into a piece of abstract sculpture.

The lacquer wall panels have not survived, and until recently the only documentation of their appearance was through written description and black-and-white period photography. In 2001 a painted plywood maquette for the bed wall turned up in the collection of one of Dunand's granddaughters. For many years, Dunand used it — turned upside down — as a shelf in a small cabinet where he stored lacquer-working tools (presumably, after showing it to Crocker, Dunand chose not to waste the wood by discarding it).[5]

Crocker died in 1948. The apartment remained intact until 1959, when it was dismantled and sold by his heirs. Kept in storage until 1972, the bedroom furnishings were then acquired by the donors.[6]

JEAN DUPAS

Bordeaux 1882–1964 Paris

Pinned to the wall of Jean Dupas's studio in Bordeaux was a quotation from Voltaire:

Decadence is produced by doing things the easy way and by being lazy about doing them well, by being sated with beauty, and by a taste for the bizarre.

The quotation was noted by Marcel Valotaire on a visit to the studio. The critic believed that it was important to point this out "if we are to form a true estimate of him."[1]

Decorative painting and sculpture—works that contribute to the atmosphere of the specific location for which they were conceived—were considered crucial elements of the Art Deco interior, and few painters were as accomplished in this arena as Dupas. One reason that his work is not better known today is that much of it was destroyed by a fire in his studio shortly before his death in 1964.

Born to a family of seamen—his father was a captain in the merchant marine—it was probably assumed that the young Dupas would follow in the tradition.[2] But Dupas changed course and decided to become a painter, attending the École des Beaux-Arts in Bordeaux and the École des Beaux-Arts in Paris. In 1910 he was awarded the Prix de Rome, though it was not until 1912 that he went to Italy, where he studied under Carolus-Duran and Albert Besnard. His stay in Rome ended abruptly with the outbreak of war in 1914. Returning to Bordeaux, he served in the French Army's auxiliary services, primarily assisting Dr. Émile-Jules Moure, an ear, nose, and throat surgeon who invented a prosthesis for facial mutilations.

Following the war, Dupas went back to Rome and picked up where he had left off. From Italy he submitted entries to the Paris Salons, notably those of the Société des Artistes Français and the Société des Artistes Décorateurs, to which he would regularly contribute for the rest of his career. Early on, Dupas settled on decorative—rather than easel—painting, developing a recognizable personal style that revealed a strong taste for classicism. In the manner of Poussin and Claude, he composed highly structured, stylized paintings with elegantly attenuated figures. Dupas's first consideration was

. . . to create a rhythm on a given surface, to build up a composition with lines, with lights and darks, with warm and cold tones; the composition absolutely determines the way in which the picture is finished. . . . I subordinate the elements of nature to the rhythm I have fixed on. . . . Why are there so many voluminous robes in my pictures? . . . Not because I have a special predilection for them, but merely because they are useful

to me. The same holds good of the very tall hats worn by certain of my figures. . . . I do not aim at a systematic deformation, which would be a formula. . . . But one must realise that a painted decoration is part of an architectural scheme, and hence it demands scale and strong vertical lines. A decoration is not an enlarged easel picture, such as Rubens painted.[3]

In his large-scale works, Dupas invariably followed the same procedure:

I first make a rapid sketch on a small scale. Then I make sketches from nature, studies of fragments, slowly built up, until I reach what I take to be the most expressive point. . . . I then make a cartoon half the projected size of the complete work. . . . Finally, I make an enlargement, either with squares or photographically, and then the execution follows, very rapidly, like a fresco, which is the best guarantee that the freshness will be preserved.[4]

Some of Dupas's best-known paintings were made for the 1925 Paris Exposition, among them *Les Perruches* (Parakeets), which was hung above the mantelpiece in the main salon of the Ruhlmann pavilion. The following year, he again collaborated with Ruhlmann on the Salon de Thé of the SS *Île de France*, for which he painted *Sylvie*, a large decorative panel inspired by the 1853 novella by Gérard de Nerval.

Dupas's creative output was varied and wide-ranging. In addition to his monumental panels, he designed posters (one for the London Underground in 1933), book illustrations, and advertising for French and American shops and department stores (Max Furs and Saks Fifth Avenue) and magazines (*Vogue* and *Harper's Bazaar*). He also supplied tapestry designs to Gobelins and decorations for porcelain blanks to Sèvres. He produced his masterwork, the History of Navigation panels for the SS *Normandie*, in 1934 (see no. 22). A monumental panel lacquered by Jean Dunand was his contribution to the French Pavilion at the 1939–40 World's Fair in New York.

After the Second World War, Dupas taught at the École des Beaux-Arts in Paris and was a curator at the Musée Marmottan. In 1926 he was made a chevalier of the Légion d'Honneur.

Intérieur du Gd. Paquebot NORMANDIE. Un Coin du Grand Salon.

Série R. 107

Richard Bouwens van der Boijen and Roger-Henri Expert. Grand salon, with Dupas glass wall panels, SS *Normandie*, ca. 1935

22 | *The Chariot of Poseidon*

JEAN DUPAS AND CHARLES CHAMPIGNEULLE
1934; glass, paint, gold, silver, palladium
leaf

The ocean liner *Normandie* was the last great expression of French Art Deco. In 1932, with the financial backing of the French government, the Compagnie Générale Transatlantique began construction of what was to be the largest, fastest, and most beautiful passenger ship on the high seas. The unprecedented cost of its production and lavish interiors was justified—or rationalized—in the midst of the worldwide financial crisis by the liner's mission to serve as an ambassador, carrying the art and glory of France to foreign lands. Just as the 1925 Paris Exposition had impressed with its unabashedly patriotic display of French luxury goods, so too the SS *Normandie* was to seduce its passengers with its sumptuous décor, fine wine and food, and various and sundry extravagances.

Designed by Jean Dupas, this extraordinary mural was one of four executed by Charles Champigneulle

in 1934 for the *Normandie*'s grand salon.[1] The series of murals, titled The History of Navigation, comprised four separate scenes: *The Rape of Europa*, *The Birth of Aphrodite*, *The Chariot of Thétis*, and *The Chariot of Poseidon*. The Metropolitan's glass panels are the only remaining complete scene; the other panels have been dispersed. Dupas designed a fifth decorative wall composition for the salon, *The Chariot of Aurora*, which extended the theme of the glass panels. Rendered in lacquer by Jean Dunand, it is now in the collection of the Carnegie Museum of Art, Pittsburgh. While navigation may be the nominal subject of the panels, the profusion of quasi-historical vessels and miscellaneous mythical creatures was clearly not intended to tell a specific story but rather to create a spectacular decorative effect. Passengers on the *Normandie* paid not so much for transportation as for atmosphere, and the first-class lounge was a temple of glamour.

The murals' mirror-like brilliance is achieved through a technique known as *verre églomisé*, in which paint and metal leaf are applied to the reverse of plate glass to which a canvas backing is then affixed.[2] The *Normandie* murals are more than twenty feet high, well suited to a room that had nearly thirty-foot ceilings.[3] "The larger the job," Dupas was quoted as saying, "the better pleased I am."[4]

Launched from Le Havre in 1935, the *Normandie* made its last voyage to New York in August 1939. Following the bombing of Pearl Harbor on December 7, 1941, the United States immediately commandeered the ship for use as a troop carrier; conversion began on Christmas Eve. On February 9, 1942, sparks from an acetylene torch ignited the life preservers that were piled high in the grand salon, and the ship went up in flames. The enormous quantity water that had been pumped into the interior to extinguish the fire was trapped below decks and froze overnight, causing the ship to capsize. The *Normandie* languished in the Hudson River, at Pier 88, for a year and a half, until it was finally righted, towed away, and sold for scrap. The glass panels, which had been removed before the fire, were sold by the U.S. government at public auction in the summer of 1942.

PAUL FOLLOT

Paris 1877–1941 Sainte-Maxime

A designer whose career began at the turn of the twentieth century and continued until the Second World War, Paul Follot was not only one of French Art Deco's longest practitioners but also one of its most important pioneers. As for many of his generation, tradition was the foundation of his work:

His canon will be the following: to produce objects that "hold their own" beside those from the past and to remain French through balance, order, logic and clarity.[1]

The son of a successful Paris wallpaper manufacturer, Follot as a young man studied under the Art Nouveau designer, graphic artist, and educator Eugène Grasset.[2] Grasset encouraged Follot's enthusiasm for sculpture, a discipline that would inform his subsequent taste for three-dimensional applied arts. In 1901, Follot was hired as a designer for La Maison Moderne. Founded in 1899 by Julius Meier-Graefe and directed by Maurice Dufrène, the gallery-cum-design studio provided competition for Siegfried Bing's L'Art Nouveau, the famous shop that gave its name to the Art Nouveau style. In addition to displaying works by well-known international designers such as Henry Van de Velde and Louis Comfort Tiffany, La Maison Moderne produced its own works, hoping to promote an alliance between art and industry. For the company Follot designed jewelry, small decorative objects mainly in bronze or silver, and textiles.

La Maison Moderne closed in 1904, and Follot opened his own studio, establishing himself as an ensemblier who could produce anything needed for a domestic interior. The same year, he joined the newly founded Société des Artistes Décorateurs, displaying his work at its first annual exhibition in what was the beginning of his active participation in the major Paris Salons and international exhibitions.[3]

Together with Dufrène, Follot became one of the first French designers to abandon the whiplash curves and organic naturalism of Art Nouveau in favor of the clean, architectonic lines of abstracted Neoclassicism. He developed a personal vocabulary filled with the garlands, latticework, floral motifs, and festooned draperies that would later inspire other tradition-minded designers such as É.-J. Ruhlmann and Süe et Mare. Although in his designs—especially for furniture—he looked to history for forms, materials, and construction techniques, they never devolved into pastiche:

He has studied in depth the works of the great eighteenth-century cabinetmakers, and one recognizes his intention of continuing [their tradition, but] at a remove. His sense of the exceptional and his sense of color have inspired him to create very personal works of all types, works in which the execution is no less important than the conception.[4]

Invariably, Follot's pieces were exquisitely made; although he was not a craftsman himself, he fully understood the production methods of everything he designed and carefully supervised every piece sold under his name. On occasion, he took on work-for-hire jobs for prestigious international manufacturers, for example designing textiles for Schumacher, ceramics for Wedgwood, and silver for Christofle. Such was his reputation that already in 1912, examples of his work were in the collection of the Musée des Arts Décoratifs. In 1914 he moved into a new studio-residence in Montparnasse. Built by the architect Pierre Selmersheim, it was fully conceived and furnished by Follot himself.

Following the war—he likely served at the front—Follot returned to his ensemblier business. In 1921 he received the prestigious commission to decorate several first-class staterooms on the new ocean liner the SS *Paris*. The first modern-style French passenger ship, it featured elegant cabins designed by well-known ensembliers as well as innovative features such as private telephones, adjacent rooms for servants, and large square portholes.

In 1923, Follot was hired by the department store Le Bon Marché to be director of its new decorating department. He named the business "Pomone" after the Roman goddess of fruit and gardens, traditional symbol for abundance and therefore well suited to a commercial enterprise. Through Pomone, Follot introduced to a wide public his luxurious, polished style. The critic Pierre Olmer praised his large and varied output as

. . . irreproachable in its execution. This meticulous artist loathes the unfinished or the overgrown; he is an aristocrat of art and himself concedes — not incorrectly, to be sure — that art is the privilege of the elite. Everything about him is refined, even precious.[5]

In the postwar years, however, Follot's ultra-refinement began to fall out of favor. Notably, the influential Bonney sisters labeled him "conservative," although they allowed that he "is credited with introducing the comfortable chair into the modern."[6]

Follot was involved with many displays at the 1925 Paris Exposition and oversaw every aspect of the Pomone pavilion. In 1928 he left Pomone to join, unexpectedly, the modernist designer Serge Chermayeff at the Paris premises of Waring and Gillow, a London-based furniture manufacturer. The venture was short-lived (the branch closed in 1931, probably the result of the economic downturn), but for the company's inaugural exhibition Follot assembled sixty room settings, experimenting modestly with new ideas such as indirect lighting.

Follot suffered from ill health during the 1930s. Nevertheless, in 1935 he managed to design a deluxe cabin for the SS *Normandie*, and the same year participated in the French display at the Brussels International Exhibition. He died in 1941.

See no. 70.

GEORGES FOUQUET

Paris 1862–1957 Paris

"Jewelry is to our clothing what gold- and silver-work are to our homes."[1] So wrote Jean Fouquet in 1931, nicely summing up the philosophy of Maison Fouquet. This renowned jewelry-making firm was founded in 1860 and run by three generations of the same family—Alphonse Fouquet, his son Georges, and his grandson Jean.[2] Alphonse Fouquet quickly established a reputation for fanciful designs in fashionable revivalist styles that incorporated figural and floral motifs. In 1895 he turned the firm over to his son Georges, himself a skilled craftsman and designer. More in tune with the tastes of his own generation, Georges favored the organic forms inspired by nature and the elaborate asymmetrical flourishes of Art Nouveau.

Like his contemporaries René Lalique and the Vever brothers, Georges Fouquet favored a mix of precious and nonprecious materials, reflecting the early twentieth-century shift from a prevailing taste for precious stones in traditional settings to a new aesthetic in which unorthodox materials were chosen less for their intrinsic value than for their contribution to the overall design. As Fouquet himself said: "A 136-carat diamond has no more right to a better place than a beryl or a topaz. The cutter's and setter's art, the search after the arrangement and setting of the stones alone count."[3]

As head of a large and successful commercial enterprise, Georges Fouquet relied on many outsiders—painters, sculptors, graphic designers, and even architects—to supply designs that were realized in the Fouquet ateliers.[4] Perhaps most notably, in 1899—likely at the behest of the actress Sarah Bernhardt, for whom Fouquet had made jewelry—Fouquet joined forces with the Czech graphic artist Alphonse Mucha to create a series of spectacular monumental jewels for the Fouquet display at the 1900 Paris Exposition Universelle. So well received was this collaboration that in 1901 Fouquet asked Mucha to design a new Fouquet showroom in the fashionable rue Royale, across the street from Maxim's restaurant. The astonishing interior, decorated with a profusion of mirrors and stained-glass panels, was dominated by a motif of preening peacocks, while the entrance front was centered on a relief sculpture by Christofle depicting an elegant woman holding handfuls of cascading jewels. In 1941, the Fouquet family donated the showroom to the Musée Carnavalet in Paris, where today it is displayed in its entirety.

After the war, changes in women's fashion inspired new forms of jewelry: short hair showed off long dangling earrings; bare shoulders were bedecked in lavish draped necklaces, replacing heavy corsages and pectoral ornaments; waistless dresses sported brooches, clips, and pins rather than elaborate stomachers. Fouquet recognized the important relationship between clothing and jewelry, and his designs of the 1920s reflected not only changes in fashion but the aesthetic shift toward the stylized abstractions of Art Deco, where simplified forms were enhanced by an increasingly bold palette and adventurous color combinations. In 1923 the critic Émile Sedeyn described Fouquet as a man "who believes in his own time and wishes to supply it" and whose work is characterized by

. . . [a] taste for color and unabashedly decorative effects. His work is not very discreet. On occasion, he is boldly daring. There is in him much of the improvisational spirit of the couturier or the ensemblier, tempered by a knowledge of and a taste for materials more for their intrinsic beauty than because their rarity makes them precious. He stays on top of fashion and most current

issues, which supply him every moment with new themes. . . . He chooses gems as a painter chooses colors. The essential thing is that his palette furnishes him at just the right moment with the necessary harmony or brilliance that he seeks.[5]

Unlike many of his contemporaries, Georges Fouquet rarely participated in the annual Salon exhibitions. Even so, the high regard in which he was held by his peers and associates led to his appointment as president of the jewelry section at the 1925 Paris Exposition. In 1929 he organized an important exhibition of jewelry and goldwork at the Musée Galliera.

In 1919, Georges's son Jean joined the family firm as a designer. The youngest Fouquet had been a student of literature and moved in intellectual circles—among his friends were the writers Louis Aragon and Paul Éluard and the architect-designers Le Corbusier and Charlotte Perriand. His designs for jewelry embraced a modernist sensibility that can be linked to that of his contemporaries Raymond Templier (see pages 228–30), Gérard Sandoz, and Paul Brandt. Even more than his father, Jean Fouquet stripped his jewels of unnecessary embellishment and experimented with unorthodox materials such as wood, chromed steel, and lacquer. He first displayed works under his own name at the 1925 Paris Expo, and in the following years at the Société des Artistes Décorateurs. In 1929 he became a founding member of the Union des Artistes Modernes.

The worldwide economic crisis of the 1930s took its toll on Maison Fouquet, which was forced to close its doors in 1936. Nevertheless, pieces made by the firm were included in the jewelry display at the 1937 Paris Exposition, which was presided over by Georges Fouquet. Georges Fouquet died in 1957; Jean Fouquet would continue making and displaying jewelry until his death in 1984.

Jewelry by Georges Fouquet, Boucheron, Lacloche Frères, Linzeler et Marchak, Mauboussin, and Paul Templier, in *L'Illustration*, December 1927

23 | Dress Ornament
ca. 1923; jade, onyx, diamonds, enamel, platinum

The American *Report of Commission* on the 1925 Paris Exposition, submitted to Secretary of Commerce Herbert Hoover in March 1926, included the following comments on the jewelry display, which had been organized by Georges Fouquet:

The jewelry exhibits at the Exposition were, as might have been expected, of great richness and beauty. Many of the creations displayed were of a distinctly modern quality. Perhaps the most notable feature about the jewelry as a whole from the American standpoint was the considerable number of large pieces in the form of brooches, pendants, drops, and girdle tassels that contained very few precious stones but gained their effect through semi-precious materials like black onyx, coral, turquoise matrix, and enamels, that were of such size as to form a distinct decorative element of the costume.[1]

The commission's assessment could easily have been a description of Georges Fouquet's own contributions to the fair. It also reflects the general design philosophy of Maison Fouquet. In the words of Georges Fouquet's son Jean:

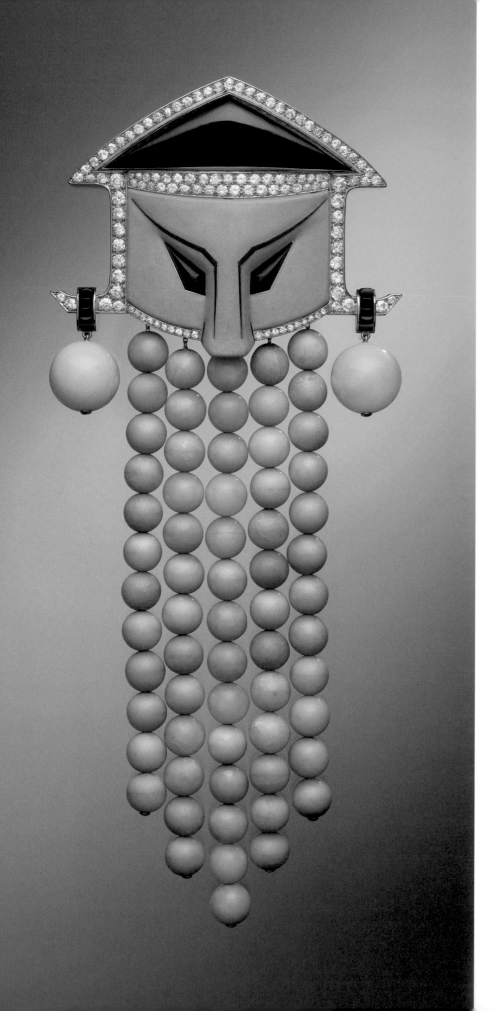

This dress ornament is anything but diminutive. Essentially a large pin with a heavy dropped fringe, it is made from jade beads, onyx, and enamel embellished with diamonds set in platinum and takes the form of a stylized Chinese mask. Although it is unclear whether it was included in the Fouquet display at the 1925 Expo, the extraordinary scale suggests that it was conceived as an exhibition piece, since its weight would easily have compromised the drape of—or even torn—a delicate dress fabric. With its striking combination of colors, unusual juxtaposition of materials, and nod to the East, it typifies the Art Deco taste for theatrical exoticism.

The Chinese motif fits well into Georges Fouquet's oeuvre of the mid- and late 1920s, when he made a number of mask-inspired jewels of both Asian and African inspiration, many of which were displayed at the 1925 Expo. The palette of *eau-de-nil* green, black, and white relates to a number of other pieces by Fouquet that were published between 1925 and 1927, including bracelets and earrings, which incorporate the same color scheme. Curator and critic Henri Clouzot noted in 1926 that Fouquet was one of the first of his generation to preach "the dogma of unity in personal adornment, rings, ear rings, pendants, being made of the same turquoise, sapphire, emerald, coral, or crystal."[3] One should certainly add jade to the list.

A color image of the ornament was published in the December 1927 issue of *L'Illustration*. Interestingly, at that time each strand of the jade ball fringe was longer by two beads. Later images show only the ornament as it appears today. Because it is such a singular (and, frankly, unwearable) piece, it is highly unlikely that more than one example was ever made.

ÉMILE GAUDISSARD

Algiers 1872–1956 Paris

Would one deny that this decorator is a poet? In front of his carpets, I myself feel an emotion closely related to what I experience when I read beautiful lines of poetry—discrete and glowing, evocative, nuanced.[1]

With these words the critic Ernest Tisserand described Émile Gaudissard in 1926. Very little has been written about Gaudissard, but a few basic facts have been established. Born and raised in Algiers, as a young man he went to Paris and enrolled at the École des Beaux-Arts, where he studied sculpture. He made several monumental sculptures for public squares in Algeria, Tunisia, and France, and he also worked in a range of media. As a painter, he displayed work at the Paris Salons d'Automne; as an architectural sculptor, he contributed decorations to private residences and to the Bon Marché department store in Paris; and as a designer of tapestries and upholstery, he was employed by the Beauvais and Gobelins manufactories. He also turned his hand to ceramics, *pâte-de-verre*, wrought iron, and lithography.

Gaudissard is best remembered today, however, as a designer of carpets. His principal manufacturers were Braquenié and Cogolin, both of which are still in operation today. Gaudissard's carpets graced some of the most prominent interiors of his day, including those of the Paris restaurants Drouant and Prunier and the French liners *Île de France*, *Lafayette*, and *L'Atlantique*. At the 1925 Paris Exposition, he designed carpets for the Ruhlmann pavilion and for René Gabriel's Chambre de Jeune Fille at the Ambassade Française.

"His carpets are altogether remarkable," wrote Tisserand. "In their number and diversity, they constitute the greater part of his decorative production." He continued by pointing out the importance of carpets in interiors, citing Gaudissard's particular skill in designing them:

It would not be insulting to say to a number of accomplished decorators that the weak point of their ensembles was the carpet—whether commissioned from collaborators who more or less follow the program set out for them, or made by themselves, in which case they generally reproduce the same design over and over again. They have a model in their mind's eye, which they hardly vary except in the tones. There just seems to be something missing. . . . Gaudissard's inventiveness [, on the other hand,] is infinite, whether drawing from nature or from geometric decoration, with which he is intimately familiar, having long lived in Muslim countries.[2]

French Art Deco is beautifully exemplified in the carpets of Gaudissard, whose profound knowledge of technique enabled the realization of his poetic fantasy and invention.

See no. 57.

MARCEL GOUPY

Paris 1886–1954 Paris (?)

Marcel Goupy is a bit of a mystery man; although he was a prolific designer of glass and ceramics, many of the facts of his life are unclear.[1] Educated at the École Nationale des Arts Décoratifs, where he seems to have studied architecture, interior design, sculpture, and painting, he set up a studio in Paris around the turn of the century. Although for a time he was engaged with silver and jewelry making, as a young man he began enameling on glass and soon turned his hand to designing patterns for glass and ceramics.

After the war, during which he served in the French Army, Goupy met Georges Rouard, owner of the eponymous retail establishment. Rouard, as it was commonly known, was a twofold business: Maison Rouard sold production-line tableware made by major international manufacturers; Galerie Georges Rouard dealt in *les arts du feu* (the arts of fire), one-of-a-kind works in glass, ceramics, and metal.

Maison Rouard's roster of ceramics manufacturers included Charles Ahrenfeldt, Théodore Haviland, Nymphenburg, Bing & Grondahl, and Wedgwood. Glass manufacturers included Baccarat, Gallé, Lalique, and Saint-Louis. Rouard also manufactured its own lines of both glass and ceramic wares, sold under the Rouard name. Clients could order from existing patterns or they could commission unique table services.

Beginning in 1913, Galerie Georges Rouard displayed works by the Artisans Français Contemporains, a group of well-known artist-craftsmen.[2] New artists were added by a vote of the group's membership. Once accepted, the new member would be given use of a vitrine for the display of his work. Exhibitions of work by members of the Artisans were presented each November at the gallery.

Goupy was hired by Rouard as principal designer for the firm. Supervising a team of seventeen workers, he oversaw the decoration of Rouard's glass and

Marcel Goupy. Glass and porcelain table service, ca. 1928, plate 29 in Gérard Sandoz, *Objets usuels* [1928]

24 | Vase

ca. 1925; glass, gold

High above a rocky landscape chiseled in silhouette, three powerful centaurs, beautifully articulated in moody tones of dark green and black—two with bows and arrows, one with a spear—boldly pursue foxes and soaring birds, creating a dynamic frieze that carries the eye around this small-necked vase. Although the centaur motif has its origin in Greek mythology, here it is treated in a way that is anything but archaeological; its bold palette and stylized imagery bring to mind not so much Attic vase painting as an exotic fantasy from the *Thousand and One Nights*.

Throughout the 1920s and 1930s, Goupy enjoyed a solid reputation as a designer of utilitarian glass and porcelain table services—plates, bowls, drinking glasses, and serving pieces painted or enameled with an aesthetic of subtle modernity—which were made for and retailed by Maison Rouard. But Goupy was himself a skilled glassmaker, and in the mid-1920s he began exploring a new avenue that allowed him greater freedom to experiment: decorative glass, mainly vases that were in every way more robust than his tableware. The new direction did not go unnoticed by critics:

Large pieces with massive silhouettes, recherché colors, a focus on materials, decoration of a new scale and purpose, and the adoption of a pseudo-primitive vocabulary mark this evolution, which may perhaps hold happy surprises in store.[1]

This vase is typical of Goupy's decorative glass and reveals his mastery of the métier. The glass body he made with broad sloping shoulders to show the frieze to best advantage. He used colorless glass to bring a sparkling play of light to the vase's surface and spray-enameled the interior in mottled tones of yellow, orange, and white to provide a luminous foil to the dark, thickly applied enamel decoration. The bands of net-like tracery at the neck and underbelly are highlighted with gold.

porcelain services, which were conceived to complement one another: "Marcel Goupy . . . composes attractive designs that find their place at the same time around his drinking glasses and in the reserves of his plates."[3] His glassware was singled out in the *Report of Commission*, submitted to the United States government by the American reporters who visited the 1925 Paris Exposition:

Marcel Goupy works entirely in enameled glass. In this case enamels of various colors are used to produce a design upon a body of clear or colored glass. Many of these productions seem more like the work of a decorator than that of a glass-maker. This work is less expensive [than that by Lalique or Marinot], and is, of course, capable of an infinite variety of forms and colors.[4]

About 1925, in addition to the utilitarian glass he designed for Rouard, Goupy began making works of decorative glass that he exhibited under his own name. In 1929 he was appointed design director of Rouard, a position he held until his death in 1954.[5] (The firm would close in 1966.) Throughout his career, both with Rouard and on his own, he was a frequent participant in the annual Salons and his work was included in many important exhibitions in France and abroad.[6] At the 1925 Paris Exposition, he displayed works in both the Rouard pavilion and the glass display at the Grand Palais.

PAUL IRIBE

Angoulême 1883–1935 Roquebrune-Cap-Martin

Although he is best remembered as an illustrator, the breadth of Paul Iribe's accomplishment was remarkable. He turned his hand to, among other things, the decorative arts, stage and screen design, advertising, and publishing, and in so doing profoundly helped to shape what would become French Art Deco. Shortly after Iribe's death in 1935, Louis Cheronnet, editor in chief of *Les Échos d'art*, described him as

> . . . *a precursor. Even before the war, it was he who laid the foundations for the simplification that is the true sign of today's art; and yet no one better represented that sort of art précieux — the refinements of which have their source both in the eighteenth century and in the style moderne of 1900 — which had its last hurrah at the Exposition of 1925.*[1]

The same year, writer Paul Morand described what in Iribe's work he believed contributed most to the formation of Art Deco: the audacity of unexpected materials, the combination of the outrageous with the refined, and the invention of extravagant forms.[2]

Shortly after Iribe's birth, his father, an engineer, left his family to work on the Panama Canal.[3] In 1889 the family moved to Madagascar, returning to Paris in 1892. Iribe's first exposure to typography and illustration — two métiers that would occupy him for the rest of his life — was as an apprentice at the newspaper *Le Temps*. He worked briefly for the architect René Binet, but by 1901 he had found his calling: satirical illustration. His first caricature was published that year in *Le Rire*, and over the next dozen years he would produce hundreds more for the many illustrated journals popular in his day, including *Le Sourire*, *L'Assiette au beurre*, *Le Canard sauvage*, and *Le Cri de Paris*. Iribe's bold, flat, mainly black-and-white graphic style was greatly influenced by the work of Aubrey Beardsley. The two also shared a decided taste for the erotic and the decadent, but Iribe's was a lighter touch. In 1906 he founded his own satirical weekly, *Le Témoin*. Impressed by the magazine, in 1908 the couturier Paul Poiret commissioned Iribe to illustrate his first catalogue, "a very beautifully produced publication, intended for the élite of Society . . . dedicated in homage to all the great ladies of the whole world." Poiret recalled that Iribe was

> . . . *an extremely odd chap, a Basque plump as a Capon. . . . He spoke in a very low voice, as if mysterious, and gave some of his words a special significance by separating their syllables; for instance, he would say, "it is — ad-mir-able." Altogether a charming and remarkable personality.*[4]

In 1913, Iribe established his own imprimatur, Éditions Paul Iribe. In his drawings, he invariably gave careful attention to background details — jewelry, furniture, textiles, patterns — that evoked the intimate, refined, and hothouse atmosphere of the feminine world. Friends, in particular the cultural arbiters painter Josep Maria Sert and his wife Misia, encouraged him to further explore this obvious but as yet uncultivated interest in the decorative arts. Iribe's first efforts, made in 1910 with the silversmith Robert Linzeler, were jewelry and dressing table accessories, which immediately attracted international press coverage. Some of the designs were subsequently produced by Cartier and marketed under the name Moderne Iribe.[5]

Iribe's 1911 marriage to the stage actress Jeanne Dirys led to commissions for theater sets and costumes. Then in 1912 he opened the tiny but sumptuous

Paul Iribe et Cie, a shop at 104, rue du Faubourg Saint-Honoré. The moody black-and-gold interior served as a dramatic setting for his jewelry, objets d'art, textiles, cushions, furniture, lamps, and myriad other treasures.[6] Iribe was not himself a craftsman, and his designs were realized by others, notably Clément Rousseau and Pierre Legrain. Also in 1912, the couturier Jacques Doucet—having sold, at the age of nearly sixty, his important collection of French eighteenth-century fine and decorative arts— engaged Iribe to supervise the decoration of his new apartment (see page 135, top). The installation would include furnishings not only by Iribe but by, among others, Legrain, René Lalique, and Eileen Gray.[7] The project would confirm Iribe and Doucet as two of the most important tastemakers of their day and establish the roster of key figures of French Art Deco. It also brought Iribe to the attention of other clients, including Baron Robert de Rothschild, the comedic actress Andrée Spinelly, the writer Claude Farrère, and the couturiere Jeanne Lanvin.

During the war, Iribe worked in a hospital at the front. In 1919, after divorcing Dirys, he moved to New York, opened Paul Iribe Designs, a short-lived venture located at 275 Madison Avenue, and married a rich American, Maybelle Hogan. He later moved to Hollywood. Hired by Paramount Pictures as an art director and costume and set designer, he worked with director Cecil B. De Mille on such films as *The Affairs of Anatole* (1921) and *The Ten Commandments* (1923).

In 1927, Iribe returned to Paris. He established a design studio and resumed his career as a graphic artist, producing a range of commercial publicity materials into the 1930s. Also during these years, he penned several strongly nationalistic polemics in support of the French cause, each with a suitably emphatic title: *Choix* (Choice, 1930), *La Marque France* (The Brand *France*, 1932), *Défense du Luxe* (Defense of Luxury, 1934), and *Parlons Français* (Let's Speak French, 1934). In 1931, Iribe's burgeoning relationship with the couturiere Coco Chanel led to the collapse of his second marriage. The following year, Chanel displayed a line of diamond jewelry heavily influenced by designs by Iribe that had appeared in *Choix*. Following Iribe's death at Chanel's villa in the South of France, Chanel took over Éditions Paul Iribe, renaming it Éditions Chanel.

Iribe was made a chevalier of the Légion d'Honneur in 1931. A selection of his furniture was included posthumously in the important exhibition "La Décor de la vie de 1900 à 1925," held in 1937 at the Musée des Arts Décoratifs. Iribe's contributions to the field of design were heralded at the time of his death by Gabriel Boissy, editor in chief of *Comœdia illustré*:

With no apparent effort, he was the first inventor of modern decorative art. . . . Well before our ensembliers produced the spindle leg, the fan, the doe's foot, the massive body on skinny legs, rich materials encrusted with delicate elements, etc.—everything that brings well-deserved glory to the Sües, the Ruhlmanns, the Rapins, the Bouchers, the Dufrènes—all of it was imagined and designed by Iribe.[8]

Paul Iribe. Cover for *Comœdia illustré*, March 1911, with Iribe's first wife, the actress Jeanne Dirys, wearing a jewel of his design

25 | *Roses*

1914; silk, metal thread

Noted as early as 1915 in *Vogue*, the rose was Iribe's signature motif:

. . . a little gold rose, the Iribe label.[1]

While Iribe was certainly not the only designer of his day to employ the motif, it was for him so ubiquitous that his particular take on it—a single stylized bloom on a long stem with two leaves—became known as "la rose Iribe" (see following page). The flower appears in countless of his satirical and fashion drawings, and he adapted its blossom for jewelry, decorative marquetry on furniture, hardware and metal mounts, embroidery on cushions, and as a pattern for textiles. One of its earliest appearances was in 1908 or 1909, when Iribe was working for Paul Poiret, who used it on his dress labels.

On this lampas textile, three leafy roses are clustered in a bowl with a tassel hanging languidly from one of its handles. Arranged in an alternating repeat pattern, the motif in metallic silver is set against a bright pink ground, inverting the expected coloration of the flowers. Although the weaving technique and flower motif are quite traditional, almost indistinguishable from those of textiles made

Paul Iribe. "La rose Iribe," detail of a dress designed by Paul Poiret, 1913. The Metropolitan Museum of Art, Milla Davenport and Zipporah Fleisher Fund, 2005 (2005.198a, b)

a century earlier, the stylization and outré palette place the textile unmistakably in the twentieth century. This combination of modernity and historical reference is characteristic of the best of Iribe's work.

Iribe designed the textile in 1914 for the Lyons silk manufacturer Atuyer, Bianchini et Férier, a firm that commissioned a number of important artists in an effort to fashionably update their goods (see no. 15). The pattern was produced in at least one other equally surprising colorway: pink, orange, and gold roses in gold vases set against a black ground.[2]

A note in the Museum's files indicates that this length came "from a costume by Callot." Callot Sœurs was a fashionable Parisian dressmaking establishment, founded in 1895 by four sisters and known for its luxurious garments made with gold and silver lamé. The textile was given to the Metropolitan in 1926 by Mrs. Morris Hawkes (née Eva Van Cortland Morris), a noted collector of French porcelain, and represents an early recognition in the United States of the designer's work.

LÉON-ALBERT JALLOT

Nantes 1874–1967 Paris

"By virtue of the high quality of his work —so pure, so French— Jallot can be defined as the classic artist of today's furniture."[1] Despite these authoritative and admiring words, written in 1926, Léon Jallot has since, for the most part, been relegated to obscurity. Nevertheless, this self-taught ensemblier created some of the most elegant and subtle designs of his era, at once completely original yet respectful of French tradition.

By the time he was twenty, Jallot had moved from his hometown, Nantes, to Paris with ambitions of attending the École des Beaux-Arts. However, unable to afford the tuition, he instead found work (of what sort is unrecorded) and studied wood carving at an atelier in Montparnasse. In his quest to become an accomplished woodworker, he also spent considerable time in museums studying historical furniture and making painstaking copies of the work displayed.

Jallot's diligence paid off. In 1899 he was hired by the influential dealer Siegfried Bing to head the furniture-making atelier of L'Art Nouveau, Bing's famous Paris shop that gave its name to the Art Nouveau style. When L'Art Nouveau closed in 1903, Jallot set off on his own, opening a workshop at 17, rue Sedaine. He first displayed examples of his furniture at the 1904 Salon of the Société Nationale des Beaux-Arts, and he continued to actively participate in Salon exhibitions until the late 1930s.[2]

Although Jallot's earliest furniture fits well into the Art Nouveau cannon, incorporating that style's characteristic curving flourishes and decorative motifs drawn from nature, it was distinguished principally by its simplicity and restraint in an age of extravagant showmanship. Rather than seeking novelty for its own sake, he became one of the first of his generation to embrace tradition, and from the beginning, grace and proportion rather than richness and embellishment informed his work. Dedicated to revealing the natural beauty of wood, Jallot for the most part restricted his surface decoration to contained areas of carved relief. In 1909 his furniture was described as demonstrating "an assured elegance, a sober richness, and a sure and delicate taste."[3]

It is unclear how Jallot spent the war years (presumably he served in the French Army), but by 1919 he had resumed his profession as a furniture maker. He later turned his hand to textiles, carpets, tapestries, hardware, stained glass, and ceramics. In short, he evolved from furniture maker to ensemblier. In the end, however, it was his carefully considered, understated furniture that endured and that most impressed the critics of his day:

There is a phrase that M. Jallot constantly has on his lips, and which he never tires of repeating . . . : balance above all, everything depends on balance. Indeed the merit of his work consists primarily in the balance of proportions. . . . True to his motto, although he sometimes allows himself to be swept away by inspiration, he instinctively returns to simplicity.[4]

Simplicity, however, does not suggest a lack of richness, and eventually Jallot came to employ a range of exquisite materials, including beautifully figured wood veneers, galuchat, leather, and lacquer (often inlaid with eggshell or mother-of-pearl) to adorn his furniture, always managing to avoid any appearance of ostentation or vulgarity. Although he instinctively shied away from novelty, Jallot was never uninventive, especially as a creator of forms. In the critical assessment of René Chavance, writing in 1924:

É.-J. Ruhlmann. Grand salon, with Jallot cabinet at right, Hôtel du Collectionneur, Exposition Internationale des Arts Décoratifs et Industriels Modernes, Paris, 1925

To find new forms, it is much less important to imagine the "never before seen" than to adapt traditional forms to modern ways and the modern spirit. What we know of M. Jallot is enough to convince us that such is his method.[5]

Jallot's furniture, be it cabinetwork or seating furniture, was invariably well suited to the world in which he lived.

In 1920, Jallot was joined in his business by his son Maurice-Raymond, and over the next twenty years they worked together making furniture and designing interiors. Notable among these were the Chambre de Monsieur at the Ambassade Française at the 1925 Paris Exposition and the 1928 interior they designed for Le Grand Dépôt, a Paris gallery and one of the most important venues for the display of modern decorative arts.[6] Jallot's furniture was also seen in America, displayed in several department store exhibitions in the 1920s — in New York at Macy's and B. Altman, and in Philadelphia at Wanamaker's.

Jallot continued to work until the Second World War, after which his son took over the business; it remained in operation until the 1950s. Jallot's important contributions were eloquently summed up in 1926 by Marcel Valotaire:

There are many modern furniture makers who, like M. Jallot, attach prime importance to the quality of wood and to that perfect finish in execution which never fails to give a rich character to each piece. But over and above this, even M. Jallot's simplest works possess the additional charm of harmony and equilibrium, of true logic — all qualities inherent in traditional French art, of which this artist, for all his creation of new forms, is a true disciple. He is the indirect heir of the great eighteenth century furnishers, whose work, moreover, he knows thoroughly.[7]

26 | Cabinet

ca. 1925; mahogany, palisander, *Verde di Levanto* marble

In the early 1920s, Jallot began making simple furniture — mainly cabinets — that relied for its decorative effect almost exclusively on the beauty of richly grained wood veneers. Critics took note:

He now chooses to reduce superimposed decorative motives to a minimum, limiting himself to a few inlays of rare woods or precious materials. . . . It is primarily in the wood itself that he seeks his decorative effects, and the valuable woods he employs lend themselves very happily to his purpose. Besides the woods to be found in France (walnut, oak and cherry), which are always fine when chosen with discernment, he uses for his more elaborate works such materials as macassar ebony, amaranthe, and amboyna.[1]

Jallot also favored palisander (sometimes called Brazilian rosewood). Generally, he book-matched his veneers, placing sheets cut from the same board adjacent to one another to create a kind of decorative repeat pattern using the natural graining and burls to create large symmetrical arabesques.

This bow-front cabinet beautifully exemplifies Jallot's approach. Its spare form is underscored by the sensitive use of materials, the mahogany structural elements offset with perfectly matched palisander veneer whose spectacular figuring suggests watered silk. Double doors meet discreetly at the seam of two veneered panels. The plain interior houses three mahogany shelves. The top is a slab of mottled *Verde di Levanto*, a rich green marble.

The cabinet formed part of the furnishings of the main salon of the Ruhlmann pavilion at the 1925 Paris Exposition, where Metropolitan Museum curator Joseph Breck first noticed it. Although the majority of the pavilion's furnishings were designed and made by Ruhlmann, a small number of works were supplied by his friends. Displayed against a wall beside the mantelpiece, Jallot's cabinet was placed on a small carpeted platform that followed the contour of the bowed front. Although a period photograph (see page 110) shows a sculpture by Alfred Janniot atop the cabinet, Ruhlmann's original sketch for the room called for a dark vessel, perhaps the ceramic vase by Émile Lenoble (see page 142), which also was acquired by the Metropolitan from the Ruhlmann pavilion.

The cabinet was put on view almost immediately upon arrival in New York at the end of 1925. In January 1927, a friend of Jallot's visited the Museum and noticed that the varnish had dulled, probably the result of exposure to humidity during transport. In April of that year, Jallot wrote to Breck requesting that the piece be French polished (a technique that involves the application of shellac to achieve a high-gloss finish) and offering to pay for the labor. Two weeks later Breck replied, assuring Jallot that the work would be done at the Museum's expense. Jallot, obviously pleased, wrote back: "I have my heart set on presenting the Americans with an impeccable piece of furniture, and I am happy to see that you are helping me obtain that result."[2]

PAUL JOUVE

Bourron-Marlotte 1878–1973 Paris

Paul Jouve is best known as a painter and sculptor of animal subjects, especially of the exotic sort.[1] The son of painter Auguste Jouve, he was fascinated from a young age by both art and animals, learning to draw from life on visits to the Paris zoo. He studied briefly at the École Nationale des Arts Décoratifs and later at the École des Beaux-Arts. At the age of sixteen, he first displayed work at the Société des Artistes Français and from that time on, until his death nearly a century later, would participate in the full range of fine and decorative arts Salons in Paris.

Jouve's first major commission was for the 1900 Paris Exposition Universelle, to which he contributed sculptures of lions to one of the main entrance gates designed by architect René Binet. In 1907 he was awarded a grant by the French government that enabled him to travel to Algeria, the first of many visits he would make to the French colonies in Africa and Asia; the flora and fauna he encountered in these faraway locales would deeply inform his choice of subjects. During the war, on a tour of duty in Greece, Jouve was introduced to Prince Alexander of Serbia (later king of Yugoslavia), who would become an important patron.

In 1921 he painted murals for the presidential study at the Summer Palace in Algiers. The following year, another grant took Jouve to Indochina; he was especially impressed there by the temples at Angkor Wat. He would make a third colonial trip, to sub-Saharan Africa, in 1931.

Jouve contributed a number of works to the 1925 Paris Exposition, mainly decorative paintings for pavilion interiors. Notable among the many private and public commissions he received throughout the 1920s and 1930s were the decorative panels for the first-class writing room on the SS *Normandie* (1935) and the murals for the Luxembourg Parliament (1938). Jouve was made a chevalier of the Légion d'Honneur in 1920 and an officer in 1926.

See no. 19.

RENÉ LALIQUE

Aÿ 1860–1945 Paris

"What is there to be said about René Lalique that has not already been said?" So asked critic Maurice Guillemot as early as 1910, on the occasion of a glass exhibition at the Musée Galliera. "His exhibition vitrines could be sent . . . to the Louvre, to be placed in the Galerie d'Apollon beside those which are already there, filled with famous jewels [of art]."[1]

René Lalique is probably the best-known figure of French Art Deco, renowned especially for his work in glass. This may be because his eponymous firm continues to operate today, but more likely it results from the enormous number of books and exhibitions that have been devoted to his work since his own time. It may also stem from the ubiquity of his prodigious output. He is the only designer in this book to fully embrace industrial production, albeit with an artistic bent; indeed, his particular skill as a designer is what allowed him to transform factory-made glass into a desirable luxury. His factories, staffed by hundreds of workers, turned out a vast range of glass both utilitarian and decorative, ranging from tiny baubles to massive architectural elements. Lalique took on private, public, and commercial projects, and he had an international distribution network that made his products readily available to consumers on at least four continents. His professional career can be neatly divided in two: the first half, from about 1880 to about 1900, when he earned his reputation as one of the most celebrated Paris jewelers, and the second, until his death in 1945, when he turned his hand to designing glass.[2] In both métiers, his work is considered among the most important of the twentieth century.

Raised in Paris, where his father worked as a commodities trader, Lalique from an early age was drawn to art. He sketched incessantly and was especially attracted to subjects from nature. His schooling was cut short by the death of his father in 1876, at which time he apprenticed with the jeweler Louis Aucoc. In 1878 he left for England to study design at Sydenham College, with the intent of establishing his own jewelry business. Returning to Paris in 1880, he opened his own firm in 1882.

As for many designers of the Art Nouveau era, artistry was for Lalique of paramount importance. He rejected the then-favored use of precious stones and conservative settings, preferring to combine semiprecious stones with unexpected materials such as enamel, horn, ivory, coral, rock crystal, and glass. He actively participated in the annual Salons and important international exhibitions, and his reputation as a jeweler led to his election to the Légion d'Honneur in 1897 as a chevalier and in 1900 as an officer.

Lalique soon turned to other areas of applied design. In 1890 he opened a second Paris atelier, for which he designed all the furnishings. At the 1900 Exposition Universelle, the exhibition cabinets he designed for his display — embellished with cast-bronze butterfly-women — drew nearly as much attention as the jewels inside. In 1902 he built for his ever-expanding family (he would eventually have four children by three different women, two of whom he married) a house in Paris, for which he designed architectural details, furniture, lighting fixtures, and textiles. But more important, in 1901 he had a small furnace installed on property he owned at Clairefontaine and, assisted by the director of the Saint-Gobain glass manufactory, he began to experiment with glass. In 1905 he opened a showroom for his glasswork on the fashionable Place Vendôme.

Lalique's early pieces in glass were for the most part one-of-a-kind bowls and vases made with the *cire-perdue* casting technique (see no. 30). In 1908, however, after being asked by François Coty to

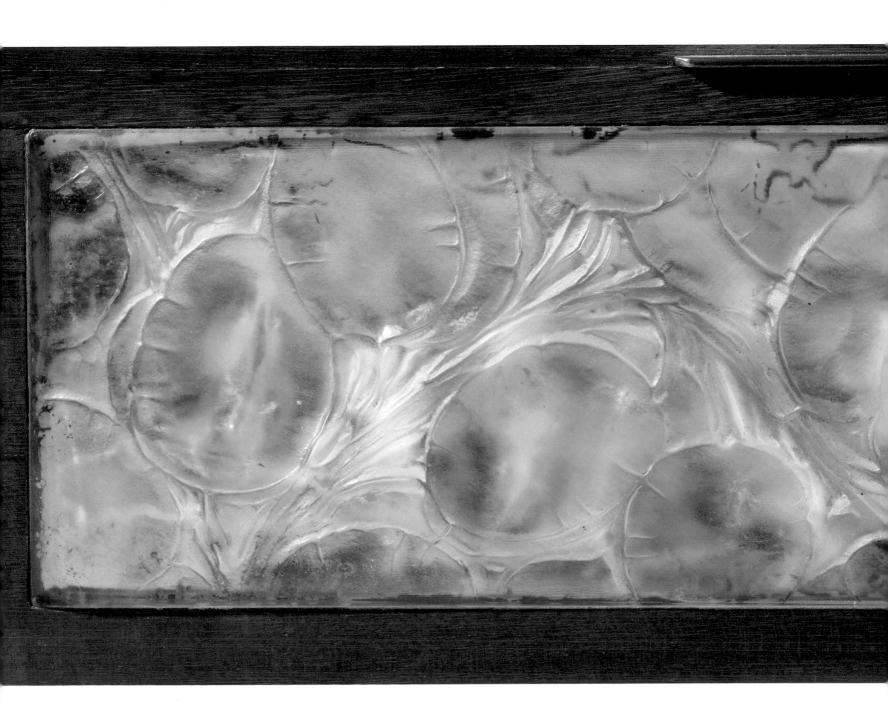

manufacture perfume bottles, Lalique began experimenting with reusable metal molds that enabled production in quantity. In 1909 he opened his first factory in Combs-la-Ville, and by the outbreak of the war he had created more than eight hundred molds for household items, lighting fixtures, and architectural fittings. He favored colorless glass, which he treated in a variety of ways: it was frosted, polished, cut, enameled, or stained. And it was widely seen at exhibitions both domestic and international.[3] Two of his most important prewar commissions were the façade of the Coty Building in New York and a pair of glass doors for the interior of the apartment of the couturier Jacques Doucet (both 1912).

During the war, the Lalique factory was put in service to the French State, producing glass for use in hospitals and by the Army.

Expanding his business, Lalique in 1921 built a second factory in the town of Wingen-sur-Moder in Alsace, a region with a long tradition of glassmaking. Focusing on industrial production, he developed and marketed lines of table and serving glass, encouraging clients to buy complete sets rather than using piecemeal combinations of different patterns. He also continued to display the full range of his production at the Salons and in exhibitions, and he accepted important commissions that brought prestige and publicity to the business. In 1922, for example, he was commissioned to create a special table service for the president of the French Republic.[4]

At the Paris Exposition of 1925, "it can be said without exaggeration that Lalique was everywhere in evidence."[5] Indeed, he was probably the fair's most prolific exhibitor. As president of the glass section, he also supervised the installation of two dedicated displays. The first was a fully furnished pavilion that demonstrated different ways glass could be incorporated into the domestic environment; outside was a monumental illuminated-glass fountain—a landmark at the fair. The second was a smaller "shop" on the rue des Boutiques, where table services and housewares were exhibited. Lalique designed a complete dining room setting for the Sèvres pavilion and bas-reliefs for the Porte d'Honneur entrance gates, and he displayed his work in no fewer than twenty other locations. Following the fair, he was made a commander of the Légion d'Honneur.

The Paris Expo only increased public interest in Lalique. His glass was sold through authorized dealers in Europe, North Africa, and both North and South America. In the United States, it could be purchased at any number of department stores, including B. Altman, Bullock's, Lord & Taylor, Saks Fifth Avenue, and Wanamaker's. By the late 1920s, more than six hundred workers were employed in Lalique's two factories. He contributed to the furnishing of ocean liners and trains, and he accepted architectural commissions from Paris to Tokyo. A state gift of a table service from the president of France to the British monarch was made by none other than Lalique. In 1933 he was given a retrospective exhibition in Paris at the Musée des Arts Décoratifs.

With the outbreak of the Second World War in 1939, both Lalique factories were closed. The Alsace factory was taken over by the occupying German forces. At Combs-la-Ville, Lalique himself continued to work, making a small number of pieces, some of which incorporated patriotic themes. Lalique died on May 5, 1945, only days before the liberation of Alsace. The factory reopened under the direction of his son Marc and his daughter Marie-Claude.

Lalique's contribution to French Art Deco was described in 1929:

He has dared to introduce his art into those departments of life which we are too often content to furnish with machine-made conveniences. He sees no reason why the doorknobs we turn, the knives and forks we use, the tools or instruments of our most ordinary moments should not be beautiful. He represents in our time the point of view . . . that the distinction between fine and applied art is false. This is at once the most democratic and the most aristocratic view of art. It assumes that all objects associated with human experience are available for the expression of beauty. It assumes also that we, the common run of men and women, would enjoy beauty if we could have it on all sides of us.[6]

Or perhaps more succinctly:

Lalique . . . has succeeded best at introducing beauty into the framework of contemporary life.[7]

27 | *Monnaie du pape* Coffer

designed 1914; glass, silver leaf, amaranth, brass

This coffer presents a charming visual pun: the molded-glass panels are decorated with Lunaria, a plant also known as a money plant or pope's money, in reference to its purpose. The box, which can be locked, was obviously intended for safekeeping valuables—but what sort of strongbox is made of glass?

The model is one of Lalique's earliest. Introduced in 1914, it remained in production until 1947 (a variant box which had only one glass panel, on the lid, was in production from 1920 to 1947). The five glass panels are made of mold-pressed colorless glass. Four different molds were used: one for the lid, one for the front panel with keyhole, one for the back panel, and one for the two side panels.

Each panel is backed with silver leaf and inserted into the wood frame. A variety of woods were used for the boxes, including maple burl, satinwood, and mahogany; in this case, it is amaranth. The catch and hinges are brass.

A box of this type was included in the 1919 exhibition of works by Lalique held at Knoedler Gallery in New York. A review in *The New York Times* described it as "a jewel box . . . covered with a plaque of crystal and then carved in a leaf design. The exquisite play of light and shade over the crystal surface and the soft glow of the general tone make it an object of abiding beauty."[1] It is unclear whether this coffer is our model, but only one other box design with a leaf motif is known.[2]

The coffer is made the same way as much of Lalique's architectural glass, though on a smaller

René Lalique. Dining room, the table set with *Haguenau* glasses, Sèvres pavilion, Exposition Internationale des Arts Décoratifs et Industriels Modernes, Paris, 1925

scale: mold-pressed bas-relief panels are set into a frame. This format was first used in 1902 for the entrance doors that Lalique made for his own house in Paris, where rectangular mold-pressed panels were individually set into a cast-iron doorframe, and again for doors made for Jacques Doucet in 1912. The coffer also relates closely to decorative panels made in 1928 for the interiors of the Côte d'Azur Pullman Express, a deluxe French train that ran for ten years beginning in 1929. Those panels were also relief-molded — with a motif of birds and figures amid grape-laden vines — backed with silver metal, and set into the paneling, of Cuban mahogany.

28 | *Haguenau* Wine Glasses
designed 1924; glass

Although Lalique had produced a limited range of glass for the table at his first factory in Combs-la-Ville, it was not until he opened his second factory, in Alsace, that he began manufacturing table services in quantity. Often he would give his patterns geographic names, many of which were from the Alsace region. The present pattern is named for Hagueneau, a town near Strasbourg. Introduced in 1924, it was in production until 1947. The full set consisted of

six stemmed glasses — water, Burgundy, Bordeaux, Champagne, liqueur, and Madeira — a decanter, and a pitcher. The flared bowl of each glass is mold-blown, while the high, square-sectioned stem with stepped, rectangular, pierced knop is mold-pressed. Industrial production meant that the glasses could be sold at fairly moderate prices. At Barker Brothers in Los Angeles in 1936, for example, a dozen glasses in this pattern were on sale for $58.50 (they normally retailed for $78, equivalent to about $1,300 today); comparable glasses made by Steuben sold for between $90 and $108 per dozen.

Lalique included the glass service in the dining room setting he created for the Sèvres pavilion at the 1925 Paris Exposition. It was also displayed in the 1933 retrospective exhibition of his work at the Musée des Arts Décoratifs.

Lalique used only colorless glass for his table services. The critic Gaston Derys took note:

[Lalique] has created refined models for drinking glasses worthy of the finest grands crus. Naturally, he has not made that unfortunate error of using color for a wine glass. A gourmet takes pleasure in admiring the robe [color] of the wine he will be enjoying. If you cloak it in a hue that alters it, you commit a heresy as lamentable as that of the Philistine who pours soda into a great Chambertin.[1]

29 | *Tourbillons* Vase
designed ca. 1925; glass

The majority of Lalique's glass was machine-made from reusable metal molds; the *Tourbillons* vase represents one of the finest examples. Although this mold-pressed model was produced in quantity, the boldness of its concept and the complexity of the finish suggest that it was made by hand. The *Tourbillons* vase was made in a variety of tonalities, but by far the most effective scheme was this one: a body of clear, colorless glass with the outer edges of the deep walls highlighted in black enamel. The strong patterning of swirling lines—the title, *Tourbillons*, translates as Whirlwinds—lends a dynamism that stands alone in his work.

Mrs. Gordon-Stables, a British writer for *Artwork*, could well have had the *Tourbillons* vase in mind when she wrote in 1927:

In contradistinction to the many glassworkers who today are running riot in bold colour, Lalique employs this very little. Barring the brownish patine [sic] . . . and an opalescent or misty effect of which he is very fond, he now confines himself for the most part to the use of black and white, the two being in a number of the new pieces most strikingly exploited, the white as background, and the black in the ornamentation. This reticence in use of all colouration, throws into fine relief the quality of his modelling and the grace of shape.[1]

There are questions as to the actual authorship and date of the model. Lalique scholar Félix Marcilhac states that the *Tourbillons* vase was first made in March 1926 after an initial drawing by Suzanne Lalique, René Lalique's eldest daughter, who was also a designer of glass and ceramics.[2] He also notes that the model was introduced at the 1926 exhibition of the Artisans Français Contemporains at the Galerie Georges Rouard, to which Lalique had been invited to participate that year for the first time.[3] Curator Carolyn Hatch, however, contends that the model was seen a year earlier, at the 1925 Paris Exposition, probably in the glass section (of which Lalique was president) at the Grand Palais.[4]

30 | Vase

1929; glass

This vase was made by the *cire-perdue*, or lost-wax, casting process, traditionally used for bronze sculpture but perfected by Lalique for glass. A full-scale model of the design carved in wax was first covered with plaster. The wax was then melted, and molten glass was blown or poured into the reserve. After the glass had solidified and cooled, the plaster casing was broken away. Although molds were used only once—effectively rendering each piece unique—a master design could be copied several times. Many of Lalique's earliest works in glass were made using this technique, which Lalique favored for art glass rather than for pieces with a more utilitarian function because of the great risk of breakage. A 1919 review of Lalique's work at Knoedler Gallery in New York described his *cire-perdue* glass: "There are also great bowls for flowers cast by the cere perdu [*sic*] method which involves an appalling amount of risk even in the hands of the most skillful."[1] Lalique continued to make *cire-perdue* glass until 1933, producing more than six hundred fifty pieces over the course of his career.

This unique mold-blown example was made (using mold no. 707) on February 11, 1929.[2] Of colorless glass with a very pale brownish patina, the body is frosted and the rim polished. The decorative motif, repeated four times, depicts a stylized upright bough of foliage arranged in the form of a leaf. Although after 1919 Lalique's wax models were sculpted under his supervision by an assistant named Amaury, there are fingerprints molded into the unfinished underside of the vase. Could they perhaps be those of the master himself?

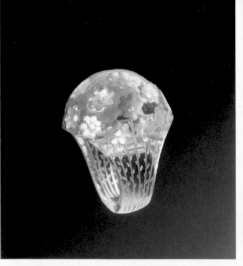

31 | Rings and Necklace

a | Rings, ca. 1931; glass

b | *Perruches* Necklace, ca. 1929; glass, silver

Lalique first made a name for himself as a jeweler of great originality—famous for incorporating unexpected materials such as glass into his designs—in the last decade of the nineteenth century. He largely abandoned jewelry when he turned to glassmaking around 1900, but in 1923 actively took up the idea again as a way to broaden the market for glass products. At that year's Salon des Artistes Français, he presented a group of glass flower-shaped brooches enhanced with enameling and diamond brilliants. He went on to produce a variety of forms, including brooches, necklaces, pendants, bracelets, rings, belt buckles, cuff links, buttons, and hatpins. Although industrialized production allowed such pieces to be easily manufactured and sold at moderate prices, they were marketed as fashionable novelties; this, in turn, encouraged the public perception of glass as a luxury material.

Lalique's glass jewelry was met with considerable interest in the press. In 1927, Mrs. Gordon-Stables, writing in *Artwork*, noted:

René Lalique is that rarest of individuals, a practical man as well as a talented artist. He likes nothing better than to produce things for use, beautiful things that may be employed every day in every type of household—lamps and vases, fruit-bowls, table glass, yes, and even inexpensive ornaments to hang around one's neck or pin in one's hat.[1]

The following year, *The New York Times* reported:

Lalique glass, which has been so popular in perfume bottles, mirror and picture frames and other odd items which delight the American visitor in Paris, is now to be found in the newest jewelry. This glassware is molded into beads with novel surface designs and in modernistic shapes. These are used to form entire chokers and necklaces in widths varying from a half inch to an inch.[2]

And Olive Gray, in *The Los Angeles Times*, enthused:

The new Paris craze, jewelry fashioned by that famous artist in glass, Lalique, bids fair to take America by storm. . . . The Lalique costume jewelry is somewhat similar to that artist's creations in art objects, much carved white opaque being used, but, in conjunction with the bright colors which are the choice of the mode—fine reds, blue, rose tints as well as lovely greens. Necklaces are matched by extremely long ear-rings, combining the colors with white, and in some instances, with pearl.[3]

The Metropolitan Museum purchased this group of jewelry from Lalique himself in 1934. The witty, colored-glass rings—informal fashion accessories rather than real jewels for evening wear—suggest cabochon gems such as sapphires and moonstones and would, indeed, have been regarded as nearly as desirable. Each was cast in a pressure mold and hand-engraved with flower and plant motifs: fern fronds on the blue ring, forget-me-nots on the colorless ring, and lilies of the valley on the smoky ring. Lalique introduced glass rings in 1931; many incorporated the same basic ball form and were decorated with one of a range of engraved floral motifs.

The *Perruches* (Parakeets) necklace is made from crystal glass beads in the form of lovebirds in facing pairs perched atop tooth-like forms. The simplified, almost fetishistic design lends a hint of exotic sophistication. The partially frosted beads were made in pressure molds; they are hand-finished and linked with silver wire. Two similar necklaces, both with sparrows atop the same tooth-like forms—on one necklace with heads raised, on the other with heads lowered—were introduced by Lalique in 1929.

ROBERT LALLEMANT

Pau 1902–1954 Davos, Switzerland,

Robert Lallemant was raised by his paternal aunt and grandmother in Dijon; his mother had died shortly after his birth, and his father, a wine merchant, worked in Russia.[1] As a young man, he was encouraged to take up ceramics by the sculptor Ovide Yencesse, with whom he studied at the École des Beaux-Arts in Dijon. After serving an apprenticeship at the atelier of the art potter Raoul Lachenal, Lallemant acquired, with the financial support of his father, a small ceramics factory in Paris, where in 1926 he began to produce his own designs. His gratitude to his father is reflected in the signature that invariably appears on his work, T R Lallemant, incorporating Théophile, the father, and Robert, the son (see page 257).

From the beginning, Lallemant rejected Lachenal's self-conscious artistry and one-of-a-kind pots. Instead, he wanted his work to express the spirit of the modern world by means of industrial production

techniques. Although his low-priced pieces made from reusable molds could be reproduced in quantity, he approached the process with the care and attention of an artisan. "He prefers casting . . . to throwing the pot," wrote the critic René Chavance:

His batch, which he likes to be as nearly white as possible, is composed of very pure potter's clay to which he adds kaolin, lime, and silica. Subjected to very hot firing temperatures . . . it provides a biscuit that is suitably hard and resonant to receive enameling. . . . After conceiving a form, he details it in a sketch. It is then made up in plaster. On the plaster model, which will serve as the matrix for a mold, he works out the décor. One model succeeds another. In the atelier where he fills his molds, they are lined up by the hundreds. But he also must control the preparation of the enamel glazes and carefully supervise the firing, because Robert Lallemant leaves nothing to chance.[2]

Chavance then goes on to describe Lallemant as a man also fully engaged with the world around him:

What would you like him to create, if not the forms with which we are obsessed, which suggest the machines and all the mechanical fervor that surround us? Inclined by temperament to create architectural constructions, he is most pleased by the equilibrium of geometric lines.[3]

Lallemant produced a range of forms for the domestic environment: vases, lighting fixtures, candle holders, table sculptures, and the like. Many were conceived as coordinated groups, such as matched table and wall lamps or sets of smoking accessories. He also devised unusual items, such as radiator caps for automobiles. When not covered with rich monochromatic glazes, Lallemant's bold forms provide surfaces for his simplified applied decoration. In addition to abstract geometries inspired by the language of Cubism — the hallmark of modernity — his favored motifs included sport, travel, and maps. Although Lallemant's production runs were never large, his pieces were small in scale and easily exported and he developed markets for his work in England and the United States.

Lallemant's work was displayed at the Salon des Artistes Décorateurs in 1927 and 1928. Also in 1928, he participated in a group exhibition at the Bernheim-Jeune gallery that included work by the architect-designer Georges Djo-Bourgeois, the jeweler Jean Fouquet, and sculptors Jan and Joël Martel. With these same colleagues, he founded the Union des Artistes Modernes (UAM) in 1929 (he was the only potter in the organization). Over the next few years, a growing interest in interior design led to commissions for residential and commercial interiors, and he founded Le Maillon (The Link), a club that brought together members of professions concerned with interiors. Around this time, Lallemant and his wife moved into a new building on the Quai d'Auteuil in Paris. It housed not only their modernist apartment (decorated entirely by Lallemant) but also kilns and a showroom, where Lallemant displayed his own work together with that of his friends from the UAM.

In 1933, Lallemant in effect abandoned his career in ceramics and interior design to join the public works business owned by his wife's family (although he did continue to exhibit his ceramics). During the Second World War, he served in the French Navy, and in 1942 he was made artistic advisor to Marshal Pétain, premier of the Fascist-dominated Vichy government. In that capacity, he was responsible for official commissions of decorative arts, including porcelains from Sèvres (a vase he designed for Sèvres was decorated with nationalistic motifs), glass from Baccarat, and silver from Puiforcat. In 1944 he returned to the Navy, serving in the Far East. Lallemant rejoined his father-in-law's firm in 1946. An avid skier, he suffered a fatal heart attack while making a run at Davos in 1954.

32 | Vase
1927; porcelain

This vase brings to mind an engine part, although it also evokes the traditional Chinese cong, in which a square-sectioned body with horizontal detailing is superimposed on a cylindrical matrix (see following page). Lallemant produced two variants of the design, a taller version with a protruding lip and a shorter version, oval in section. Made from his specially formulated off-white clay, it is covered with an even, glossy black glaze. The cylindrical form is accentuated by raised vertical rows of horizontally grooved prismatic detailing. Two rows run the full height of the vase; the other two are fragmented. While this feature may have been conceived with practicality in mind — it provides a grip on an otherwise slick surface — more likely Lallemant's concern was with aesthetics.

Although Lallemant never abandoned figural and abstract painted decoration, he experimented with rich monochromatic glazes, especially black, white, gold, and platinum, which lend his work an almost industrial character. Lucie Delarue-Mardrus, writing in *Art et industrie* in 1928, described Lallemant as a young artist,

. . . filled with the present and with the future. . . . In looking at his works, it is impossible not to feel that they have emerged from the very period we are passing through. The influence of the machine . . . is revealed at every moment, as much in the forms of his pots as in the motifs that decorate them.

There is something of the connecting rod, the screw head, the motor, the rail, even the ammunition shell, in the ceramics of Robert Lallemant. The angles so beloved of Cubism are often found in them; and the fractured line inspired by lightning — a particular sign of our age which lacks tranquility — pleases his inventive fingers.

His black vases, which are of a solid brilliant black, demand a strong contrast [provided by] the brightly colored flowers that will be placed in them, and are best seen against a brightly lit background, all the brighter to show off the gleaming dark-as-night enamel glaze.[1]

Critic René Chavance also spoke of the importance of context in Lallemant's ceramics, citing his interest in interior design:

When he conceives a decorative object, he thinks instinctively of its likely destination. Because he cannot separate his work from daily life, he envisions an object within its setting, aware of the effect its color note and strong silhouette will make against the sober background of a modern interior. Furthermore, who knows if, some day or another, he might not be tempted to arrange this very setting with his own furniture designs and décor? The individual parts call forth the whole.[2]

Jade cong. Liangzhu culture, China, ca. 2400 B.C.
The Metropolitan Museum of Art, Purchase, Sir Joseph
Hotung Gift, 2004 (2004.52)

JACQUES LE CHEVALLIER

Paris 1896–1987 Fontenay-aux-Roses

RENÉ KOECHLIN

Le Vésinet 1888–1972 Grenoble

Restaurant Chiquito, Paris, with glass ceiling designed by Le Chevallier, 1928

Although most prolific as a maker of decorative architectural glass, Jacques Le Chevallier is today perhaps better known for the extraordinary modernist table lamps he designed with René Koechlin during the late 1920s and early 1930s.[1] The son of a businessman (who took an interest in architecture and art collecting) and a painter, he studied at the École Nationale des Arts Décoratifs in Paris until the outbreak of the war, during which he served as an ambulance driver.

In 1920, Le Chevallier joined the architectural glassworks of Louis Barillet, whose eponymous firm specialized in architectural glass such as windows, decorative panels, and screens. Best known for their graphic, modernist designs made primarily with molded and frosted colorless glass offset with areas of black (an austere, limited palette that was nonetheless especially well suited to admitting bright, diffused light), Barillet commissions included glassworks for several pavilions at the 1925 Paris Exposition, the villa of the Vicomte and Vicomtesse de Noailles in Hyères (1925), and the Paris house-studio of sculptors Jan and Joël Martel (1927).[2] Le Chevallier eventually became a *maître verrier* (master glassmaker), supervising the design and execution of many Barillet projects up until the Second World War.

The Barillet firm also carried out many religious commissions. Le Chevallier, a devout Catholic, belonged to a number of organizations that promoted the revival of religious art, including the Artisans de l'Autel (Artisans of the Altar) and the Ateliers d'Art Sacré (Ateliers of Sacred Art). Religious-themed stained-glass windows would increasingly dominate Le Chevallier's interests.

In 1926, Le Chevallier joined forces with René Koechlin to design a series of experimental lighting fixtures.[3] Very little is known about Koechlin.

Trained as a naval architect, after an illness he took on small engineering projects in his studio near Grenoble. In their work together, Le Chevallier was responsible for the visual aesthetic of the lamps, Koechlin for the technical aspects. Their collaboration was highly successful. Between 1926 and 1932, they made twenty different models, uncompromisingly modernist in design and intended for mass production. Nevertheless, although a small number of models were put into limited production with the backing of Louis Barillet, and selected designs were produced by and sold through Décoration Intérieur Moderne (DIM), no model was ever produced in quantity.[4]

Le Chevallier was a founding member, in 1929, of the forward-looking, reform-minded Union des Artistes Modernes, while his interest in religious art continued undiminished. To the Pavillon Pontifical at the 1937 Paris Exposition, he contributed stained-glass windows that were later installed in the cathedral of Notre-Dame de Paris (he would create additional windows for the cathedral in the 1960s). Like many of his contemporaries, Le Chevallier followed a broad range of artistic pursuits, including painting, printmaking, tapestry design, and wood engraving, as well as being an avid lecturer, writer, and teacher, concerned with imparting to his audiences the importance of art in the modern world.[5] His work was seen at the annual Salons, including the Salon d'Automne and the Société des Artistes Décorateurs.

In 1938, Le Chevallier set up his own studio in Fontenay-aux-Roses, designing stained glass, mosaics, and tapestries. He later expanded the studio to include a glassmaking atelier where he produced stained-glass windows into the late 1960s. In 1948 he revived the Ateliers d'Art Sacré, renamed the Centre d'Art Sacré, which supported postwar reconstruction of cathedrals in Angers, Besançon, and Toulouse and promoted continuing development of the stained-glass industry. In 1958 he was elected a chevalier of the Légion d'Honneur.

33 | Lamp
1926–27; aluminum, ebonite

Of the twenty lamp models that Le Chevallier and Koechlin produced between 1926 and 1932, Type 4, the present model, is the most radically abstract. All twenty were made with aluminum, some with details in wood or ebonite.[1] Although aluminum had the advantages of being inexpensive and suitable for mass production, with a surface that created a soft, evenly diffused light, its use was quite unusual for domestic interiors at that time.

The bulb in Type 4 is housed in a construction of three intersecting aluminum discs that rest in a hoop base with cylindrical legs. Set at angles, and held in place with exposed brass screws and ebonite braces, the cut and bent discs create complex sculptural juxtapositions. No effort has been made to conceal the bulb or the socket, although the cradle base allows the housing to be turned at will, directing or obscuring the light source as desired.

The lamp, while functional and machine-like in appearance, also reveals a lyrical, even mysterious quality, the silvery light reflected on its ever-changing arrangement of surfaces suggesting the segmented shapes of the moon in its various phases. In this evocation, the lamp becomes a visual metaphor for nighttime light, both natural and artificial, as a source of illumination. The lamp also presents a virtual essay in Cubist design: the deconstruction of the sphere into a series of angular planes heightens the perception of its round volume.

An article that appeared in *L'Art vivant* in 1930 noted:

The lighting designer must . . . conceive his fixtures in such a way that they remain works of art, just as beautiful in full daylight as when, at night, they throw off their expected light. . . . [Le Chevallier and Koechlin are among] those sophisticated artists who use metal and mechanical forms for their lamps, wall sconces, and chandeliers, in which we know not whether logic or strangeness prevails, but which are [ultimately] quite alluring.[2]

Type 4 was conceived in October 1926; a prototype was completed in time for the 1927 Salon d'Automne. By 1929 the model had been put into limited production by Décoration Intérieur Moderne (DIM), the modernist ensemblier.[3] Le Chevallier and Koechlin were not happy with DIM's production, and only a small number were made. After 1930 further examples were made by Koechlin in a range of different materials, including nickel, brass, zinc, and duralumin.

PIERRE LEGRAIN

Levallois-Perret 1889–1929 Paris

Transported by his creative gifts, by an imagination that favors the most unexpected forms and materials, Legrain from the very start of his projects would provoke a kind of despair among the courageous craftsmen charged with realizing them: "But Monsieur Legrain, it is impossible, it has never been done!" "I should hope not," he would reply, unruffled, and, pencil in hand, patient and gentle, he would set out to convince them [it could be done], and he always succeeded.[1]

Without a doubt, Pierre Legrain was one of the most inventive and original designers of the French Art Deco period. Despite the brief span of his career—it lasted little more than a decade—he nonetheless produced a considerable body of work that ranged from bookbindings to gardens. His inventive aesthetic—which drew inspiration from African art, Asian art, and Cubism, among other sources—represents the most advanced taste of his day, while sumptuous materials and superb craftsmanship place his work soundly in the realm of French Art Deco.

The son of a distillery owner, Legrain was raised in Paris.[2] An enthusiastic athlete, he nevertheless suffered from various heart-related ailments that afflicted him throughout his life. He studied art—focusing on drawing and sculpture—at the École Germain-Pilon in Paris, but had to leave the school when the distillery business failed and Legrain's father died, leaving the family with no means of support. To make ends meet, Legrain submitted drawings to several illustrated magazines, including Paul Iribe's satirical review *Le Témoin*. Iribe liked Legrain's work, hired him in 1908, and, recognizing his multifaceted skills, eventually had him assisting with designs for stage sets, jewelry, objects, and furniture. Although never credited,

Legrain appears to have made contributions to a 1912 commission by the couturier Jacques Doucet to supervise the decoration of his apartment (see page 135, top). Legrain's work for Iribe ended at the beginning of the war.

Declared physically unfit to serve at the front, Legrain spent the war years in Paris, assigned to various clerical posts. In 1917 he contacted Doucet (who was unaware of Legrain's contributions to the decoration of his apartment), asking for work. His timing was excellent. Long a bibliophile, Doucet was in the process of building a library of contemporary literature under the guidance of writers Louis Aragon, André Bréton, and André Suarès, and he wanted appropriately modern bindings for the books. Although Legrain had no experience as a bookbinder, in need of income, he agreed to take on the project. The commission introduced Legrain to a skill that would come to define his career. Rejecting traditional binding embellishments such as complicated interlaces and fleurons, intricate dentil borders, and elaborate bandings, he employed instead an abstract geometric vocabulary—usually offset with bold typography—through which he was able to establish a relationship to the book's subject matter. Over time, Legrain would create covers for more than three hundred fifty of Doucet's books and nearly a thousand for other clients, including French prime minister Louis Barthou, bibliophile collectors Georges and Auguste Blaizot, Florence Blumenthal, and Baron Robert de Rothschild. His bindings were first exhibited at the Salon des Artistes Français in 1919 and the Salon des Artistes Décorateurs in 1920.

Legrain opened his own workshop in 1923, in the atelier of decorators Briant et Robert at 7, rue d'Argenteuil. Here, he not only continued with bindings but expanded his repertoire to include picture frames and furniture, with designs that often combined strong African and Cubist influences and incorporated unusual materials such as exotic woods, animal skins, metal, and glass. Doucet and another of Legrain's early clients, the milliner Jeanne Tachard, clearly influenced his taste, since both were important collectors of African and Cubist art. In 1924 he was commissioned by Tachard to furnish her villa in La Celle-Saint-Cloud, for which he also designed an extraordinary modernist garden that in plan resembled one of his bookbindings.[3]

In the late 1920s, Legrain designed furniture and interiors for such clients as the Vicomte de Noailles and the American railroad and banking heir Templeton Crocker. He also took work-for-hire jobs, including furniture for Louis Vuitton, camera cases for Kodak, an automobile for Delage, and at least one textile for Maurice Lauer (it was used for the curtains of the smoking room on the SS *Île de France*). In 1928 he designed the sets for *L'Éventail de Jeanne*, a ballet set to music by multiple composers, including Georges Auric, Darius Milhaud, Francis Poulenc, and Maurice Ravel, which was presented at the Opéra de Paris in 1929.

Legrain was an active participant in the annual Paris Salons, especially that of the Société des Artistes Décorateurs. At the 1925 Paris Exposition, his bindings and other work graced several rooms of the Ambassade Française, the Ruhlmann pavilion, the Art et Industrie du Livre pavilion, and the leatherworking section in the Grand Palais. He was awarded a Prix Blumenthal about 1925. In 1926, discouraged by the conservative nature of many of the displays at the 1925 Expo, he was a founding member of Les Cinq, a group of five designers who explored a more aggressive modernity in their work.[4]

Legrain's final project was also his client's: in 1929 he supervised the installation of Doucet's formidable collection of modernist art, furnishings, and literature in his now famous studio in Neuilly, much of which had been created by Legrain himself (see page 135, bottom). Not only did this project represent the culmination of Legrain's career, it was in many ways the apogee of French Art Deco taste. Both Doucet and Legrain died shortly after its completion, heralding the end of an era.

The editors of *Plaisir de bibliophile* paid eloquent tribute to Legrain following his fatal heart attack in 1929:

If the gift of invention, that is to say, the creative imagination, is for the artist the supreme faculty and essential condition of genius, Legrain will be ranked among the masters who have expressed in a new way the harmony of lines and colors. Served by an astute intelligence and refined taste, he always subordinated the fantasy of his vision to the critique of reflection; his mind, which liked difficult problems, was never satisfied with mundane solutions.[5]

34 | Stool
ca. 1925; palisander

In addition to his important collections of modern paintings, sculpture, decorative arts, and literature, Jacques Doucet owned numerous works of Asian and African art. When Legrain began designing furniture for Doucet in 1923, he clearly kept his patron's eclectic tastes in mind. Even after the work he did for Doucet, most of Legrain's furniture would to some degree incorporate a combination of the avant-garde and the exotic, not to mention luxury materials, a mix that lent his work a unique character: "Anyone who knows [Legrain's] work, who has followed his varied output . . . can distinguish it at a glance from that of a thousand others."[1]

Legrain's stool derives its form from furniture made by the Ashanti people of Ivory Coast and Ghana—specifically, carved wood stools and headrests with concave oval tops set on blocky, sculptural bases. Doucet was known to have Ashanti art in his collection, and indeed shortly after the Museum acquired this stool, art historian Henry Sorensen informed curator Henry Geldzahler:

As for your Legrain stool, it may interest you to know that Marcel Coard (who of course knew Doucet very well) told me that Doucet had, amongst his African items, an African stool quite similar to yours from which Legrain took the greater part of his inspiration—or, in other words, he practically copied it.[2]

Ashanti stools were traditionally ceremonial rather than utilitarian in use, which may explain Legrain's conception: a seat that is essentially non-functional. Too low to sit on with any degree of comfort, it is rather a mood-making abstract sculpture for the domestic environment. "Creating an atmosphere—that is for Pierre Legrain the preeminent concern, whether for a bookbinding or for a modern interior."[3] While both form and decoration are clearly based on the African model, Legrain has so abstracted and regularized its component details that the design is his own.

The stool, made of solid palisander, has a concave oval seat with a carved border of stepped molding and bands of triangles. The tapered mid-section with projecting, triangular step details rests on a base with two pierced block feet carved with horizontal ribbing. Although undoubtedly made for Doucet's Paris apartment, it was installed again in 1928 or 1929 in the main room of his Neuilly studio. Legrain made a second version of the stool for Doucet's friend the milliner Jeanne Tachard, a fellow collector of African art.[4]

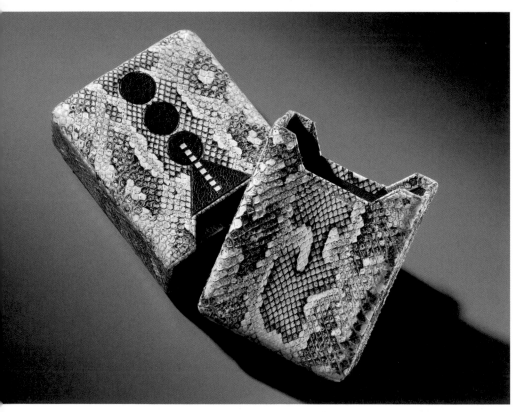

35 | Portfolio and Cigarette Cases

a | Portfolio, ca. 1925; dyed leather, chrome-plated metal, gold leaf

b | Cigarette Case, ca. 1925; dyed and tooled leather, gold leaf

c | Cigarette Case, ca. 1925; snakeskin, dyed and tooled leather, gold leaf

In 1917 couturier Jacques Doucet commissioned Legrain to design bindings for his extensive collection of books by contemporary writers. Although untrained in bookbinding, Legrain learned quickly and soon proved his expertise. Indeed, Legrain's abstract designs, unexpectedly contrasting colors, unusual spatial compositions, and use of rare and exotic materials make his bindings among the most advanced creations of the Art Deco style. These three works employ the same aesthetic vocabulary and materials as his bookbindings, but on a smaller scale.[1]

The teal leather folding portfolio has front and back half-covers of chrome-plated metal with five rows of horizontal and ten rows of vertical perforations, each centered with a gilt dot. The interior has two leather pockets on each side and is lined with blue moiré silk. Its exact purpose is unclear, though it may have been intended as a large wallet. Each of the two slipcase cigarette boxes has an outer box with notched edges for gripping the inner box, which is similarly notched. One box is made of maroon-dyed leather with areas of abstract geometric patterning in browns and oranges embellished with gilt details. The other is covered in tan and brown snakeskin, and inlaid with geometric areas in brown and green leather, also embellished with gilt details.

The donor of all three works was Ethlyne Seligman, widow of French-American art dealer Germain Seligman (1893–1978). Seligman was the son of the Paris dealer Jacques Seligmann (1858–1923). Seligmann senior opened a New York branch in 1904 (the younger Seligman dropped the final "n" from his name when he became an American citizen in 1943). During the 1920s, Germain Seligman, whose interest was modern art, began selling decorative arts by French designers such as Legrain, Jean Dunand, Claudius Linossier, Maurice Marinot, É.-J. Ruhlmann, and Jean Serrière. All three works were included in a 1926 exhibition devoted to the work of Legrain and the glassmaker Maurice Marinot at the Jacques Seligmann gallery in New York.

Legrain seems to have designed other cigarette cases. Long after his death, Legrain's schoolmate the painter Robert Bonfils recalled that he had made "cigarette boxes for Lucky Strike and Camel."[2] In fact, he may have been referring to two other cigarette boxes included in the Seligmann exhibition, each with decoration adapted from the two famous brands. Neither logo on these boxes seems to have been an accurate rendering but instead a somewhat abstract evocation.[3]

The design of the portfolio may have been adapted from a binding Legrain made in 1924 for Doucet's copy of *Les Amis nouveaux*, by Paul Morand. Nearly identical, it too was made with teal leather and perforated chrome-plated metal panels offset by gilt dots.[4] Legrain seems to have made at least one other variant of the design: a larger desk blotter or folio cover in tan leather with perforated chromed-metal half covers and gilt dots.[5]

Salon, Jacques Doucet residence, 46, avenue du Bois (today avenue Foch), Paris, ca. 1913

Salon, Jacques Doucet studio, 33, rue Saint-James, Neuilly, ca. 1929

JULES-ÉMILE LELEU

Boulogne-sur-Mer 1883–1961 Paris

Jules Leleu seems to be one of those who has best understood the needs of his contemporaries, even as he remembers the great French traditions. . . . His work [has already become] so important both here and abroad, where he has often been the ambassador of French good taste.[1]

Thus was Leleu described in 1932, when he had not yet arrived even at the midpoint of his career as a furniture designer and ensemblier. More conservative than that of many of his contemporaries, such as Ruhlmann or Süe et Mare, Leleu's nonetheless sophisticated and refined aesthetic—original yet strongly rooted in French tradition—held a wide appeal. Such was its reputation that the Leleu firm, founded in 1909, remained in operation until 1971, with clients around the world.

After attending the École des Beaux-Arts in Boulogne-sur-Mer, the École Germain-Pilon in Paris, and the art academy in Brussels, Leleu in 1909, with his brother Marcel, took over their father's house-painting business, adding a furniture-making and decorating atelier.[2] Both brothers served in the Army during the war, Jules in the air division.

In 1922, Leleu first submitted his furniture to several Salon exhibitions, and the following year his display at the Salon des Artistes Décorateurs brought him the public and critical attention necessary for him to establish his own business independent of the family firm; Maison Leleu opened in 1924. Early on, he established an international roster of noteworthy clients, including Gonzalo Zaldumbide, the Ecuadorian ambassador to France, and Prince Pierre of Monaco, father of Rainier III, who appreciated the suave simplicity of his Directoire and Louis-Philippe–inspired furniture.

Although he had been in business for only a year, Leleu took a stand in the 1925 Paris Exposition; the commode later acquired by the Metropolitan Museum (no. 36) was among the many works on display. He also contributed furniture to the Ambassade Française.

Like much French Art Deco, Leleu's forms, materials, techniques, and decorative motifs—not to mention his design process—recall but do not replicate eighteenth-century precedents, linking his original designs to those of his nation's past. "It seems to me," wrote critic Simonne Ratel in 1927,

. . . that Jules Leleu is the direct heir to the great French craftsmen, the Boulles, the Rieseners, who conceived furniture as though it were a living being. Their first concern was the material, which they wanted rare and flawless. Then they endeavored to bring the body and soul [of the piece] into harmony—the intrinsic beauty of the woods and marbles and the ideal beauty of line and ornamentation. Finally, they believed in adapting the design of their furniture both to its function and to the atmosphere of the place it would occupy. In this way their work was formed gradually, making its way toward perfection by a process of evolution.[3]

Although invariably conceived with a respect for the past, Leleu's harmonious, elegant, well-made furniture is always original, never veering—like less accomplished work of his era—either to the bizarre or to historicism:

French tradition and certain French constants undoubtedly give life to the work of Leleu, and there is certainly no reason to criticize him for that. But we will not find, overall or in the details [of his work], anything that can be considered even remotely a copy or a pastiche.[4]

In the late 1920s and 1930s, Leleu's sons André and Jean and his daughter Paule joined the firm, which expanded to provide the full interior decoration services of an ensemblier. Their clientele represented a worldwide Who's Who of the era—nobility, royalty, industrialists, and bankers, some as far afield as Japan.[5] Notable among their public commissions were interiors for the ocean liners *Île de France* (1927), *Normandie* (1935), and *Pasteur* (1939) and for the Salon des Ambassadeurs at the League of Nations in Geneva (1936) and the new French Embassy in Ankara, Turkey (1939). In the United States, Leleu's furniture was seen in museum and department store exhibitions—at Macy's and B. Altman in New York—and in the French Pavilion at the 1939–40 New York World's Fair.[6]

During the Second World War, Leleu served as a reservist in the War Ministry. He later resumed the full scope of his work, albeit for a diminishing clientele. In 1947 he furnished a dining room at the Élysée Palace, the official residence of the French president. The following year, he opened an office in New York at 55 East Fifty-Seventh Street, a venture that lasted until 1969. Leleu died in an automobile accident in Paris in 1961. The firm continued to operate for another ten years, when it merged with Maison Jansen, another high-end Parisian decorating firm.

It is the simplicity of line—which is in no way barren—and the knowing technique that give [Leleu's] creations the enduring quality which guarantees that later, much later—when Time has rejected the awful and hasty output of would-be artists—the works of Jules Leleu will remain among the purest expressions of the decorative art of our time.[7]

36 | Commode

1925; amboyna, ivory, *fleur de pêcher* marble, brass, mahogany, birch plywood

This elegant commode typifies Leleu's work. While virtually every aspect of its composition—the form, the precious veneers, the floral motif of the marquetry—suggests the eighteenth century, its reductive simplicity speaks to a twentieth-century aesthetic. The frame is mahogany; the birch plywood sides and doors are veneered with amboyna burl, and a cluster of ivory roses is inset at the center of the front panel. Further ivory detailing appears on the drawer pulls, on the legs, and along the bottom edge of the body. The top is a slab of pinkish grey *fleur de pêcher* marble. Each of the three mahogany-veneered compartment interiors is fitted with two mahogany shelves. The two drawers are also made of mahogany.

Part of Leleu's display at the 1925 Paris Exposition, the commode was one of at least four similar

pieces he designed between 1923 and 1927.[1] The earliest, which also had two ivory ring drawer pulls and an ivory floral motif, was presented at the 1923 Salon des Artistes Décorateurs. At least one variant of the present model was made; it is identical except for a modified ivory floral motif.[2]

Following its display in Paris, the commode was seen in the United States in the American Association of Museums' traveling exhibition of selected works from the 1925 Paris Expo. It was presumably after this that it was acquired by Agnes Miles Carpenter, a Francophile American heiress (she died in 1958).[3] Carpenter seems to have been much taken by modern French decorative art. In 1926 she

moved into a new apartment at 950 Park Avenue in New York, which she furnished at least in part with contemporary French furniture.[4] Most notable was a dining room suite in forged iron, made to her specifications by Edgar Brandt.[5] The commode was also part of the apartment furnishings, though it is not clear in which room it was used. Carpenter decided to give it to the Metropolitan Museum in 1946, a period when Art Deco had fallen out of fashion, although that fact seems not to have diminished her love for the piece. "I abandon it with reluctance," she wrote to curator Preston Remington, "but cannot [place it] in a better way than at the Museum under your care."[6]

ÉMILE LENOBLE

Choisy-le-Roi 1875–1939 Morgat

"One could say that Lenoble was born a potter," wrote the critic Léon Deshairs in 1924.[1] And indeed from an early age, Émile Lenoble found his calling in ceramics.[2] That the celebrated potter Ernest Chaplet was a neighbor in Lenoble's hometown of Choisy-le-Roi must certainly have played a part. Lenoble enrolled at the École Nationale des Arts Décoratifs in Paris when he was about twenty, but left after two years to work for Jules Loebnitz, an industrial manufacturer of tin-glazed earthenware. In 1903 he returned to Choisy-le-Roi to become Chaplet's assistant—and also to marry his daughter. Chaplet was one of a number of late nineteenth-century French potters who had brought new life and artistry to stoneware—traditionally considered a coarse medium reserved for utilitarian pottery—achieving astonishing effects through their experimentation with clay, glaze, and firing formulas.

Around 1904, Lenoble's friend the painter Henri Rivière showed him examples of archaic Korean, Chinese, and Japanese pottery from his private collection: "I was struck by them," Lenoble recalled. "Without a doubt, they inspired me."[3] Lenoble's first efforts were displayed to acclaim at the Galerie Georges Petit in Paris in 1905, and by 1914 his pots were being seen in the annual Paris Salons, museum exhibitions, and internationally at world's fairs.[4]

From the start, Lenoble limited his repertoire of materials, forms, and decoration. He worked exclusively with stoneware batch that he formulated himself. He threw all his own pots, working out the details of the design directly on the potter's wheel rather than on paper beforehand, and restricting his forms mainly to those that could be created on the wheel; only rarely did they include such additions as handles. Accordingly, he often had to make pieces in two or more parts, joined seamlessly with slip.

In 1909 the critic Maurice Pillard Verneuil noted that Lenoble's forms were "generally strong, robust, and powerful, well-balanced and stable, truly suited to the character of the stoneware that constitutes his ceramic material."[5] In similar vein, Lenoble tailored his decoration specifically to his medium:

Where Lenoble is truly himself, where one could never mistake the paternity of one of his pots, is in decorating his pieces. His system of ornamentation is very sober and simple in its lines; most often it remains purely linear, but sometimes—though rarely—he is tempted by flowers.[6]

For his decoration, Lenoble favored two techniques: painting and carving. Because stoneware is fired at high temperatures, painted decoration can melt and streak unless carefully controlled. Lenoble developed glazes that allowed his motifs to remain intact. With carved decoration, he cut bas-relief patterns into the body, often covering the raised elements with a differently colored slip or clay to highlight the motif. He restricted his palette to natural, earthy tones.

Lenoble was drafted at the onset of the war. Wounded at the front, he was interned as a prisoner of war, first in Germany and later in Switzerland. When he returned to his studio in Choisy-le-Roi, he quietly resumed his work, experimenting in particular with blue and celadon glazes, his style evolving though changing little through the 1920s and 1930s. During this period he continued to participate in the Paris Salons. He also exhibited at the Galerie Rouard and at the Paris Expositions of 1925 and 1937.[7]

In 1930 an entire issue of *Les Albums d'art Druet* was dedicated to Lenoble, placing him in the company of such artists such as Bonnard and Cézanne, Degas, Gauguin, Manet, and Van Gogh. The introductory essay was written by Léon Deshairs:

I admire the pots of Lenoble for their beautiful material, their balance, their vitality, their full and robust harmony. I would say that they are "brawny," if that epithet were not too vulgar to characterize these grands seigneurs whose quiet power is never unrefined. . . . Such simplicity in richness, such refinement in strength, such a happy alliance of order and life — all this protects Lenoble's work from the vicissitudes of taste.[8]

37 | Three Vases

a | Vase, 1925; glazed stoneware

b | Vase, ca. 1925; glazed stoneware

c | Vase, ca. 1913; glazed stoneware

Hand and fire have joined together to bestow on Lenoble's pots that essential quality: life. Personal without affectation, independent of all fashion, executed with skill and love, they have the quiet radiance of classical works. Let us have no fear: they will endure.[1]

Such was the high praise of critic Léon Deshairs in 1924. Lenoble was one of the first modern ceramists to elevate stoneware from a base material, traditionally suitable only for disposable utilitarian wares, to a material worthy of the highest artistic expression.

His successful marriage of refined ornamentation with the dense raw material is a testament to his creativity and skill. Lenoble's ornament is infused with a naïveté celebrated by contemporary artists who sought inspiration in primitive and vernacular traditions. Deshairs was a particular champion of Lenoble's work. Of such ornament he wrote:

I will not describe Lenoble's decorations, for they can be seen. Indeed, I would not have the words to define without circumlocution his chevrons, traceries, torsades, scales, spirals, waves, leaves, his flowers pared down to their most essential characteristics. It would take someone very clever to recognize the exact source of each of these motifs, to distinguish in them the part that is nature, the part that derives from Greece or the Orient, the part that is the artist's invention.[2]

Lenoble's motifs were, for Deshairs, timeless:

They belong to humanity's oldest ornamental repertoire. They have for centuries been in common use and yet they have not become hackneyed. In adapting them to his works, Lenoble has made them his own.[3]

Similarly, his forms are

. . . from every country and from every age; the most serene, the most enduring, always fresh because they do not belong to any particular fleeting fashion.[4]

Metropolitan Museum curator Joseph Breck purchased the small greyish white-and-blue crackle vase (opposite, right) from Galerie Rouard in 1922. The two larger vases were probably acquired by the New York collector Aline Meyer Liebman at the 1925 Paris Exposition. Both vases sat atop a bookcase in Mrs. Liebman's New York living room and were eventually given to the Museum by her son (see page 56). The taller of the two (at center) has a cylindrical neck set on a spherical body; its deep brown glaze is offset with bands of orange decoration carved around the neck, shoulder, and underside of the belly. The shorter, ovoid vase (at left) is embellished with a frieze of stylized prunus blossoms.

É.-J. Ruhlmann. Design for the grand salon, with cabinet by Léon Jallot, Hôtel du Collectionneur, Exposition Internationale des Arts Décoratifs et Industriels Modernes, Paris, 1925

38 | Vase

1925; glazed stoneware

This beautiful pot, which seamlessly combines material, form, and ornament, embodies what critic Léon Deshairs called

. . . the essential character of Lenoble's great talent: equilibrium and vitality. However expressive the form, however personal the decoration, however unusual the material, a vase by Lenoble never gives the impression of labor or effort. Everything about it seems easy, natural, created in joy.[1]

More important, it epitomises Lenoble's achievement as an artist:

What is emblematic of the true artist is that he puts into a work everything that is necessary, but nothing more. In this, Lenoble is most profoundly an artist. His pieces show no excess, but neither do they show any lack.[2]

It was surely these qualities that drew Metropolitan Museum curator Joseph Breck to this vase when he saw it in the Ruhlmann pavilion at the 1925 Paris Exposition. Ruhlmann, like many other ensembliers at the fair, approached friends and colleagues to help him round out the furnishing of his display, and their ceramics, glass, and sculptures filled vitrines or were placed on furniture throughout the building. He included several pieces by Lenoble. Most of Lenoble's work was exhibited in the vestibule, but this vase may have been placed — at least temporarily — atop a cabinet by Léon Jallot (see no. 26) in the pavilion's grand salon.

Like his pots, Lenoble himself seems to have been quite understated in character and in his expression. "When he said, 'This is a pot!'" wrote Deshairs, "he said it all."[3] Well, *this* is a *pot*.

CLAUDIUS LINOSSIER

Lyons 1893–1953 Lyons

Like the creation of a beautiful vessel of stoneware, the execution of an object in hammered metal represents a passionate struggle between the artist and the material. Under repeated blows of the hammer, the medium yields, becomes manageable, and is transformed. Without using molds or measuring tools, and only with a steady hand and a precise eye, the maker can form—from a flat sheet of copper—a vase with a slender neck, whose walls are often further shaped in relief, with moldings and harmonious decorative motifs.[1]

If the revival of traditional skills was a fundamental aspect of French Art Deco, no craftsman better exemplifies this development than Claudius Linossier, a metalworker who excelled in dinanderie. The term derives from Dinant-sur-Meuse, a town near Liège, Belgium, where hand-worked metalware had been produced since the Middle Ages. Although the most famous dinandier of the era was Jean Dunand (see pages 73–89), Linossier deserves to be considered his equal and together they were instrumental in reviving an age-old technique that had become nearly obsolete with the advent of industrialization. Although historically dinanderie was used to make utilitarian objects such as cooking utensils—which in the modern world could be machine produced using presses and dies—over time this laborious métier had evolved from a humble craft into a prestigious art reserved for ornamental metalwork.

Born in Lyons, the son of a *canut*, or textile weaver, Linossier apprenticed from the age of about eleven with a locksmith-ironworker, and later worked for Berger-Nesme, a local silversmith specializing in religious wares.[2] After military service during the war, he was hired in 1919 by the prestigious if somewhat conservative Paris firm Maison Cardeilhac, which specialized in silver cutlery and tableware, and where he did enamel and inlay work. Later that year he entered the dinanderie atelier of Jean Dunand, working under the supervision of Francesco ("Kéco") Zambon. His three-month stay at the workshop, though brief, was crucial to the development of his appreciation for metalwork as an art form. In Paris he often visited the Louvre:

Of all the impressions that struck the young provincial in Paris, none was stronger than that of discovering ancient Greek pottery at the Louvre. The purity of its forms, the sobriety of its decoration, the nobility of its style—all would stay in his head as perfect models and give direction to his art.[3]

In 1920, Linossier returned to Lyons and set up his own workshop. From the start, he limited his repertoire of materials, techniques, and decorative vocabulary, restricting himself principally to abstract geometric and archaic figural decoration. He favored copper, though he also used brass, silver, nickel silver, and other alloys, and he experimented with hammering, inlay, and patination to achieve a variety of surface and color effects. Unlike other dinandiers, he never enameled or lacquered his pieces but relied solely on acid and fire for his distinctive patinas. And while he preferred vessel forms—vases, bowls, and plates—none were conceived with utility in mind. Most significantly, each piece was unique. Linossier's narrow range of artistic expression was criticized by some as lacking in innovation, but others recognized his persistent efforts to achieve perfection: "M. Claudius Linossier never rests on his laurels; he endlessly renews the elements of his inspiration . . . revealing the spirit of an obstinate seeker."[4]

From 1921 until the Second World War, Linossier was an active participant in the annual Paris Salons.

In the early 1920s, he was represented in Paris by Galerie Hébrard and later by Rouard, and his work was featured in several pavilions at the 1925 Paris Exposition.[5] Between 1924 and 1930, his work was also included in many important international exhibitions.[6] He was made a chevalier of the Légion d'Honneur in 1932.

Linossier's most prolific period—also considered his finest artistically—was from 1923 to 1932. During this decade he made over a hundred pieces each year, never employing more than two assistants. He explored sculpture briefly around 1925.

As early as 1923, his work was eloquently described by an admiring—and prescient—critic:

Like the best works from times past, those by Linossier attest to a fine balance between craft and art. In any object made by this artist, one senses that the work has been touched by an ideal. Hence these vases, perfect in their construction, balance, power, and grace. . . . Linossier's work allows us to declare that contemporary decorative art is beginning to fully realize itself.[7]

39 | Vase
ca. 1923; copper, silver

This vase typifies Linossier's mastery of dinanderie. The process involves raising a form from a thin, flat sheet of metal (usually brass or copper) by hammering it over an anvil or a shaped form. Reheating prevents the metal from becoming brittle and fracturing. A sulfuric acid bath and beating with a flat-headed mallet eliminates hammer marks from the surface.

Linossier was also particularly skilled with inlay and patination, two techniques he used to decorate his dinanderie. Inlay involves precisely cutting sheet metal, hammering it into channeled grooves in the body of a vessel, and passing the surface under a blowtorch, causing the two metals to fuse. In patination, the vessel is submerged in an acid bath or exposed to controlled flame, which oxidizes the metal alloys and changes their color. After considerable experimentation, Linossier was able to achieve a wide range of colors and tones, from reds and oranges to greys and blacks, even purples and yellow-greens. Using fire and specialized alloys, he effectively created abstract paintings in metal.

The elegantly shaped body of this vase swells outward and upward, cinched below a dramatic flared lip. In an architectonic pattern of inlaid silver patinated to a brassy grey, riblike columns of spirals alternate with columns of diamond lozenges, enhancing the verticality of the graceful silhouette; a triple banding of dots circles the neck beneath the lip.[1] Linossier's understated aesthetic was described by critic Luc Roville in 1923:

As taste is refined by looking at masterpieces, simplicity becomes an increasingly essential quality for a work of art. Linossier has made a rule of this: no ornament ever disturbs the profile of his vases. If ever the idea of adding relief to them occurred to him, he would never allow himself to do so. The decoration of his pieces always strictly addresses their forms, and often seems to be used only as a way to emphasize and highlight their curves. . . . It is to geometric designs that he habitually returns, and in this he displays an inexhaustibly fertile imagination. There is nothing but lines, waves, squares, diamonds, circles, dots, meanders, and chevrons, but he intermixes them and arranges them with an endlessly renewed artfulness, and above all relates them closely with form: around his vases he wraps opulent necklaces and marvelous belts. . . . It is perhaps in the colors of his decoration that Claudius Linossier's true and original merit becomes apparent. The means at his disposal, however, seem quite limited. He uses neither enamels nor lacquers. He seeks his colors only from inlaid metals patinated with the blowtorch: silver, copper, brass, white metal, and nickel silver.[2]

The vase was displayed at the 1924 exhibition of the Société des Artistes Décorateurs in Paris, where it was acquired by Florence Blumenthal, the wife of George Blumenthal, a director of the Paris-based investment bank Lazard Frères and a trustee of the Metropolitan Museum from 1909 to 1941 (he served as president after 1934). The Blumenthals were major patrons of the French Art Deco designers, most notably Armand-Albert Rateau (see pages 177–81), who completed several interiors for their residences in New York and France. In 1919 they established the American Foundation for French Art and Thought, an organization that awarded financial grants to French artists and writers. Linossier was a recipient in 1922.

JOSEP LLORENS ARTIGAS

Barcelona 1892–1980 Gallifa

Josep Llorens Artigas, perhaps the most renowned Spanish potter of the twentieth century, trained in Barcelona at the Escola de la Llotja, the Cercle Artístic de Sant Lluc, and the Escola Superior dels Bells Oficis.[1] His education was grounded in the spirit of Catalan Noucentisme, a movement that encouraged the revival of traditional handcraftsmanship. In the spirit of French Art Deco, the Catalan concept of the *obra ben feta* — the "well-made work" — was an essential part of its philosophy: an artisan should be both a designer and a fabricator, mastering all aspects of his métier. As a young man, Llorens Artigas developed a reputation as a potter specializing in elegant wheel-turned pots with a range of subtle and sophisticated glazes. He traveled

to Paris in 1922, establishing a studio in the suburb of Charenton-le-Pont the following year. There he joined fellow Spanish artists — Paco Durrio, Pablo Gargallo, Pablo Picasso, and Ignacio Zuloaga — and became an active participant in the art scene. His friendship with Salvador Dalí and Luis Buñuel led to his playing the role of Governor in the notorious Surrealist film *L'Age d'or* (1930).

Llorens Artigas left Paris in 1939 for the town of Céret in the Pyrenees, and two years later he returned to Spain, where he taught ceramics at Barcelona's Escola Massana. Throughout his career, he collaborated with painters — among them Albert Marquet, Raoul Dufy, Georges Braque, and Joan Miró — creating with them both pots and ceramic tile murals.

See no. 16.

MAURICE MARINOT

Troyes 1882–1960 Troyes

"Marinot is often referred to by his countrymen as possessing the greatest artistic genius of any of the workers in decorative glass." These words introduced Maurice Marinot to the American public in 1926.[1] Interestingly, Marinot had no experience with glass until he was nearly thirty.[2] The son of a bonnet manufacturer in north-central France, he studied painting at the École des Beaux-Arts in Paris. His fellow students included André Derain, André Dunoyer de Segonzac, Charles Despiau, André Mare, and Jacques Villon, all of whom would be lifelong friends. In 1905, Marinot submitted his paintings to the Salon d'Automne, joining, among others, Henri Matisse, André Derain, Albert Marquet, and Kees van Dongen, a group referred to by the critic Louis Vauxcelles in his review of the exhibition as Les Fauves (The Wild Beasts). Marinot would continue to paint in the bold, vibrantly colored style of the Fauves for nearly ten years, regularly participating in annual Salon exhibitions. He moved back to Troyes, where he settled permanently, in 1908.

In 1911 his childhood friends Eugène and Gabriel Viard bought a factory that produced drinking glasses and other functional glass wares in the town of Bar-sur-Seine. The brothers invited Marinot to visit, and, fascinated as he watched the workers blow and shape the glass at their furnaces, he decided to give glassmaking a try. Initially decorating blanks made at the factory—mainly utilitarian forms like vases and jars—with brilliantly colored enameled motifs such as nudes, animals, fruit, and flowers, he was soon conceiving his own forms.

Marinot introduced his enameled glass to the public at the Salon des Indépendants and the Salon des Artistes Décorateurs in 1912, and later that year he contributed to La Maison Cubiste, an architectural installation presented by his colleagues Jacques Villon and André Mare at the Salon d'Automne.[3] It was most likely at the Maison Cubiste that his glass was first seen by Adrien Hébrard, owner of the Galerie Hébrard in Paris; in 1913, Hébrard became Marinot's sole agent.

Marinot served as a hospital attendant in Troyes during the war, following which he returned to the Viard factory, where he began to develop his own idiosyncratic style and technique. Having earlier worked with thin, light, clear glass, by 1920 he began to experiment with thick-walled forms made with heavy, "imperfect" glass. He stopped enameling—formerly his specialty—in the belief that enamel obscured the natural beauty of the material. And he began to incorporate what had been traditionally considered flaws—internal bubbles and cracking—accentuating them to astonishing effect. He generally treated his massive forms in one of two ways: either with acid etching or with overlaid layers of internally decorated glass. Although he always made utilitarian forms (bottles, vases, and bowls), over time his pieces became increasingly abstract and were not intended for use.

Between 1920 and 1937, Marinot produced nearly two thousand pieces, each one unique. His work was displayed internationally in galleries and museum exhibitions and avidly acquired by both museums and private collectors.[4] At the 1925 Paris Exposition, it was shown at three pavilions, and eight pieces were included in the American Association of Museum's traveling exhibition that followed in 1926.[5] Marinot was made a chevalier of the Légion d'Honneur in 1924.

In 1937, Marinot gave up glassmaking. The Viard factory closed that year, and working at the glass furnaces for so many years had taken a physical toll. However, he was able to return to his first love,

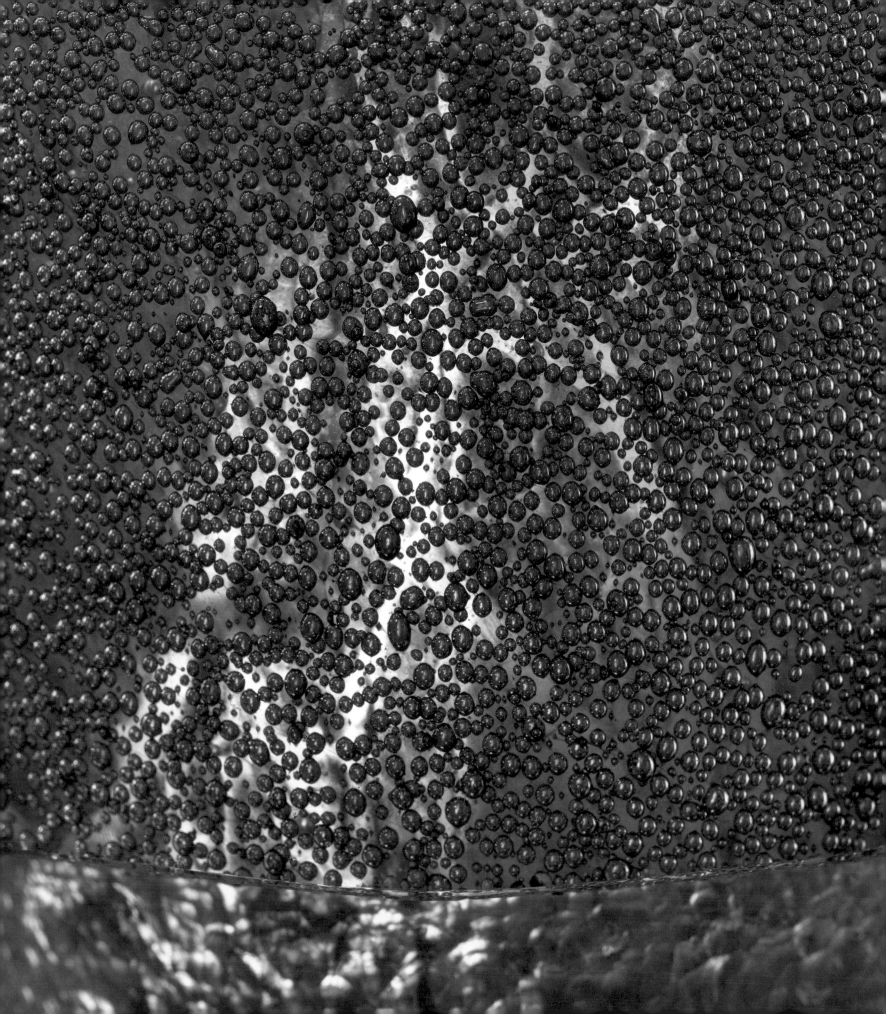

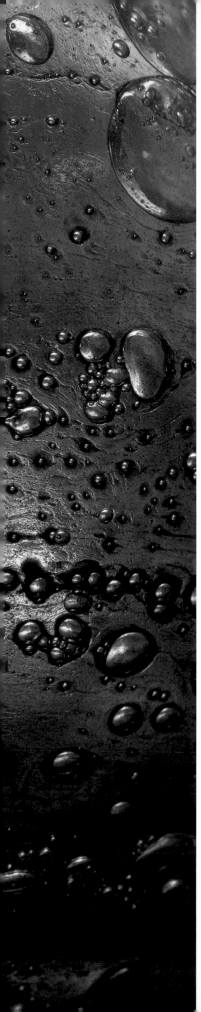

painting, and to exhibit successfully in such galleries as Charpentier. Marinot's studio in Troyes was bombed during the Second World War. Thousands of paintings and works in glass were destroyed.

Marinot considered each piece that he made an expression not only of the métier of glassmaking but of human creativity, indeed life itself:

I think that a good piece of glassware preserves, at its best, a form reflecting the human breath which has shaped it, and that its shape must be a moment in the life of the glass fixed by cooling.[6]

40 | Three Bottles and Bowl

a | Bottle with Stopper, 1922; glass

b | Bottle with Stopper, 1923; glass

c | Bottle with Stopper, 1924; glass

d | Bowl, 1923; glass

The Metropolitan Museum purchased its first examples of Marinot glass in 1923 and 1924, from the Galerie Hébrard in Paris. The first piece to be acquired was the smoke-colored bubble-glass bottle (opposite, top left). Marinot described it as a "flacon méplat chinoise poétique"—a flattened, poetic Chinese bottle. The bubbles were produced by adding metallic flakes to the glass in the process of blowing; the brownish grey coloration is known in French as *bistre dégradé.* The bottle has a tiny colorless ball-shaped stopper which recalls those on Chinese snuff bottles, perhaps a source for Marinot's inspiration, and the reason they were known as "à la chinoise"—in the Chinese style.[1]

The second bottle (top center) is made from frosted, colorless glass. The deeply etched strip streaked with red that winds around the body was created by applying hydrofluoric acid to the thick walls. Marinot described this as a "flacon à spirales gravé"—a bottle with engraved spirals. The bottle's ball-shaped stopper is of red and colorless glass.

The third bottle (top right) is made with colorless glass that suggests cracked ice. To achieve this effect, Marinot used a technique traditional to Venetian glass. The process involves submerging the still-hot semifinished piece in water, causing fissures to appear. The piece is then reheated in the furnace and enlarged by further blowing, which stretches the re-fused fissure marks. This bottle has a square neck with intaglio carving and a ball-shaped colorless stopper. Marinot described it as a "flacon méplat blanc à col carré givré à l'interieure"—a flattened colorless bottle with a square neck rimmed on the interior.

The "bol vert gravé d'une onde" (bottom), a heavy green glass bowl, is deeply acid-etched with a wave pattern. Such pieces impressed the critics. Gabriel Mourey, for example, wrote that Marinot "gets extraordinary effects by engraving with acid on very thick surfaces of crackled or frosted glass: geometrical or architectonic motifs incomparably magnificent in their powerful reliefs."[2] And curator and critic Henri Clouzot sang his praises:

Maurice Marinot has but one muse in his service: pure art. This fine craftsman produces only rare objects, the pride of museums and of great private collections. . . . Marinot has resolved the difficult problem of giving his vases the qualities of robustness and volume without taking away from the material its brilliance, its gleam, or its transparency. In spite of his ingenious experiments, such as the distribution of air bubbles and colored powder in the body mass, his works still remain "glass." His forms are simple but harmonious. One senses that they were born naturally from the end of the [glassmaker's] rod . . . [and] that they express the very qualities of the métier. To say they were made by the hand of a worker is undoubtedly the greatest praise that one can bestow upon them. . . . His eminently personal talent leads imitators to despair.[3]

41 | Four Vessels

 a | Lidded Urn, ca. 1925; glass

 b | Bottle with Stopper, ca. 1925–29; glass

 c | Jar, 1927; glass

 d | Lidded Jar, ca. 1925; glass

In 1964, Maurice Marinot's daughter Florence gave a quantity of his glass to the Victoria and Albert Museum, marking not only the beginning of a revival of interest in his work but, more generally, a renewed interest in French Art Deco, which had been out of fashion for a quarter of a century. The gift was hailed in *Connoisseur* magazine as a significant one, and Marinot's works were described as being

. . . not vases and bowls made for use at the dining-table or for decoration on the mantelpiece [but] free and expressive works of art, made with the most ambitious artistic aims and exploiting to the fullest extent the aesthetic possibilities of the material.*[1]

Marinot was said to have employed color "in the same bold and expressive way" as the Fauves. His work was described as having "the intellectual austerity of the Cubists." Indeed, proclaimed the critic, "much of his glass is really pure sculpture."[2]

A few years later Marvin D. Schwartz, writing in *The New York Times*, noted:

Glass collectors, always the first to push up the date limit for desirable antiques, are getting serious about flapper-era glass. They began the quest for art glass of the eighteen-eighties long before most collectors would consider furniture, silver, or ceramics made after 1830. . . . [Now] those intent on acquiring glass have got involved with fine design of the twenties.[3]

He cited Marinot as a key figure of the period.

cover has a squared finial. Marinot made several similar pieces between 1923 and 1925. The urn form—a covered vase without handles—was conceived in antiquity as a receptacle for the ashes of the dead.

The jar at right was made with three layers of glass: a dark green crackled layer with small bubbles sandwiched between a thick colorless outer wall and an orange-yellow lining visible through the fissures. In 1927 the jar was illustrated in *"The Studio" Yearbook*, where it appeared with a shallow domed colorless glass stopper that has since disappeared.[4]

The small but very heavy bottle at center comprises a layer of colorless glass over a lining of densely bubbled dark brown glass; it is topped, discreetly, by a clear glass ball-shaped stopper, a style referred to by Marinot as "à la chinoise."

The lidded jar at left was a bequest to the Metropolitan by the Marquise Raoul de Saint Cyr (see no. 19c and page 81). The red-orange underlayer is covered with a colorless, bubbled outer layer that has been deeply acid-etched, creating vertical ribs and raised panels. The raised surfaces are polished smooth, while the recessed surfaces are irregularly pitted, harmonizing with the internal occlusions.

In 1971 a gallery in the Museum was installed with many of the Metropolitan's finest French Art Deco works. "The style," noted Marvin D. Schwartz,

These four vessels were acquired by the Metropolitan Museum in or after 1970. In scale, form, and decorative treatment, they are even more remarkable than the four works purchased in the 1920s (see no. 40). While curator Joseph Breck looked for typically representative works, fifty years later curator Henry Geldzahler instead sought exceptional and outstanding ones.

The three pieces shown opposite were part of a large group of French Art Deco works Geldzahler purchased from the Galerie Sonnabend in Paris. They included the vase by Argy-Rousseau (no. 1) and the two bronze cobras by Dunand (no. 17), as well as a cabinet and bedside table by É.-J. Ruhlmann (acc. no. 1970.198.4, .5) and a glass vase by the Établissements Gallé (acc. no. 1970.198.9).

The massive covered urn at left is made from layered colorless glass internally decorated with bubbles and fine black trails. The deep bowl is set on a thick stem and a square foot, and the substantial

. . . has been rediscovered with great enthusiasm by antiques collectors. Many approach tongue in cheek and favor mass-produced work that is reminiscent of the settings once provided in Hollywood films for shady ladies. The museum selection features prize-winning examples that reveal the directions the most adventuresome designers and craftsmen took.

The half-dozen pieces of glass by Maurice Marinot that are shown add a dimension to our understanding of the designs of the period. . . . The geometric patterns that are considered standard for Art Deco were rarely employed by Marinot. He concerned himself with bold squat forms that were in the spirit of the best work of the style.[5]

JAN MARTEL

Nantes 1896–1966 Paris

JOËL MARTEL

Nantes 1896–1966 Paris

For a sculpture to be interesting, it must be an object of interpretation in which anatomy — in the relationships implied by its lines — plays only a secondary role. [The works of] Egyptian, Roman, and Khmer artists offer prototypes for such interpretations . . . [and,] together with examples from the archaic Greek period, [they can be classified as] among the most accomplished manifestations of plastic art.[1]

Louis-Charles Watelin, writing in 1926, went on to say that the sculptures of Jan and Joël Martel exemplified such "objects of interpretation" in the contemporary world and, like their historical precedents, represented an artistic achievement of the highest level.

Born in Nantes, the identical twin brothers were raised at a family estate in the nearby town of Mollin. Following the death of their mother, in 1911 they moved to Paris with their investor father and, the following year, enrolled at the École Nationale des Arts Décoratifs, from the start focusing their studies on sculpture.[2] They would later be described by critic Paul Fierens:

Four hands at work; a single thought in their two minds. . . . One must speak of Jan and Joël Martel only in the singular. These two young men together comprise one artist — and one of the best constituted of our times.[3]

And indeed, although they would have families of their own, the two brothers remained exceptionally devoted to each other, living under the same roof and working closely together. Perhaps the only time they took separate paths was during the war, when Jan fought at Verdun while Joël was exempted from service because of a chronic hip condition. The many commissions for memorial monuments that they received following the war not only allowed them to develop their idiom of simplified, stylized realism but brought their work to the public and gained them critical acclaim.

Back in Paris, the Martel brothers were fully engaged in the art scene, befriending painters, architects, musicians, and dancers. Among their circle were the architects Jean Burkhalter (whose sister Joël married in 1926), Georges Djo-Bourgeois, Le Corbusier, Robert Mallet-Stevens, and Pierre Patout. Indeed, architecture would provide a context for much of their work; many of their sculptures were conceived as part of architectural schemes (decorative bas-reliefs form a major portion of their oeuvre) or were architectonic in scale and treatment

Robert Mallet-Stevens. Garden with Cubist tree sculptures by Jan and Joël Martel, Exposition Internationale des Arts Décoratifs et Industriels Modernes, Paris, 1925

planar sculptures. In 1929 they were founding members of the Union des Artistes Modernes and, like fellow member Jean Puiforcat, they discovered the writings of the Romanian mathematician Matila Ghyka, which expounded on the Golden Section, a formula based on geometry for ideal proportions and harmonious formal relationships. Thenceforth, geometry would be the underlying principle of their work. "Cubism without esotericism, hierarchy without rigidity, orthodoxy without dogmatism, mathematic but not lacking in fantasy"[5] was how critic Paul Fierens summed up their work.

The work of the Martel brothers extended to radiator caps for the Sizaire automobile company, advertising posters in bas-relief, and models for table sculptures (mainly animal figurines) produced in porcelain at the Sèvres factory. In the 1930s their architectural sculptures were displayed at the 1931 Exposition Coloniale and the 1937 Exposition Internationale. And in 1935 they were awarded the prestigious commission for the bas-relief altar in the chapel aboard the SS *Normandie*. In tandem, they were made chevaliers of the Légion d'Honneur in 1966. Jan died in March of that year in an automobile accident. Joël fell ill soon after and died in September.

(most notably, their war monuments of the 1920s and 1930s).

Beginning in 1919, Martel sculpture was seen regularly at the Paris Salons. A maquette for a monument honoring Claude Debussy, which would be installed in the Bois de Boulogne in 1932, was exhibited at the 1924 Salon d'Automne. At the 1925 Exposition, they exhibited both freestanding sculptures and bas-reliefs in no fewer than twelve locations.[4] The most impressive was the garden designed by Mallet-Stevens, for which they created four reinforced concrete Cubist trees.

In 1926 they commissioned Mallet-Stevens to design a studio-residence. Completed the following year, the building was one of several by the architect in the rue Mallet-Stevens, a street he developed in the Sixteenth Arrondissement. The Martel house not only served as an atelier but comprised three apartments, one for each brother and his family and one for their father.

The brothers worked in a range of media, including traditional sculpting materials — plaster, bronze, and stone — but also ceramic, aluminum, mirror glass, and reinforced concrete. Although by the mid-1920s their work had evolved from stylized realism to abstraction, they never fully abandoned figural work. In the late 1920s they experimented with sheet metal, cutting, bending, and folding it to create calligraphic,

42 | Maquette for a Cubist Tree
1925; painted wood

Although the 1925 Paris Exposition purportedly showcased modern decorative arts and design, most of the works exhibited were stylistically rooted in tradition. One radical exception was the Martel brothers' installation of four Cubist tree sculptures in a small garden designed by architect Robert Mallet-Stevens. Not at all popular with visitors to the fair, the display generated a heated response:

Trees of reinforced concrete! There they are, on the Esplanade des Invalides . . . in the Mallet-Stevens garden. They carry the signature of those artists — curious in so many ways — the brothers Martel: Joël and Jan. Well, the uncomprehending crowd passes by and is astonished, it cries out, it protests, it rants and raves, believing it to be merely an architectural stunt. Trees of reinforced concrete, indeed![1]

Standing more than sixteen feet high, each of the four identical sculptures had a cruciform trunk supporting quadrangular planes attached vertically and at angles to suggest the massing of foliage, their abstract modern sensibility clearly derived from the Cubist aesthetic.[2] They were set in a pair of rectangular beds bordered with low hedges, planted with flowers, and separated by a gravel path. Mallet-Stevens had first considered using real trees, but the extensive network of utilities and rail lines that ran beneath the site prevented the planting of suitably large trees. Furthermore, the fair's early spring opening meant that trees would not yet be in leaf.[3] Mallet-Stevens approached the two sculptors, who chose to bypass nature and create their own abstract tree forms. That year, Joël Martel explained that the composition had to be seen

. . . in the first place as a technical demonstration of the refined construction that can be achieved with reinforced concrete and, in the second, as the pursuit of a decorative and plastic scheme. . . . In such a composition, the play of volumes creates a play of sunlight. And as for our sculptural quest, our aim in deliberately using abstraction is to break with the habit of those who want always to judge a work by comparison [with nature] — ever ready to applaud imitation and protest invention.[4]

Charles Fegdal was more appreciative in his 1925 critique than the early visitors to the fair:

I am well aware that art lovers, gardeners, designers, and even critics are rebelling against these "immutable" trees. But these trees, which they accuse of being immutable, are no more so than the façades of houses whose broad planes, severe friezes, and sharp, precise angles catch the light and are marvelously brought to life by the ever-changing brilliance of sunshine and the eternal softness of moonlight.[5]

The sculptures were destroyed when the exhibition closed. They are known today only through period photographs and surviving maquettes, such as this one in cream-painted wood — a satisfying and fully resolved sculpture in its own right.[6]

HENRI ÉDOUARD NAVARRE

Paris 1885–1971 Paris

Henri Navarre is an all-around artist. With the same ease he handles the pencil, the chisel, the brush, the glassmaker's rod. . . . Nothing that Henri Navarre does leaves you indifferent.[1]

Born to a family of architect-decorators, Navarre from an early age spent time on construction sites.[2] His initial training was in sculpture, metalwork, stained glass, and mosaic. In 1906 he took a job as an architectural and decorative stonecutter; he also modeled large-scale terracotta figural sculptures, probably also for building façades. By 1911, Navarre had decided to become a sculptor. He first made a name for himself in 1922, when he contributed the carved bas-relief panels to a monument to the war dead at Pointe de la Grave. The following year, he was awarded the commission for a monument to the aviator Georges Guynemer in the city of Compiègne. At the same time, he created small-scale sculptures which he displayed at the Paris Salons.

In 1924, Navarre turned his hand to glass. His first commission was for decorative windows in the offices of the newspaper *L'Intransigéant*. Instead of using traditional leaded panes, he made solid panels of glass engraved and painted with motifs from modern life. It was probably this project that piqued Navarre's interest in the medium; the same year, he began to work on small-scale sculptural pieces, including a series of decorative cast-glass masks.[3]

Navarre's glasswork generally comprises thick-walled vessels internally decorated with bubbles, swirls of color, and granulations. Although it bears a superficial resemblance to that of Maurice Marinot (see nos. 40, 41), Navarre's approach was quite different. Marinot employed the traditional method of glassblowing, while Navarre, a sculptor, made minimal use of the blowpipe, instead shaping molten glass with hand tools such as wooden spatulas. Apart from works cast in *pâte-de-verre* by glassmakers such as Argy-Rousseau and Décorchemont (see nos. 1, 12, and 13), before Navarre there was no tradition of sculpture in glass since the material could not be shaped by carving or chiseling.

Navarre first exhibited his glass at the Galerie Edgar Brandt, and later was represented by Georges Rouard. His work was seen regularly at the annual exhibitions of the Société des Artistes Décorateurs through the 1930s and in both national and international exhibitions. In New York it was displayed at Macy's International Exposition of Art in Industry (1928) and in the American Federation of Arts' "Contemporary Glass and Rugs" (1929–30). In 1927, Navarre made what is perhaps his best-known sculptural work in glass: a mysteriously luminous, monumental figure of Christ on the cross for the chapel of the SS *Île de France*. The ocean liner also had, in the first-class dining room, a Navarre fountain made from silvered and gilt-metal tubes.

While most of his work of the 1920s and 1930s was in glass, Navarre continued to make architectural sculpture in other media. At the 1925 Paris Exposition, he created a series of metal bas-relief panels for Edgar Brandt's Porte d'Honneur entrance gates adjacent to the Grand Palais. His bas-relief panel for the proscenium arch of the Théâtre de la Michodière in Paris was likely of plaster. And the monumental lion sculptures made for Jean Prouvé's entrance gate to the Palais des Colonies at the 1931 Exposition Coloniale were carved in granite.

Navarre stopped working in glass after the Second World War (he would take it up again briefly in the 1960s), focusing instead on architectural sculptures for churches and schools throughout France. He was made a chevalier of the Légion d'Honneur in 1947.

glassmaker gathers the molten paste on the tip of a blowpipe, the iron tube into which he blows to obtain a hollow ball, whose walls become thinner as it inflates. By turning the blowpipe, by touching the ball with another rod, he does more or less what the potter does on his wheel: it is the work of a modeler. Henri Navarre has understood everything an artist can draw from that simple but difficult technique. Favoring heavy forms, he blows minimally into the batch, leaving his vases thick as mortars. . . . And it is in the very thickness of the walls that he seeks decorative effects. By infusing [the body with] air bubbles, he obtains a kind of luminous opaline that he is able to use, marvelously, as streaks, as clouds, as spirals, to adorn the transparent mass. With oxidation or with jets of sand, he gives infinite variation to the appearance of these precious vessels.[1]

The precious vessels that Gallotti referred to were later described by Henri Classens as

. . . more blocks of glass than vases in the strictest sense. Some, in fact, have only an insignificant central cavity that is virtually unusable. There is a logical intention here that should be pointed out: because it is understood that a piece of art glass has no utilitarian purpose and that to fill it with water and flowers is to defile it, why persist in respectfully preserving the element that renders it a receptacle?[2]

An entry on Navarre that appeared in the featured "Dictionnaire des artistes décorateurs" in a 1954 issue of *Mobilier et décoration* describes him as "a Renaissance man":

. . . gold- and silversmith, medal engraver, sculptor . . . an artist with a craftsman's feel for the material, for the métier. "Everything" he says, "is in the hands."[4]

43 | Vase
ca. 1928; Glass

Navarre's working process was described in 1932 by the critic Jean Gallotti:

A sculptor, [Navarre] does not blow the glass, he models it. Neither does he resort to casting. We know that the

This bottle-shaped vase has an upper portion of palest violet translucent glass masterfully filled with trapped air bubbles created by rolling molten glass in metal oxides and refiring. The lower portion is irregularly flashed with rich, purple-black manganese glass. The ring-shaped neck with tiny cavity does indeed preclude any functional use for the vase. Bought by Metropolitan Museum curator Joseph Breck from the Galerie Georges Rouard in 1928, it was included two years later in a solo exhibition of Navarre's glass, sculpture, and drawings organized by the Ehrich Galleries in New York and installed on the fourth floor of Bergdorf Goodman. "In Paris," exclaimed the reviewer in *The New York Times*, "he is best known for his magnificent blown glass—not only a craft but also an art—beautiful as sculpture, as emotionally beautiful."[3]

PIERRE PATOUT

Tonnerre (Yonne) 1879–1965 Rueil

"Architecture: Keystone of all the arts." Engraved on the decorative exterior panel of the Paris apartment building Pierre Patout designed and where he lived from 1934 until the Second World War, this motto neatly sums up the philosophy of the renowned architect who would also turn his hand to the related disciplines of urban planning, interiors, and furniture design. Born in the north-central region of Burgundy, Patout was the son of a surveyor; his father's work may have sparked his interest in what would be his chosen calling.[1] In 1896 he entered the atelier of Jean-Louis Pascal, an architect trained in the classical tradition, and the following year he enrolled at the École des Beaux-Arts

in Paris. When he was twenty, during his military service, he met É.-J. Ruhlmann (see pages 186–203), who would become a lifelong friend.

About 1910, together with fellow pupils from the Beaux-Arts, Patout set up an architectural practice they named Art et Construction, attracting prominent clients such as the airplane and automobile manufacturer Gabriel Voisin. From the beginning of his career, he regularly displayed his architectural drawings at the annual Salons.

Patout opened his own firm after the war, and over the next twenty years would carry out a wide range of residential, commercial, and urban projects. Notable among these were the offices (1923) and a house (1923–26) for textile manufacturer François Ducharne (see no. 14); the offices (1926–29) and furniture workshops (1927) of his friend Ruhlmann; the studio-residence of the painter Alfred Lombard (1928); the interior of the Nicolas wineshop (1928); and a house for the politician André Tardieu (1930). He also designed numerous apartment buildings around Paris. Overall, despite superficial overtones of modernism, such as a preference for blank white walls and horizontal detailing, Patout always maintained a healthy respect for tradition and classicism; above all, he favored symmetrical compositions, regular rhythms, and monumentality.

Patout designed several of the most prominent buildings at the 1925 Paris Exposition. His circular peristyle served as an entrance gate at the Place de la Concorde. With Ruhlmann he designed the pavilion of the Hôtel du Collectionneur, and with André Ventre, the Sèvres pavilion. He was actively involved with the Société des Artistes Décorateurs (for which he created architectural settings for the display of furniture), and designed its pavilion at the 1937 Paris Exposition.

Pierre Patout. Façade of Les Galeries Lafayette, Paris, 1932, in *L'Architecture* (1934), p. 398

In 1926, Patout received the first of three commissions from the Compagnie Générale Transatlantique (CGT), the builder of French Line passenger ships: the first-class dining room, main foyer, and grand staircase for the *Île de France*. The two commissions that followed were interiors and furniture for *L'Atlantique* and the *Normandie*, the benchmark of glamour in the era of ocean travel (see no. 46).

Patout's work for the CGT would greatly influence some of his later projects. In 1932 he won the competition to redesign the façade of the Galeries Lafayette department store on the Boulevard Haussmann. The new façade had a receding, stepped roofline that evoked the decks of a ship perched above a massive hull (the main body of the building), and the two round roof towers suggested ship funnels (see previous page). Even more ship-like was the Paris apartment house Patout built for himself in 1934. Again, a series of stacked horizontal floors suggesting decks was surmounted by vertical projections along the roof. The low, pointed terrace that opened out from Patout's own apartment served as the building's prow.

One of Patout's last major architectural projects was the French pavilion at the 1939–40 New York World's Fair, designed with Roger-Henri Expert. In 1940, Patout closed his Paris office. Throughout the 1930s, however, he worked on several urban planning projects—among them, the Longchamp corniche in the resort town of Saint-Lunaire (1931) and the new axial road linking Paris to the suburb of Saint-Germain-en-Laye (1935). These led eventually to his 1946 appointment as head architect for the reconstruction of the heavily bombed city of Tours where, in 1957, he built a new public library.

44 | Pair of Armchairs

1934; mahogany, gilt bronze, wool upholstery

Together with architect Henri Pacon, Patout was responsible for the layout and decoration of a number of the spectacular first-class public spaces on the ocean liner *Normandie*, including the vast dining room (more than 300 feet long and 28 feet high, it could seat 700 people at 150 tables). Because it was an interior space with no windows, Patout and Pacon made up for the lack of natural light by covering the walls with thick slabs of reflective, translucent glass, which created a spatially ambiguous ambience. The walls, lined with tall, columnar lamps, together with the twelve illuminated glass "fountains" by René Lalique, further enhanced the atmosphere of cool glamour.

Food and especially wine were important on the *Normandie*, and the first-class tableware included extensive silver, glass, and porcelain services that were both elegant and sturdy. Luc Lanel designed the silver-plated flatware, manufactured by Christofle. Glasses were supplied by Daum. Two porcelain services, one designed by Suzanne Lalique and the other by Jean Luce, were manufactured by Haviland, in Limoges.[1]

Patout designed the tables and chairs.[2] Each barrel-form mahogany chair has a high narrow back with a rolled crest rail. The broad, heavy seat has an exaggeratedly deep seat-rail, carved with reeded detailing. Curved armrests follow the contour of the seat and terminate at the saber-shaped front legs with brass sabots. Designed by Raymond Quibel and manufactured by Cornille et Cie, the

machine-woven upholstery incorporates a red shield with two lions passant, the heraldic device symbolizing the French province of Normandy, for which the liner was named and where her home port of Le Havre is located.

The chair's design is based on one Patout made in 1926 for the first-class dining room of the SS *Île de France*. The high, narrow back evokes *caquetoire* chairs of the French Renaissance, while the rolled back, saber leg, and use of mahogany bring to mind Restauration and Louis-Philippe chairs of the early nineteenth century. Each chair originally had a buckle mechanism under the seat, required by the CGT for all seating furniture, which was used to secure it to the deck when the seas were particularly rough.

Pierre Patout and Henri Pacon. Drawing of first-class dining room with Patout armchairs, SS *Normandie*, in *L'Illustration*, hors série, 4813*bis*, June 1935

PAUL POIRET

Paris 1879–1944 Paris

The English-language title of Paul Poiret's autobiography, *King of Fashion*, perhaps more accurately describes this major player in the Art Deco era than does the original *En habillant l'époque* (While Dressing the Era).[1] While the French title aptly identifies him as a couturier—and indeed he was one of the most important of the twentieth century—the translation better defines his lofty position as an arbiter of style in Paris at the height of the fashionable 1910s and 1920s:

If he had not turned out a dressmaker, he would have been an artist, or a musician, or an interior decorator, or a writer of ballads, or an actor. And the amazing truth is that he is all of those things now. . . . A man of sports, a singer of ballads, a player of the violin, an Oriental scholar, a maker of rare perfumes, a decorator of houses and yachts, and now, the latest of all his achievements, he is to produce amazing ballets![2]

He was also an important art collector and patron of architects, a gourmand and writer of cookbooks, an inveterate party giver, a theatrical impresario, and a nightclub owner, effectively inventing the concept of "lifestyle," and in the process creating an overarching, recognizable Poiret brand.

The son of a successful Paris cloth merchant and draper, Poiret knew textiles from the outset. After an uneventful childhood, he served as an apprentice to an umbrella maker. Charged with repairing holes in the silk, he used the leftover scraps to fashion miniature costumes for a wood mannequin. He also began making sketches for dresses, which he shopped around as he delivered umbrellas. His work so impressed Jacques Doucet that in 1898 he landed a job with the preeminent Parisian couturier. Poiret created many garments for Doucet, but

it was the black tulle and taffeta mantle embroidered with mauve irises, made for the actress Réjane in the play *Zaza*, that established his reputation. In 1901, after a year of military service, he joined Worth, the famous house of haute couture, where he remained until setting up his own business in 1904. During the war, Poiret served as a tailor in the French Army. In 1905 he married Denise Boulet, a woman who would serve as his creative muse throughout their marriage (they would divorce in 1928); together they had three children.

Success came easily to Poiret, owing in part to his iconoclastic approach to fashion design but in no small measure to his skill for self-promotion. He was among the first to encourage women to abandon their corsets, and his radical designs reshaped the feminine silhouette. He mined a range of sources for ideas—classical antiquity, the Directoire, and Orientalism, especially as seen through the lens of the sets and costumes of the Ballets Russes. A smart entrepreneur, he had his designs reproduced in two luxuriously printed albums, *Les Robes de Paul Poiret*, illustrated by Paul Iribe (1908), and *Les Choses de Paul Poiret*, illustrated by Georges Lepape (1911), copies of which he sent not only to ladies of society but to the crowned heads of Europe. Thus did he develop a large and devoted clientele, which enabled him to open two related businesses, each named for one of his two daughters. Rosine, established in 1908, manufactured perfumes. Martine, established in 1911, focused on interior decoration.

This school of decoration . . . is a generation younger than I am. So is my girl. Martine is a generation younger than the present one in thought, and the house and the baby will be full grown when I am an old man.[3]

Atelier Martine. Colored photograph of dining room, ca. 1925

Poiret opened Martine following a trip in 1910 to Austria and Germany, where he had been impressed by the modern design work he encountered there, especially that produced at the Wiener Werkstätte. Under the direction of architect-designer Josef Hoffmann, the designers' cooperative, founded in 1903 on the principles of the British Arts and Crafts movement, was dedicated to the creation of the "total work of art," wherein every element of the domestic environment was designed with a vision of aesthetic unity. Clothing and fashion accessories, for example, were designed to harmonize with their surroundings, a fact not lost on Poiret; he based Martine largely on this Viennese model.

Martine comprised École Martine, Atelier Martine, and La Maison Martine. École Martine, housed in the Poiret premises on the rue d'Antin, was an experimental art school for working-class girls. Under the guidance of design educator Marguerite Gabriel-Claude Sérusier, they would sketch plants and animals in local parks and zoos. Poiret bought the best of their drawings, which were then adapted for use by Atelier Martine, the design studio.

Initially, Atelier Martine produced only textiles and wallpapers, but it soon expanded to produce carpets, lighting, glassware, ceramics, and other small items (including oversize dolls outfitted by Poiret; see page 164). Furniture and interior decorating services were later introduced under the direction of Guy-Pierre Fauconnet. Although most of the designs were realized by outside manufacturers, hand-decorating of the glassware and hand-knotting of the deep pile carpets were done by the students.[4]

La Maison Martine, located first at 107, rue du Faubourg-Saint-Honoré, and from 1924 at 1, rond-point des Champs-Élysées, was the retail and interior design service. By the early 1920s, branches had opened in Marseilles, Cannes, Biarritz, Deauville, and La Baule, as well as in London and Vienna. Martine products were also promoted and sold in department stores in the United States and Germany.

Martine drew a number of clients who were often as theatrical as the interiors they commissioned, including American dancer Isadora Duncan, American movie star Valeska Suratt, French aviator Baron de Précourt, French actress Andrée Spinelly, and Dutch painter Kees van Dongen. Many were also patrons of Poiret's couture business. "If you are the sort of person who would like to be dressed by Poiret," claimed the Bonney sisters, "you might expect to consult him in this other field."[5] Well-publicized commercial projects included the Paris beauty salon of Helena Rubinstein, the first-class Chantilly suite on the SS *Île de France*, set designs for theater and film, and the décor of Poiret's night-club, L'Oasis.

Although Poiret participated in the annual Salon exhibitions, he did so sporadically. His most notable display was at the 1925 Paris Exposition, to which he contributed three lavishly decorated barges moored on the banks of the Seine. *Amours* (Loves) showcased designs by Martine. *Délices* (Delights) offered

Atelier Martine. Colored photograph of La Maison Martine, interior with oversize doll, ca. 1925

perfumes by Rosine and had a restaurant. And *Orgues* (Organs) displayed Poiret's fashions and housed a luminous pipe organ that was played at concerts.

Poiret's extravagances soon led to financial setbacks. Although Martine remained open until 1934, Poiret was forced to explore new opportunities for revenue. In the late 1920s, he signed a contract for a line of furniture for Contempora, a New York–based company dedicated to introducing modern design to the American public. The other principal designers were the Germans Bruno Paul and Lucian Bernhard and the American Rockwell Kent. Their products were sold in department stores across the country. For its inaugural exhibition in 1929, Poiret designed a brilliantly colored suite of lacquered bedroom furniture in keeping with Contempora's philosophy of "harmonized rooms." Unlike Martine, Contempora was committed to mass production and geared toward consumers of average means, reflecting a new economic climate. Contempora's catalogue advised that "easy accessibility of good design, through quantity production, is no more destructive of individuality than is the growing tendency to standardize dress," and it specifically recommended Poiret's contributions to those "who wish to

carry their feeling for fashion into the furnishings of their homes."[6] Contempora marked Poiret's last venture in the decorative arts. An article in *The Los Angeles Times* describes him in 1934 as having been jobless for eighteen months, "living on charity and a 70-cent daily employment dole."[7] Bankrupt, he retreated from public life.

45 | Four Textiles

    a | Textile, ca. 1919; printed silk

    b | Textile, ca. 1920; printed linen

    c | Textile, ca. 1920; printed silk

    d | Textile, ca. 1920; printed linen

In a class by himself is Martine, none other than our old friend Poiret. . . . He dared the world to use color in decorative effects. . . . He flung it all over his cretonnes with such a wicked hand that you probably remember the time when your American decorator pulled a sample from behind a screen, apologetically, saying: "Here is a new cretonne which is popular in France, but it is rather loud for us. However, since you want something unusual, look at this." Almost like bootlegging. It was the rare person who accepted them at first, for the really lovely things that they were. On stage—with the Russian ballet, of course, but in the home!! Hardly. Only a few years ago—and now the cheapest and most popular textiles in the basements of stores are riots of color.[1]

The brilliant colors and simple imagery of these printed textiles are typical of Martine, and were the keynote of any Martine interior:

What characterizes . . . the textiles of Martine is the presentation of natural forms, but with a simplified look. Any literal copying of nature is rigorously rejected. . . . Thus reduced to a purely ornamental state, flowers [are used to create] an indication of mass, with a robust and harmonious effect.

    The other characteristic of Martine textiles lies in the poetry of their color. The forms are embellished with fresh and vibrant hues, handled with such delicacy that they do not assault our sensibilities.[2]

civilization, to the childhood of art: indeed, this feeling is a reality, as the little workers have no idea of what art is and are not even told what is good and what is bad in their work. It is their feeling, their sensitiveness, that is expressed in what they do, and it is also the true expression of their comprehension and appreciation of the things, the way they really see them. To them a rose or a peony is a red or pink round spot, a daisy or marigold, a sort of star or wheel, and so on. The inner nature of the worker is revealed by what she does, and the main characteristic throughout the work is the display of the Latin love of color.[3]

Poiret was especially well known for juxtaposing violent, clashing colors. As he explained in his florid but entertaining autobiography, when he began his career,

. . . there were absolutely no tints left on the palettes of the colourists. The taste for the refinements of the eighteenth century had led all the women into a sort of deliquescence, and on the pretext that it was "distinguished," all vitality had been suppressed. Nuances of nymph's thigh, lilacs, swooning mauves, tender blue hortensias, niles, maizes, straws, all that was soft, washed-out, and insipid was held in honour. I threw into this sheepcote a few rough wolves: reds, greens, violets, royal blues, that made all the rest sing aloud.[4]

Poiret's interest in floral printed textiles developed after his 1910 visit to the Wiener Werkstätte. The regimented patterns of its textiles, however, did not appeal. What did interest him was its revival of the naïve simplification and bold colors seen in folk and children's art. The young students of the École Martine achieved this very expression, as recognized in 1914 by a reviewer for the *New-York Tribune*:

To our eyes, accustomed to the highest refinement in art, the first impression is that one is carried to the root of

Martine produced a range of printed textiles, in silk, cotton, and linen, and sold yardage for decorating and dressmaking needs, both through La Maison Martine and internationally through independent retailers.[5] In the 1910s and 1920s, Martine's textiles were astonishing and new—"Martine has struck the world of decoration a blow in the face, just as the house of Poiret struck a blow to the world of dress"[6]—but by the early 1930s they seemed passé:

L'École Martine was above all a school of the art of color, at a time when color was given precedence over line. Line has now regained the upper hand, and it is in this sense that one can say, taking care to not overgeneralize, that we are in a classical period. Poiret, an artist who is too personal, too romantic, finds himself today without employment.[7]

FRANÇOIS POMPON

Saulieu 1855–1933 Paris

The story of François Pompon is as improbable as his family name.[1] Indeed, one would be hard-pressed to find a less appropriate name for a sculptor who was described as unassuming, unpretentious, and simple in his habits, and who achieved recognition only at the age of sixty-seven. But his name, which, as noted in 1923, evokes "a natty cockade . . . is not, as one might be tempted to believe, the cheerful pseudonym of the aged master [but rather] an actual patronymic . . . indisputably authentic."[2]

Pompon was an animalier, a sculptor of animals. As a genre, French animalier sculpture reached its height in the mid-nineteenth century, with the work of Antoine-Louis Barye. Its popularity, albeit principally as a form of decoration, lasted well into the twentieth. Called the King of Sculptors of Animals, Pompon drew generous praise from the critics:

Together with Barye, Pompon is the greatest modern animalier. But whereas Barye is a romantic, Pompon is a classicist who excels at giving the simplest, most assured, but also the most essential and truest image of the most humble [creatures]. He envelops his little animals in light, bathes them in shadowless brilliance; the volumes are full and the surfaces entirely smooth, so that light flows over their contours.[3]

Pompon's gift for sculpting animals led to his reputation as a sort of spiritual brother to Saint Francis of Assisi and the fabulist Jean de La Fontaine, while his Montparnasse atelier—filled with sculptures, maquettes, studies, and sketches of animals—was frequently referred to as a modern Noah's Ark.

Born in the heart of Burgundy, a region traditionally known for its sculptors, Pompon was the son of a joiner, and by his father's side Pompon learned the basics of wood carving. "From that time," wrote Julien Léonard in 1923, "he has retained his love for wood, and one of his great joys is on occasion to abandon marble or bronze to carve some beautiful block of grained cedar or amboyna wood."[4]

At the age of fifteen Pompon moved to Dijon, where he earned his living as a marble cutter for the funerary trade while at night he attended classes at the École des Beaux-Arts. In 1875 he moved to Paris, where his life differed little from that in Dijon: marble cutting by day with art classes at night. In 1879 he began to display his (mainly figural) sculptures at the annual Salon exhibitions—but to little acclaim. He left the marble-cutting trade around 1880, and for the next four decades took studio jobs for a number of well-known sculptors, including Albert Bartholomé, Camille Claudel, Alexandre Falguière, Antonin Mercié, Auguste Rodin, and René de Saint-Marceaux. The low-paying work kept him busy, but he managed to find time and materials to produce his own sculptures. While he had addressed animal subjects in the 1890s, around 1906 he turned from the human figure to focus on them, probably in part because models (especially local birds) were abundant, available, and free of charge. He went frequently to the Paris zoo, in the Jardin des Plantes, to observe the animals there. Although the stylized naturalism of his animalier sculptures, which he made in plaster, clay, wood, marble, bronze, and occasionally porcelain, proved more salable than his earlier figural works, he seems not to have had his first solo exhibition—at the Galerie Hébrard in Paris—until 1919.

Everything changed for Pompon in 1922, when his contribution to the Salon d'Automne brought him instant fame: "Such a brouhaha, the banquets and the Légion d'Honneur and the reviews now making such a fuss over him."[5] His life-size plaster sculpture of a

striding polar bear was an immediate hit. Pompon's work was from this time forward featured prominently in exhibitions and art publications, and was sought out by private collectors and public institutions (including the Metropolitan Museum and, in Paris, the Musée du Luxembourg), "commanding high esteem and equally high prices."[6] Indeed, he was hailed as a near-genius.

Sculpture, like painting, was considered an integral part of the French Art Deco interior, and after 1922 Pompon received additional exposure by showing his work in domestic environments that emphasized their decorative character, such as the room settings at the annual Salon des Artistes Décorateurs. Galleries that specialized in decorative arts, such as Charpentier, Edgar Brandt, and Hébrard, took an active interest in his sculpture, while the celebrated É.-J. Ruhlmann, a close friend, often placed

his sculptures in his interiors and included them in exhibitions at his fashionable showroom.

When Pompon died in 1933, the many articles that mourned the loss of this gifted artist lamented as much the loss of a kind, modest man surprised by the good fortune that had come to him late in life. It is recounted that when fame at last arrived, a friend advised Pompon to increase the price of his works.

"Why?" the sculptor asked. "I am not in need." The man suggested that he use part of the enormous sums that his now-renowned talent deemed him to be worth to relieve the poverty of less fortunate artists. "I'll think about it," said Pompon. And in fact, shortly thereafter he raised his prices, and after his death a brief look at the books revealed that, from that day forward, a few of his fellow artists were indebted to him for the greater part of their livelihood.[7]

46 | *Polar Bear*
ca. 1923; marble

Polar Bear is the sculpture that brought fame to Pompon at the age of sixty-seven. Although he had explored the subject since before 1920, he first showed a life-size plaster version of a striding bear at the 1922 Salon d'Automne. It met with critical and popular approval, and the following year he displayed a smaller marble variant. The Metropolitan's *Polar Bear* is one of twelve known marble examples of this smaller version.[1] The enormous popularity of these two sculptures led him to produce both models in a variety of sizes, from tabletop to full-scale, and in a range of media including plaster, marble, bronze, and porcelain. Pompon either made or directly supervised the production of all of them, with the exception of the molded porcelain version. In all, 632 porcelain *Polar Bear*s were manufactured at Sèvres between 1924 and 1934; the mold was broken in 1940. The sculpture in one or another version was included in many international exhibitions during the 1920s. In the United States, it was seen at the Exhibition of Contemporary French Art at Polk Hall in San Francisco in January 1923 and in the American Association of Museums' 1926 traveling exhibition of works from the 1925 Paris Exposition.

The figure is stylized and abstracted to create a heightened natural effect. Pompon opted for an ultrasmooth surface and voluptuous form to express

. . . the rigor and complexity of structure under the vast folds of thick, snowy fur. From the large rear paw to the end of the muzzle, the visible curve of the clearly indicated spine unrolls, solid, supple, and — it must be said — living. [It is in this quality of living that] the art is revealed, bypassing blind fidelity in its modeling to arrive, through infidelity, at a truth of interpretation that affirms his genius.[2]

Polar Bear has a decidedly tactile quality: one wants to run one's hands over its smooth, gleaming form. Pompon believed that this quality was specifically suited to what he called "room sculpture," small-scale sculpture used in the domestic environment. He particularly loved the fact that one "can appreciate his animals as much by touching them as by looking at them."[3]

The model proved popular with many contemporaneous French decorators, especially Pompon's friend É.-J. Ruhlmann, who featured it prominently in many of his interiors, most notably two room settings he designed for the 1925 Paris Expo: a small version atop a center table in the main salon of his own Hôtel du Collectionneur and a full-scale version in the entrance hall of the Ambassade Française. In 1931 the Compagnie Maritime des Chargeurs Réunis considered commissioning a life-size *Polar Bear* in bronze for the décor of its new liner, *L'Atlantique*. Although the piece was never realized, it would have provided a somewhat baffling juxtaposition to Jean Dunand's vast lacquer murals in the first-class dining room, which depicted a steamy jungle scene.[4] Pompon himself also adapted *Polar Bear* for decorative use. In 1930 he made a full-scale bronze version of the bear's head, which he mounted on the front door of his Montparnasse studio to serve as an instantly recognizable beacon for his visitors

É.-J. Ruhlmann. Entrance hall, with Pompon *Polar Bear*, Ambassade Française, Exposition Internationale des Arts Décoratifs et Industriels Modernes, Paris, 1925

JEAN PUIFORCAT

Paris 1897–1945 Paris

If the name Puiforcat is recognized today, it is in part because the firm is still in business. More important, however, is the reputation of Jean Puiforcat, the company's greatest practitioner and one of the most accomplished French silversmiths of any age. During the 1920s and 1930s, he brought an artist's eye and the disciplined mind of a mathematician to the production of silver—orfevrerie—transforming conventionally utilitarian objects into masterworks of abstract, sculptural perfection.

Born in 1897, Puiforcat came from an established family of silversmiths.[1] The firm was founded in 1820 by three cousins, including his maternal great-grandfather, Émile Puiforcat. His mother, Laure Puiforcat, married the silversmith Louis-Victor Tabouret, who took charge of the business in 1902, orienting it toward luxury production aimed at a rich yet conservative clientele that favored updated versions of eighteenth-century models.[2] In 1915, Tabouret changed his family name to Puiforcat.

Much of Jean Puiforcat's childhood was spent in his father's atelier. In 1914 he enlisted in the Army, and after the war he began a formal apprenticeship with his father.[3] His *maîtrise* (presented by an apprentice to demonstrate mastery of his craft) was, not surprisingly, a replica of a Louis XIV tureen. He also studied sculpture in Paris under Louis-Aimé Lejeune, who introduced him to such artistic concepts as volume, form, and the necessity of eliminating the superfluous, all of which would eventually inform the work he did in silver.

Puiforcat did not share his father's historicism. Even his earliest work indicates an aesthetic of abstraction and simplification. In general, he eschewed surface embellishment, especially hammer marks (traditionally a sign of the handmade), preferring plain, smooth surfaces that would reflect light. Shifting light, which could alter the perception of a surface, was decoration enough. At the same time, he delighted in introducing unexpected materials, contrasting silver with ivory, exotic woods, or stones such as jade, carnelian, and lapis lazuli. He would later offset silver with glass or areas of gilding.

In 1921, Puiforcat first displayed his work—two tea and coffee services—at the Salon des Artistes Décorateurs. Indeed, throughout his career functional objects—tea and coffee sets, flatware, tureens, candlesticks, and the like—were his stock-in-trade. But his overarching consideration was artistry: "A teapot must pour properly and accomplish its task, but it is also a companion in the home. It must be a work of art in its own modest sphere; it must elevate the soul by its beauty."[4]

Puiforcat's early work, which incorporates bulbous forms and floral details, is characterized by a kind of stylized naturalism. In the mid-1920s, he began to develop a new aesthetic vocabulary, one more suited to the demands and preferences of modern life. Increasingly, he favored simple geometric shapes—cubes, cylinders, spheres, cones, polyhedrons—and straight lines that reveal the beauty of the silver. It is this purity, achieved through precision of conception and quality of execution, that separates Puiforcat's work from that of his contemporaries.

Throughout the 1920s, Puiforcat was an active participant in a number of international exhibitions; his work was seen in Paris, Brussels, Antwerp, Milan, Madrid, Tokyo, Buenos Aires, San Francisco, New York, Montreal, and Barcelona. At the annual Paris Salons, where he was routinely represented, and at the 1925 Paris Exposition, he played a variety of roles: contributor, admissions juror, awards juror, and reporter.[5] In 1926 he joined four like-minded

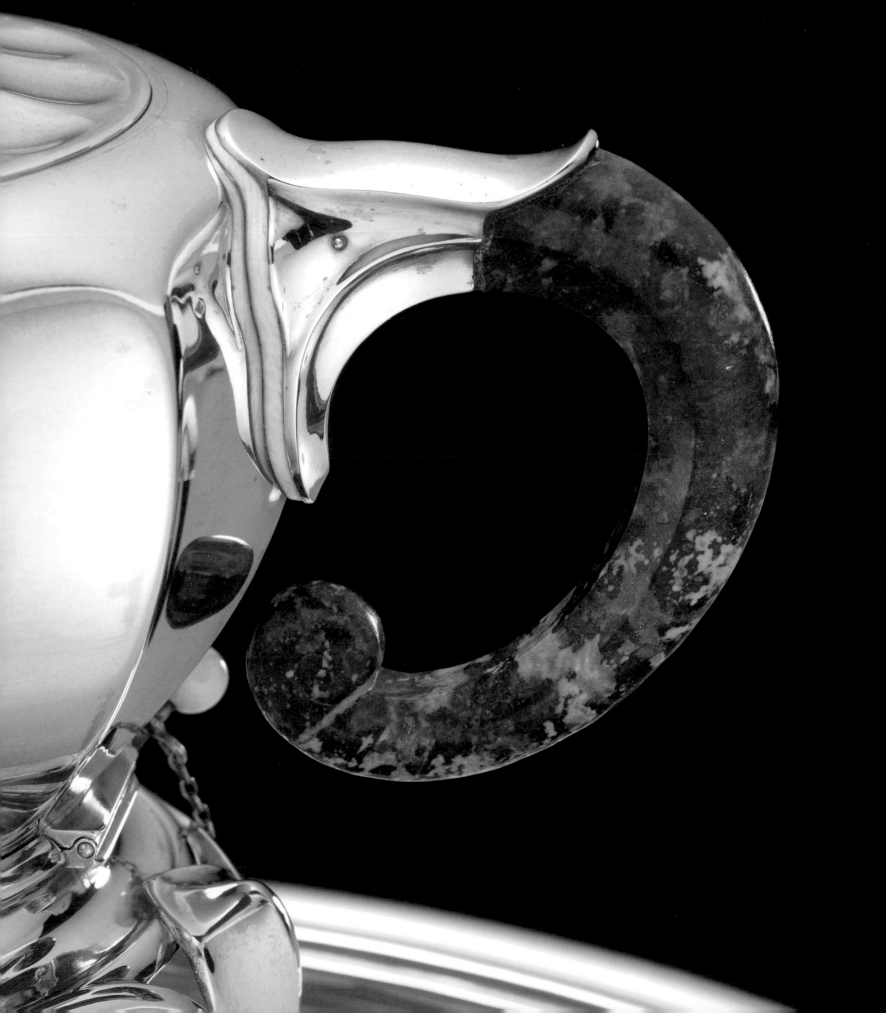

designers—Pierre Chareau, Pierre Legrain, Raymond Templier, and the ensemblier firm of Dominique—to form a group known as Les Cinq (The Five). In contrast to what they considered the *retardataire* uniformity of works shown at the Paris Expo and at the Salons, they explored a more aggressive modernism in works they exhibited at independent Paris galleries such as Barbazanges, Renaissance, and Georges Bernheim.

By 1929, Les Cinq had disbanded and its members had joined the larger and more radical Union des Artistes Modernes (UAM), an organization that promoted forward looking reform. Its motto was "Le Beau dans l'utile" (Beauty in Utility), and its members advocated mass production as a way to bring good design to the general public. However, Puiforcat—and he was not alone—was never able to fully accept this aspect of the charter. Unwilling to sacrifice quality for mass appeal, he took further offense when his vision of purity was misconstrued as representing a machine aesthetic: "The machine," he asserted, "is not French. It is not French in spirit."[6]

Over time, Puiforcat's work became increasingly intellectualized and esoteric. His interest in geometry led him to Plato and Pythagoras and to the contemporary Romanian mathematician Matila Ghyka, from whom he learned about the Golden Section. Used since antiquity, the principle was central to his work of the 1930s, which is characterized by a complex formal interplay between an object's component parts. Although based on mathematical precision, Puiforcat's designs, which combine the aesthetic and the philosophical with the functional, were never soulless.

In the late 1920s, Puiforcat returned to sculpture. A champion tennis player and a member of both the national soccer and rugby teams and the French ice hockey team at the 1920 Olympics, he was drawn to the theme of sport and created a number of sporting pieces. Among these were the monumental athletic figures for the Pierre de Coubertin and Yves du Manoir Stadiums in Paris. His well-known love of sport led in the 1930s to numerous commissions for trophies.

Despite the worldwide economic crisis, the 1930s were busy years for Puiforcat. In 1936 he opened a large Paris showroom with an elegant, spare décor by fellow UAM member René Herbst. Among his clients were the Maharaja of Indore, for whose palace in India he designed tablewares, and the Compagnie Générale Transatlantique, which commissioned him to design flatware for the SS *Normandie*. At the Exposition International des Arts et Techniques dans la Vie Moderne of 1937, he created a chapel setting with a full range of liturgical objects—a display that spoke to Puiforcat's devout Catholicism.

Following the rise of Fascism in France, in 1940 Puiforcat moved to Mexico, where he established a workshop in 1942. His work during the war years was retailed mainly in North America. Returning to Paris in 1945 at the end of the war, he suffered a fatal heart attack at the age of forty-eight.

Puiforcat's contributions to his field cannot be overstated. "If a contemporary silversmithing style exists," wrote the critic René Chavance in 1938, "it is in great part due to Jean Puiforcat."[7] The sentiment was echoed by Henri Clouzot:

One can say that French orfevrerie has regained the worldwide supremacy it held in the grandes époques [of the eighteenth and nineteenth centuries]. It behooves us, in order to assure the worldwide demand for French goods, to retain this supremacy. Over the last twenty-five years, through his incessant artistic creation, Jean Puiforcat has shown us how to do just that.[8]

47 | Tea and Coffee Service
ca. 1922; silver, lapis lazuli, ivory, gold

From early in his career, Puiforcat was known for the elegant simplicity of his forms and the unexpected combination of flawless metal with brilliantly polished hardstones, ivory, exotic woods, and glass. Made shortly after he earned his *maîtrise* in 1920, this tea and coffee service shows one of his earliest attempts to break away from the preceding generation's organic naturalism; the only vestiges that remain are the lapis lazuli blossoms that serve as knops on the lids. As Art Nouveau gradually evolved into Art Deco during the first decades of the twentieth century, designers adapted these motifs to the simplified stylizations that were a hallmark of the new aesthetic. The vaguely melon-shaped bodies of the vessels (here fluted rather than lobed) recall French and English silver of the early nineteenth

century and reflect Puiforcat's solid knowledge of traditional forms.[1]

An especially nice conceit is the bluebell form of the knops, rendered in an appropriately colored material (see page 21). The introduction of lapis lazuli is not only decorative but practical. In addition to the insulating effect of the ivory spacers that separate the handles from the heat of the tea-, coffee-, and waterpots, the hardstone handles remain cool to the touch, even when the vessels are filled with hot liquid.

Puiforcat introduced this service with ivory details in his debut exhibition at the 1921 Salon des Artistes Décorateurs:

At the Décorateurs of 1921, one noticed the vitrine of a silversmith who was breaking away from old traditions. Jean Puiforcat surprised the visiting public with his ample, generous, sculptural forms, somewhat heavy perhaps but which tended toward simplicity and had good proportions. The impeccable technique revealed a perfect knowledge of the métier, which has since developed further, allowing the artist to assert himself and to refine his workmanship.

He is an innovator, but at the same time it is through his very innovations that he remains within this most noble of traditions. Since then, one discovers in his work "well-balanced and supple lines, the arrangement of which satisfies both the eye and the mind."[2]

The following year Puiforcat showed this second version with lapis lazuli details, which he again displayed at the 1925 Paris Exposition. A single coffeepot from the second version was acquired from Puiforcat by the Musée des Arts Décoratifs in 1922. The Metropolitan acquired its complete set in two separate purchases: three pieces in 1923 and the remaining four in 1925.

48 | Bowl

1934; silver, glass

The pendulum swing of taste is a curious thing. By the time Puiforcat made this handsome bowl (probably intended as a table centerpiece) in the early 1930s, he was deriding his earlier work of the 1920s (see no. 47) as merely "chic."[1] By today's taste, it is probably this later work that would be considered more glamorous. Puiforcat's rationale was that in the early 1920s he had yet to discover the Golden Section, the ancient formula for ideal proportion that shaped his work in the 1930s. As well as any other, this bowl demonstrates both Puiforcat's exquisite understanding of proportion and the perfection of his finish.

Only three examples of this model were made. The Metropolitan's bowl was acquired in 1934 by curator John Goldsmith Phillips, who wrote:

In his regard for the essential quality of his material, in his emphasis on form and proportion, and in his avoidance of naturalistic decoration, Puiforcat works in the present-day tradition. . . . [This bowl is] typical of his most recent work [in which he] joins sparkling crystal and highly polished silver in a strikingly effective union.[2]

While overall the bowl appears to be devoid of ornament, Phillips points to the "six curved segments of amber-colored glass . . . attached to the base, apparently as supports, although actually their chief function is decorative."[3] Although the glass manufacturer Baccarat is known to have supplied Puiforcat with glass components for his silver, it is unclear who produced this glass.

The bowl reflects not only the reductivist style Puiforcat favored after he joined the Union des Artistes Modernes in 1930 but also the concurrent shift in consumer taste toward bold simplicity. With regard to such pieces, the jeweler Jean Fouquet had this to say:

The secret of Jean Puiforcat, sculptor of silver, lies in the construction and the proper relation of the object to its function. The harmony of the proportions shows to best advantage his volumes and the materials he joins to the silver, in keeping with the best traditions. . . . He was among those who have restored honor to the polished beauty of metalworking.[4]

49 | Soup Tureen
ca. 1937; silver, gold

I continue to believe that the circle, which explains the world in its entirety, is the ideal figure, and the curve, which relates to it, is more noble than the straight line.[1]

This *soupière* (soup tureen) not only illustrates this belief but also epitomizes Puiforcat's oeuvre. Although utilitarian, it has an abstract, monumental, even sculptural presence and takes its pleasing form from simple geometric shapes — flattened spheres, stepped conical sections — and an elegantly flared lip. The subtle color effect is achieved by the addition of gilded banding. In conception and execution, the piece is exquisite and flawless.[2]

Puiforcat favored plain surfaces as a way of exploiting the interplay of light, shadow, and reflection, here highlighted in the sophisticated combination of warm gold and cool silver. Although gilding is used to enhance only specific elements — finial, lip, and foot — its effects are optically multiplied in the reflections created by the precise arrangement of the stacked forms.

The tureen makes an interesting, if possibly unintentional, connection with precedent, its form recalling traditional Asian rice bowls, in which a larger bowl is covered by a smaller inverted one. The form was popular in eighteenth-century European and American silver, especially for sugar bowls. Puiforcat's use of it may reflect both his knowledge of historical silver and the general growing awareness, following the 1931 Exposition Coloniale, of the arts of the French colonies in Asia. The flared lip, in particular, provides an elegant and evocative grace note. Such details did not escape the critic René Chavance, who in 1938 wrote:

On occasion, his visible humor and his fantasy take pleasure in complicating the rhythm of the volumes in an unexpected way, even reshaping the forms somewhat sharply.[3]

But he added that even

. . . his most whimsical inventions do not make him forget rational harmonies. Although he conceives with a quasi-romantic exuberance, his realizations are classic.[4]

HENRI RAPIN

Paris 1873–1939 Paris (?)

The work of the multitalented Henri Rapin—painter, illustrator, decorator, and designer—forms an important part of the French Art Deco canon.[1] Possibly the son of painter Alexandre Rapin, the young Rapin is known to have studied painting under both Jean-Léon Gérôme and Joseph Blanc at the École des Beaux-Arts in Paris. He began showing his work at the annual Salons of the Société des Artistes Français in 1898. At the 1900 Salon he added examples of leatherwork, suggesting a burgeoning interest in applied art. By 1904 he was designing and exhibiting furniture, marking the start of his career as an ensemblier. It is likely that around this time he began studying design, probably under the Swiss-born Eugène Grasset. Grasset was a founding member of the Société des Artistes Décorateurs, and it was perhaps his encouragement that led Rapin to include his furniture at that organization's annual Salon exhibitions beginning in 1910. Rapin was already a successful ensemblier before the war, able to address any aspect of an interior, from the architecture to the smallest decorative object. Never a craftsman himself, he established relationships with specialist workers who could realize his vision.[2]

It is unclear how Rapin spent the war years, but he likely served in some capacity. He later resumed his design career, but also took on other professional responsibilities. In 1918 he was appointed artistic director for the ladies' atelier at the school of the Union Centrale des Arts Décoratifs in Paris, where he expanded the curriculum limited to traditional women's pursuits—mainly textiles—to include a range of design classes. In 1920 he was hired as an artistic advisor to the Manufacture Nationale de Sèvres, a position he held until 1934. For Sèvres, he designed a series of ceramic blanks, including one decorated by René Crevel.

The wide display of Rapin's work at the 1925 Paris Exposition had an important impact on his career.[3] Most notable were his contributions to the Ambassade Française, in which he installed a salon and a dining room, and to the Sèvres pavilion, for which he designed not only a series of translucent porcelain lighting fixtures and fountains but furniture and a garden setting. Both pavilions were visited by Prince Asaka Yasuhiko and his wife, Princess Nobuko, daughter of the emperor of Japan. Rapin's work impressed the royal couple, who subsequently commissioned him to design for them an Art Deco residence in Tokyo. The architectural components of the project were carried out by the Japanese court architects in consultation with Rapin. Most of the furnishings were designed and manufactured in France under Rapin's direct supervision (he never traveled to Japan). For the project, Rapin called on some of his collaborators from the Ambassade Française, including René Lalique (who supplied glass door panels and lighting fixtures) and Raymond Subes (who supplied various metal grilles, panels, and lighting fixtures). Completed in 1933, the Asaka Residence established Rapin as an ensemblier of the first rank. It comes as no surprise that in 1928 he also contributed furniture (a suite of "feminine furniture" probably intended for a lady's boudoir) to the important exhibition of French decorative arts at the Tokyo Imperial Museum.

Although Rapin continued to participate in the annual Salons through the mid-1930s, he gradually played a less prominent role. His last official project was as coorganizer of the *métiers* display at the 1937 Paris Exposition. Rapin was made a chevalier of the Légion d'Honneur in 1920, and an officer in 1926.

See no. 9.

ARMAND-ALBERT RATEAU

Paris 1882–1938 Paris

America was introduced to the work of Armand-Albert Rateau in the catalogue of the American Association of Museums' 1926 traveling exhibition of works from the 1925 Paris Exposition:

Rateau has only lately produced works in the modern spirit. For many years he has carried on an important establishment where reproductions of old French woodwork and furniture were made for an exclusive clientele.

Turning to creations in the modern manner he has retained the spirit of the older French styles but has introduced a new note in his treatment of wood and in the construction of bronze furniture. The woodwork and furniture designed by him for the Pavillon d'Elégance constituted one of the few highly successful interior effects at the Exposition.[1]

The introduction was necessary. Rateau had always worked independently, never joining professional organizations or displaying his work at the Salons; accordingly, his name rarely appeared in the design press.[2] Nevertheless, he developed a small, loyal, international clientele that responded to his very personal vision of modern design.

The son of a shoemaker, Rateau at the age of twelve enrolled at the École Boulle in Paris, where he studied drawing, sculpture, and the history of art.[3] By 1898 he seems to have been working as a freelance draftsman and designer. One of his earliest employers was Georges Hoentschel, a noted Paris decorator whose dual mastery of traditional and contemporary design exposed him both to design history and to the practice of interior decoration. In 1905 he was hired to supervise the studios of Maison Alavoine et Cie, a large firm that specialized in the sort of historicist interiors then in fashion. At Alavoine, Rateau supervised commissions for an international roster of important residential and commercial clients, including the French perfumer François Coty, the jewelers Boucheron and Tiffany & Co., the art dealers Knoedler and Seligmann, and perhaps most important, the banker George Blumenthal and his wife, Florence.

After serving in the French Army during the war, Rateau returned briefly to Alavoine, but left in 1919 to establish his own interior decorating business. The same year he traveled to America. On his transatlantic crossing, fortuitously, he met the Blumenthals. In 1914 the couple had built a large town house in New York on the corner of Park Avenue at Seventieth Street, and Rateau's first commission was the decoration of the ballroom and indoor swimming pool. Rateau's work for the Blumenthals reflects the dual nature of his design sensibility: the ballroom recalled the elegant atmosphere of eighteenth-century Venice, while the decidedly modern grotto-like room that housed the swimming pool was filled with his own distinctive bronze furniture. Over the next ten years, Rateau would design interiors for their houses in France, as well as for those of Florence Blumenthal's sisters.

In 1920, Rateau attracted two other important clients, the French couturiere Jeanne Lanvin and the Spanish Duke and Duchess of Alba. Lanvin not only commissioned Rateau to design interiors for several of her houses but also hired him as director of Lanvin Décoration, a short-lived business that oversaw, among other projects, the decoration of her couture showrooms and the Théâtre Daunou, a small private theater in Paris built by comedic actress Jane Renouardt (an important client of Lanvin's) in 1921.[4] Together with Paul Iribe, Rateau designed an emblem for the Maison Lanvin, which depicts Lanvin herself reaching down to her daughter Marguerite. The

motif was introduced in January 1923 on Lanvin's
Arpège perfume bottle, and remains today one of the
most recognized logos in the rarefied world of fashion. The Duke and Duchess of Alba commissioned
a suite of rooms for the Palacio de Liria in Madrid,
including a bathroom (opposite), completed in 1926,
which would become one of Rateau's most widely
published interiors.

Rateau's work for these clients dominated the
early 1920s, establishing his reputation and serving
to develop his very original design sensibility, which
was based on his thorough understanding of historical precedent and his training as a sculptor and
draftsman. His two primary modes of expression
were carved wood furniture that echoes the refinement of eighteenth-century France and cast-bronze
furniture that evokes classical antiquity expressed
in elegant forms, exquisite details, and skillful handling of stylized natural motifs — mainly flowers,
trees, and animals. He generally placed his furniture in rooms paneled with richly carved wood or
gilt lacquer, although theatricality was offset by the
sensitivity and wit of his designs:

*The art of M. Rateau, decorator, is in not indiscrimi-
nately mixing modes, masculine and feminine, styles,
sources, flowers, and scrollwork. He creates, but he creates by seeking moderation rather than lavishness or fri-
volity. And for that he must be praised without reserve.*[5]

Rateau was an ensemblier, not a craftsman.
To bring to realization the many components of
his interiors, he turned to the Ateliers Neuilly-
Levallois, a workshop on the outskirts of Paris that
met all his needs, from architectural paneling and
furniture to textiles, lighting fixtures, and small
decorative objects. There were studios for stone,
wood, and metalwork, as well as for lacquer and
gilding. Rateau's reliance on the workshop was such
that he bought it outright in 1922, and by 1929 there
were more than two hundred workers in his employ.

The 1925 Paris Exposition brought Rateau wide
recognition. As an independent designer he was not
eligible to exhibit in pavilions of design associations
such as the Société des Artistes Décorateurs. He
did, however, contribute furnishings to a number
of displays, mainly related to the fashion industry,
notably the Pavillon de l'Élégance, in which mannequins wearing dresses by Callot Sœurs, Jenny,
Lanvin, and Worth were posed on Rateau's furniture.[6] While none of his contributions were credited
in the Exposition's official catalogue, they did not go

unnoticed in the press.[7] The following year he was made a chevalier of the Légion d'Honneur.

Rateau's business thrived in the late 1920s, when he developed an international roster of clients and took on a number of projects. Among these were the design of the music room in Cole Porter's Paris apartment (with Jean-Michel Frank); the living room and oval salon at Dumbarton Oaks, the home of Mr. and Mrs. Robert Woods Bliss in Washington, D.C.; a logo for the Young-Quinlan department store in Minneapolis; and suites at the Hôtel de Crillon.

The 1930s were less kind. The international economic crisis caused a significant drop in business, although several commissions were forthcoming from the French government: furniture for the French Legation in Belgrade (1934), the French Embassy in London (1934), and the Commerce Ministry in Paris (1936). But by the late 1930s, there was little demand for Rateau's work. Although he designed furniture for the Expositions Committee building at the 1937 Paris Exposition, his participation in the exhibition "Le Décor de la vie de 1900 à 1925" at the Musée des Arts Décoratifs was perhaps more telling, suggesting that his work was now relegated to history.

50 | Dressing Table and Hand Mirror

> a | Dressing Table, ca. 1925; bronze, black limestone, Carrara marble, mirror glass
>
> b | Hand Mirror, ca. 1925; bronze, ivory, mirror glass

In 1914, Rateau traveled to southern Italy. Captivated by the ancient bronze furniture he saw at Pompeii, he later adapted its forms and decorative motifs for his own cast-bronze furniture, lighting, and decorative accessories. Referring to this work, a 1925 article in *Vogue* described Rateau as "a modern artist who knows how much of the past enters into the present, since one is the logical continuation of the other, and that genius consists in discovering the simple lines which connect the two."[1]

Antiquity certainly provided inspiration for this dressing table, although Rateau may have borrowed its peacock motif and stylized floral decoration from

Rateau conceived the original model, which had a round-edged marble top, for the fantastical bathroom he designed in 1921 for the Duchess of Alba at the Palacio de Liria in Madrid (now destroyed).[2] He made at least three subsequent versions: one for his wife, one for the bathroom of couturiere Jeanne Lanvin, and the present one, acquired by the Metropolitan Museum.[3] An example was included in the Pavillon de l'Elegance at the 1925 Paris Exposition, although it is unclear if it was any of the above.[4]

Recognizing the importance of the Alba commission, in June 1925 Rateau reconstructed the bathroom at the Arnold Seligmann gallery in Paris. Because the Alba furniture was already in Spain, Rateau used later versions of many of the pieces for the installation. It was at the gallery that Metropolitan curator Joseph Breck saw the dressing table and decided to acquire it for the Museum. In gratitude, Rateau offered the charming hand mirror (shown opposite resting on the table and at left) to the Museum as a gift. In a letter dated July 8, 1925, Rateau wrote to Breck:

Monsieur A. Seligmann has just informed me that you have decided, on behalf of the Metropolitan Museum of Art, to purchase the dressing table that was displayed in his gallery this past June.

I hasten to express to you, along with my feelings of gratitude, all the pleasure that your decision brings me.

It is for me a great honor to appear in that fine museum of your great country, and that public recognition gives me the most valuable encouragement for the future.

I hope you will allow me to add to your purchase one hand mirror, which I am happy to offer you, free of charge, to complement the ensemble.

I am preparing these objects for you right now, so that they will present all the most desirable qualities.[5]

The oval hand mirror incorporates the same peacock motif that appears on the dressing table. Like the table, it is a later version of a model first conceived for the Duchess of Alba.[6] The original was made of cast bronze in its entirety; later examples, including the present one, have handles of ivory.

Persian miniature painting. The dressing table itself is a witty metaphor of vanity, which lends the design its special appeal and originality. Each pair of attenuated, antler-shaped cast-bronze legs takes the form of a hairpin. They are adorned at the top with a pair of preening peacocks — emblems of *l'amour-propre* — that support the black limestone top inlaid with white Carrara marble, where a woman, presumably of means and beauty, would herself preen in admiration of the image reflected in the mirror. Another pair of peacocks forms the support for the double-faced mirror, held in place with acanthus-leaf brackets and floral rivets.

CLÉMENT ROUSSEAU

Saint-Maurice-la-Fougereuse 1872–1950 Neuilly-sur-Seine

One of the most interesting aspects of French Art Deco is the revival and updating of traditions from preindustrial France, whereby formal and decorative vocabularies as well as materials and techniques were mined and reinvented in a way that appealed to modern sensibilities. The work of Clément Rousseau is a perfect case in point.[1]

Although trained as a sculptor, Rousseau is today best known for household furnishings that incorporate galuchat, a durable leather-like veneer made from the tanned skins of rays and other fish.[2] Usually referred to in English as shagreen, this material has been used since ancient times, principally as a covering for dagger sheaths and sword scabbards, which explains why French galuchat workers are known as *gainiers*, or sheath-makers.[3]

The use of fish skins for veneer originated in eighth-century Japan. By the eighteenth century, Asian objects with galuchat were being seen in the West. They were regarded as exotic and as precious as lacquer or porcelain. Seeking to imitate them, French artisans used the material to cover a range of small-scale wares such as sewing boxes, telescope covers, and traveling sets. Among the first Frenchmen to excel in the technique was Jean-Claude Galluchat (d. 1774), whose name was adopted for the veneer. During the eighteenth century, galuchat was avidly collected, but by the late nineteenth century the technique had been essentially forgotten.

Paul Iribe is generally credited with initiating the twentieth-century revival of the technique in France. Around 1912 he seems to have bought a small eighteenth-century galuchat object, which piqued his interest in the material. By chance, shortly thereafter he came across a batch of old skins and decided to use them on a commode he had designed for the couturier Jacques Doucet. Not being a cabinetmaker himself, Iribe asked his friend Rousseau to experiment with them. Through trial and error, Rousseau became the first French craftsman of the modern era to master the complex technique, which involved first stripping, cleaning, and preserving the skins; then sanding and staining them; cutting and gluing them onto a structure; and finally varnishing.

Eighteenth-century galuchat was generally stained green. Rousseau experimented with vegetable dyes to develop a wider spectrum of colors, including greys, pinks, and blues. For visual and textural contrast, he frequently offset the skins with other exotic materials imported from the colonies. His preferred woods were macassar ebony, rosewood, and palmwood, and he often incorporated accents of ivory and mother-of-pearl. The elegantly curving forms of his furniture were often based on eighteenth-century models that showed the galuchat to its best advantage.

Rousseau's output was not large, and only occasionally did he participate in the annual Salons of the Société des Artistes Français. He did, however, contribute a number of works to the 1925 Paris Exposition.[4] In 1926 he was given a one-man show at the Galerie Charpentier in Paris. It included sixty works that ranged from large-scale furniture to small objects such as clocks and lamps and a marble sculpture titled *Le Rire* (Laughter) set atop a galuchat base. In the exhibition's catalogue, Rousseau described himself as a sculptor, although he had built his reputation as a gainier and furniture maker. He seems to have worked mainly on commission. The Charpentier catalogue noted:

Clément Rousseau can reproduce all the furniture and works of art displayed and, according to the wishes of the client, can accommodate any modification demanded,

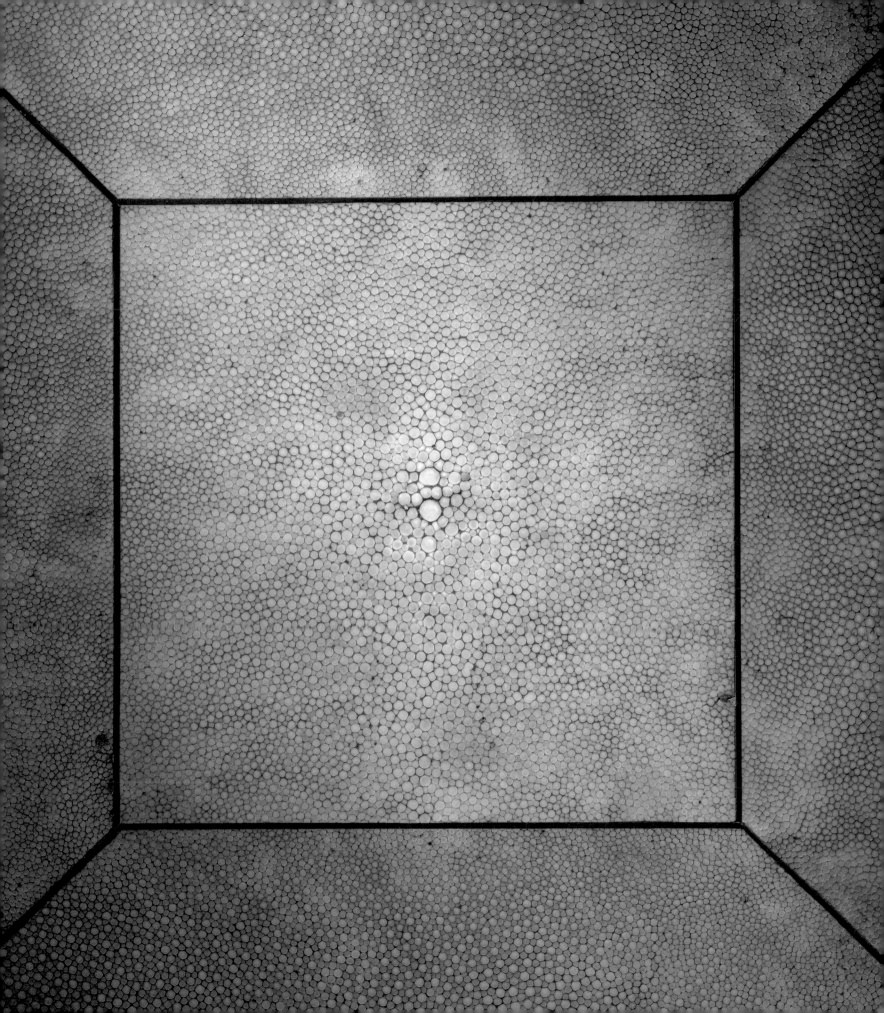

or he can create new forms for which he will furnish the design, plans, and estimates.[5]

Rousseau's client list included such well-known collectors as Doucet, Baron Robert de Rothschild, and Henriette, duchesse de Vendôme.[6]

If Iribe was the first modern French designer to take an interest in galuchat, Rousseau must be given full credit for its revival and popularization, and in this his contribution to the French Art Deco aesthetic was significant. It is not known whether he instructed other furniture makers in the technique, but directly or indirectly his influence can be felt in the work of the many who used galuchat during the 1920s and 1930s.

51 | Table

1924; ebony, galuchat, ivory, brass

Rousseau made this strange and extraordinary table (there is always something vaguely sinister about using skin—of any kind—as a covering for furniture) in 1924 for the couturier and collector Jacques Doucet's Paris apartment at 46, avenue du Bois. Doucet probably later moved it to his famous studio in the suburb of Neuilly, completed in 1928. The original model was not created for Doucet; that earlier version, described as a *table à journaux* (newspaper table), was made in 1921 for Baron Robert de Rothschild.[1] Presumably, the day's papers were laid out on the table, which was light enough to be picked up and moved to wherever one wished to read them.

Contrasts of material, texture, and color are typical of Rousseau's work. Here, dark macassar ebony is offset by areas of green-stained galuchat and detailing in ivory, all materials that would have been imported from French colonies in Africa and Asia. The central square of the galuchat-veneered top is surrounded by a wide mitred border, with each panel made from a separate but closely matched skin, the joints delineated by delicate ebony stringing.[2] The top is set into an ebony frame carved with lark's tongue chamfered edges, and the integrated legs and handles are formed of tapering hairpin arches made of ebony, the curved tops of which are partially veneered in galuchat terminating in carved ivory rings; the feet are also ivory.

If the aesthetic is exotic, the concept is more traditionally European. Small, easy-to-move furniture—while certainly not invented there—reached a level of perfection in France during the late eighteenth century, when evolving social customs brought an increased informality to the domestic environment. Rooms often served a variety of purposes, with portable furniture moved about as needed. As a collector of eighteenth-century French decorative arts, Doucet would have understood the table's links with the past. And as a connoisseur, he would have recognized its refined proportions, beautiful materials, and exquisite craftsmanship—not to mention its eminent utility (galuchat is impervious to water)—as the equal of anything made in the eighteenth century.

Doucet died in 1929. Soon thereafter, his widow gave away or sold off many of the paintings in his collection. His furnishings, however, remained in the Neuilly studio until her death thirty years later, when several pieces were bequeathed to the Musée des Arts Décoratifs. Others were kept by Doucet's nephew Jean Dubrujeaud, who stored them in a warehouse until 1972, when his son sold them at auction.[3]

In 1973, after the table arrived at the Museum, a curious discovery was made by conservators during a routine cleaning. Under one of the brass leg braces, a small religious medal was found inserted behind a plug of wood. The medal depicts Saint Thérèse of Lisieux.[4] The inscription on the verso reads, in translation: "I wish to spend my time in heaven doing good on earth." It is not known who placed the medal there, or what its meaning might be in relation to the table.

Medal of Saint Thérèse of Lisieux, set into the underside of the table frame

É.-J. RUHLMANN

Paris 1879–1933 Paris

Perhaps the most renowned French designer of his day, É.-J. Ruhlmann is considered the preeminent exponent of high-style French taste following the First World War.[1] Aesthetic refinement, luxury materials, and impeccable construction techniques place his work on a par with the finest examples from the eighteenth century, a source for many of his designs. Although best known today for his furniture, he was in fact an ensemblier, able to provide any aspect of a décor from the architectural framework to the upholstery textiles.[2]

Ruhlmann was raised to inherit the household contracting firm founded by his mother's family in 1827, which provided straightforward services of the building trade: housepainting, drywalling, wallpapering, and mirror-glass making. He served there as an apprentice, and after his father's death in 1907 took over the business, quickly setting about to reinvent its mission and ultimately turning it into one of the most renowned decorating enterprises of its day. With his partner, Pierre Laurent, Ruhlmann added design studios, cabinetmaking and upholstery workshops, and a showroom. At its peak, the business employed upwards of fifty designers, craftsmen, and administrative staff. Accordingly, the Établissements Ruhlmann et Laurent could produce much of their work in-house. The weaving of carpets and textiles and the manufacture of porcelains and glass, they contracted out — Cornille and Prelle for textiles, Desfossé & Karth for wallpapers, and Sèvres for ceramics.

Ruhlmann functioned as something of an editor, if not actually designing then supervising and overseeing every aspect of a commission down to the smallest detail. In the tradition of the great architect-designers of the late eighteenth and early nineteenth centuries, he took as much interest in details such as molding profiles and the proportions of bronze mounts as he did in practical specifications like joinery techniques and the selection of wood veneers, or even how color and lighting would affect the senses.

Ruhlmann's first realized designs were a series of wallpapers he displayed at the 1911 Salon d'Automne. In 1913 he presented his first interior — a dining room — also at the Salon d'Automne.[3] About this time he also began designing *meubles précieux*, delicately attenuated furniture often decorated with figural motifs. Such pieces hardly qualified as practical household furnishings, and very few were made; indeed, most of his earliest projects for furniture and interiors exist only on paper.[4] The drawings, however, reveal an attention to overall settings and atmosphere. From the beginning Ruhlmann created total environments, complete in their conception and harmonious in their sophisticated and pleasing combinations of vivid colors and bold patterns and in the richness of their furnishings. Some of his more theatrical interiors recall set designs of the Ballets Russes.

Illness prevented Ruhlmann from serving during the war, and chronic health problems would plague him throughout his life. After the war, Ruhlmann established an international reputation as a designer of great originality and skill. His furniture was acquired by the French State as early as 1922, and by the Metropolitan Museum in 1923. His work was also widely represented in exhibitions both at home and abroad.[5] His private clients, who were mainly French, represented a veritable Who's Who of figures in industry and business, and overseas they included the King of Siam and the Maharaja of Indore.[6] His many commissions for commercial projects ran to interiors for the SS *Île de France*, fashionable restaurants such as Drouant, and the Chamber of Commerce and Industry in Paris.

Ruhlmann's made-to-measure furniture and interiors were extremely expensive, and Ruhlmann addressed his design practice to a rarefied clientele:

The rich client wants to possess only furniture that is impossible for the less rich to acquire. This furniture must therefore be costly, being difficult to execute and using precious materials that no knock-off can simulate.[7]

To underscore this point, he often spoke of the enormous sums paid by the French nobility for furniture by such eighteenth-century masters as André-Charles Boulle and Jean-Henri Riesener:

If you remark to J.-E Ruhlmann that he is not, in the strictest sense, in sync with his time, or rather with the trends of his time, he will readily remind you that the ancien régime created its masterpieces by throwing money at them, that Boulle received 95,000 livres for a cabinet for the Grand Dauphin, and Riesener 73,000 for Louis XV's desk.[8]

Through such references, Ruhlmann not only compared himself with the greatest *ébénistes* of the past but also linked his patrons with royalty, a connection they were not likely to refute.

Ruhlmann's work of the 1920s, considered his finest period, was a combination of tradition and innovation:

What artist of this generation has been able to produce the high-end luxury furniture of today, which a princess of royal blood or an archduchess would choose if such titles still signified artistic culture and wealth? . . . Without a doubt, their choice—because of the sumptuous, lofty, even majestic style of his works—would be the ébéniste Jacques Ruhlmann. Not because Ruhlmann leans toward flashy and excessive ornament, but because his furniture, by its austere grace and technical perfection, often attains the Grand Style. It must be said that his displays in the various Salons are subtle and unusual: neutral grounds against which, isolated and proud, a costly and beautiful piece of furniture stands, illuminated, its simple lines, spare curves, and discreet ornamentation having been achieved only after great efforts; the piece as a whole, as well as the most minute details, executed with refinement. . . . That his style . . . recalls the Empire style—nothing could be

more true; yet a heightened sensitivity in the contour of the lines and the addition of precious materials make his furniture entirely modern.[9]

Ruhlmann welcomed technical and material invention—for example, he preferred artificial spray to natural lacquer—and enthusiastically addressed modern design problems, such as the incorporation of radiators and other modern conveniences into the elegant interior. He took on projects that required his participation as an interior architect, reconfiguring existing spaces and advising on new buildings.[10] His approach to architecture was as historically inspired as his furniture, his rooms tending toward symmetry in both plan and elevation, with a strong emphasis on verticality to create a sense of grandeur.

Of all Ruhlmann's projects, perhaps the most successful—and the one that best reflects his philosophy as a designer—was his pavilion at the 1925 Paris Exposition, known alternately as the Pavillon du Collectionneur and the Hôtel du Collectionneur. Designed to give the impression of a private mansion, it was described at the time as "a happy compromise between a real private house and an exhibition pavilion."[11] Official credit for the building and its contents was given to the Groupe Ruhlmann, an association of more than forty designers, artists, and craftsmen working under Ruhlmann's supervision. The purported occupant of the house was an idealized collector—the sort of person the Exposition was engineered to attract.

Although the building was designed by Ruhlmann's lifelong friend the architect Pierre Patout (see pages 159–61) with an eye to the elegant pavilions of eighteenth-century France, it was Ruhlmann who created its look. While each room was treated with the same degree of attention, the undisputed centerpiece was the domed grand salon, with luxurious furnishings that recalled the majesty and formality of the Empire and Louis-Philippe periods (see page 12). While Ruhlmann himself designed the majority of the furnishings, he also—in the manner of his "ideal collector"—included works by his contemporaries, Brandt, Décorchemont, Dunand, Jallot, Lenoble, Puiforcat, and Rapin among them (see nos. 12, 26, and 38).[12] In addition to his own pavilion at the Exposition, Ruhlmann contributed furnishings to the Ambassade Française and the Grand Palais (see no. 55).

The worldwide economic crisis dealt a profound blow to the luxury trades, and Ruhlmann's most notable projects of the late 1920s and early 1930s were, not surprisingly, public rather than private commissions. Grand spaces such as the gala reception rooms of the Chamber of Commerce and Industry of Paris or the study for the French colonial minister at the 1931 Exposition Coloniale were intended to project a sense of security and confidence in a period increasingly characterized by rapid change and financial panic.

For his contributions to French culture, Ruhlmann was made a chevalier of the Légion d'Honneur in 1925 and an officer in 1932. The year after his death in 1933, a memorial exhibition was presented at the Louvre.[13] His contemporaries readily acknowledged his contributions to modern design:

[Ruhlmann] shows us that one can love Versailles, sumptuous creations, beautiful materials, luxury, and rare and precious things and at the same time incorporate in one's present-day work the telephone, indirect lighting, scientific devices, central heating. But Ruhlmann never wished to depart from the principle of elegance. He sought not to interpret machine forms but rather to establish the primacy of man and of taste over the machine—and that constitutes the most confounding problem of our time.[14]

52 | Textile and Wallpaper

a | *Sarrazin* Textile, ca. 1917; printed linen

b | *Sarrazin* Wallpaper, ca. 1917; printed paper

Ruhlmann's first endeavors as a designer were wallpapers, several of which were exhibited at the 1911 Salon of the Société des Artistes Décorateurs. It was an appropriate beginning, since wallpapering was one of the services that had long been offered by the Ruhlmann family firm and was the aspect of design that Ruhlmann would have known best. No traces of these papers have survived.

Two years later there was another display, of both wallpapers and textiles, at the 1913 Salon d'Automne. Many of these featured variations of

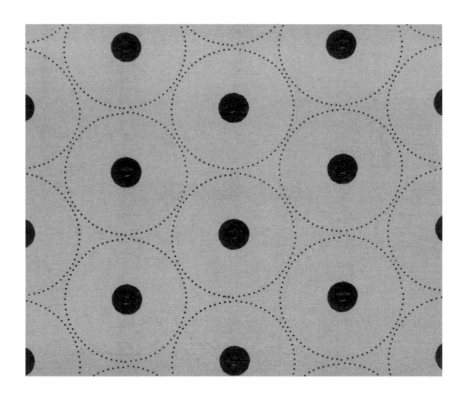

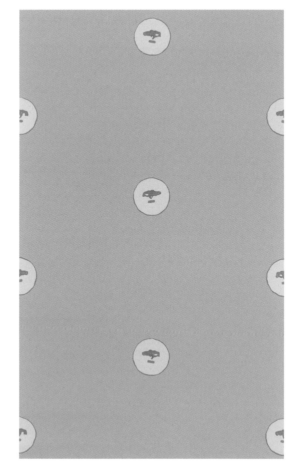

É.-J. Ruhlmann. Dining room, textiles and wallpapers with rondel motif, Salon d'Automne, 1913

pattern printed for Ruhlmann by the Paris wallpaper manufacturer Desfossé & Karth in 1917.[4] Over the years, Ruhlmann worked with various printers in the production of his wallpapers and textiles, including Desfossé & Karth, Follot, Hans, and Essef.[5] Ruhlmann's wallpapers were retailed under the Établissements Ruhlmann et Laurent brand, the more profitable contracting side of his company, which offset the financial losses of the furniture-making business.

53 | *David-Weill* Desk

ca. 1918–19; amboyna, ivory, galuchat, silk, metal, oak, lumber-core plywood, poplar, walnut, birch, macassar ebony

This desk is based on French and English kidney-shaped desks of the late eighteenth century, known as *rognon* (kidney) or Carlton House desks.[1] The link to historical precedent would have been obvious— and desirable—to the client who commissioned it. David David-Weill (1871–1952) was an American-born French financier who worked at Lazard Frères, his family's bank. A serious art collector, he served as the president of the Musées Nationaux and vice president of the Union Centrale des Arts Décoratifs. In his will, he bequeathed more than two thousand works of art to French and American museums. His house, filled with antique furnishings, was testament to his passion: the arts of eighteenth-century France. Accordingly, Ruhlmann designed this desk to harmonize with them:

The starting point was one of those pieces of eighteenth-century furniture whose nickname, rognons, though hardly euphonious, does capture its rather nice shape. The owner, M. David-Weil [sic], was attached by ingrained habit to the proportions and interior arrangements of this desk [form]. The idea was therefore to draw on that old model to create a deluxe modern version.

M. Ruhlmann was not averse to that plan. . . . [Indeed,] he believes that to make an original work, it is not necessary to obliterate tradition. One doesn't get very far by starting from scratch.[2]

With this desk David-Weill paired a Louis XVI armchair, and with its elegance, luxury materials, and

a specific decorative treatment, a graphic repeat motif of flowers, plants, and birds set within an irregular rondel; sometimes the repeat motif was embellished with patterns of dots (the furniture and architectural features of Ruhlmann's display were also decorated with meandering lines of dots).[1] At least one of these designs, a pattern of abstracted flowers, was produced as both a wallpaper and a printed cotton-and-silk velvet textile.[2] Ruhlmann clearly had a fondness for such rondels; they would reappear many years later on his business letterhead, encircling his name and address set against a field of flowers.

The *Sarraẓin* pattern relates closely to Ruhlmann's 1913 designs. It incorporates the same basic motif—a stylized Cedar of Lebanon tree set within an irregular circle—on both the wallpaper and the textile, though on the textile each motif is offset by an added circle of dots. Ruhlmann produced the pattern in alternate colorways.[3] The name of the pattern, *Sarraẓin*, is perhaps a variant spelling of the French *sarrasin*, meaning Saracen—an antiquated term for Arabs of Middle Eastern countries (such as Lebanon). Although the manufacturers of the Metropolitan's wallpaper and textile remain unknown, the use of dot circles recalls a similar

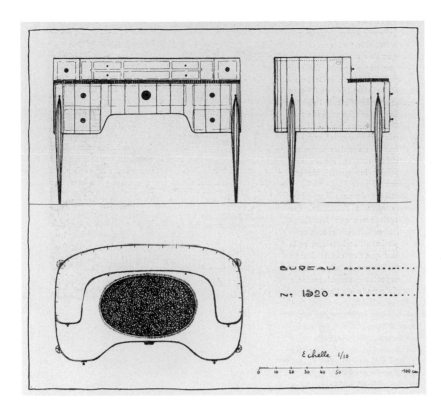

É.-J. Ruhlmann. Design for *David-Weill* desk, in *Art et décoration*, January 1920

The desk marks a rare opportunity to trace every step of Ruhlmann's design process, from preliminary sketch to small-scale and full-scale drawings made in his atelier, and ending with a finished piece. The sketch was published in a 1920 article in *Art et décoration*.[6] Its form is virtually identical to the finished model. Some kind of decoration was indicated at the top of the superstructure (hastily drawn scrolls suggest either the graining of galuchat or a pattern of veneer he called *cailloux*, or pebbles). This sketch would have been given to a draftsman in his office to make more resolved 1:10 scale drawings. Highly detailed full-scale drawings would then have been made. Plans, elevations, and separate sheets devoted to details such as the ivory hardware and the galuchat marquetry are housed in the Ruhlmann Archive at the Musée des Années Trente, Boulogne-Billancourt. It is interesting to note that none of the drawings include the horizontal bands and spirals of dots that appear on the finished piece, and it is possible that this motif was a last-minute addition.

The desk is veneered on all sides with amboyna burl inset with ivory fillets to suggest vertical boards. The veneer completely disguises the construction. The body, which has five drawers, appears effortlessly raised on four *fuseau* (spindle-shaped) legs — a Ruhlmann invention — each with twelve tapering facets separated by ivory stringing. Each leg terminates in a small ivory ball at the top and a faceted ivory sabot at the bottom. The work surface, set back slightly from the edge of the desk, is raised on a frieze of ivory rectangles that suggest dentils, and the inset writing surface is of grey-tinted galuchat. The drawer pulls are simple ivory balls with circular backplates, with the exception of the pull for the large drawer at the front, which is an ivory ring fastened to a circular backplate with a metal chain wrapped in green silk threads.

magnificent craftsmanship, Ruhlmann's piece held its own against the earlier furniture masterworks.

Traditional *rognon* desks are generally flat-topped worktables with independent superstructures, known as *cartonniers*, that rest on top of the work surface. Ruhlmann's superstructure, by contrast, is fully integrated. Drawings from his sketchbooks include a variety of kidney-shaped desks and suggest that he had been working out ideas for them as early as 1913.[3] Indeed, he made a similar desk, without the superstructure, for the actress Fernande Cabanel in 1918–19, a variant of which appears in an undated drawing of a proposed salon commissioned by Baron Lambert.[4] The *David-Weill* desk must be seen as having evolved from these two earlier models.[5]

54 | *Tibattant* Desk

ca. 1923; macassar ebony, ivory, leather, aluminum leaf, silver, silk, oak, lumber-core plywood, poplar, mahogany

In November 1923, Metropolitan Museum curator Joseph Breck installed a gallery with recent acquisitions of modern French decorative arts. He included this small desk by Ruhlmann, which he had purchased directly from Ruhlmann et Laurent earlier the same year. It was the first work by Ruhlmann to enter the Metropolitan's collection, and indeed one of the first of his works to enter a public institution. The almost exaggerated delicacy of this diminutive piece relates closely to the *meubles précieux* (precious furniture) that had occupied Ruhlmann during the war years. Drawings for similar drop-front desks appear in Ruhlmann's sketchbooks from 1913 and 1917.[1] This desk takes inspiration from the eighteenth-century *bonheur-du-jour*, a type of lady's desk that was small enough to be easily moved about. The name of the model, *Tibattant*, is possibly

a contraction of the French words *petit* and *abattant*, loosely translated as "little drop-front," and is an instance where Ruhlmann did not name a piece after the model's first owner.[2]

Ruhlmann first presented this model at the 1921 Salon of the Société des Artistes Décorateurs, and displayed it again in a 1923 exhibition of decorative arts held in the Pavillon de Marsan (now the Musée des Arts Décoratifs). Critic René Chavance described it in 1924:

The purity of [Ruhlmann's] taste is seen here not only in the harmony of lines but in the choice of colors. . . . this little desk in tones of pink, delicately planted on aristocratically svelte legs, whose drop front opens to reveal an array of charming little drawers embellished with silvered leather.[3]

The desk's frame is constructed from oak and poplar, with two layers of macassar ebony veneer offset with ivory detailing. The back too is finished, suggesting the piece was conceived to stand in the center of a room. The drop-front panel is inlaid with a thin decorative ivory oval and has an ivory oval keyhole escutcheon. The top, veneered in a diamond pattern, is raised on a gallery bordered with ivory pseudo-dentils. The single front drawer has two ivory pulls set with tassels. And the gracefully attenuated cabriole legs, traditional in inspiration, are carved from solid blocks of macassar ebony inlaid with ivory fillets, their thinness accentuated by concave surfaces. The sabots are also of ivory. Lined in deep pink-red morocco leather tooled with silvery aluminum leaf, the interior has two small drawers with ivory ball pulls; a closed compartment has an ivory pull set with a tassel of silk with silver threads.[4]

Steam heating caused damage to the veneers of the desk soon after it arrived at the Museum, and it was restored to Ruhlmann's own specifications in 1928. The ivory volutes are modern replacements. So, too, are the two tassels on the front drawer.

The model was produced in a variety of veneers and with different details.[5] Another example is in the collection of the Philadelphia Museum of Art. An interesting feature of the Metropolitan's example is the secret locking mechanism for the front drawer. By turning the proper left ivory knob clockwise, the drawer is unlocked.[6]

55 | *État* Cabinet

designed 1922, manufactured 1925–26;
macassar ebony, amaranth, ivory, oak, lumber-
core plywood, poplar, chestnut, mahogany,
silvered brass

This cabinet is a tour de force, displaying the astonishing skill and artistry achieved by French furniture
makers in the Art Deco period. Every aspect was
specifically conceived to be as complex as possible.
Its realization not only demonstrates Ruhlmann's
mastery of his métier but proclaims him an artist of
the highest order.

The outline is deceptively simple: apart from the
top and back (the cabinet was designed to be set
against a wall), there are no planar surfaces. The
entire visible exterior is veneered in an elegant combination of macassar ebony, amaranth, and ivory.
It is difficult enough to properly veneer a flat surface; when the surface curves, the process is further
complicated, all the more so when a complex pattern is employed. The bombé front is framed by
concave chamfered projecting corners that rest on
short cabriole legs, each with an ivory-set volute
at the top and an ivory sabot. The cabinet has a
shallow recessed gallery raised on a band of ivory
pseudo-dentils. The mahogany-lined interior has
four mahogany shelves.

The most distinctive aspect of the cabinet is
the front door panel, which is delineated along
the outer edge with a band of ivory dots. At the
center is an oval marquetry design in amaranth and
ivory that depicts a vase filled with and surrounded
by cascading flowers. So as not to interrupt the
inlaid motif, Ruhlmann left the panel in one piece,
rather than dividing it vertically into two doors.
This construction effectively renders the cabinet
unusable: because the door is so wide and so deep
(to accommodate the recessed gallery), its weight
causes the cabinet to tip forward when swung
open. When the model was first displayed, it was
presented on a small carpeted platform, lending
it an architectonic presence and underscoring its
conception as a work of art rather than as a piece
of furniture intended for use.

Ruhlmann developed this cabinet in 1922, from
a more functional earlier version: a three-legged
corner cabinet with the same inlaid door, the first
example of which was made in 1916. Four examples
of each version, all with variations in materials and
marquetry details, are known.[1] The triangular form
of the earlier model provided for a body deep and
heavy enough to counter the weight of the solid
panel door. Ruhlmann introduced the four-legged
rectangular version at the 1922 Salon d'Automne,
from which it was purchased by the French State.
Because the state was presumably the first client to
acquire this model, Ruhlmann assigned it the name
État. The cabinet was exhibited the following year
at the important Mostra Internazionale delle Arti
Decorative in Monza, Italy, and again at the 1925
Paris Exposition, where it was shown at the Grand
Palais together with other furniture by Ruhlmann
and tapestries by Gobelins.

It was at the 1925 Paris Expo that curator Joseph
Breck saw the cabinet. Although—or perhaps
because—he had purchased the *Tibattant* desk (see
no. 54) for the Metropolitan in 1923, he was eager to
acquire more works by Ruhlmann for the collection.
He had considered the monumental *Élysée* cabinet,
which was on display in the Ambassade Française,
but deemed the price of 65,000 francs prohibitive.
Instead, he opted to commission a less expensive version of the *État* cabinet—together with a
Fuseaux cabinet (acc. no. 25.231.2) and a *Drouant*
side chair (acc. no. 25.231.3a–c).

É.-J. Ruhlmann. Rectangular
version of *État* cabinet (at left),
Grand Palais, Exposition Internationale des Arts Décoratifs et
Industriels Modernes, Paris, 1925

In early July 1925, Ruhlmann informed Breck that it would take five months to complete the cabinet; work presumably began at that time. Hoping to include it in an installation of new acquisitions of modern decorative arts at the Metropolitan scheduled to open in early 1926, Breck wrote to Ruhlmann on December 30, asking when he could expect it to be delivered. A letter from Ruhlmann et Laurent of January 12, 1926, assured Breck that the cabinet had been delivered for shipment on January 4. The cabinet did not in fact arrive in time for the February opening, but it was installed in March.[2]

By 1927, the cabinet (together with the other veneered pieces by Ruhlmann that the Museum had acquired) was suffering from condition problems: veneers were beginning to lift, probably the result of steam heat. Breck wrote to Ruhlmann, asking how best to address the issue. Mortified, Ruhlmann supplied the name of a New York cabinetmaker—a Mr. D. Tomitch of 177 East Eighty-Seventh Street—who repaired the veneers at Ruhlmann's cost.

Ruhlmann died in November 1933. A record receipt for the cabinet was sent the following month to the Museum by Ruhlmann's office. The accompanying letter, dated December 11, was stamped posthumously with Ruhlmann's signature:

Messieurs,
I thought it would be good for our clients to have, for the furniture produced in our ateliers and which they have acquired, certificates that document their origin.

These certificates bear the number of the piece, the name of the model, the date of completion, the specifics of the piece, and a precise reproduction of the signatures and marks branded on the piece itself. Made in triplicate, the [clients'] certificates have been removed from a logbook; the master copies will be deposited at the Bibliothèque du Musée des Arts Décoratifs and the second copies will remain in our archives.

I have therefore the pleasure of enclosing the documentation for the work you have in your collection.

Yours respectfully,
Ruhlmann[3]

Curiously, the receipt states that the cabinet was completed in March 1926; this date may more accurately reflect the date it was delivered to the Museum.

56 | Pair of *Duval* Cabinets

designed 1924; Brazilian rosewood, ivory, amboyna burl, mahogany, oak, plywood

In his furniture of the mid-1920s, Ruhlmann accentuated his subtle forms with abstract decorative patterning; diamonds, pseudo-dentils, and rows of dots are typical motifs. Yet despite the linear, geometric quality of the decoration, he rarely used straight lines, preferring gentle curves that were technically difficult to execute.

The boxy bodies of this handsome pair of cabinets are veneered with Brazilian rosewood over an oak frame. The slightly bowed double door fronts, punctuated by an ivory keyhole escutcheon, are delineated by a diaper pattern of inlaid ivory stringing, outlined

with a broad ivory fillet, and framed by a stepped surround. Each cabinet is surmounted by a recessed gallery and raised from a platform base on bobbin-shaped ivory balusters. The interiors are veneered with amboyna burl detailed with mahogany. One (above left) is divided horizontally by two shelves above three shallow drawers; the other (above right), into nine pigeonholes, one with three stacked drawers. The high quality of the interior finish suggests that the doors were intended to be kept open.

Ruhlmann made the first example of this model in 1924.[1] Of the first client, we know only that his name was Duval—hence the name of the model. In 1925 a version was exhibited in the bedroom of Ruhlmann's pavilion, the Hôtel du Collectionneur, at the 1925 Paris Exposition. And the following year another version, with a tortoiseshell-and-ivory front and an interior lined in suede embossed with gold leaf, was displayed at the Salon d'Automne. Period

photographs show the latter being used to house small decorative objects.[2] Ruhlmann seems to have made a version with a tortoiseshell front for his own use. Included in the 1934 Ruhlmann retrospective at the Louvre, it was bequeathed to the museum by his widow in 1957.[3]

Eleven versions of the original 1924 model are believed to have been made before 1932.[4] The Museum's cabinets are unusual, not only by virtue of their Brazilian rosewood veneer (Ruhlmann generally used macassar ebony, amboyna, or amaranth) but because they form a matched pair. One of the fundamental principles that Ruhlmann applied in his interiors, especially those of the 1920s, was symmetry. Accordingly, he often specified pairs in his architectonic furnishing plans, using pedestals, tables, and cabinets to flank centrally positioned doors or windows. Curiously, no other pairs of this model are known.

57 | Carpet

É.-J. RUHLMANN AND ÉMILE GAUDISSARD
ca. 1925; wool, cotton

While the furniture of Ruhlmann et Laurent is noted for the subtle richness of materials, refinement of line, and exquisite craftsmanship, their patterned designs—for carpets, textiles, and wallpapers—are more flamboyant. The vivid palette and motion-filled design of this carpet are typical of Ruhlmann's taste for vibrant color and pattern. Pink, orange, red, ecru, grey, and blue are juxtaposed in scrolling swirls of stylized plant and flower motifs on a field encircled by a geometric border. The integration of color and pattern shows close ties to other avant-garde arts of the period, from Fauve paintings to the sets and costumes of the Ballets Russes.

The model seems to have been created for the intimate round boudoir of the Ruhlmann pavilion at the 1925 Paris Exposition.[1] The fair's official catalogue cites Émile Gaudissard as the sole designer, but because working drawings survive in the Ruhlmann Archive, it is more likely to have been a collaborative effort between the two designers.[2] Indeed, the design can be said to show both their hands. Ruhlmann had been sketching round carpets with floral and spiral motifs since before the war, and similar stylized leaf and geometric forms can be found in carpets by Gaudissard. During the mid-1920s, Ruhlmann decorated the apartment of the British newspaper publisher Lord Rothermere and his wife, Margaret Hunam Redhead, on the Champs-Élysées, and for their round boudoir he used the same model carpet.[3]

In 1925, Metropolitan Museum curator Joseph Breck considered the acquisition of another Ruhlmann carpet, one that was displayed in the study of the Ruhlmann pavilion at the 1925 Paris Expo. Designed in collaboration with the painter and illustrator Léon Voguet, it was decidedly more modern, with a meandering irregular pattern of calligraphic black lines set on a creamy white ground.[4] An employee by the name of Rousseau at Ruhlmann et Laurent wrote to Breck in July 1925, expressing his regret that Breck had decided against buying it.[5]

É.-J. Ruhlmann. Boudoir, with Ruhlmann–Gaudissard carpet, Hôtel du Collectionneur, Exposition Internationale des Arts Décoratifs et Industriels Modernes, Paris, 1925

58 | Lamp

ca. 1926; gilt bronze, alabaster

Ruhlmann often adapted forms and decorative motifs to meet a variety of needs. One form to which he returned time and again was the inverted bell, which he used, varying its proportions, for vases, teacups, lampshades, and other small objects.[1] The shape was realized in many materials, including metal, porcelain, or, as in this case, alabaster. On occasion, it was also set right-side-up when used for a textile lampshade.

This lamp comprises a translucent alabaster shade raised on a high gilt-bronze tripod base. The attenuated legs (open on the inside), one of which houses the electrical cord, taper inward toward the shallow domed foot. The shade rests on a heavy reeded collar that houses the bulb socket. When the bulb is illuminated, the mottled alabaster casts a warm outward ambient glow, while brighter, more focused light is directed upward.

Indirect lighting, in which the lighting source is hidden, was a new concept in the 1920s. Ruhlmann designed a number of lighting fixtures that used inverted-bell shades to conceal the light source, including wall sconces, table lamps, and monumental standing lamps.[2] Some shades were a shallow bowl, others a deep vase. The overall conception of this lamp probably derives from the *athénienne*, a Neoclassical form popular in late eighteenth-century France. Little more than a bowl (sometimes with a cover) raised on three legs, the *athénienne* served multiple purposes: it could be used as a planter or torchère, a perfume burner, a washstand, or the like. Generally made of metal (to withstand both fire and water), the fanciest *athéniennes* were made of gilt bronze by master metalworkers such as Martin-Guillaume Biennais (1764–1843), Pierre Gouthière (1732–1813), and Pierre-Philippe Thomire (1751–1843).

Ruhlmann's first documented use of this lamp was in 1926, in the home of the industrialist Henri Fricotelle, where a pair was placed on the dining room sideboard.[3] In 1930, another pair was displayed on a sideboard in the Ruhlmann et Laurent showrooms, in an exhibition that juxtaposed Ruhlmann's modern furnishings with eighteenth-century French paintings, sculpture, and silver. The gilt-bronze lamps were a perfect complement to the three Rococo-era paintings in carved and presumably gilded wood frames that hung behind them.

Ruhlmann et Laurent showroom, with Ruhlmann lamps, 1930

Martin-Guillaume Biennais (1764–1843). Gilt-bronze and mahogany *athénienne* made for Napoleon I, ca. 1804–14. Château de Fontainebleau (F24C)

JEAN SERRIÈRE

Nancy 1893–1968 Paris

While the name Jean Serrière is now unknown to all but the most dedicated students of French Art Deco, in his day he was considered an artist-craftsman of considerable interest, and his work was frequently and enthusiastically covered in the press.[1] He seems to have been something of a jack-of-all-trades, in the manner of such nineteenth-century industrial designers as the British Christopher Dresser (1834–1904) and the Dutch T.A.C. Colenbrander (1841–1930), who turned their hands to a wide range of design projects as they came their way. What separates Serrière from these designers was his skill as a craftsman (industrial designers rarely realized their own designs). More important, he considered himself not only a designer but an artist:

In reality . . . there is art as such, which cannot be learned, and métiers, which must be taught if they are to be in the service of art. Although the métier does not make the artist, the practice of a skill can bring some artists to life, even as others remain craftsmen . . . , whatever their pretensions to art.[2]

Born in Nancy, Serrière moved to Paris to study painting and sculpture. After the war, he decided to learn a métier, and found himself naturally drawn to metalworking:

Although I was not born hammering metal, I have — ever since I could hold a pencil or a brush — at least drawn and painted. But I also wanted to have a métier. I began modeling my objects in wax, then gradually I learned to produce them myself in copper or silver. I try to make metal objects that are "sculpture" and not simply decorations on forms.[3]

Serrière's efforts to bring together the fine and decorative arts were praised by the critic Guillaume Janneau in 1923:

He is a sculptor, indeed an architect; he likes bold lines, bold masses, bold forms. His silver vases . . . are less silverwork than statuary.[4]

Serrière quickly mastered both silversmithing and dinanderie, and was recognized as one of the most accomplished metalworkers of his day. His early training as a painter would afford him a successful career in that field as well, and with both skills he designed fans, tapestries, ceramics, furniture, and enamels. As luck would have it, Serrière's mother was secretary to Adrien-Aurélien Hébrard, owner of the Hébrard bronze foundry and the Galerie Hébrard in Paris. Hébrard took an interest in his work, and beginning in 1919 Serrière annually displayed both metalwork and paintings at the gallery.

Every year . . . Jean Serrière exhibits his most recent work at the Galerie Hébrard. And it is always with the same refined pleasure that lovers of art rediscover the works of that sensitive and informed artist.[5]

At the 1925 Paris Exposition, Hébard paid Serrière the compliment of displaying his works alone within the gallery's small pavilion.

During the 1920s, Serrière participated in the Salon d'Automne and in many of the exhibitions of the Société des Artistes Décorateurs. In 1922 the French State acquired one of his dinanderie works, and in 1923 the Metropolitan Museum purchased his chalice (opposite). Serrière's metalwork was included in the Inaugural Exposition of French Art at the California Palace of the Legion of Honor in San Francisco

in 1924–25, in the American Association of Museums' traveling exhibition of works from the 1925 Paris Exposition, and at the Macy's International Exposition of Art in Industry in New York in 1928.

Serrière first began working in enamel in the mid-1920s. In 1928 he made two large enameled wall panels for the SS *Île de France*, and he continued to explore the medium until his death in 1968. He was made a chevalier of the Légion d'Honneur in 1938.

59 | Chalice
ca. 1923; silver

This elegant chalice has great presence. Its impressive scale is matched by the simplicity of its form and the boldness of its decoration: a plain hemispherical bowl and inverted bell-form foot offset with an exuberant repoussé stem depicting grapes on a vine. The form is a traditional one, steeped in ceremony and meaning, and Serrière's choice of motif further relates it to wine, if not specifically to the celebration of the Eucharist. Indeed, it is possible that Serrière conceived this piece as a communion cup.

Serrière first displayed the model in a 1922 exhibition held at the Musée Galliera in Paris, where it was reviewed by critic Guillaume Janneau:

M. Jean Serrière is exhibiting, in addition to a silver flagon, two admirable pieces of silver: a chalice and a ciborium. M. Jean Serrière is one of those rare craftsmen who possess a sense of the plastic. His intelligent hammer knows how to avoid the thinness of form that takes away voluptuousness, without which there is no art.[1]

The following year the Metropolitan Museum acquired this example, which may have been the same one displayed at the Musée Galliera. Another critic, Armand Dayot, had already considered Serrière's contributions representative of the best modern French design:

His works in silver, with bold and appealing decorations, often borrow their lines from our handsome models of times past. . . . [Yet] all his work is filled with new accents, unexpected and gracious, and with an elegance that is altogether French. No foreign influence here; everything derives from the purest national tradition, reinvented with perfect and very personal taste, within a thoroughly modern decorative conception. . . . Everything is at once new and traditional, but essentially personal. From today, we hail his appearance with joy and with hope.[2]

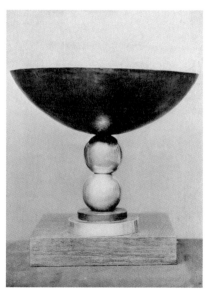

Jean Serrière. Silver coupe, plate 28 in Gérard Sandoz, *Objets usuels* [1928]

HENRI SIMMEN

Montdidier 1879–1963 Nice

EUGÉNIE JUBIN, KNOWN AS O'KIN

Yokohama, Japan, 1880–1948 Nice

Although each had specialized skills and an established reputation, husband and wife Henri Simmen and Eugénie Jubin frequently collaborated with one another. Simmen was a renowned potter, while Jubin excelled in *tabletterie*, carving and turning delicate materials such as ivory, tortoiseshell, horn, and wood to make fans, combs, buttons, chess pieces, and the like. Perhaps because their work is characterized by an understated elegance, it has tended to be overlooked—but it is just this quality that makes it extraordinary.

Born in the northern French town of Montdidier, Simmen trained initially as an architect while also taking courses in pottery at the Conservatoire des Arts et Métiers in Paris.[1] Soon after 1900 he was studying with the noted French art potter Edmond Lachenal, under whose influence he discovered traditional French vernacular pottery. About 1907 he established his own studio in Meudon, a suburb of Paris. Simmen's work from this period—mostly salt-glazed stoneware—was usually decorated with geometric or pictorial friezes; sometimes it had flambé glazes. In 1907 he first displayed his work at the Société des Artistes Décorateurs and was a regular participant in its annual Salons. His career was interrupted by the war, during which he served at the front.

In 1919, Simmen embarked on a three-year journey to China, Japan, and Korea to study local pottery techniques. He returned to Europe in 1921 and established a new studio in Montredon, near Marseilles. Profoundly influenced by what he had seen in Asia, for the rest of his career he used only traditional methods and materials, rejecting the use of modern technology. His work was described by the architect and critic Frantz Jourdain:

It is . . . to the Orient that Simmen owes a part of his formation. Drawing inspiration from primitive Asian techniques, he uses only natural materials: rocks, minerals, lavas, basalt, oak ash, camellia, and bamboo, never making use of modern chemistry. He never refines the minerals he uses in his glazes—copper, iron, chromium, and cobalt—but grinds them just as they are, with all their natural impurities, which, when fired, create unexpected results. . . . Simmen has studied with [potters] in China and Japan. His stoneware, made without the use of a potter's wheel, is high-fired, and shows in its very carefully considered forms a painted decoration whose beauty develops harshly under the violent action of a scorching fire that sometimes burns them too roughly, too passionately, but which marks them with an allure, a power, and an incomparable beauty.[2]

Works made at the Montredon studio are characterized by an Asian-inspired subtlety. Simmen's hand-thrown pots were sometimes modeled in low relief or engraved with geometric motifs, though he also drew formal inspiration from nature, shaping some vessels like strange fruits or vegetables. He favored milky and irregular monochromatic glazes in rich tones of red, green, yellow, and white. He also experimented with aventurine glazes. Pieces were sometimes adorned with delicately carved wood or ivory stoppers, lids, or stands made by his wife. In the 1930s he began to make ceramic sculptures, using text as decoration.

Simmen participated in three world's fairs: the 1911 International Exhibition in Turin and both the 1925 and 1937 Paris Expositions, and during his lifetime his work was included in a number of museum exhibitions.[3] Beginning in 1921, he was represented primarily by the galleries Rouard and

La Crémaillère in Paris. Illness forced Simmen to stop making pottery after the Second World War.

Eugénie Jubin was born in Yokohama, Japan, in 1880. She appears to have moved to France by the early years of the twentieth century. While her European name suggests that she had a French father, it is likely that her mother was Japanese.[4] Professionally—perhaps to call attention to her non-European roots—she used the exotic-sounding name O'Kin.[5] It is unclear when she and Simmen were married.

Although sometimes referred to as a sculptor or an ivory worker, O'Kin was in fact a *tablettière*, trained in the full range of *tabletterie* under the renowned Henri Hamm.[6] It is not known if she maintained her own studio, but it is safe to assume that she accompanied Simmen on his travels.[7] While she often collaborated with him, O'Kin is today best known for her precious, tiny-scaled ivory work, which recalls Japanese netsuke carving. She first exhibited her work—jewelry, hair combs, and buttons—in 1907, participating that year in three of the most prestigious of the annual Salons, those of the Société Nationale des Beaux-Arts, the Société des Artistes Français, and the Salon d'Automne. In 1924 she took part in an exhibition at the Ruhlmann showrooms, probably contributing small decorative objects for an ensemble titled "Furniture for a Young Lady." And at the 1925 Paris Exposition, she contributed a group of sculptural ivories—bottles, bas-reliefs, and pendants—to the Ruhlmann pavilion; they were displayed in vitrines at the building's entrance.

Both Simmen and O'Kin were advocates for the artist-craftsman. In 1924, in anticipation of the 1925 Expo, Simmen commented:

There is no doubt that the role of each [of us] in the creation of an object must be clearly defined. . . . Artist-craftsmen are becoming rarer by the day, and it is only right to bring their work to the public's attention with a special notice: "Designed and executed by the maker." The extensive study and considerable effort needed to master the technique of their art must not allow [their works] to be confused with [those by] designers who have their works made [by others].

My wife, Mme O'Kin, who works in the same manner as I, also recommends establishing precisely defined categorizations.[8]

60 | Lidded Jar

HENRI SIMMEN

1921–23; salt-glazed stoneware

This tiny covered jar in the form of an abstracted pinecone, each of its scales clearly demarcated, is made from salt-glazed stoneware, the traditional French vernacular pottery medium in which Simmen specialized. Although he produced many such works at his first studio in Meudon before the war, the stylized naturalism of this piece is probably Asian in inspiration, supporting a date after his 1921 return from China, Japan, and Korea. The form may also represent a holdover from Art Nouveau, which was characterized by the incorporation of organic motifs. As Art Nouveau gradually evolved into Art Deco during the first decades of the twentieth century, designers adapted such motifs to reflect the simplified stylizations that were a hallmark of the new taste.

61 | Lidded Jar

HENRI SIMMEN AND O'KIN
ca. 1929; aventurine-glazed stoneware, wood,
ivory, gold leaf

This diminutive jar is arguably the most exquisite French Art Deco ceramic in the Metropolitan's collection. It is a collaboration between Simmen, who created the vessel, and O'Kin, who carved and gilded the lid. Although the overall conception of the piece—an Asian-inspired shouldered jar with a wood cover—is traditional, nothing about it is ordinary.

The jar represents an outstanding example of the sort of pottery Simmen produced at his Montredon studio during the 1920s. The simplicity of its form and the modesty of its material are offset by the seductive shimmer of the orange-brown aventurine glaze, which transforms a humble object into a precious and elegant work of art. Simmen experimented with this technique after his return from Asia in 1921 and used it on a number of pieces. The effect was likely achieved by introducing certain minerals—in this case, probably hematite, which lends sparkle to aventurine quartz—to the lead-based glaze medium. Shortly after the jar was acquired by the Metropolitan, curator Joseph Breck wrote:

Around the beginning of the seventeenth century there was invented at Murano a variety of yellowish or brownish glass in which are fused little particles of copper or silicate of copper that gleam like gold. The composition having been discovered by accident, the glass was called avventurino, or in English, aventurine. Pottery covered with a glaze resembling this sparkling aventurine glass is now being made by the French ceramist, Henri Simmen, and a beautiful example of his work is included among the new purchases. The carved ivory cover of the vase is by the artist's wife, Mme Okim [sic].[1]

The precious quality of Simmen's jar is augmented by O'Kin's delicate lid, a netsuke-like ivory carving attached to an ivory disc foot, which in turn is set atop a stepped wood lid. The apparent charm of the iconography is deceptive. Peeking out from beneath a leafy curl are what look to be enchanting miniature fruits or flower buds. In fact, they are sea anemones. Closely related to jellyfish, these predatory undersea creatures use venom-filled tentacles to ensnare their prey and draw it into a central mouth cavity (here represented by a gilded dot at the center of each anemone). Swirling tentacles carved into the ivory foot seem to wave gently, as if beckoning from a watery seabed. A subtle detail on the lid reveals itself only on close inspection: the outer edge of the lip which fits into the jar's opening is lightly gilded. Until the cover is removed, one is unaware of this unnecessary but altogether luxurious detail.

Like the sea anemone itself, this covered jar has a strange, otherworldly beauty. Its dazzling allure suggests something vaguely unsettling and dangerous. It is a vamp of the decorative arts.

SÉRAPHIN SOUDBININE

Nijni-Novgorod, Russia, 1867–1944 Paris

Séraphin Nikolaevich Soubdinine, born in Russia in 1867, was a man of many talents and careers.[1] He first trained as an opera singer in Russia, under the renowned Feodor Chaliapin (whom he would later sculpt). Around 1902 he moved to Paris, where he studied sculpture with Auguste Rodin. His work was displayed at the Salon d'Automne as early as 1906. He continued to work as a sculptor, in the stylized, figural mode, into the mid-1920s.

Soudbinine made at least three trips to New York between 1923 and 1926. During this time he collaborated with Jean Dunand on an important pair of lacquered screens for the Long Island house of Mr. and Mrs. Solomon R. Guggenheim (see no. 20). In 1926, the Reinhardt Galleries in New York displayed three of his screens. The screens were lacquered, but because Soudbinine was not a lacquer artist, it is likely that they too were made with Dunand. While in New York, Soudbinine is believed to have visited the Metropolitan Museum, where he encountered Asian ceramics, an experience that prompted him to abandon his career as a sculptor and devote himself to pottery. In Paris he set up a studio and kiln, both destroyed in the Second World War. He is best known today for his sculptural works in stoneware.

See no. 20.

LOUIS SÜE

Bourdeaux 1875–1968 Paris

ANDRÉ MARE

Argentan 1885–1932 Paris

"'*Evolution* within *tradition*.' A complete manifesto in two words."[1] With this phrase, critic Jean Gallotti concisely summed up the work of Louis Süe and André Mare.[2] Although each designer was successful in his own right, it was their joint direction of La Compagnie des Arts Français from 1919 to 1928 that brought them their greatest recognition. And while their ensemblier business was dedicated to reviving the traditional arts of France, their respect for tradition was tempered by an understanding of the tastes and requirements of the modern world. Conceived as a collaborative venture, the firm employed the talents of many artists and craftsmen to create grand interiors for a rich and highly sophisticated clientele. Theirs were among the first examples of Art Deco furniture to be acquired by the Metropolitan Museum in 1923.

Louis Süe, the older of the two, was born to a family of prosperous wine merchants. He showed an early interest in art and moved to Paris in 1895 to enroll in the École des Beaux-Arts, where he studied painting and architecture and befriended the painters Pierre Bonnard, Roger de La Fresnaye, André Derain, and André Dunoyer de Segonzac. His paintings were displayed at the Salon des Indépendents and the Salon d'Automne in 1902.

In 1903, Süe founded an architectural partnership with Paul Huillard, a classmate from the École, and over the next nine years, they would realize a number of projects — mainly residential — in and around Paris. From the start, Süe's work was characterized by duality, demonstrating a thorough knowledge of history and respect for tradition and a keen interest in the new.

About 1909, Süe was commissioned by the couturier Paul Poiret (see pages 162–66) to remodel an eighteenth-century house that served as his atelier, showroom, and residence. Süe's proposed renovations (the project was never realized) drew heavily on recent avant-garde design from Vienna, namely that of the Wiener Werkstätte, a designers' cooperative founded in 1903 and dedicated to the creation of the "total work of art," where every element of the domestic environment was overseen by a master designer with the objective of achieving aesthetic unity. In 1910, Süe and Poiret themselves went to Vienna to visit the Werkstätte; it would later serve as the model for both Poiret's Atelier Martine and Süe's Compagnie des Arts Français.

About the same time, Süe was exposed to Cubism, probably through his painter friends, many of whom were members of the Puteaux Group, a collective of painters, sculptors, poets, and critics who gravitated around the three Duchamp brothers, Jacques Villon (born Gaston Duchamp), Raymond Duchamp-Villon, and Marcel Duchamp, whose studio was in Puteaux, a suburb of Paris. The members of the group, which came together around 1911, were united in their attempt to reconcile Cubism with expressionist color theory and in their belief that in their compositions the fractured abstractions of Cubism would become stronger and more harmonious through the application of the principles of the Golden Section, the ancient formula for ideal proportion.

Although the influence of Cubism is not evident in Süe's painting, Cubistic simplification and abstraction are explicit in his architectural designs, underscoring his belief that construction and geometry form the basis of any successful design. He first presented complete room settings at the 1910 Salon d'Automne and would throughout his career participate regularly in the annual Paris Salons.

In 1912, Süe dissolved his architectural association with Huillard and, with Roger de La Fresnaye, André Groult, Gustave Jaulmes, André Mare, and the brothers André and Paul Vera, among others, established L'Atelier Français, an ensemblier business loosely modeled on the Wiener Werkstätte. Rather than following the direction of a single master designer, however, each member of the group worked independently, though with a shared point of view. Their philosophy was formalized in a 1912 manifesto written by André Vera, which set forth their objective of bringing clarity, order, and aesthetic unity to interior design through a combination of tradition and modernity.[3] While inspiration was drawn from the forms, decorative motifs, materials, and techniques of preindustrial France (especially from the era of Louis-Philippe), the rigorous simplifications and geometric stylizations of Cubism informed their designs, enlivened by a boldly modern color palette. The Atelier Français was short-lived, ending with the advent of war in 1914.[4] During the war years, Süe served with the French Army in southern Greece.

André Mare was Süe's junior by ten years. Like Süe, he moved to Paris to study painting and sculpture, first at the École Nationale des Arts Décoratifs and later at the Académie Julian. He exhibited his work at the Salon d'Automne and the Salon des Indépendants. In 1905 he set up a painting studio with his childhood friend Fernand Léger, taking an active part in the Paris art scene, especially among the artists who made up the Puteaux Group. Mare's first efforts in the decorative arts were motifs for bookbindings — mainly bouquets and vases of flowers — which he exhibited at the Salon d'Automne in 1909. Like Süe, he would be an active participant in the Paris Salons. In 1910 he assisted the ensemblier André Groult with his display at the Salon d'Automne and by the following year was presenting his own fully furnished room settings. The year 1912 brought a collaboration with the Puteaux Group in the creation of the notorious Maison Cubiste, presented at the Salon d'Automne.[5] The same year, he joined Süe's Atelier Français.

Mare's war service included the development of Cubist-inspired camouflage patterns to disguise artillery. He survived mustard-gas poisoning and was seriously wounded, which severely compromised his health; he died at the age of forty-seven.

In the spring of 1919, having returned to civilian life in Paris, Süe and Mare received a commission, together with the painter Gustave Jaulmes, to design a memorial cenotaph and decorate the triumphal route along the Champs-Élysées for a victory celebration parade. They also formalized the organization of Belle France, an atelier that several months later would evolve into La Compagnie des Arts Français. Under the direction of Süe and Mare, with premises at 116, rue du Faubourg Saint-Honoré, the business was from the beginning known as Süe et Mare.[6]

Süe et Mare was a classic ensemblier establishment, meeting the needs of its clients in all areas of the built environment: architecture, interior decoration, furniture, carpets, textiles, wallpapers, lighting, and decorative accessories. Furniture was made in the studio; textiles, wallpapers, lighting, ceramics, glass, and hardware were generally produced by outside workshops. Among its first commissions was the decoration, in 1919, of the French Embassy in Washington D.C. The firm not only worked on custom projects but also, hoping to help manufacturers that were failing in the wake of the war, explored serial production of inexpensive yet elegant furniture made with standardized elements.

The company's philosophy was essentially that of the Atelier Français, combining modernity with a respect for tradition. The critic Léon Deshairs, writing in 1920, described the singular collaboration of the two designers:

Having only just returned to peacetime work, M. Süe and M. Mare have exhibited, under their dual signature . . . both "unique" furniture and "mass-produced" furniture: clean, simple, and intelligible, like the clear expression of a sure thought, pleasing in its singular mix of innovation and tradition.

[Their designs are] obviously not the work of improvisers submissively following fashion or driven by their own imagination. A precise will manifests itself.[7]

He went on to quote Süe and Mare themselves:

When we study the masterpieces of architecture and the arts that adorn it, we see that their harmony resides in a more or less hidden geometry. Certain proportions and certain lines have special properties. Not all triangles,

not all rectangles, and not all ovals are equally beauti-
ful. . . . It is the presence, visible or concealed, of such
figures . . . [with] their contrasts and relationships, that
brings to a façade or a piece of furniture its rhythm and
harmony.[8]

The designers explained their specific preference for
the Louis-Philippe period as a source of inspiration:

The Louis-Philippe style, long in favor in our prov-
inces, is the last of the [truly] French styles. It is a bit
ungainly, but serious, logical, welcoming. [The style]
responded to needs that we still have today. Its forms are
so rational that even the carriage maker of today who
designs a bucket seat for an automobile unintentionally
stumbles upon them once more. We are not taking up the
style again; we are not continuing it to make a point; we
rediscover it in seeking simple solutions, and through it
we reestablish ties to our magnificent past. We are not
producing a fashionable art.

Some modern interiors are conceived in such a way
that it is impossible to bring in an eighteenth-century
engraving in an antique frame without creating a mis-
match of styles. By contrast, we would like any beauti-
ful piece of furniture from the past to be at home amidst
our furniture, to be received there as a relative and not
as an intruder.[9]

Süe et Mare's clients included the couturier
Jean Patou, the actress Jane Renouardt, the Duke
of Medinaceli, the jeweler Robert Linzeler, Fontaine
et Cie (a high-end locksmith and hardware manufacturer), Parfumerie d'Orsay, and the F. Pinet shoe
company. The firm designed first-class staterooms
on the SS *Paris* (1921) and the first-class salon on
the SS *Île de France* (1927). It also designed the Salle
Moderne in the sportswear department at Bergdorf
Goodman in New York, probably in 1927.

At the 1925 Paris Exposition, Süe et Mare had
its own pavilion — Un Musée d'Art Contemporain — prominently situated on the Esplanade des
Invalides (see nos. 65, 66); across the Esplanade
was the nearly identical pavilion of Fontaine et
Cie, which the firm also furnished. Süe et Mare was

further responsible for the decoration of the Salle
des Fêtes in the Grand Palais and supplied works to
other pavilions, including the Ambassade Francaise.

Although Süe et Mare did not often participate
in international exhibitions, its work was included
in both the American Association of Museums'
traveling exhibition of works from the 1925 Paris
Expo and the exhibition of French decorative arts
held at the Tokyo Imperial Museum in 1928. In 1925
both designers were made chevaliers of the Légion
d'Honneur. Süe would be elected an officer in 1936.

Despite its productivity, the cost of the business
was prohibitive. In 1922, La Compagnie des Arts
Français found a financial backer in Gaston Monteux,
owner of the Raoul shoe manufacturing company.
Before his death in 1928, Monteux sold the company
to the Galeries Lafayette department store, which
brought in the modernist designer Jacques Adnet.
Adnet's design proclivities ran counter to those
of Süe and Mare. They left the business in 1928,
although it continued to operate until 1960.

Mare returned to painting. Süe went on to work
as a successful independent architect and decorator, with a fashionable international clientele that
included Daisy Fellowes, Comtesse Jean de Polignac, and Helena Rubinstein. He designed a suite
for the SS *Normandie* and ventured into theater,
creating stage sets for the Comédie-Française. An
active participant in exhibitions of the Société des
Artistes Décorateurs, he was elected vice president
in 1939. During the Second World War, Süe lived
in Istanbul, where he was a lecturer at the Institute
of Fine Arts. He returned to France in 1945 and
resumed his work as an architect, forming a partnership with his nephew Gilbert-Olivier Süe in 1947.

In its nine years under Süe and Mare's direction,
La Compagnie des Arts Français produced nearly
two thousand designs for approximately sixty different projects. Jean Gallotti praised their work:

In it, we see admirably resolved the problem posed by
those three words: modern, local, and traditional. . . .
We like refreshing our eyes on works where the smile
of our native land is reflected in youth and vitality.[10]

62 | Side Chair

LOUIS SÜE

designed ca. 1912, manufactured ca. 1920;
walnut, silk velvet

About 1910 many French designers began to mine their national past. The historical styles of the late eighteenth and early nineteenth centuries provided not only formal and ornamental sources for new designs, but also manufacturing techniques and materials that recalled an era when objects were handmade by guild-trained craftsmen rather than by machines. The conscious linking of modern design to the preindustrial past was key to the desire to reestablish the traditional role of France—dating from the eighteenth century—as the leader in the luxury trades.

Foremost among these designers were several associated with L'Atelier Français—particularly its founder, Louis Süe, and his collaborators André Mare and the brothers André and Paul Vera. For inspiration, they looked to the era of Louis-Philippe I (r. 1830–48), which corresponded with the rise of the middle class, in the belief that the decorative arts produced during that time—in contrast to the aristocratic preciousness of those of the eighteenth-century ancien régime—were best suited to the requirements of the modern world.

This charming and unpretentious side chair (Süe et Mare model no. 208) exemplifies their approach. Sturdily constructed from solid walnut (rather than more expensive imported wood such as mahogany),

its Neoclassical form and decoration are stylish yet restrained. The back splat is carved in low relief with a woven basket filled with garden roses. The crest rail is edged in a twisted rope design that terminates in carved tassels. The curved stiles evolve into saber-shaped rear legs, while the tapered forelegs are vertically grooved. The stretchers form an integral part of the design. Not only do they add strength to the chair's construction, they project an image of down-to-earth provinciality that ties the chair to French tradition. The brown silk velvet upholstery is original. The basket-of-flowers motif, while designed by Süe alone, typifies the work of L'Atelier Français and relates closely to motifs by André Mare that were used to illustrate the Atelier's manifesto of 1912.[1]

It is unclear when Süe conceived this specific model, although in 1912 he designed a nearly identical variant for the Atelier Français, which he presented the same year at the Salon d'Automne. That chair's painted back splat featured a squatter basket resting on a horizontal band of diamond-patterned openwork.[2] The Metropolitan's later example was made after Süe and Mare formed La Compagnie des Arts Français in 1919. The chair was shown in the Süe et Mare display at the 1921 Salon of the Société des Artistes Décorateurs, and it is possible that Süe made the modifications to his earlier design at that time.

In an article that appeared in 1922, the American writer Leo Randole spoke of the wedding of art and industry that found expression in the work of Süe et Mare:

In a nation where the gift of art is as traditional as it is innate, even the most revolutionary modernist turns constantly to the past for his inspiration, his justification. The modern decorator in his intellectual asceticism penetrates the past through the logic of geometry, which so infallibly defines the equilibrium of all harmony. . . . It is to such men as the Süe et Mare group, who have become craftsmen without ceasing to be artists, that is assigned the leading place to-day in this era of renaissance in the decorative arts through which France is passing. . . . The mating of creative minds, imbued with the aesthetic impulse, to the commercial skill which makes possible the wide distribution of beautiful objects is a characteristic of the hour in which we may all rejoice.[3]

63 | Four Textiles

a | *Abondance*
ANDRÉ MARE
designed ca. 1911; manufactured
after 1918; silk

b | *Draperies*
ANDRÉ MARE
ca. 1919; cotton

c | *Bouquets*
LOUIS SÜE
ca. 1919; silk

d | *Paris*
LOUIS SÜE
ca. 1919; silk

Louis Süe and André Mare. Grand salon, alcove with *Abondance* textile by André Mare, Un Musée d'Art Contemporain, Exposition Internationale des Arts Décoratifs et Industriels Modernes, Paris, 1925

Like many artists of his day, painter André Mare expanded his repertoire to the decorative arts as a means of augmenting his income. At the 1909 Salon d'Automne, he presented designs for bookbindings, many employing a recurring motif: a bouquet, basket, or bowl of flowers, usually roses. Although his use of this traditional motif was not unique—Paul Iribe (see no. 25) and the Vera brothers used it extensively—the stylized uniformity of his compositions made them new and entirely his own. He would develop floral motifs into repeat patterns for textiles and wallpapers, some of which were put into production before the war. During the war, when Mare was serving abroad, his wife oversaw their continued production. They were later manufactured for and retailed through Belle France and La Compagnie des Arts Français.

Probably the earliest documented textile is *Abondance* (Süe et Mare pattern no. 1003), an exuberant composition of bowls of fruit surrounded by curling leaves and cornucopias filled with flowers, which Mare used as a wall hanging in his display at the 1911 Salon d'Automne. It is unclear who the prewar manufacturer was, but after the war it was produced as a damask by two Lyons silk weavers: Lamy & Gautier and Lauer.[1] Süe and Mare included a full-page reproduction in their 1921 manifesto *Architectures*. They also used it as a wall covering in their pavilion at the 1925 Paris Exposition (see above). The Metropolitan's sample consists of two lengths in vivid yellow-green, sewn together side by side to make a double repeat.

Draperies (pattern no. 1308) is a printed cotton percale with similar baskets of fruit and bowls of flowers, although here they are surrounded with swags of drapery. It is unclear when the pattern was originally designed—though it would reasonably date to the same time as *Abondance*—or first produced; the manufacturer is also unknown. According to notes from Süe and Mare in the Museum's files, the textile was exhibited in 1922, probably in their display at the Salon of the Société des Artistes Décorateurs. The Metropolitan's length is executed in tones of blue and grey on a neutral ground.

While Süe's prewar textile designs tend toward the rigidly stylized and architectonic, the postwar designs are downright theatrical.[2] *Bouquets* (pattern no. 1004) presents a dense pattern of clustered flowers tied with ribbons. The Metropolitan's silk damask is woven in gold against a puce ground. Like Mare's *Abondance*, *Bouquets* was produced in Lyons by both Lamy & Gautier and Lauer.[3]

Süe's *Paris* silk damask (pattern no. 1007), here woven in tones of blue and grey, is perhaps the most spectacular of the group. Bunches of flowers tied with knotted bows are set against folding fans and feathered plumes. The curling feathers generically suggest a fleur-de-lis (lily flower), traditional symbol of the French Bourbon monarchy. Süe probably selected the motif to evoke the grandeur of the eighteenth-century ancien régime.

64 | Commode and Mirror

a | Commode
LOUIS SÜE, ANDRÉ MARE, AND PAUL VERA
ca. 1918; oak, lumber-core plywood,
chestnut, *Verde di Levanto* marble, paint,
gold leaf

b | Mirror
LOUIS SÜE AND ANDRÉ MARE
designed ca. 1919, manufactured 1923; cherry
or pearwood, mirror glass, paint, gold leaf

Members of La Compagnie des Arts Français seem to have exhibited works together even before they formalized their association as such in 1919. In May 1918 several designers displayed works at the Galerie Devambez in Paris, including a commode of this design decorated in a black-and-gold scheme. A review of the exhibition described the commode as "semiclassical in inspiration, while remaining very modern and perfectly original."[1] Although attributed solely to Paul Vera, the commode was in fact a collaborative effort between Vera, Louis Süe, and André Mare. Süe et Mare showed the same commode again the following year, at the 1919 Salon of the Société des Artistes Décorateurs. Critic Roger Allard described the contributions of each designer:

M. Louis Süe, with his sumptuous taste that is evolving from a somewhat precious mannerism to [an appreciation for] fullness of form . . . M. André Mare, with all the gifts of an exquisite and robust colorist, and M. Paul Vera, with the ingenuity of a true ornamentalist have together juxtaposed the French "look"—at once stylish and tasteful—with the delicious and splendid fantasies that are currently in fashion.[2]

In other words, Süe provided the form, Mare the color scheme, and Vera the decorative program. The 1919 display also included an oval mirror, hung above the commode. La Compagnie des Arts Français used both models again in its display at the Mostra Internazionale di Arte Decorative in Monza, Italy, in 1923.

The Metropolitan's commode and mirror are variants of those shown in 1919 and 1923. Süe's two-drawer commode (a variant of Süe et Mare model no. 501) is traditional in inspiration, with faceted octagonal legs, a band of decorative gadrooning along the bottom edge, and a *Verde di Levanto* marble slab top with beveled edges.[3] Mare's green-and-gold color scheme specifically recalls *vernis Martin*, an imitation lacquer developed in the 1730s by French craftsman Guillaume Martin and his brothers. And Vera's lavishly gilded decoration presents the mythological story of the Judgment of Paris. Having been summoned as judge, to choose the most beautiful of the three goddesses Hera, Athena, and Aphrodite, the shepherd Paris is shown awarding the golden apple to Aphrodite.

Vera may have first conceived the motif as a simple woodcut; he used a close variant as an illustration for his brother's 1919 book *Les Jardins*.[4] Here, he expands the composition with sketchy clouds and a heavy floral swag. The motifs on the side panels—one depicting a hand mirror and the other a fan (opposite), both set with flowers—also relate closely to the woodcuts for *Les Jardins*.[5] The decoration was probably applied to the commode's green-painted surface by a specialized craftsman using a stencil.

Süe and Mare conceived the green-and-gold oval mirror (a variant of Süe et Mare model no. 802) to be shown with the commode. The lower half is composed of twin cornucopias—with a scrolled detail at the point where they meet at the bottom—from which springs an arc of gilded flowers. The design is a variant on the earlier black-and-gold version, and was made to order for the Metropolitan in 1923, when the Museum decided to purchase the commode.[6] Of the acquisition, curator Joseph Breck wrote in the Museum's *Bulletin* that year:

The rocket-like career of l'art nouveau was a warning too conspicuous to be disregarded; and a period of sober experimentation ensued in which problems of design were studied with closer reference to historical precedent and originality was sought with more discretion. This furniture has many virtues but rarely charm. The pursuit of this elusive quality—surrounded by pitfalls for the unwary—preoccupies the contemporary designer.

A commode and mirror . . . have this charm in no small measure. Both pieces are lacquered in dark green; the mirror is richly carved and gilded; the commode decorated in gold lacquer with a composition representing The Judgment of Paris. The commode and mirror were designed by Louis Süe and André Mare; the lacquer decoration is by Paul Vera. These three artists, with other kindred spirits, compose an association known as La Compagnie des Arts Français. In the work of these designers . . . a tendency to return to the style of Louis-Philippe as a "point de départ" for original creation is evident.[7]

65 | Desk and Chair

a | Desk, ca. 1925; ebonized wood (probably
beech), oak, zebrawood, gilt bronze, leather

b | Desk Chair, ca. 1925; ebonized wood
(possibly walnut or beech), pigskin

This desk and chair were placed at the very center of the grand salon—a large rotunda—of the Musée d'Art Contemporain, Süe et Mare's pavilion at the 1925 Paris Exposition; on top of the desk was a copy of *Architectures*, the designers' manifesto from 1921. There, they were seen by Metropolitan Museum curator Joseph Breck, who immediately arranged for their purchase. In a letter to Breck, giving his assurance that the two pieces would be packed and shipped directly to the Museum at the close of the fair, Mare added, "We are happy that you appreciated our efforts and would like to express our great satisfaction at being represented at the Metropolitan Museum by such an important work."[1]

Robert W. de Forest, director of the Museum, was himself planning a trip to Paris, and Breck encouraged him to visit the pavilion:

Another [*pavilion*] *which you must be sure to see, is 13—Musée d'art contemporain—in reality, the work of Sue et Mare and their collaborateurs who form the Compagnie des Arts Français. In my opinion the furniture shown here is the best in the exhibition—traditional in the best sense—yet distinct with personality. Here you will see my chief purchase—the desk in ebony and ormolu, with chair to match, which occupies the central portion in the exhibit. It is a striking piece—beautiful in line and most effective in the contrast of ebony and gold. Ask the vendeuse to let you go into the rotunda where it is shown so that you can see it closely.*[2]

The desk and chair perfectly embody Süe et Mare's philosophy of "evolution within tradition." The desk (Süe et Mare model no. 737) is a *bureau plat*—a flat-surfaced writing table of a type introduced in France in the early eighteenth century, although both the proportions and detailing have been exaggerated, abstracted, and stylized to a degree that make it impossible to mistake for anything but twentieth century.[3] Like its precedents, it is finished on all four sides so that it can be placed at the center of a room.[4] The swelling bombé contours of the four sides are finished in pristine ebonized wood.[5] A shallow central drawer is flanked by heavy side compartments. Jib doors swing open to reveal the spectacular zebrawood interior. Like many mid-eighteenth-century examples, this desk has S-curved cabriole legs; unlike earlier models, however, the legs here are made of ormolu (gilt bronze). Historically, elegant but durable ormolu mounts were applied to vulnerable points on precious furniture—corners, knees, and feet—as decoration and protection. Here, they are combined into a single, massive, wing-like design, transforming the mount into a leg itself.[6] A further band of ormolu edges the orange-stained leather writing surface. Both the desk and chair have replacement pigskin upholstery; by the 1940s the original skin had begun to split, and in 1982 the pieces were re-covered.

The chair (Süe et Mare model no. 82) has a frame of solid ebonized wood and its orange-stained pigskin upholstery matches that of the desk. The front is carved in an elegant continuous grooved arc that unites the armrests with the front seat-rail, which is reeded beneath the arc. The squared legs terminate in cubic volutes.

Louis Süe and André Mare. Grand salon, with Süe et Mare desk and chair, Un Musée d'Art Contemporain, Exposition Internationale des Arts Décoratifs et Industriels Modernes, Paris, 1925

In the February 1926 issue of the Metropolitan's *Bulletin*, Breck cites this desk and chair as the "most important" of his recent acquisitions of modern decorative arts, calling it

a fine achievement. . . . The bold contrast between the simple, un-ornamented planes of the ebony and the play of light and shade in the modeling of the ormolu mounts, the massive forms, and the largeness of the design are thoroughly in the modern manner.[7]

Breck put both pieces on view that year and their allure was not lost on others, including the anonymous writer for *The Christian Science Monitor*, who described "a flat-top desk of astonishing beauty, made by Süe and Mare":

The play of light between the ebony and the metal is like that between black wind clouds and a hurrying moon. The design is massive and as simple as a canvas by Cézanne.[8]

66 | Carpet
1925; wool

This carpet was commissioned by curator Joseph Breck after his visit to the Paris Exposition in 1925. Having purchased the desk and chair from the Süe et Mare pavilion (see no. 65), he wanted a carpet to accompany it. Given the scale of the pavilion's rotunda, the original carpet was presumably too large, and indeed may already have been sold by the time Breck saw it. The Metropolitan's hand-knotted carpet (Süe et Mare model no. 2023) recalls the richness of the original (which had a fully patterned ground), but with a different composition. Here, decoration is confined to the edges: on a plain black ground, large bouquets of flowers are set in each corner, linked with heavy floral garlands and fluttering ribbons. At the center is a gold sunburst medallion. The predominantly gold-and-black scheme was designed to harmonize with the furniture. Although no manufacturer is recorded, the Metropolitan's carpet was probably made by Établissements Lauer in Aubusson, the same manufacturer that supplied the pavilion's carpet.

On July 4, 1925, Breck wrote to the Museum's director, Robert W. de Forest:

I spent hours trying to find a rug which would go well with the Süe et Mare bureau but without success. I have finally arranged that the same artists who designed the desk should submit a drawing for a carpet to be made specifically for the desk.[1]

On July 17, André Mare wrote to Breck, enclosing a maquette for a carpet "2.5 m by 2.7 m, in knotted buttonhole stitch, for placement under the desk you purchased."[2] He wrote again on July 22 to say that it would take three months to make the carpet, and that he would await Breck's approval.[3]

Breck responded on August 6, officially ordering the carpet according to the maquette's specifications.[4] Breck added that he hoped the carpet would be finished in time to ship along with the desk and chair after the Exposition closed at the end of October. It did not happen.

"How are you getting on with the carpet which the Museum ordered last August?" asked Breck in his letter of December 3 to La Compagnie des Arts Français. "I hope it is nearly finished as I planned, you will remember, to show it with the desk which I purchased at the Exposition."[5] He wrote again on December 30:

The desk and chair have been received and were passed by the Customs yesterday. . . . I am disappointed that the carpet has not yet been delivered. When I ordered it on August 6, I understood that it would take about three months for completion. Will you not please make every effort to have the carpet finished and delivered not later than the end of January, as I am anxious to show it with other recent purchases of modern decorative arts at an exhibition in the Museum early in February.[6]

Breck, in exasperation, had this to say in the Museum's February 1926 *Bulletin*:

[This] new installation will be marked by the first display of some of the purchases made by the Museum this summer at the Paris Exposition. Others have not yet been received.

He cites the Süe et Mare furniture as the most important acquisitions, adding "a carpet which is being made specially to go with this desk has not yet been completed. Furniture is always seen at a disadvantage when the surroundings are not appropriate.[7]

67 | *David-Weill* Chair
designed 1923, manufactured probably late 1920s; palisander, oak, wool

Süe and Mare designed this chair (Süe et Mare model no. 45) in 1923 as their entry in the Concours David-Weill, a competition organized by David David-Weill, then vice president of the Union Centrale des Arts Décoratifs (see no. 53). Organized to stimulate interest in the decorative arts on the eve of the 1925 Paris Exposition, the competition required French designers to submit proposals for modern chairs in three categories: a salon armchair, a dining room chair, and a bedroom chair. There were few other restrictions, but, as the case would be at the Exposition, "any copy, any pastiche of old styles will be disqualified by the Jury."[1]

Typically, however, Süe et Mare looked to history for inspiration. The chair's deep, rounded back recalls the *chaise en gondole*, or gondola chair, a form popular in the late eighteenth and early nineteenth centuries. Their entry did not win, but the model proved to be a warhorse for its designers. Over the years, they used it in many interiors both domestic and commercial, including those of the Parfumerie d'Orsay (1923), the Paris town house of couturier Jean Patou (1924), and their own pavilion at the 1925 Expo. The model may also have been used in the Salle Moderne, the fashionably modern salesroom for sportswear at Bergdorf Goodman in New York that Süe et Mare is credited as having designed.[2]

Süe et Mare adapted this model, originally conceived without arms, as an armchair, which was in turn revised as the Metropolitan's desk chair about 1925 (see no. 65).

The wood elements of the chair are carved from palisander. The shell-form splat connects to

the front legs with curving supports that terminate at the top in bas-relief scrolls. The legs are saber-shaped, and also terminate in scrolls top and bottom. The seat-rails are carved from oak and veneered with palisander. The chair is unusual in retaining its original wool needlepoint upholstery, a pattern called Tulipes et Œillets (*Tulips and Carnations*) designed by Mare (probably Süe et Mare pattern no. 2513).[3] Both the motif of a floral bouquet tied with ribbons and the soft palette set against a black ground recall Süe et Mare's designs for woven textiles and carpets (see nos. 63 and 66).[4] Here, the design perfectly conforms to the chair seat, with ribbons cascading down the front. It is not known who made the cover, although other covers by Süe et Mare were supplied by such workshops as Beauvais. Other examples of this chair have either plain velvet or silk (damask or brocade) upholstery.[5]

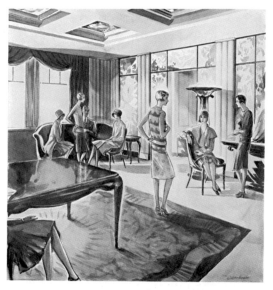

THE SALLE MODERNE AND ITS SMART IMPLICATION

Advertisement for the Salle Moderne at Bergdorf Goodman, New York, with furnishings designed by Süe et Mare, in *Vogue*, July 20, 1929

RAYMOND TEMPLIER

Paris 1891–1968 Paris

"Raymond Templier's jewelry creations belong to our age in the same way as a poem by Paul Valéry, a building by Le Corbusier or Mallet-Stevens, or a cubist painting by Braque or Picasso" was the critical assessment of Paul Sentenac in 1932, at the height of Templier's career.[1] Templier was born into a family of jewelers. His grandfather, Charles Templier, founded the family firm in 1849, and after his death in 1884 his son Paul took over.[2] Under Paul Templier's direction the firm prospered, participating in many world's fairs including those in Glasgow (1901), St. Louis (1904), Brussels (1910), Turin (1911), and San Francisco (1915).

Raymond Templier, Paul's son, studied the fundamentals of design at the École Nationale des Arts Décoratifs in Paris. It is likely, however, that he learned jewelry-making techniques in his father's workshops. In 1911—a year before he earned his diploma—he began displaying work under his own name at the Paris Salons. His submissions at the 1911 exhibition of the Société National des Beaux-Arts were a gold and enamel hair comb with a nautilus and wave motif and a gold and topaz pendant in a vaguely Asian pattern, with a silk cord and tassel.

The war put Templier's career on hold, as it did with most young men of his generation. Because Templier suffered from asthma, he remained in Paris, where he served as an interpreter and a driver. After the war, he resumed making jewelry and small silver objects under his own name, selling them from the Templier shop. He joined the family firm as a designer in 1922, at which time it was renamed Paul Templier et Fils.

During the first half of the 1920s, Templier seems to have experimented with a range of idioms, as he searched for a vocabulary that best expressed his sensibilities. In many of his early works he incorporated stylized floral motifs, though he explored geometric abstraction as well. In 1923, the Metropolitan Museum acquired the arresting mirror with masked face (no. 68). The year 1924 saw the fabrication of jewelry for Marcel L'Herbier's modernist film *L'Inhumaine* (the two would collaborate again in 1929 for the film *L'Argent*). In 1925, at the Paris Exposition, Templier was represented by both silverwork and jewelry, and later that year the Musée des Arts Décoratifs acquired a brooch. Invariably, Templier combined precious and nonprecious materials in such a way that attention was focused more on the overall artistic composition than on any of its component parts, such as gemstones.

By the second half of the 1920s, Templier was working exclusively in the abstract, geometric mode that would bring him renown. Critic Henri Clouzot wrote at this time:

Planes, lines, compartmentalizations. . . . No more large stones, whose obvious effect catches the eye at the expense of the setting. No more borrowing of natural or architectonic forms. Raymond Templier's jewelry is a slate with strict contours, a fascinating polygon placed onto the feminine form. . . . Technique, material, color—everything is personal and new without veering toward eccentricity.[3]

Critics recognized Templier's unique gifts:

Each piece is composed in and of itself, forming a bold yet well-balanced whole. Consequently, these pieces do not belong only to the present; they transcend fashion by virtue of the thought and care that have gone into their conception. *In this regard, they are classics and will in the future retain their charm and merit.*[4]

Paul Sentenac compared Templier's jewels to sculpture, saying they should be

. . . considered from all angles. . . . They are conceived and treated not only frontally but also from their many sides and in perspective. They present a succession of planes and a combination of volumes on which light comes to play. They glint not only because of the sparkling stones; they glitter on all their surfaces by means of opposing areas of light and shadow.[5]

In 1926 Templier, with fellow designers Pierre Chareau, Dominique (the firm of André Domin and Marcel Genevrière), Pierre Legrain, and Jean Puiforcat, formed the group Les Cinq. These committed modernists abandoned the Salon showings, displaying their work instead at a series of exhibitions at the Galerie Barbazanges. In 1929, joined by a number of other like-minded designers, they founded the Union des Artistes Modernes. Templier was the organization's first secretary and treasurer. The same year, Paul Templier acknowledged his son's important contributions by renaming the family firm Paul et Raymond Templier, and the business moved to larger, more prestigious premises on the Boulevard Malesherbes. By 1929, women of fashion in New York were purchasing Templier's jewelry at Saks Fifth Avenue.

During the 1930s, Templier took a newfound interest in the human figure. A lifelong love of sport led to his designing trophies and posters for sporting events, and figures of athletes began to appear in his work; the motif would linger into the 1940s. Templier participated in both the 1931 Exposition Coloniale and the 1937 Paris Exposition. He continued to show at the Paris Salons and in galleries until his death in 1968. He was made a chevalier of the Légion d'Honneur in 1938.

Templier's work was neatly summed up in a 1926 article in *La Renaissance de l'art français*:

A happy alliance between skill and intellect: it is thus — definitively — that the sumptuous and refined art of M. Raymond Templier can best be characterized.[6]

68 | Mirror
1921; silver, gold, carnelian, enamel, pewter

Every curator hopes to make a great discovery at some point in his career, whether a long-forgotten masterpiece or an important new talent. In the 1920s, Metropolitan Museum curator Joseph Breck was no exception, and when he found this diminutive mirror — it stands only 4½ inches high — he considered Templier a significant discovery. It is unclear when and where Breck first came across Templier's work. As he made yearly trips to Europe,

By June 1923, Breck had seen the mirror and instructed Templier to send it to New York. The acquisition appears to have been the first of Templier's work by a major museum. Templier wrote back:

Dear Mr. Breck,
Thanks for your letter of the 1st. As you suggest I will engrave my name and date of execution on the rim of the mirror you purchased. As settled I will send it by post registered value at the end of June to the Metropolitan Museum — New-York - .
I am glad you appreciated my work and remain
Sincerely yours,
Raymond Templier[2]

The oval mirror, set into a silver frame, is held in place with a border of gilded petal-shaped prongs. The back is inlaid with a niello (blackened silver) mask with gold-plated tie ribbons that cascade like ringlets of hair. The voluptuous, realistically modeled lips are inlaid carnelian. The mirror rests on a pewter stand with strap-shaped supports.

Because Templier is best known for his abstract geometric jewelry from the late 1920s and 1930s, not only is the figural imagery on this early mirror very unusual, but so too is its hand-mirror form. The war years were in many ways liberating for women, as they assumed new roles and became more independent. At the same time, it became acceptable for women in society to smoke and to wear makeup. Jewelers responded by creating a range of new products — vanity cases, lipstick and rouge cases, cigarette cases, lighters, and of course mirrors. Not only were these precious objects made for use in public, they were considered an integral part of a lady's toilette.

Templier here evokes, with an economy of means, the contemporary woman's made-up face, dressed for a masquerade. Perhaps suggesting the mask — both literal and metaphorical — created by makeup, the image hints also at the promise and excitement of the unseen and unknown.

he may have seen examples at the Salon des Artistes Décorateurs. Émile Sedeyn, in his review of the 1923 Salon, described Templier as "having come from a long line of noteworthy jewelers" and his jewelry as revealing

. . . the bold, sure taste of a decorator not only very familiar with the techniques of jewelry making but obsessed with drawing from them expressions that are at once new and logical. [His works] are of value for the originality of their conception and for their masterly realization. They also argue for an artistic renaissance in jewelry, all the more because the artistry [of his pieces] is free of the fleeting influence of fashion, allowing it to be guided only by eternal laws.[1]

VAN CLEEF & ARPELS

Founded in Paris, 1906

Ten years after the 1896 marriage of Alfred Van Cleef and Estelle Arpels, the jewelers Van Cleef & Arpels in 1906 opened their doors on the place Vendôme.[1] By the early 1920s, the firm had branches in a number of French cities and fashionable resorts: Cannes, Deauville, Dinard, Lyons, Nice, and Vichy. In 1929–30, a New York outpost enjoyed a brief existence on Fifth Avenue at Thirty-Third Street. It reopened in 1939 at Rockefeller Center, and in 1942 the business moved to its present location at Fifth Avenue and Fifty-Seventh Street.

From the beginning, Van Cleef & Arpels provided a smart international clientele with a full range of jewelry and bejeweled objects in the latest styles. An article published in 1923 in *La Renaissance de l'art français et des industries de luxe* pays tribute to the firm's role in helping shape those styles:

For the past twenty or twenty-five years, the tyranny of fashion has singularly shaped the evolution of jewelry. Classic sets of rubies, emeralds, or sapphires, as well as jewels lovingly inspired by nature—insects or stylized plants—have given way to understated pearl necklaces and stones set as solitaires. The elegant ladies of the rue de la Paix, just like their sisters on Fifth Avenue, prefer jewelry that is more expensive but with simpler lines to the overworked masterpieces by followers of Benvenuto Cellini. In this, their taste follows the same stylistic evolution as furniture and clothing.

At the same time, these ladies are not averse to arousing a bit of envy, wearing their parures less out of a love for gems than for the personal satisfaction of one-upping other women.

Need we say that the role of a jeweler such as M. Van Cleef comes not from researching and haggling over diamonds, gemstones, and pearls? A stone, however perfect it may be, is just a stone. In its setting, however,

it becomes a jewel. The art of the jeweler derives its value from its settings and mountings. In his skilled fingers, a jewel seems to lose its rigidity, to become flexible, to yield to the movement that the designer has given to its composition. That is where one finds the triumph that justly can be called "the art of the rue de la Paix"—that unique art which has made Paris the world marketplace for jewels and gems.[2]

Two designers dominated the firm during the 1920s and 1930s: René Sim Lacaze and Renée Puissant (the daughter of Alfred Van Cleef and Estelle Arpels). While the firm had its own workshops, certain jobs were turned over to outside specialists, in particular the design and manufacture of small jeweled boxes, which were supplied by the *boîtiers* (box makers) Alfred Langlois and Strauss, Allard, Meyer. Two influential Van Cleef & Arpels inventions, however, set it apart from its rivals: the minaudière and invisibly set gemstones.

The minaudière is a small, handheld, hard-case box that a lady could carry in lieu of an evening bag. The name derives from the verb *minauder*, meaning to use affectation, and was patented in 1930.[3] The interior was customized according to the needs of the client, but usually included some combination of powder and rouge compartments, a lipstick, a comb, a mirror, a cigarette case and lighter or match holder, and a clock.[4] Although most Van Cleef & Arpels minaudières were exquisite, expensive objects, embellished with enamels and set with gemstones, by the mid-1930s (perhaps in response to the worldwide economic crisis), less expensive versions with finishes that included rhodium, gold plate, and black enamel set with rhinestones were being retailed internationally through department stores.[5]

The innovation of invisible settings, which were marketed as Mystery Settings, did away with the unsightly prongs that traditionally held stones in place. The stones were cut with a special channel groove, allowing them to be slipped along concealed settings, like train tracks. Rows of such invisibly set stones could be used to effectively pave entire surfaces of a jewel. Initially, only soft gemstones like rubies, emeralds, and sapphires were used; it was not until 1990 that diamonds could be cut with the necessary grooves.

Unlike its competitors, such as Templier or Fouquet, Van Cleef & Arpels was an unapologetically commercial firm. Accordingly, it did not participate in the "artist-decorator" annual Salons. Its work was, however, seen in a number of important exhibitions, including the 1924 "Exposition: Arts, Commerce and Industries of France and Her Colonies," held at the Grand Central Palace in New York, and Georges Fouquet's 1929 exhibition of jewelry and goldsmiths' work at the Musée Galliera in Paris. Van Cleef was represented at the 1925 Paris Exposition, the 1931 Exposition Coloniale, and the 1939–40 New York World's Fair.

Over the years, its clientele has included many well-known and glamorous figures, including the Maharani of Baroda, Nancy Cunard, Marlene Dietrich, Doris Duke, Daisy Fellowes, Greta Garbo, Florence Gould, Barbara Hutton, Grace Kelly, Eva Peron, Marjorie Merriweather Post, Elizabeth Taylor, and the Duchess of Windsor.

69 | Vanity Case

ATTRIBUTED TO ALFRED LANGLOIS
FOR VAN CLEEF & ARPELS, PARIS
ca. 1928; gold, enamel, jade, diamonds

Small jeweled boxes for cigarettes and cosmetics were developed in the 1920s, when it became acceptable for women to smoke and to apply makeup in public. Jewelers promoted these vanity cases, *nécessaires*, and minaudières as an important part of an evening parure, or jewelry set. Although modeled on eighteenth-century gem-encrusted snuffboxes, modern boxes were feats of ingenuity that included a wide range of features corresponding to a client's needs.

This flashy and exotic vanity case presents a somewhat indiscriminate mix — typical for its time — of Asian and Near Eastern influences. The jade panel set into the cover is carved with a flowering fruit-tree motif that evokes both traditional Chinese jades and Persian miniature paintings; the rich green color recalls Mughal emeralds; the intricate open-work piercing, set against a polished gold ground, suggests Islamic screens. Because green and red are complementary colors, the vermilion enamel case provides an eye-catching contrast to the jade. The cover is composed like a Persian carpet, the floral field expanding into a cartouche by the addition of stepped pyramids made from baguette and rose-cut diamonds and cabochons of grey jade and by the articulation of the four corners with additional diamonds and jade. The sides and underside of the box incorporate inlaid gold in a vaguely Chinese fret-work pattern, again articulated with diamonds and grey jade. The case is opened with a diamond push button to reveal a polished gold interior with a mirror. The central powder compartment is engraved with a date, above which is a smaller compartment for rouge. A hinged lipstick (with a bayonet mechanism) springs up when the case is opened. The piece retains its original leather protective slipcase.

The case was likely made for stock rather than as a special commission. Although it is engraved with the year 1938, its manufacture probably dates to the mid- or late 1920s. That comparable examples were made by the *boîtier* Alfred Langlois after 1925 leads to the case's attribution.[1]

The taste for fashionable exoticism, which reached its height in the early 1920s, lingered into the 1930s. The cosmetics company Elizabeth Arden, for example, promoted "Chinese" makeup in an advertisement that appeared in 1936:

You must match your skintones not only with powder but with rouge, lipstick, cosmetique and nail varnish as well. . . . The keynote of the Chinese make-up is a warm amber tone that makes you look like a Manchu princess.[2]

Walter L. Richard (1886–1964) bought the case as a second wedding anniversary gift for his second wife, Annette Shelby Bracy, whom he married on February 8, 1936. Richard was a man of many careers. After an early stint as an investment banker, he became a manufacturer of silk goods. When he retired at the age of forty, he turned to more amusing pursuits:

Because his father excelled in several sports, Richard made himself excel in all: golf, tennis, bobsledding, shooting, skating, badminton, polo, chess, all manner of cards and parlor games, amateur magic, etc. When polo palled, Richard organized a motorcycle polo team and went on until the polo ball lodged in the front forks, throwing him and breaking three ribs.[3]

He is best known for resurrecting the long-forgotten game of backgammon, and was the author of the definitive *Complete Backgammon*, first published in 1931.

PAUL VERA

Paris 1882–1957 Saint-Germain-en-Laye

Paul Vera was born into a family of accomplished artists.[1] His father was the architect Gustave Léon Vera, and his older brother was the design theorist and garden designer André Vera. Raised in Paris, Vera from an early age was interested in painting. He frequently went on plein-air excursions with Louis Abel-Truchet, an artist friend of the family. After a decade studying to become a painter—at the Académie Julian, the École des Beaux-Arts, and the Académie Ranson—he presented his first works at the Salon d'Automne in 1904.

Vera's circle of friends, many of whom he met while a student, included, among others, Roger de La Fresnaye and André Mare, artists who gravitated around the Puteaux Group. Together with his brother André, Vera was drawn to the group's efforts to reconcile modernity with tradition. In 1912 the two brothers joined Louis Süe's Atelier Français,

an association that also included La Fresnaye and members of the Puteaux Group.

Like many other artists, Vera served during the war in the camouflage corps of the French Army, devising covers for artillery and observation posts. When he returned to Paris, he joined the newly formed Compagnie des Arts Français, the designers' collective founded in 1919 by Louis Süe and André Mare based on the principles of the Atelier Français (see pages 212, 214). For the Compagnie, Vera took on projects that allowed him to develop his uniquely expressive style, mainly decorative programs for forms conceived by others: painted decoration on furniture (see no. 64), patterns for wallpapers and textiles, illustrations and other graphic designs for printed materials, bas-relief panels, and tapestry cartoons. His repertoire of geometrically abstracted motifs was limited to a narrow range of traditional themes, many horticultural, such as the four seasons, flowers and fruit, fountains, and cornucopias. He also favored allegorical and mythological figures:

It is the great merit of this artist to have understood that there are no hackneyed subjects; it is simply a question of giving them new life [so they become] twice as charming as and considerably more unexpected than those that have yet to be sanctioned by the profound aspirations of mankind. . . . Paul Vera has created a style and has rendered concrete something that had become nothing more than an abstraction.[2]

Vera contributed many works to the two pavilions that had been designed by the Compagnie des Arts Français at the 1925 Paris Exposition. In the Musée d'Art Contemporain he displayed objects in bronze, including an inkwell and several small medallions, and in the pavilion of Fontaine et Cie (a hardware manufacturing company), a terracotta bas-relief panel set into the mantelpiece. Vera's Beauvais tapestry screen *Les Jardins* (no. 70), made independently of La Compagnie des Arts Français, was displayed at the Grand Palais.

In 1927, Vera ended his association with La Compagnie. Throughout the 1920s and 1930s, however, he worked productively as a work-for-hire designer and continued to participate in the Paris Salons. He made tapestry cartoons for the Beauvais, Gobelins, and Aubusson manufactories, designed ceramic table services and sculptures for Sèvres, and created painted and bas-relief decorative panels for interior design projects. Commissions included a panel for an *appartement-de-luxe* on the SS *Île de France* (1927) and a ceiling for the Coty perfume shop in London (1934). He also painted a series of murals for La Thébaïde, the house in Saint-Germain-en-Laye that he shared with André.

About 1923 the two brothers together began to design gardens, hoping to rejuvenate the art of landscape gardening, which they believed had been one of France's great creative achievements. Their gardens, both private and public, like Vera's other work, combined French traditions with a modernist sensibility — formal parterres, for example, laid out in Cubist patterns and planted with flowers of boldly contrasting colors.

Vera spent the years of the Second World War in Saint-Germain-en-Laye, although the occupying German military had requisitioned La Thébaïde. He continued to work as a designer until his death in 1957. Vera's lifelong commitment to tradition in modern design was described by François Fosca:

Vera reflects equally the nobility of the Louis XIV style, the grace of the Louis XV style, and the elegance of the Louis XVI style. Leaving audacity and excess to others, he seeks continuity and connections. Rather than being drawn to what breaks with French tradition . . . he prefers what is related to it. . . . In art, above all in our time, the moderate is no less necessary than the revolutionary. And in matters of the decorative arts, it is even more essential.[3]

70 | *Les Jardins* Folding Screen

PAUL VERA AND PAUL FOLLOT
1923–24; wool, silk, mahogany

In 1932, Metropolitan Museum curator Joseph Breck wrote that by 1917, when Jean Ajalbert of the Académie Goncourt was made director of the Manufacture Nationale de Beauvais, "that famous institution had [already] fallen upon evil times."[1] Although the factory still employed highly skilled workers, demand for tapestries was at an all-time low. Few new designs — cartoons — had been initiated in nearly half a century. Ajalbert was determined to change that:

The manufactory must renew its contact with contemporary art; the designs for the weavers must come not from dusty storerooms and the scavengers of past styles, but from artists who are creating the living art of our own time.[2]

Ajalbert approached approximately twenty artists, including Vera, to make cartoons for new tapestries:

Among the artists who have supplied cartoons to Beauvais in recent years, none . . . has been more successful than Paul Vera. A versatile artist, whose activities have included architectural and garden design as well as work in many fields of the applied arts, he well deserves the high reputation he holds as a leader of the modern movement. His style, although wholly personal and original, is based upon a thorough knowledge of the past. To a magistral capacity for pure design he adds a gayety of spirit and a freshness of invention that are distinctly his own.[3]

Les Jardins was first conceived in 1921. The cartoon was by Vera, and the frame by Paul Follot.[4] It was woven in 1923–24 and shown at the 1925 Paris Exposition in the Gobelins and Beauvais display.[5] The garden motif reflects Vera's interest in horticulture. It may also represent the four seasons. Indeed, the design may have been adapted from a gold-and-black lacquered four-panel screen (date unknown) made for La Compagnie des Arts Français, which depicted similar compositions titled *Le Pain* (Bread), *Les*

Légumes (Vegetables), *Le Vin* (Wine), and *Viandes et Poissons* (Meats and Fish). Here, each panel depicts a trophy-like arrangement of figures, fruit, flowers, and garden tools.

The trophy has its origins in ancient Greece, where it was used to commemorate a victory. Armies would affix the weapons of their defeated enemies to trees or posts. Such displays were later adapted as decorative ornaments, replacing the symbols of military spoil with more peaceful signs of abundance, as on these screens, where fruit, flowers, vines, and vegetables are arranged around gardening implements — rakes and shovels, scythes and pitchforks, ladders and pinwheels (to drive away birds). Vera's robust, ruddy figures — in contrast to the elegant, lithe sophisticates generally associated with Art Deco — personify the very spirit of France as embodied in the stalwart yet humble peasants who for centuries worked the land.

Breck noted the "suggestion of the eighteenth century in the decorative motives":

. . . these charming groups of fruits, flowers, and garden utensils, so happily combined with figures of women and children. But here the resemblance stops. The scale is bolder, the modeling more forceful, and in the choice of colors, which form a rich, full orchestrated harmony, there is a greater range of hues.[6]

The range of colors could be achieved only with synthetically dyed threads, which had been introduced in the early years of the twentieth century.

These bright, singing colors may come somewhat as a surprise to those who have never seen the backs of old tapestries, where the original colors have been protected from the light. . . . Very wisely the modern Beauvais tapestries are keyed to a brilliancy of color which not only is in keeping with contemporary taste but which also will allow these fabrics to grow old gracefully in their turn.[7]

Vera's panels, rather than having "grown old gracefully," have happily retained their full, original brilliance.

Gobelins and Beauvais display, Grand Palais, Exposition Internationale des Arts Décoratifs et Industriels Modernes, Paris, 1925

NOTES

FRENCH ART DECO: AN OVERVIEW

1. For a survey of Art Deco in its broadest sense, see Charlotte Benton, Tim Benton, and Ghislaine Wood, eds., *Art Deco, 1910–1939* (London: V&A Publications, 2003).

2. The most complete scholarly examination of French Art Deco can be found in Nancy J. Troy, *Modernism and the Decorative Arts in France* (New Haven: Yale University Press, 1991).

3. Henri Verne and René Chavance, *Pour comprendre l'art décoratif moderne en France* (Paris: Hachette, 1925), p. 8.

4. See Katharine Morrison Kahle, *Modern French Decoration* (New York: G. P. Putnam's Sons, 1930), pp. 29–30.

5. Léon Deshairs, quoted in ibid., p. 7. The dates are those of two Universal Expositions at which the style was most prominently seen.

6. Verne and Chavance, *Pour comprendre l'art décoratif moderne*, pp. 10–11.

7. "The first important presentation of the new movement occurred at the International Exposition held in Paris in 1900, where among other novel expressions the *Art Nouveau* creations of the Establishment Bing attracted universal attention. The new motives became at once the vogue with the result that manufacturers in large numbers hastened to gain profit from their popularity. To give the new quality to their productions designers of all degrees of capacity were called upon with the result that motives requiring the hand of a master were soon vulgarized and cheapened and the whole movement reduced to absurd and fantastic exaggerations." *Report of Commission: Appointed by the Secretary of Commerce to Visit and Report upon the International Exposition of Modern Decorative and Industrial Art in Paris, 1925* (Washington, D.C., 1926), p. 13.

8. About 1900, a number of designers' organizations were founded in Germany to promote the alliance of art and industry, including the Vereinigte Werkstätten für Kunst im Handwerk (1897) and the Deutscher Werkbund (1907). The success these groups had in producing well-designed, affordably priced, industrially manufactured objects for a broad public quickly became a source of competitive concern for French designers, especially after their work was seen in Paris in 1910 at the prestigious Salon d'Automne. The traditionally inspired, aesthetically unified German room settings drew inspiration from the reductive elegance of the early nineteenth-century Biedermeier style; each interior was conceived and overseen by a single master designer. Nevertheless, while French pride was sensitive to any hint of supremacy by another culture, many French designers looked to and learned from avant-garde trends in Germany in their effort to regain dominance in the design industry.

9. In 1912, it was noted in *Vogue*: "It has come to be quite the fashion for designers to combine in one establishment, millinery, novelties, bags, belts, caps, and a hundred other accessories; and that these things are an important, even an essential part of the wardrobe . . . that gives the final touch of elegance that makes or mars the toilette, is undeniable; but certainly couturiers have never before insisted that chairs, curtains, rugs, and wall-coverings should be considered in the choosing of a dress, or rather that the style of the dress should influence the interior decoration of a home." "Poiret's New Kingdom," *Vogue* 40, no. 1 (July 1912), p. 16.

10. Frances B. Schaefer, "French Interior Decoration," *Arts and Decoration* 1 (March 1911), pp. 202–4.

11. Thérèse Bonney and Louise Bonney, *Buying Antique and Modern Furniture in Paris* (New York: Robert M. McBride & Company, 1929), p. 27.

12. Quoted in Léon Moussinac, *Le Meuble français moderne* (Paris: Librairie Hachette, 1925), p. 67.

13. For a complete history of this important organization, see Yvonne Brunhammer and Suzanne Tise, *The Decorative Arts in France: La Société des Artistes Décorateurs, 1900–1942* (New York: Rizzoli, 1990).

14. Gaston Quénioux, *Les Arts décoratifs modernes (France)* (Paris: Librarie Larousse, 1925), p. 3.

15. *Report of Commission*, p. 16.

16. The pavilion was funded by the French government, which took possession of its unsold furnishings at the close of the fair. Brunhammer and Tise, *Decorative Arts in France*, p. 96.

17. The full regulations for the fair can be found in *Exposition Internationale des Arts Décoratifs et Industriels Modernes: Catalogue générale officiel* (Paris: Imprimerie de Vaugirard, 1925), pp. 18–22. This English translation appears in *Report of Commission*, pp. 17–18.

18. Léon Deshairs, *L'Art décoratif français, 1918–1925* (Paris: Éditions Albert Lévy, 1925), p. xi.

19. *Report of Commission*, p. 20.

20. Kahle, *Modern French Decoration*, pp. 24–25.

21. Ibid., pp. 25–26.

22. See Bonney and Bonney, *Buying Antique and Modern Furniture in Paris*, pp. 27–30.

23. Representative titles are *Pour comprendre l'art décoratif moderne en France* (1925), by Henri Verne, director of the Musées Nationaux and the Musée du Louvre, and René Chavance, a critic who worked for *Mobilier et décoration* magazine; *Les Arts décoratifs modernes* (1925), by Gaston Quénioux, inspector general of design education in France; *L'Art décoratif moderne et les industries d'art contemporaines* (1925), by Charles Henri Besnard, head architect of the Monuments Historiques; and the series L'Art français depuis vingt ans, published under the direction of Léon Deshairs, which included volumes on furniture (1921), metalwork (1921), painting (1921), architecture (1922), books (1922), theatrical decoration (1922), fashion (1925), textiles, tapestries, and carpets (1926), ceramics and glass (1928), and sculpture (1928).

24. These included *Art et décoration*, *Art et industrie*, *L'Amour de l'art*, *La Renaissance de l'art français et des industries de luxe*, *La Revue de l'art ancien et moderne*, *L'Art et les artistes*, *L'Art vivant*, *Le Bulletin de l'art ancien et moderne*, *Le Bulletin de la vie artistique*, *Les Arts de la maison*, and *Mobilier et décoration*. Many women's magazines, such as *Fémina* and *Vogue*, avidly covered the subject as well. American and British publications, such as *Arts & Decoration*, *Good Furniture*, and *The Studio*, presented the subject to English-language readers.

25. Because the majority of French Art Deco interiors were photographed only in black-and-white, such folios are often the only records of the color schemes. They included: *Architectures* (1921), *Harmonies: Intérieurs de Ruhlmann* (1924), *Intérieurs de Süe et Mare* (1924), *Une Ambassade française* (1925), *Intérieurs en couleur* (1925), *Répertoire du goût moderne* (1928–29), and *Choix* (1930).

26. Thérèse Bonney was an American photographer and journalist who lived and worked in Paris; her older sister, Louise, served as her representative in New York. In their book, the sisters recommended that Americans with an interest in Art Deco but who were unable to travel to France visit a French liner while it was docked at an American port. Katharine Morrison Kahle was a lecturer at the University of California, San Diego; her book included contributions from Léon Deshairs. Another guide, published by the Chemins de Fer de l'État—the French national railway—was . . . *and Blondes Prefer PARIS*, by Jacques Deval (Paris: Devambez, n.d. [ca. 1930]).

27. Many of these were organized by such French institutions as the Association Française d'Action Artistique and the Comité Français des Expositions à l'Étranger. A partial list includes exhibitions in Barcelona (1923, 1929), Brussels (1935), Bucharest (1928–29), Buenos Aires (1912, 1935), Cairo (1928), Liège (1930), Lisbon (1933), London (1933), Madrid (1922), Monza (1923, 1925), New York (1918, 1924, 1939–40), San Francisco (1915, 1924–25, 1939), Tokyo (1928), and Turin (1911). In the United States, groups such as the American Association of Museums

(1926) and the American Federation of Arts (1928, 1929, 1930) organized several traveling exhibitions that included French Art Deco.

28. French Art Deco was exported to far-flung establishments such as the Galerie Taourel in Algiers and the Maison des Arts Français in Buenos Aires. The United States provided a surprisingly strong market. During the 1920s, in New York alone one could find works at Beaux Arts Shade, Brummer Galleries, de Hauke & Co., Jacques Seligmann & Co., M. Knoedler & Co., and the Park Avenue Galleries, to name but a few. For an in-depth examination of French works shown at American department stores, see Marilyn F. Friedman, *Selling Good Design: Promoting the Early Modern Interior* (New York: Rizzoli, 2003).

29. In 1930, members of the Bauhaus were invited to display their modernist household furnishings at the Salon des Artistes Décorateurs, sparking both considerable interest and outrage among the French.

30. Members included Pierre Chareau, Le Corbusier, René Herbst, Eileen Gray, Gabriel Guévrékian, Robert Lallemant, Robert Mallet-Stevens, Jan and Joël Martel, Charlotte Perriand, and Jean Puiforcat. The organization, which was founded in 1929 and published its first manifesto in 1934, was active until 1959.

31. A notable exception was the 1931 Exposition Coloniale Internationale, sponsored by the French government, which revived the taste for exoticism.

32. Several articles from the 1950s—especially in French publications—showed a continued appreciation for French Art Deco design. *Mobilier et décoration*, for example, ran a series of biographies of prominent artist-craftsmen.

33. "Les Années '25': Art déco/Bauhaus/Stijl/Esprit Nouveau" was presented at the Musée des Arts Décoratifs from March to May 1966. The exhibition in Minneapolis included more than 1,400 works. Entitled "The World of Art Deco," it was organized by Bevis Hillier. Hillier's 1968 publication *Art Deco of the 20s and 30s* is considered the first to use the term "Art Deco."

34. For an examination of the post-1970 interest in Art Deco, see José Alvarez, *Histoires de l'art déco* (Paris: Éditions du Regard, 2010).

FRENCH ART DECO IN THE METROPOLITAN MUSEUM OF ART

1. "Recognition for Modern Art," *Bulletin of The Metropolitan Museum of Art* 17, no. 7 (July 1922), p. 146.
2. Ibid., p. 147.
3. A brief biography of Breck can be found in Timothy B. Husband, "Creating the Cloisters," *The Metropolitan Museum of Art Bulletin* 70, no. 4 (Spring 2013), p. 19.
4. "Modern Art Show at Metropolitan," *The New York Times*, February 10, 1923, p. 12.
5. Joseph Breck, "Modern Decorative Arts," *Bulletin of The Metropolitan Museum of Art* 18, no. 2 (February 1923), p. 34.
6. Breck's appreciation of their work was such that in 1925 he specifically recommended them to Mrs. Vincent Astor: "At these two places you will see some of the finest modern French furniture, and I think you will find a visit worth while." Joseph Breck to Mrs. Vincent Astor, December 10, 1925; Archives, The Metropolitan Museum of Art.

7. Joseph Breck to Robert de Forest, July 4, 1925 (with addendum dated July 7, 1925); Archives, The Metropolitan Museum of Art.
8. Joseph Breck, "Modern Decorative Arts: A Loan Exhibition," *Bulletin of The Metropolitan Museum of Art* 21, no. 2 (February 1926), p. 37.
9. Edward C. Moore Jr. to Metropolitan Museum of Art director Edward Robinson, May 3, 1926; Archives, The Metropolitan Museum of Art.
10. Phillips acquired several examples of glass, including jewelry, by Lalique and silver by Puiforcat (see nos. 31 and 48).
11. Henry Geldzahler to Thomas H. Hoving, February 27, 1970; Archives, The Metropolitan Museum of Art.
12. Ibid.
13. Notable among Geldzahler's acquisitions were the suite of lacquered bedroom furniture made by Jean Dunand for Templeton Crocker (no. 21), the Jean Dupas wall panels from the SS *Normandie* (no. 22), and furniture by Pierre Legrain and Clément Rousseau from the estate of Jacques Doucet (nos. 34 and 51). Other acquisitions include nos. 1, 17, 41, 44, and 53.
14. These include "Cartier: 1900–1939" (1997), "Jean Dunand: Master of Art Deco" (1998), "Art Deco Paris" (2004), and "Ruhlmann: Genius of Art Deco" (2004).

GABRIEL ARGY-ROUSSEAU

1. Argy-Rousseau sold his work at several galleries in Paris, including Goupil et Cie, Briche, Manoury, and the Salon des Arts Ménagers. In 1910, it was included in the glass exhibition at the Musée Galliera.
2. Notably, his work was included in the 1934 glass exhibition at the Musée Galliera and in the 1937 Exposition Internationale des Arts et Techniques dans la Vie Moderne.

1 | *Eurythmics* Vase

1. Janine Bloch-Dermant, *G. Argy-Rousseau: Glassware as Art* (New York: Thames and Hudson, 1991), pp. 95, 222.
2. Quoted from a leaflet produced for Les Pâtes de Verre d'Argy-Rousseau; Bloch-Dermant, *Argy-Rousseau*, p. 27.

GEORGE BARBIER

1. Edith A. Standen, "Instruments for Agitating the Air," *The Metropolitan Museum of Art Bulletin*, n.s., 23, no. 7 (March 1965), p. 257.
2. On Barbier, see Barbara Martorelli, ed., *George Barbier: The Birth of Art Deco* (Venice: Marsilio Editori, 2008).
3. Francis de Miomandre, "George Barbier," *L'Art et les artistes* 19 (June 1914), p. 177.
4. "Their coats are pinched in a little . . . at the waist, their ties are spotless, and their boots immaculate; a bracelet slipping down over a wrist at an unexpected moment betrays a love of luxury . . . might almost be, indeed, the insignia of the group." Anon., "Art: Beau Brummels of the Brush; A Dozen of the Gilded Youth of Paris . . . Dub Themselves Knights of the Bracelet . . ." *Vogue* 43, no. 12 (June 15, 1914), p. 35.
5. Barbier produced two albums of drawings based on Ballets Russes productions: *Nijinsky* (1913; with text by Francis de Miomandre) and *Karsavina* (1914; with text by Jean-Louis Vaudoyer); each depicted its title dancer in his or her most famous role.

6. Barbier met Louÿs about 1910, when he illustrated *Les Chansons de Bilitis* (1894), the author's most famous work, which was inspired by ancient Greek poetry. Louÿs praised Barbier as a "truly Greek painter" (Standen, "Instruments for Agitating the Air," p. 256). The two remained lifelong friends.
7. It was at this point that Barbier resumed using his own name to sign his work.
8. For reproduction, Barbier's delicate drawings and watercolors were transposed into woodcuts and pochoir prints by fellow artists François-Louis Schmied and Jean Saudé.
9. Marcel Valotaire, "George Barbier," *The Studio* 93 (1927), pp. 406, 409.
10. Miomandre, "George Barbier," p. 178.
11. Judy Rudoe, *Cartier, 1900–1939* (New York: Harry N. Abrams, 1997), p. 241.
12. Miomandre, "George Barbier," p. 183.

2 | Fan

1. *Journal des dames et des modes*, no. 21 (December 20, 1912).
2. Madame Paquin may have printed this album in response to two similar albums produced by Paul Poiret: *Les Robes de Paul Poiret*, illustrated by Paul Iribe (1908), and *Les Choses de Paul Poiret*, illustrated by Georges Lepape (1911). Iribe designed two of the fans included in Paquin's album.
3. Miomandre, "George Barbier," p. 182.
4. Ibid., pp. 179–80.
5. It is unclear which tomb Miomandre is referring to, since there is none with the name that he cites. Several tombs, however, have paintings of dancers and musicians, such as the Tomb of the Triclinium and the Tomb of the Leopard.
6. Millicent Veronica Willson (1882–1974) married the newspaper baron William Randolph Hearst in 1903. Although they never divorced, the couple became estranged around 1921 after Hearst began a relationship, which he publicly flaunted, with the actress Marion Davies. Millicent Hearst is best known for her charitable work for children.

VALÉRY BIZOUARD

1. On Bizouard and Tétard Frères, see Dedo von Kerssenbrock-Krosigk, ed., *Modern Art of Metalwork: Bröhan-Museum, State Museum of Art Nouveau, Art Deco and Functionalism (1889–1939), Berlin* (Berlin: Bröhan-Museum, 2001), pp. 439, 570.
2. Henri Clouzot, *L'Art français depuis vingt ans: Le Travail du métal* (Paris: F. Rieder et Cie, 1921), p. 66.
3. Georges Rémon, "Orfèvrerie d'argent: Les Dernières Créations de Tétard Frères; Oeuvres de Valéry Bizouard, de Tardy et de Jean Tétard," *Mobilier et décoration* 10, no. 1 (January 1930), pp. 197–208.
4. *Vogue* 71, no. 9 (May 1, 1928), p. 87, and Florence Taft Eaton, "A White and Silver Christmas for the Hostess," *Vogue* 72, no. 12 (December 8, 1929), p. 138.

3 | Flatware

1. Rémon, "Orfèvrerie d'argent," p. 204.
2. In 1977, Metropolitan Museum curator Penelope Hunter-Stiebel saw a set of the same model with the marks of Tétard Frères in their original box, marked "Cristalleries de Baccarat, 30 bis rue de Parades." A set of dressing-table bottles made by Baccarat

and Tétard was published in *Vogue* 7, no. 9 (May 1, 1928), p. 87.

3. Called *Paraison*, the service was designed by Georges Chevalier, artistic director at Baccarat.

EDGAR BRANDT

1. Joseph Breck, "Accessions and Notes: Modern Decorative Arts," *Bulletin of The Metropolitan Museum of Art* 19, no. 11 (November 1924), p. 275.
2. For an in-depth biography, see Joan Kahr, *Edgar Brandt: Master of Art Deco Ironwork* (New York: Harry N. Abrams, 1999).
3. Henri Clouzot, "Une Oeuvre d'Edgar Brandt à New York/The Work of Edgar Brandt in New York," *La Renaissance de l'art français et des industries de luxe* 9 (January 1926), pp. 4, 6 (English translation included with original article).
4. Ibid., p. 4.
5. The ensemble was purchased from the fair by a South American collector. The interior screen Brandt made for the Ruhlmann pavilion was purchased by the Portuguese Count of Vizela, who had it installed in his house in Porto.
6. These included, in Philadelphia, Wanamaker's department store (1924), the American Federation of Arts' traveling exhibition of works from the 1925 Paris Exposition, which toured eight American cities (1926), the Jacques Seligmann Gallery, New York (1926), Macy's department store (1927), Lord & Taylor (1928), the Park Avenue Galleries (1928), and the American Federation of the Arts' Third International Exhibition of Contemporary Industrial Art, which traveled to four American cities (1930–31).
7. In collaboration with artist Paul Jouve, Brandt made a monumental pair of silvered bronze doors for the Paris Musée Permanent des Colonies; for the SS *Normandie* he designed serving pieces and decorative vases.

4 | *Perse* Grille

1. Société du Salon d'Automne (Paris), *Catalogue des ouvrages* (Paris, 1923), p. 108, no. 227.
2. The second grille differs from the Metropolitan's in having three small caps above each of the scrolling triglyphs at the bottom edge.
3. Henri Verne and René Chavance, *Pour comprendre l'art décoratif moderne en France* (Paris: Hachette, 1925), p. 111.
4. *A Selected Collection of Objects from the International Exposition of Modern Decorative and Industrial Art at Paris 1925* (Washington, D.C.: The American Association of Museums, 1926), p. 4.
5. Walter Rendell Storey, "Cool Settings for the Summer Diners," *The New York Times*, June 30, 1929, p. SM17.

RENÉ BUTHAUD

1. Marcel Valotaire, *La Céramique française moderne* (Paris: Les Éditions G. van Oest, 1930), p. 35.
2. On Buthaud, see Jacqueline du Pasquier, *René Buthaud* (Bordeaux: Horizon Chimérique, 1987). A concise English-language biography may be found in Alastair Duncan, "Buthaud's Decorative Art," *The Connoisseur* 208, no. 836 (October 1981), pp. 153–55.
3. Du Pasquier, *René Buthaud*, p. 50.
4. Ibid., p. 67.

5. Jean Dunand, one of the jurors, acquired several pieces for himself; Florence Blumenthal, patron of the prize, did not share his enthusiasm. When Buthaud thanked Blumenthal for the grant, she informed him that had she been a member of the jury, he would not have won. Ibid., p. 68.
6. Coal-fired kilns attain higher temperatures than wood-fired kilns, allowing the potter a wider range of firing techniques.
7. Guillaume Janneau, "Les Poteries de René Buthaud," *Art et décoration* 51 (January–June 1927), p. 58.
8. Rouard represented Buthaud until the gallery closed in 1961. After 1930, as a way to identify works not sold through Rouard, Buthaud signed them "J. Doris," most likely in homage to the ancient Greek vase painter Douris.
9. French exhibitions include those held at the Musée de la Céramique, Sèvres (1924 and 1931), and the Louvre (1937). International exhibitions include the American Association of Museums' traveling exhibition of works from the 1925 Paris Exposition (1926) and the American Federation of Arts' International Exhibition of Ceramic Art of 1928–29.

5 | Three Vases

1. Valotaire, *La Céramique française moderne*, p. 35.
2. Ibid.
3. Lillian Nassau to Henry Geldzahler, December 24, 1969; Archives, The Metropolitan Museum of Art.

6 | Statuette

1. Henri Menjaud, "Nouvelles Céramiques de Buthaud," *Art et décoration* 65 (1936), p. 110.

7 | Study for an Athlete

1. The program included the construction of a municipal swimming pool, a trade union, and schools, as well as the updating of the city's sewer system and streetlights. Marquet, initially a socialist, would later serve as minister of state and minister of the interior under the right-wing Vichy government of Philippe Petain during the Second World War.
2. In 2001 the stadium was renamed Stade Chaban-Delmas, after the politician Jacques Chaban-Delmas, mayor of Bordeaux from 1947 to 1995.

ÉDOUARD CAZAUX

1. On Cazaux, see Mireille Cazaux-Charon, *Édouard Cazaux: Céramiste-sculpteur art deco* (Saint-Rémy-en-l'Eau: Éditions Monelle Hayot, 1994); and, in English, Bernadette Boustany, "Édouard Cazaux: Master of the Kiln," in *Bordeaux années 20–30: From Paris to Aquitaine* (Paris: Éditions Norma, 2008), pp. 90–99.
2. Clément Morro, "Édouard Cazaux," *La Revue moderne des arts et de la vie* 21, no. 3 (April 30, 1921), p. 18.
3. C. de Cordis, "Les Céramiques d'Édouard Cazaux," *La Revue moderne des arts et de la vie* 22, no. 2 (January 30, 1922), p. 15.
4. His work was included in the international expositions in Barcelona (1929) and Paris (1937), as well as in exhibitions at the Musée de la Céramique (Sèvres) and the Musée Galliera (Paris); in Paris, he exhibited at the galleries Reitlinger, Le Grand Dépôt, and Georges Rouard. At the 1925 Paris Exposition,

his ceramics were displayed in the Ambassade Française, the Arthur Goldscheider pavilion, and the stand of the decorating firm Sormani-Charles Thiebaux.
5. Cristalleries de Compiègne would supply the glass wall panels for the first-class dining room of the SS *Normandie* (see page 18).
6. De Cordis, "Les Céramiques d'Édouard Cazaux," p. 16.

8 | Vase

1. Morro, "Édouard Cazaux," p. 18.
2. De Cordis, "Les Céramiques d'Édouard Cazaux," p. 15.

RENÉ CREVEL

1. E. Bénézit, *Dictionnaire critique et documentaire des peintres, sculpteurs, dessinateurs et graveurs*, new ed. (Paris: Librairie Gründ, 1976), vol. 3, p. 273.
2. Illustrated in Gaston Quénioux, *Les Arts décoratifs modernes (France)* (Paris: Librairie Larousse, 1925), p. 506.
3. Together, Crevel and Follot also supervised the installation of the Exposition's textile display in the Grand Palais.
4. After it opened in 1928, Sèvres ceramics were also sold in Paris through Le Grand Dépôt; it is unclear whether this had anything to do with Crevel, who was then working for both firms.

9 | Lidded Vase, 1926

1. Joseph Breck to Lockwood de Forest, July 4, 1925; Archives, The Metropolitan Museum of Art.
2. Hard-paste is also known as "true" porcelain because its formulation follows that of traditional Chinese porcelain. The batch is made from kaolin and feldspathic clay, which, when fired at a high temperature, becomes extremely hard, durable, and resonant with a glassy surface.
3. The 1932 Sèvres trade catalogue depicts five of these; a sixth pattern appears in Yvonne Brunhammer, "Éléments pour une histoire d'Henri Rapin," in *Āru deco yōshiki no Sēburu jikiten: 20-seiki no ereganzu; Tōkyō-to Teien Bijutsukan Kaikan 10-shūnen kinen/Sèvres: Pour célébrer le dixième anniversaire du Musée Teien; Élégance du 20ème siècle, L'Exposition des porcelains de Sèvres du style art déco* (Tokyo: Tōkyō-to Bunka Shinkōkai, 1993), p. 48, no. 45.
4. Two examples (with lids) were sold at Christie's, New York, *Fine Art Nouveau and Art Deco*, June 15, 1985, lot 451; two other examples (missing lids) were sold at Sotheby's, New York, *Important 20th Century Design*, June 12, 2013, lot 80.

ÉMILE DECŒUR

1. *A Selected Collection of Objects from the International Exposition of Modern Decorative and Industrial Art at Paris 1925* (Washington, D.C.: The American Association of Museums, 1926), p. 9.
2. W. B. Dalton, "Émile Decœur: An Appreciation," *Ceramic Age* 59, no. 5 (May 1952), p. 22.
3. In spite of the great admiration for his work, little has been written on Decœur. The most complete biography is Michel Giraud and Fabienne Fravalo,

Émile Decœur, 1876–1953 (Paris: Galerie Michel Giraud Éditions, 2008).

4. He exhibited works at the international exhibitions in Milan (1906), Copenhagen (1908), Brussels (1910), and Turin (1911). His work was also included in ceramics exhibitions at the Musée Galliera in Paris (1908 and 1911).
5. Decœur and his wife enjoyed a long marriage. Augustine died in 1943. Decœur remarried the following year.
6. His work was included in the Inaugural Exposition of French Art at the California Palace of the Legion of Honor in San Francisco (1924–25), the American Association of Museums' traveling exhibition of works from the 1925 Paris Exposition (1926), the exhibition of French art in Bucharest (1928), and the American Federation of Arts' International Exhibition of Ceramic Art (1928–29). É.-J. Ruhlmann showed Decœur's work at his Paris showroom in 1927 and 1931.
7. René Chavance, *La Céramique et la verrerie* (Paris: Les Éditions Rieder, 1928), pp. 30–32.
8. Guillaume Janneau, "Les Céramiques d'Émile Decœur," *Art et décoration* 45 (January–June 1924), pp. 42, 44.
9. Ibid., p. 44.

10 | Jar and Two Vases

1. Joseph Breck, "Accessions and Notes: Modern Decorative Arts," *Bulletin of The Metropolitan Museum of Art* 24, no. 10 (October 1929), p. 269.
2. Dalton, "Émile Decœur: An Appreciation," p. 23.
3. Ibid., p. 24.
4. Ibid.

11 | Vase

1. It is not known where Decœur first discovered the pottery of the Tang and Song dynasties (7th–13th centuries), but his first exposure was possibly through reproductions. Several important volumes on this subject were published in France in the early twentieth century and would have been available to him.
2. This quotation and those following are taken from Dalton, "Émile Decœur: An Appreciation," p. 23.

FRANÇOIS-ÉMILE DÉCORCHEMONT

1. René Chavance, "Les Pâtes de verre de Décorchemont," *Art et décoration* 49 (March 1926), p. 75.
2. Ibid., p. 80.
3. On Décorchemont, see Véronique Ayroles, *François Décorchemont: Maître de la pâte de verre* (Paris: Éditions Norma, 2006).
4. Décorchemont's work was shown at the Musée Galliera in Paris (1908, 1910, 1923) and included in the important exhibition "Le Décor de la vie de 1900 à 1925," held at the Musée des Arts Décoratifs in 1937. In 1923, his work was displayed by É.-J. Ruhlmann and DIM and at the Galeries Lafayette department store, and in 1925 at the Galerie Edgar Brandt. Décorchemont also contributed work to the 1931 Exposition Coloniale Internationale and the 1937 Exposition Internationale des Arts et Techniques dans la Vie Moderne.
5. His work was displayed in the Grand Palais, the Rouard pavilion, the Ambassade Française, the Ruhlmann pavilion, and the "Clos Normand"

pavilion. Several pieces were also included in the 1926 traveling exhibition of works from the Exposition organized by the American Association of Museums.
6. Décorchemont contributed works to international exhibitions in Milan (1906), Bucharest (1906), Tokyo (1909), Brussels (1910), Turin (1911), and New York (1939–40). Works were also shown in the Inaugural Exposition of French Art at the California Palace of the Legion of Honor in San Francisco (1924–25) and the American Federation of Arts' traveling International Exhibition of Contemporary Glass and Rugs (1929–30). His work was sold in New York at Haviland & Co. and at the Jacques Seligmann Gallery, in Algiers and Oran at the Taourel Galerie d'Art Contemporain, and in Buenos Aires at La Maison de l'Art Français.

12 | Bowl

1. Henri Lavedan, 1912, quoted in Ayroles, *François Décorchemont*, p. 315.
2. Examples can be found in the collections of the Musée des Arts Décoratifs, Paris, and the Corning Museum of Glass, Corning, New York.
3. Henri Clouzot, "Verreries françaises modernes," *Art et décoration* 44 (July–December 1923), pp. 110–11.

13 | Bowl

1. Chavance, "Les Pâtes de verre de Décorchemont," p. 80.
2. All variants were produced in 1928. Ayroles, *François Décorchemont*, p. 277.

MICHEL DUBOST

1. Colette's words were used in a print advertisement for Ducharne silks that appeared in Paul Poiret's publicity compendium *PAN: Annuaire du luxe à Paris* (Paris: Devambez, 1928).
2. Silk lingerie and undergarments (which previously tended to be made from linen or cotton) first became popular at this time, as did silk pajamas and silk shirts for men. The post–World War I period also saw an important shift from handwoven to machine-woven silks.
3. For a history of the Ducharne firm, see *Les Folles Années de la soie* (Lyons: Musée Historique des Tissus, 1975) and Rosalind Pepall, "François Ducharne: An Exceptional Client," in *Ruhlmann: Genius of Art Deco* (Paris: Somogy Éditions d'Art, 2004), pp. 218–23.
4. On Dubost, see Henri Clouzot, "Un Dessinateur de soieries: Michel Dubost," *Art et industrie* 7, no. 9 (September 1931), p. 21.
5. Located in central eastern France at the convergence of the Rhône and Saône Rivers, Lyons was ideally positioned as a center of commerce and during the Renaissance developed an active silk trade with Italy. By the early nineteenth century, an important silk manufacturing industry had been established, which employed nearly half the city's population.
6. P. A., "La Formation des dessinateurs en soieries et l'École Lyonnaise des Beaux-Arts," *La Soierie de Lyon* 2, no. 15 (August 1, 1919), p. 241.
7. Ibid., pp. 240–41 (English translation included with original article).
8. Henri Clouzot, "L'Art de la soie au Musée Galliera, II: L'Art moderne de la soie," *La Renaissance de l'art*

français et des industries de luxe 10 (August 1927), p. 382 (English translation included with original article); and M. R. B., "The Romance of French Fabrics," *Vogue* 65, no. 3 (February 1, 1925), p. 110.

14 | L'Oiseau dans la lumière

1. "Les Soieries de Ducharne," in *L'Exposition Internationale des Arts Décoratifs et Industriels Modernes, Paris 1925* (Paris: Les Éditions G. Crès & Cie, 1925), p. 175.
2. Clouzot, "Un Dessinateur de soieries," p. 22.

RAOUL DUFY

1. On Dufy's work in design, see *Raoul Dufy*, exh. cat. (London: The Arts Council of Great Britain, 1983); and *Raoul Dufy: Le Plaisir*, exh. cat. (Paris: Musée d'Art Moderne de la Ville de Paris, 2008).
2. Paul Poiret, *King of Fashion: The Autobiography of Paul Poiret*, trans. Stephen Haden Guest (Philadelphia and London: J. B. Lippincott Company, 1931), p. 164.
3. Ibid., pp. 164–65. Philippe de la Salle was a noted eighteenth-century textile designer. Oberkampf refers to Christophe-Philippe Oberkampf, owner of the textile manufactory in Jouy-en-Josas that printed the famous pastoral *toiles de Jouy*.
4. Dufy's textiles were featured in the Bianchini-Férier display in the Grand Palais, and used as furnishing fabrics in both the Lyons pavilion and the Alpes-Maritimes pavilion. The ceramic fountain was made for the pavilion of the magazine *La Renaissance*.

15 | Four Textiles

1. Paul T. Frankl, *Form and Re-Form: A Practical Handbook of Modern Interiors* (New York: Harper and Brothers, 1930), pp. 103–5.
2. Henri Clouzot, "Les 'Tissus modernes' de Raoul Dufy," *Art et décoration* 38 (July–December 1920), pp. 177–78.
3. Ten of Dufy's designs were put into production at that time.
4. Clouzot, "Les 'Tissus modernes' de Dufy," pp. 181–82.
5. Geoffrey Rayner, *Artists' Textiles: Artist Designed Textiles, 1940–1976* (Woodbridge: Antique Collectors' Club, 2012), p. 11.
6. Clouzot, "Les 'Tissus modernes' de Dufy," p. 182.

16 | Five Swimmers

1. Dufy and Llorens Artigas were probably introduced in 1922 by their mutual friend the Spanish sculptor-ceramist Francisco "Paco" Durrio.
2. André Warnod, "Raoul Dufy," *Art et industrie* 3, no. 2 (February 1927), p. 37.
3. Dufy seems not to have assigned titles to his pots. The Metropolitan's descriptive title was specified by the donor, James H. Stubblebine, in his will. From 1957 until his death in 1987, Stubblebine was a professor of art history at Rutgers University, specializing in early Renaissance painting.

JEAN DUNAND

1. On Dunand, see Félix Marcilhac, *Jean Dunand: His Life and Works* (New York: Harry N. Abrams, 1991).
2. *A Selected Collection of Objects from the International Exposition of Modern Decorative and Industrial*

Art at Paris 1925 (Washington, D.C.: The American Association of Museums, 1926), p. 13.

3. Amalie Busck Deady, "The Unique Metal Work of Jean Dunand," *The Craftsman* 19, no. 4 (January 1911), p. 407.

4. Sugawara had arrived in Paris as part of a delegation for the Japanese display at the Exposition Universelle in 1900 and stayed to ply his trade. Another of his European students was Eileen Gray.

5. Dedo von Kerssenbrock-Krosigk, ed., *Modern Art of Metalwork: Bröhan-Museum, State Museum of Art Nouveau, Art Deco and Functionalism (1889–1939), Berlin* (Berlin: Bröhan-Museum, 2001), p. 408.

6. *The New York Times*, March 30, 1925, p. 6.

7. At the 1925 Expo, he presented a smoking room in the Ambassade Française; works in both metal and lacquer at the Ruhlmann pavilion, the Pavillon de l'Élégance, and the Pavillon des Artistes Français Contemporains, among others; and lacquered jewelry, which was worn by models at the fashion shows.

8. Among the international exhibitions in which Dunand participated were the Universal Exhibition in Brussels (1910), the Exhibition of Contemporary French Art at Polk Hall in San Francisco (1923), the Inaugural Exposition of French Art at the California Palace of the Legion of Honor in San Francisco (1924–25), the American Association of Museums' traveling exhibition of works from the 1925 Paris Expo (1926), the exhibition of French decorative arts at the Tokyo Imperial Museum (1928), the Universal Exhibition in Barcelona (1929), the Third International Exhibition of Contemporary Industrial Art (1930–31), and the world's fairs held in San Francisco and New York (1939–40). His work was exhibited in New York at Cartier Gallery (1923), Jacques Seligmann Gallery (1926), Reinhardt Gallery (1926), Park Avenue Galleries (1928), Lord & Taylor (1928), Macy's (1928), and Rosenbach Gallery (1930). It was also displayed at the I. Magnin department store in San Francisco (1939).

9. Maximilien Gauthier, "Vingt Minutes avec Jean Dunand," *La Renaissance politique, littéraire, et artistique*, n.d. [ca. 1923], n.p.

18 | Five Vases

1. Inlay involves carving channeled grooves into the surface of a vessel and then hammering a secondary metal — generally a softer one, such as silver — into the grooves. Patination alters the color of metal with acids, metal oxides, or naked flame, transforming gold, silver, and copper into tones of green, brown, or black; though not as precise as inlaying, the subtle effects can be equally elegant. Dunand's earliest incorporation of lacquer was often done in combination with other techniques such as inlay, patination, gilding, and embossing.

19 | Three Lacquered Panels

1. In its liquid state, natural lacquer is toxic and can cause severe skin rashes even by indirect contact. For Dunand's lacquer-working processes, see Mechthild Baumeister "Jean Dunand: A Master of Art Deco Lacquer," in *Ostasiatische und europäische Lacktechniken/East Asian and European Lacquer Techniques*, Arbeitshefte des Bayerischen Landesamtes für Denkmalpflege 112 (Munich: Lipp, 2000), pp. 207–18. A group of lacquer samples made by Dunand, together with

some of his tools, is preserved in the Sherman Fairchild Objects Conservation Department at the Metropolitan Museum.

2. During the war, Dunand experimented with lacquer to strengthen and protect wood military airplane propellers. His success prompted the French government to establish a lacquer workshop, the Société des Lacques Indochinoises, for this purpose in Boulogne-sur-Seine in 1917.

3. Thérèse Bonney and Louise Bonney, *Buying Antique and Modern Furniture in Paris* (New York: Robert M. McBride & Company, 1929), p. 45.

4. Ibid., p. 46.

5. Joseph Breck, "Accessions and Notes: Decorative Arts," *Bulletin of The Metropolitan Museum of Art* 19, no. 11 (November 1924), p. 275.

6. This panel was owned by Templeton Crocker (see no. 21). It is unclear where he used it, as it does not appear in any period photographs of his residence. A related panel with a nearly identical composition depicts a woman with a patterned turban and dress, her face revealed in a mirror; see Marcilhac, *Jean Dunand*, p. 227, no. 238.

7. In an article titled "In Paris You Must Have a Lacquer Portrait," in which several portraits by Dunand are illustrated, the unidentified author notes, "This is quite a vogue and quite new with a curious sort of interest between the use of lacquer and the use of the brush in one portrait." *Arts and Decoration* 27 (October 1927), p. 134.

20 | *Fortissimo* and *Pianissimo* Screens

1. The house was designed by Howard Van Buren Magonigle, with gardens by Ferruccio Vitale. For a complete history, see Paul J. Mateyunas, *North Shore Long Island Country Houses, 1890–1950* (New York: Acanthus Press, 2007), pp. 180–91.

2. After meeting Hilla Rebay in 1927, Guggenheim would begin collecting contemporary art. He founded the Museum of Non-Objective Painting in 1939; the Solomon R. Guggenheim Museum opened in 1959.

3. Burdon-Muller to Metropolitan Museum curator John McKendry, February 19, 1973; Archives, The Metropolitan Museum of Art.

4. Burdon-Muller to Metropolitan Museum curator James David Draper, December 4, 1971; Archives, The Metropolitan Museum of Art.

5. Augusta Owen Patterson, "The Revision of a Long Island Residence," *Town & Country* 81, no. 3954 (February 15, 1927), pp. 47–48.

6. Burdon-Muller to McKendry, February 19, 1973. The pair of double doors are now in the collection of the Cooper-Hewitt, National Design Museum, Smithsonian Institution, New York.

7. Soudbinine to Burdon-Muller, December 15, 1925; Archives, The Metropolitan Museum of Art.

8. "Spring Days in the Art Galleries," *The New York Times*, April 25, 1926, p. x12.

9. The titles appear, handwritten, in Mrs. Guggenheim's signed offer of gift, dated May 15, 1950; Archives, The Metropolitan Museum of Art.

21 | Bedroom Furniture and Wall Maquette made for Templeton Crocker

1. Mary Ashe Miller, "A Twentieth Century Apartment," *Vogue* 74, no. 3 (August 3, 1929), p. 31.

2. Bonney and Bonney, *Buying Antique and Modern Furniture in Paris*, p. 43.

3. Ruby Ross Wood. "A Decorator Looks at California," *Vogue* 93, no. 8 (April 15, 1939), p. 138.

4. Miller, "Twentieth Century Apartment," p. 31.

5. Information supplied to the author in 2002 by Christian Dougoud, the husband of one of Dunand's granddaughters.

6. Rita Reif, "Antiques: Paris Enigma," *The New York Times*, January 4, 1975, p. 20.

JEAN DUPAS

1. Marcel Valotaire, "Jean Dupas: His Work and Ideas," *Creative Art* 2, no. 6 (June 1928), pp. 386, 389.

2. The most complete biography of Dupas can be found in Jacqueline du Pasquier, *Affiches de Jean Dupas*, exh. cat. (Bordeaux: Musée des Arts Décoratifs de la Ville de Bordeaux, 1987).

3. Valotaire, "Jean Dupas," pp. 386–89.

4. Ibid., p. 389.

22 | *The Chariot of Poseidon*

1. Few facts are known about the life of Charles Champigneulle (1907–1955), a fourth-generation glass painter whose family firm, Maison Champigneulle, produced stained-glass windows for French churches. This was probably the only reverse-painted glass the firm produced.

2. The glass for the SS *Normandie* panels was manufactured by Saint-Gobain.

3. The Metropolitan Museum recently received as a gift one of the salon's wall lights (acc. no. 2013.45.1). Made of brass with faceted glass reflectors, they were designed by Auguste Labouret and set into the grid of the glass panels.

4. Quoted in Valotaire, "Jean Dupas," p. 386.

PAUL FOLLOT

1. Guillaume Janneau, "L'Exposition des arts techniques de 1924, IV.: La Participation des artistes," *Le Bulletin de la vie artistique* 3 (July 1, 1922), p. 297.

2. On Follot, see Jessica Rutherford, "Paul Follot," *The Connoisseur* 204 (June 1980), pp. 86–91. Curiously, some period publications on Follot's work refer to him as Charles Follot; writers may have confused the ensemblier with a wallpaper manufacturer of that name.

3. Follot contributed works to the international exhibitions in Brussels (1910), Turin (1911), and Munich (1913).

4. Émile Sedeyn, *Le Mobilier* (Paris: F. Rieder et Cie, 1921), p. 56.

5. Pierre Olmer, *Le Mobilier français d'aujourd'hui* (Paris: G. van Oest, 1926), p. 30.

6. Thérèse Bonney and Louise Bonney, *A Shopping Guide to Paris* (New York: Robert M. McBride & Company, 1929), p. 178.

GEORGES FOUQUET

1. Jean Fouquet, *Bijoux et orfèvrerie* (Paris: Éditions d'Art Charles Moreau, 1931).

2. On Maison Fouquet, see A. Kenneth Snowman, ed., *The Master Jewelers* (New York: Harry N. Abrams, 1990), pp. 157–72.

3. Quoted in Henri Clouzot, "La Parure à l'exposition des arts décoratifs," *La Renaissance de l'art français et des industries de luxe* 9, no. 1 (January 1926),

p. 42 (English translation included with original article).

4. During his career, Fouquet would collaborate with, among others, architect Eric Bagge, graphic designer Cassandre, sculptor Jean Lambert-Rucki, and painter André Léveillé.

5. Émile Sedeyn, "Des Bijoux nouveaux," *Art et décoration* 43 (May 1923), pp. 146–47.

23 | Dress Ornament

1. *Report of Commission Appointed by the Secretary of Commerce to Visit and Report upon the International Exposition of Modern Decorative and Industrial Art in Paris, 1925* (Washington, D.C., 1926), p. 62.

2. Jean Fouquet, *Bijoux et orfèvrerie*, p. 1.

3. Clouzot, "La Parure à l'exposition des arts décoratifs," p. 40 (English translation included with original article).

ÉMILE GAUDISSARD

1. Ernest Tisserand, "Un Décorateur poète: Émile Gaudissard," *L'Art et les artistes* 14 (October 1926–February 1927), p. 30.

2. Ibid., pp. 29–30.

MARCEL GOUPY

1. The most complete biographical information can be found in Victor Arwas, *Glass: Art Nouveau to Art Deco* (New York: Harry N. Abrams, 1987), pp. 154–57.

2. The artists included Laure Albin-Guillot, Georges Bastard, René Buthaud, Maurice Daurat, Émile Decœur, François-Émile Décorchemont, Auguste Delaherche, Jean Dunand, Denise Germain, Louis Jouhaud, Reneé Kieffer, René Lalique, Gaston Le Bourgeois, Émile Lenoble, Léonard Limosin, Claudius Linossier, Jean Mayodon, Guillaume Met de Penninghen, Henri Navarre, O'Kin, Jean Puiforcat, Georges Serré, and Henri Simmen.

3. René Chavance, *La Céramique et la verrerie* (Paris: Les Éditions Rieder, 1928), p. 115.

4. *Report of Commission Appointed by the Secretary of Commerce to Visit and Report upon the International Exposition of Modern Decorative and Industrial Art in Paris, 1925* (Washington, D.C., 1926), p. 56. Goupy's best-known enameler was Auguste Heiligenstein. Hired in 1919, he left Rouard in 1921 to work under his own name.

5. While most sources cite 1954 as the date of Goupy's death, it has also been given as 1977 and 1980.

6. Goupy participated regularly in the Salons of the Société des Artistes Décorateurs and the Salon d'Automne. His work was included in glass exhibitions at the Musée des Arts Décoratifs and the Musée Galliera (both 1923). Examples were displayed in the Inaugural Exposition of French Art at the California Palace of the Legion of Honor in San Francisco (1924–25), the American Association of Museums' traveling exhibition of works from the 1925 Paris Exposition (1926), the American Federation of Arts' International Exhibition of Ceramic Art (1928–29), the International Exhibition of Contemporary Glass and Rugs (1929–30), and the Milan Triennale (1936). Rouard mounted displays at international expositions in Amsterdam (1922), Monza (1923), Barcelona (1923 and 1929), Madrid (1927), Athens (1928), and Rotterdam (1928), as well as in Paris at the 1931 Exposition Coloniale Internationale and the Exposition Internationale des Arts et Techniques dans la Vie Moderne of 1937.

24 | Vase

1. Léon Rosenthal, *La Verrerie française depuis cinquante ans* (Paris: G. Vanoest, 1927), p. 33.

PAUL IRIBE

1. [Louis Cheronnet], "Informations et nouvelles: Paul Iribe," *Art et décoration/Les Échos d'art* 64 (1935), p. 43.

2. Paul Morand, "Adieux à Paul Iribe," *Le Figaro littéraire*, September 28, 1935, p. 5.

3. On Iribe, see Raymond Bachollet, Daniel Bordet, and Anne-Claude Lelieur, *Paul Iribe* (Paris: Éditions Denoël, 1982).

4. Paul Poiret, *King of Fashion: The Autobiography of Paul Poiret*, trans. Stephen Haden Guest (Philadelphia and London: J. B. Lippincott Company, 1931), pp. 98–99.

5. See Robert Carsix, "Bijoux dessinés par Iribe," *Art et décoration* 29 (January–June 1911), pp. 27–32, and "Jewels Designed by a French Artist," *Arts and Decoration* 1, no. 11 (September 1911), pp. 426–27.

6. A description of Paul Iribe et Cie, which closed in 1914, appears in Bachollet, Bordet, and Lelieur, *Paul Iribe*, p. 124. See also "Cushioned Ease," *Vogue* 45, no. 6 (March 15, 1915), pp. 66–68.

7. For the apartment (see p. 135, top) , Iribe designed two low armchairs and a commode (Musée des Arts Décoratifs, Paris), as well as a desk and armchair (Bibliothèque Jacques Doucet, Paris).

8. Quoted in Bachollet, Bordet, and Lelieur, *Paul Iribe*, p. 120.

25 | Roses

1. "Cushioned Ease," p. 66.

2. A textile with this colorway was acquired by the Musée Historique des Tissus in Lyons sometime before 1929. It is described in the museum's catalogue as a silk brocade with a composition by Paul Iribe "representing coupes decorated with two roses and arranged in an alternating pattern." Henri d'Hennezel, *Musée Historique des Tissus: Catalogue des principales pièces exposées* (Lyons: Société Anonyme de l'Imprimerie A. Rey, 1929), p. 121.

LÉON-ALBERT JALLOT

1. Pierre Olmer, *Le Mobilier français d'aujourd'hui (1910–1925)* (Paris: G. van Oest, 1926), p. 29.

2. Jallot contributed on a regular basis to the Salon des Artistes Décorateurs, the Salon d'Automne, and the Salons of the Société des Artistes Français and the Société Nationale des Beaux-Arts.

3. Maurice Pillard Verneuil, "Les Meubles de Jallot," *Art et décoration* 25 (January–June 1909), p. 131.

4. René Chavance, "Léon Jallot," *Art et décoration* 46 (July–December 1924), pp. 82–83.

5. Ibid., p. 86.

6. The bedroom was designed in collaboration with Georges Chevalier. Jallot father and son also contributed furniture to, among other venues, the Ruhlmann pavilion and to Henri Rapin's grand salon in the Ambassade Française.

7. Marcel Valotaire, "M. Léon Jallot's Furniture," *The Studio* 92 (1926), p. 412.

26 | Cabinet

1. Valotaire, "M. Léon Jallot's Furniture," pp. 410–12.

2. Correspondence between Jallot and Breck, April 25–May 23, 1927; Archives, The Metropolitan Museum of Art.

PAUL JOUVE

1. See Félix Marcilhac, *Paul Jouve: Peintre, sculpteur, animalier, 1878–1973* (Paris: Les Éditions de l'Amateur, 2005).

RENÉ LALIQUE

1. Maurice Guillemot, "La Verrerie au Musée Galliéra," *Art et décoration* 28 (1910), p. 22.

2. On Lalique, see Félix Marcilhac, *René Lalique, 1860–1945: Maître-verrier*, 4th ed. (Paris: Les Éditions de l'Amateur, 2011).

3. Lalique glass was shown at the International Exhibitions of Turin (1902 and 1911), Saint Louis (1904), Brussels (1910) and San Francisco (1915). It was also included in the important glass exhibition of 1910 at the Musée Galliera.

4. In 1923, Lalique glass was included in exhibitions at the Musée Galliera and the Musée des Arts Décoratifs. Pieces were also shown at the Brooklyn Museum and at Knoedler Gallery in New York (both 1919), the Inaugural Exposition of French Art at the California Palace of the Legion of Honor in San Francisco (1924–25), the American Association of Museums' traveling exhibition of selected works from the 1925 Paris Exposition (1926), the exhibition of French art in Bucharest (1928), the American Federation of Arts' traveling International Exhibition of Contemporary Glass and Rugs (1929–30), and the Ideal Home Exhibition in London (1931).

5. Gabriel Mourey, "Lalique's Glassware," *Commercial Art* 1 (1926), p. 35.

6. Adeline L. Atwater, "Lalique: Modernist in Glass," *The Atlanta Constitution*, April 14, 1929, p. H12.

7. René Chavance, *La Céramique et la verrerie* (Paris: Les Éditions Rieder, 1928), p. 91.

27 | Monnaie du Pape Coffer

1. "Art Notes: René Lalique's Jewelry on Display at Knoedler's," *The New York Times*, April 9, 1919, p. 10.

2. Marcilhac, *René Lalique*, p. 285.

28 | Hagueneau Wine Glasses

1. Gaston Derys, "L'Exposition de l'œuvre de René Lalique," *Mobilier et décoration* 13 (March 1933), p. 101.

29 | Tourbillons Vase

1. Mrs. Gordon-Stables, "Lalique," *Artwork* 3, no. 9 (March–May 1927), p. 34.

2. Marcilhac, *René Lalique*, p. 433.

3. Ibid., p. 106.

4. Carolyn Hatch, *Déco Lalique: Creator to Consumer*, exh. cat. (Toronto: Royal Ontario Museum, 2006), p. 95.

30 | Vase

1. "Art Notes: Lalique's Jewelry at Knoedler's," p. 10.
2. Marcilhac, *René Lalique*, p. 1054.

31 | Rings and Necklace

1. Gordon-Stables, "Lalique," p. 34.
2. "Lalique Glass Is Used in New Paris Jewelry," *The New York Times*, June 17, 1928, p. 107.
3. Olive Gray, "The New in Stores & Homes," *The Los Angeles Times*, September 2, 1928, p. C21.

ROBERT LALLEMANT

1. On Lallemant, see *Céramiques de Robert Lallemant*, exh. cat. (Bordeaux: Musée des Arts Décoratifs, 1992).
2. René Chavance, "À propos de quelques céramiques nouvelles de Robert Lallemant," *Mobilier et décoration* 9, no. 7 (July 1929), pp. 135–36.
3. Ibid., p. 136.

32 | Vase

1. Lucie Delarue-Mardrus, "Les Céramiques noires de Robert Lallemant," *Art et industrie* 4, no. 6 (June 10, 1928), p. 44.
2. Chavance, "À propos de quelques céramiques nouvelles de Lallemant," p. 139.

JACQUES LE CHEVALLIER AND RENÉ KOECHLIN

1. See Jean-François Archieri, *Jacques Le Chevallier, 1896–1987: La Lumière moderne*, exh. cat. (Roubaix: Gourcuff Gradenigo, 2007).
2. At the 1925 Exposition, under the Barillet name, Le Chevallier created windows for the Pavilion of Tourism Information and the Ambassade Française. As a member of Les Artisans de l'Autel, he oversaw the group's contribution, a small chapel in the Village Français display.
3. Our René Koechlin is sometimes confused with another French engineer of the same name. René Koechlin (1866–1951) worked on the Simplon Pass tunnel and the Paris Métro among other civic and national projects.
4. Three of the twenty were included in the American Federation of Arts' Third International Exhibition of Contemporary Industrial Art in 1930–31 and in the exhibition "Métaux dans l'art" of 1932, held at the Musée Galliera in Paris.
5. Le Chevallier taught in Paris at the École des Beaux-Arts and at the Centre d'Art Sacré.

33 | Lamp

1. The group included table lamps, reading lamps, desk lamps, piano lamps, and wall lamps; there was also a dressing-table lamp, an altar lamp, and a hanging lamp. Ebonite is a hard rubber compound first made in 1839 by Charles Goodyear for use in writing instruments and bowling balls.
2. "Esthétique du luminaire," *L'Art vivant* 14, no. 144 (December 15, 1930), p. 939.
3. DIM produced a range of Le Chevallier and Koechlin's lighting designs, as well as models by other designers, inluding Jean Prouvé.

PIERRE LEGRAIN

1. Jacques Anthoine-Legrain, "'Souvenirs' sur Legrain," in Jacques Millot et al., *Pierre Legrain, relieur* (Paris: Librairie Auguste Blaizot, 1965), p. xv.
2. On Legrain, see Millot et al., *Pierre Legrain, relieur*.
3. Legrain also designed a tomb at Montparnasse Cemetery for Tachard's son, Louis, who was killed during the war.
4. His co-founders were Pierre Chareau, Jean Puiforcat, Raymond Templier, and the ensemblier firm of Dominique. In 1929, Les Cinq disbanded and its members joined the larger Union des Artistes Modernes. Although Legrain died before the UAM mounted its first exhibition, he designed its distinctive logo.
5. "Sur la tombe de Pierre Legrain," *Plaisir de bibliophile*, 1929, p. 132.

34 | Stool

1. Gaston Varenne, "Quelques Ensembles de Pierre Legrain," *L'Amour de l'art* 5 (December 1924), p. 401.
2. Henry Sorensen to Henry Geldzahler, January 19, 1973; Archives, The Metropolitan Museum of Art. The furniture maker Marcel Coard, like Legrain, worked for Doucet.
3. Varenne, "Quelques Ensembles de Pierre Legrain," p. 401.
4. Sold at Christie's, Paris, June 8, 2006, lot 111.

35 | Portfolio and Cigarette Cases

1. The Metropolitan Museum owns several book bindings by Legrain; they are housed in the Department of Drawings and Prints.
2. Robert Bonfils, "Pierre Legrain, décorateur créateur," in Millot et al., *Pierre Legrain, relieur*, p. xxvii.
3. The two boxes are reproduced on the website of the Archives of American Art, www.aaa.si.edu /collections/jacques-seligmann--co-records-9936.
4. Yves Peyré and H. George Fletcher, *Art Deco Bookbindings: The Work of Pierre Legrain and Rose Adler* (New York: The Princeton Architectural Press, in association with The New York Public Library, 2004), pp. 64–65. The Morand binding has only four horizontal and nine vertical rows of perforations; the spine has gilt detailing and lettering.
5. Sold at Sotheby's, New York, December 15, 2011, lot 84. This cover has seven horizontal and nineteen vertical rows of perforations, each centered on a gilt dot.

JULES-ÉMILE LELEU

1. Magdeleine A.-Dayot, "Jules Leleu," *L'Art et les artistes*, n.s., 24 (March–July 1932), pp. 277–78.
2. On Leleu, see Françoise Siriex, *The House of Leleu: Classic French Style for a Modern World, 1920–1973*, trans. Eric A. Bye (New York: Hudson Hills Press, 2008).
3. Simonne Ratel, "Un Classique moderne: Jules Leleu," *La Demeure française* 3, no. 1 (Spring 1927), pp. 26–27. The author refers to the famous French furniture makers André-Charles Boulle (1642–1732) and Jean-Henri Riesener (1734–1806).
4. Bernard Champigneulle, "Leleu," *Mobilier et décoration* 16 (1936), pp. 46–48.
5. Among Leleu's clients were Enguerrand de Vergie (the French maker of *La Suze* liqueur), the de Wendel family (French mining and steel magnates), Albert Lespinasse (the French head of the Banania instant-beverage company), Prince Takamatsu (brother of Japanese Emperor Hirohito), and Michael Winburn (the American-born founder of the French Cadum pharmaceutical business).
6. Leleu was represented in the American Association of Museums' 1926 traveling exhibition of selected works from the 1925 Paris Exposition. In New York department stores, his furniture was included in the exhibition "Art in Trade" at Macy's (1928) and the "Exhibition of 20th Century Taste" at B. Altman & Co. (1928). He also contributed a cabinet to the exhibition of French decorative arts at the Tokyo Imperial Museum (1928).
7. Dayot, "Jules Leleu," p. 280.

36 | Commode

1. Pierre E. Benoit, "Commodes modernes par J. M. Leleu," *Art et industrie* 3, no. 2 (February 1927), pp. 46–47. The commode was probably shown in Leleu's stand in the furniture section, rather than in the Ambassade Française, as stated in Th. Harlor, "L'Exposition des Arts décoratifs modernes: L'Aménagement intérieur et le mobilier," *Gazette des beaux-arts*, n.s., 12 (December 1925), p. 372. The fair's *Catalogue générale officiel* gives no indication that such a piece was displayed in the Ambassade Française.
2. See Viviane Jutheau, *Jules et André Leleu* (Paris: Éditions Vecteurs, 1989), p. 29. The author mistakenly identifies the variant as belonging to the Metropolitan Museum.
3. Carpenter was a frequent client of the French couturiers. Many of her dresses are now in the collection of the Metropolitan's Anna Wintour Costume Center.
4. The dining room of the house in Bar Harbor, Maine, that Carpenter inherited was redecorated by the French-born Baron Adolphe de Meyer; http:// thedowneastdilettante.blogspot.com/2011/10/ sittin-on-dock-of-bay.html.
5. Joan Kahr, *Edgar Brandt: Master of Art Deco Ironwork* (New York: Harry N. Abrams, 1999), p. 180.
6. Agnes Miles Carpenter to Preston Remington, May 4, 1946; Archives, The Metropolitan Museum of Art.

ÉMILE LENOBLE

1. Léon Deshairs, "Émile Lenoble," *Art et décoration* 46 (July–December 1924), p. 100.
2. On Lenoble, see Anne Lajoix, *La Céramique en France, 1925–1947* (Paris: Éditions Sous le Vent, 1983).
3. Quoted in Charles Fegdal, "À l'atelier de Lenoble," *L'Art et les artistes* 13 (March–July 1926), p. 316.
4. Lenoble exhibited at the Salon des Artistes Décorateurs and the Salon Nationale des Beaux Arts; his work was included in the 1911 Universal Exposition in Turin, and the same year at the Musée Galliera in Paris.
5. Maurice Pillard Verneuil, "E. Lenoble, céramiste," *Art et décoration* 26 (July–December 1909), p. 101.
6. Ibid., p. 102.
7. At the 1925 Paris Exposition, Lenoble's ceramics were displayed at the Grand Palais, the Rouard pavilion, and Ruhlmann's Hôtel du Collectionneur. At the 1937 Paris Exposition his works were shown in the Palais des Céramiques. Lenoble's pots were included in the American Association of Museums' 1926 traveling exhibition of works from the 1925 Paris Expo and the American Federation of Arts'

1928–29 traveling International Exhibition of Ceramic Art.

8. Léon Deshairs, *Les Albums d'art Druet*, vol. 27, *Émile Lenoble: 24 phototypies* (Paris: Librairie de France, 1930), pp. [1, 4].

37 | Three Vases

1. Deshairs, "Émile Lenoble," p. 106.
2. Ibid., p. 104.
3. Deshairs, *Les Albums d'art Druet*, p. [4].
4. Ibid., p. [2].

38 | Vase

1. Deshairs, "Émile Lenoble," p. 97.
2. Pillard Verneuil, "E. Lenoble: Céramiste," p. 103.
3. Deshairs, *Les Albums d'art Druet*, p. [1].

CLAUDIUS LINOSSIER

1. Henri Verne and René Chavance, *Pour comprendre l'art décoratif moderne en France* (Paris: Hachette, 1925), pp. 194–95.
2. On Linossier, see Roger Froment, *Claudius Linossier Dinandier (1893–1953)* (Lyons: Musée des Beaux-Arts, 1979); and Dominique Forest and Marie-Cécile Forest, *La Dinanderie française, 1900–1950* (Paris: Les Éditions de l'Amateur, 1995).
3. Luc Roville, "Claudius Linossier," *Art et décoration* 44 (July–December 1923), pp. 146–47.
4. Yvanhoé Rambosson, "Le Salon des artistes décorateurs," *La Revue de l'art ancien et moderne* 50 (June–December 1926), p. 106.
5. These include the Grand Palais, the Lyons–St. Étienne pavilion, the Ambassade Française, and Ruhlmann's Hôtel du Collectionneur.
6. These include, in the United States, the Inaugural Exposition of French Art at the California Palace of the Legion of Honor in San Francisco (1924–25), the traveling exhibition of works from the 1925 Paris Exposition (1926), the International Exposition of Art in Industry at Macy's department store in New York (1928), and the traveling Third International Exhibition of Contemporary Industrial Art, organized by the American Federation of Arts (1930–31). Displays elsewhere include international exhibitions in Athens (1928), Barcelona (1929), and Monza (1930).
7. "Claudius Linossier Orfèvre," *Les Arts de la maison* 1 (Winter 1923), p. 54.

39 | Vase

1. A nearly identical vase (slightly taller and with banding of diamond lozenges) sold at the Hôtel Drouot, Paris, *Art Nouveau—Art Déco*, November 16, 1994, lot 1.
2. Roville, "Claudius Linossier," pp. 147–48.

JOSEP LLORENS ARTIGAS

1. On Llorens Artigas, see Francesc Miralles, *Llorens Artigas: Catalogue de l'œuvre personnel et créations avec Dufy, Marquet, Miró* (Paris: Éditions Cercle d'Art, 1993). Llorens Artigas's family name sometimes appears as Llorens i Artigas, in the traditional Catalan format.

MAURICE MARINOT

1. *A Selected Collection of Objects from the International Exposition of Modern Decorative and Industrial Art at Paris 1925* (Washington, D.C.: The American Association of Museums, 1926), p. 27.
2. On Marinot, see Olivier Le Bihan et al., *Maurice Marinot, Troyes 1882–Troyes 1960: Penser en verre*, exh. cat. (Paris: Somogy Éditions d'Art; Troyes: Musée d'Art Moderne, 2010).
3. Although a maquette of the Maison Cubiste was displayed at the Armory Show in New York in 1913, Marinot's glass was not included.
4. Marinot's work was included in exhibitions at the Musée Galliera (1921, 1923, 1934) and the Musée Luxembourg (1924) in Paris. It was shown at the Inaugural Exposition of French Art at the California Palace of the Legion of Honor in San Francisco (1924–25) and in the American Federation of Arts' traveling International Exhibition of Contemporary Glass and Rugs (1929–30). In Paris his work was displayed at the Hébrard and Barbazanges galleries, and in the showrooms of the Compagnie des Arts Français and Ruhlmann. In New York it was seen at De Hauke & Co., at Les Arts Modernes Inc., and at the Brummer Gallery.
5. At the 1925 Expo, Marinot's glass was displayed in the Galerie Hébrard pavilion, the Ambassade Française, and in Louis Süe and André Mare's Musée d'Art Contemporain.
6. Gabriel Mourey, "A French Glassmaker: Maurice Marinot," *The Studio* 93 (1927), p. 247.

40 | Three Bottles and Bowl

1. Léon Rosenthal, *La Verrerie française depuis cinquante ans* (Paris: G. van Oest, 1927), p. 32.
2. Mourey, "French Glassmaker: Marinot," p. 248.
3. Henri Clouzot, "Verreries françaises modernes," *Art et décoration* 44 (July–December 1923), pp. 102–4.

41 | Four Vessels

1. Ada Polak, "Maurice Marinot's Glass," *The Connoisseur* 159, no. 639 (May 1965), p. 21.
2. Ibid.
3. Marvin D. Schwartz, "Antiques: Glass of the 20's," *The New York Times*, April 5, 1969, p. 24.
4. C. Geoffrey Holme and Shirley B. Wainwright, eds., *Decorative Art, 1927: "The Studio" Yearbook* (London: The Studio, Ltd., 1927), p. 137.
5. Marvin D. Schwartz, "Antiques: Marinot Glass," *The New York Times*, October 9, 1971, p. 28.

JAN AND JOËL MARTEL

1. Louis-Charles Watelin, "Les Animaux des frères Martel," *L'Art et les artistes* 21, no. 70 (October 1926), pp. 98–100.
2. See *Joël et Jan Martel: Sculpteurs, 1896–1966*, exh. cat. (Paris: Gallimard/Electa, 1996).
3. Paul Fierens, "Jan et Joël Martel," *L'Art et les artistes* 32, no. 168 (June 1936), p. 295.
4. They printed a card that identified the twelve venues—including the entrance gate at the Place de la Concorde, the Tourist Information pavilion, the Sèvres pavilion, and the Ambassade Française—and the works shown at each one; see *Joël et Jan Martel: Sculpteurs*, p. 58.
5. Fierens, "Jan et Joël Martel," p. 300.

42 | Maquette for a Cubist Tree

1. "La Nature en ciment armé," *Le Bulletin de la vie artistique* 6, no. 15 (August 1, 1925), p. 328.
2. The trees were realized by the construction company Auger et Bonnet, with the support of the Société de Ciment Français.
3. Dorothée Imbert, *The Modernist Garden in France* (New Haven: Yale University Press, 1993), pp. 38, 40.
4. Quoted in "La Nature en ciment armé," p. 329.
5. Charles Fegdal, "L'Art du 'jardin moderne,'" *La Revue des beaux-arts*, ser. 4, no. 437 (October 1, 1925), p. 1.
6. Two other examples are known: one painted (Musée des Beaux-Arts et de la Dentelle, Calais), the other unpainted (private collection, France). A full-scale reproduction is installed in the Musée des Années Trente, Boulogne-Billancourt.

HENRI ÉDOUARD NAVARRE

1. Henri Classens, "Henri Navarre," *L'Art et les artistes* 29 (October 1934–February 1935), p. 56.
2. Very little has been written on Navarre. The most useful sources are Classens, "Henri Navarre," pp. 56–59, and "Dictionnaire des artistes décorateurs," *Mobilier et décoration* 34 (January–February 1954), p. 34.
3. The masks are illustrated in Jean Gallotti, "Un Artiste de verre: Henri Navarre," *Art et décoration* 61 (1932), pp. 42, 43.
4. "Dictionnaire des artistes décorateurs," p. 34.

43 | Vase

1. Gallotti, "Un Artiste de verre," p. 46.
2. Classens, "Henri Navarre," p. 58.
3. R. G. H., "Work in Various Mediums," *The New York Times*, November 16, 1930, p. X11.

PIERRE PATOUT

1. The Patout archive is held at the Institut Français d'Architecture in Paris. For biographical information, see the institute's website: http://archiwebture .citechaillot.fr/fonds/FRAPN02_PATPI.

44 | Pair of Armchairs

1. Examples from the table services by Lalique (acc. no. 1985.430.16), Lanel (acc. nos. 1985.430.1ab–.15, 2010.183.1ab-5), and Luce (acc. no. 1985.430.19) are in the collection of The Metropolitan Museum of Art.
2. It has been suggested that they were designed with Maurice Pré, who worked at Patout's atelier, although it is unclear what his role might have been; see Frédéric Ollivier, Aymeric Perroy, and Franck Sénant, *À bord des paquebots: 50 ans d'arts décoratifs* (Paris: Éditions Norma, 2011), p. 332.

PAUL POIRET

1. Paul Poiret, *King of Fashion: The Autobiography of Paul Poiret*, trans. Stephen Haden Guest (Philadelphia and London: J. B. Lippincott Company, 1931); Paul Poiret, *En habillant l'époque* (Paris: B. Grasset, 1930). In addition to Poiret's autobiography, there are a number of excellent biographies, notably Yvonne Deslandes, *Paul Poiret, 1879–1944*, trans. Paula Clifford (New York: Rizzoli, 1987), and

Palmer White, *Poiret* (New York: C. N. Potter, 1973). In 2007 the Metropolitan Museum organized an exhibition devoted to the designer. This essay is adapted from the author's contribution to that catalogue; see Jared Goss, "Paul Poiret and the Decorative Arts," in Harold Koda et al., *Poiret*, exh. cat. (New York: The Metropolitan Museum of Art, 2007), pp. 43–44.
2. "Poiret, Creator of Fashions, Here," *The New York Times*, September 21, 1913, p. x3.
3. Ibid.
4. These include the printers Paul Dumas and Desfossé & Karth for wallpapers, the cabinetmaker Adolphe Chanaux for furniture, and Murano workshops for glassware.
5. Thérèse Bonney and Louise Bonney, *Buying Antique and Modern Furniture in Paris* (New York: Robert M. McBride & Company, 1929), p. 45.
6. *Contempora Exposition of Art and Industry*, exh. cat. (New York: Contempora, 1929), n.p.
7. "Paul Poiret Takes Dole as Jobless," *The Los Angeles Times*, August 16, 1934, p. 3.

45 | Four Textiles

1. Bonney and Bonney, *Buying Antique and Modern Furniture in Paris*, p. 44.
2. *Les Arts de la maison*, Winter 1923, p. 48.
3. "Martine Decoration," *The New-York Tribune*, February 1, 1914, p. B9.
4. Poiret, *King of Fashion*, p. 93.
5. In New York, retailers included Paul T. Frankl's Frankl Galleries, and in London, Marcel Boulestin's Décoration Moderne.
6. "Poiret, Creator of Fashions, Here," p. x3.
7. André Billy, Review of *En habillant l'époque*, *La Femme de France*, no. 820 (January 25, 1931), p. 20.

FRANÇOIS POMPON

1. On the life of Pompon, see Catherine Chevillot, Liliane Colas, and Anne Pingeot, *François Pompon, 1855–1933*, exh. cat. (Paris: Gallimard/Electa; Réunion des Musées Nationaux, 1994).
2. Julien Léonard, "Pompon: Sculpteur, animalier," *L'Art et les artistes*, n.s., 8, no. 42 (October 1923–February 1924), p. 150.
3. Paul Doncoeur, "Revue des livres," *Études* 65, no. 196 (August 1928), p. 638.
4. Léonard, "Pompon: Sculpteur, animalier," p. 151.
5. A.-H. Martinie, *La Sculpture* (Paris: Les Éditions Rieder, 1928), p. 73. Pompon would be made a chevalier of the Légion d'Honneur in 1925.
6. Quoted from Pompon's obituary in *The New York Times*, May 7, 1933, p. 31.
7. "Le Coeur de Pompon," *L'Oeil de Paris* 7, no. 270 (January 6, 1934), p. 8.

46 | *Polar Bear*

1. On the earlier model, the bear's paws are separated; on the later, two paws touch.
2. Paul Doncoeur, "François Pompon, animalier," *Études* 70, no. 214 (March 1933), p. 320.
3. Martinie, *La Sculpture*, p. 74.
4. Several other models by Pompon were also considered: *Hippopotamus*, *Panther*, and *Deer*. It is not clear where on the ship the piece was to be placed, although a monumental sculpture of Diana the Huntress — considerably larger than life — by

Raymonde Rivoire dominated the vast first-class Salon Carré.

JEAN PUIFORCAT

1. On Puiforcat, see Françoise de Bonneville, *Jean Puiforcat* (Paris: Éditions du Regard, 1986).
2. Tabouret assembled an important collection of antique silver that provided inspiration for the historicist designs for which Puiforcat was known in the early twentieth century. This collection is now housed at the Musée des Arts Décoratifs, Paris.
3. For his wartime service, Puiforcat was awarded two Croix de Guerre and a Médaille de Verdun; he was later made a chevalier of the Légion d'Honneur.
4. René Herbst, *Jean Puiforcat: Orfèvre, sculpteur* (Paris: Flammarion, 1951), p. 27.
5. Among the many venues where his work was exhibited was the metalwork display in the Grand Palais, the Ruhlmann pavilion, and the Ambassade Française.
6. Herbst, *Jean Puiforcat: Orfèvre, sculpteur*, p. 26.
7. René Chavance, "La Richesse inventive de Jean Puiforcat," *Mobilier et décoration* 18, no. 3 (March 1938), p. 97.
8. Quoted in Jean Fouquet, "Jean Puiforcat et l'orfèvrerie française," *Art et décoration*, n.s., no. 3 (March 1946), p. 160.

47 | Tea and Coffee Service

1. Gail S. Davidson, "Perfection: Jean E. Puiforcat's Designs for Silver," *The Magazine Antiques* 163, no. 1 (January 2003), p. 176.
2. Fouquet, "Jean Puiforcat et l'orfèvrerie française," p. 151.

48 | Bowl

1. Herbst, *Jean Puiforcat: Orfèvre, sculpteur*, p. 18.
2. John Goldsmith Phillips, "New Accessions of Contemporary French and Swedish Decorative Arts," *Bulletin of The Metropolitan Museum of Art* 30, no. 1 (January 1935), pp. 3–4.
3. Ibid.
4. Fouquet, "Jean Puiforcat et l'orfèvrerie française," p. 151.

49 | Soup Tureen

1. Quoted in Herbst, *Jean Puiforcat: Orfèvre, sculpteur*, p. 22.
2. At least four other examples are known: one each in the Musée des Arts Décoratifs, Paris, the Bröhan-Museum, Berlin, and the Montreal Museum of Fine Arts; the example from the Andy Warhol Collection was sold at Sotheby's, New York, in 1988.
3. Chavance, "La Richesse inventive de Jean Puiforcat," p. 101.
4. Ibid., p. 103.

HENRI RAPIN

1. On Rapin, see Yvonne Brunhammer, "Éléments pour une histoire d'Henri Rapin," in *Āru deco yōshiki no Sēburu jikiten: 20-seiki no eregansu; Tōkyō-to Teien Bijutsukan Kaikan 10-shūnen kinen/Sèvres: Pour célébrer le dixième anniversaire du Musée Teien; Elégance du 20ème siècle, L'Exposition des porcelains de Sèvres du style art*

déco (Tokyo: Tōkyō-to Bunka Shinkōkai, 1993), pp. 17–20.
2. Brunhammer cites the *ébénistes* Gagnant, Vasseur, and Gilly, the glassmakers Gaudin and Armand Paris, and the sculptor Charles Hairon as among those who worked for Rapin in the prewar years; ibid., p. 18.
3. In addition to his work at the Ambassade Française and the Sèvres pavilion, Rapin presented his own stand in the fair's Ensembles-Mobiliers pavilion. For the education section of the Grand Palais, he organized an exhibition of work by his students from the Union Centrale des Arts Décoratifs. He also helped several fellow exhibitors — including É.-J. Ruhlmann, Arthur Goldscheider, Paul René, and the Librairie Industrielle des Arts Décoratifs — with their displays.

ARMAND-ALBERT RATEAU

1. *A Selected Collection of Objects from the International Exposition of Modern Decorative and Industrial Art at Paris 1925* (Washington, D.C.: The American Association of Museums, 1926), p. 36.
2. The rare exceptions were his contributions to the Salon des Arts Ménagers of 1933 and 1935.
3. On Rateau, see Franck Olivier-Vial and François Rateau, *Armand-Albert Rateau: Un Baroque chez les modernes* (Paris: Les Éditions de l'Amateur, 1992).
4. A suite of three rooms that Rateau designed for Lanvin's Paris town house in the early 1920s is now housed in the Musée des Arts Décoratifs, Paris, given by one of her heirs, Prince Louis de Polignac, in 1965.
5. Albert Flament, "Le Pavillon de l'Élégance," *La Renaissance de l'art français et des industries de luxe* 8, no. 7 (July 1925), p. 317.
6. He also provided furniture for the couture and jewelry section of the Grand Palais, the pavilion of the magazine *La Renaissance*, and the Siegel & Stockmann Réunis (manufacturer of mannequins) stand in the Galerie des Boutiques.
7. For a review of Rateau's work in the Pavillon de l'Élégance, see Flament, "Le Pavillon de l'Élégance," pp. 304–17.

50 | Dressing Table and Hand Mirror

1. "The Bathroom of a Palace," *Vogue* 66, no. 10 (November 15, 1925), p. 83.
2. In a letter to curator Joseph Breck dated July 23, 1925, Rateau stated: "This dressing table is part of a set of furniture that was created at the same time as the bathroom of the Duchess of Alba at the Liria Palace in Madrid." Archives, The Metropolitan Museum of Art.
3. The Lanvin table, now in the collection of the Musée des Arts Décoratifs, Paris, has a yellow marble top and towel racks attached to the sides; the mirror was mounted separately on a marble wall bracket above the sink. Madame Rateau's table appears to be identical to the Metropolitan's. Another dressing table identical to the Metropolitan's, from the collection of Claude and Simone Dray, was sold at Christie's, Paris, June 8, 2006 (lot 51). The Duchess of Alba's table (missing its mirror) was sold at Christie's, Paris, May 23, 2013 (lot 123).
4. See Héléne Guéné, *Décoration et haute couture: Armand Albert Rateau pour Jeanne Lanvin, un autre art déco* (Paris: Les Arts Décoratifs, 2006), p. 207, for what could be the example owned by Madame Rateau.

5. Armand-Albert Rateau to Joseph Breck, July 8, 1925; Archives, The Metropolitan Museum of Art.

6. Albert Flament, "Salle de bains moderne," *La Renaissance de l'art français et des industries de luxe* 8, no. 5 (May 1925), p. 234.

CLÉMENT ROUSSEAU

1. On Rousseau, see Lison de Caunes and Jean Perfettini, *Galuchat* (Paris: Les Éditions de l'Amateur, 1994). Very little is known about Rousseau's early life. As a young man, he seems to have studied under the sculptor Léon Morice.

2. Galuchat is sometimes misleadingly defined as sharkskin; rather, it is either the skin of *Dasyatis sepehen* rays (sometimes referred to as "real galuchat" and characterized by large graining) or of dogfish or gulper shark ("false galuchat," characterized by its small graining).

3. The term "shagreen" derives from the Turkish *çâghrī*, or tanned leather.

4. Rousseau's work was included in the Tabletterie-Maroquinerie (the crafts of carving, turning, and leather-work) display in the Grand Palais.

5. Quoted in Jean Perfettini, *Le Galuchat: Un Matériau mystérieux, une technique oubliée* (Dourdan: Éditions H. Vial, 1988), p. 67.

6. Although he had many other clients, only these three can be documented. Rothschild, a collector with broad tastes, had a particular interest in contemporary design and architecture and owned furniture by Rousseau, Süe et Mare, and É.-J. Ruhlmann, among others. He served as an advisor to the Union Central des Arts Décoratifs and on the board of the Musée des Arts Décoratifs. The Duchesse de Vendôme was the sister of Albert I of Belgium.

51 | Table

1. The earlier table, together with several other pieces made by Rousseau for the Baron de Rothschild, is now in the collection of the Musée des Arts Décoratifs, Paris. It is identified there as a *table à journeaux*.

2. Penelope Hunter-Stiebel described the table as "a seven-shark table, because Rousseau wanted the central segment of the skin — the belly, from which the imbrications radiate — to be an element repeated in the pattern"; see Penelope Hunter-Stiebel, *The Fine Art of the Furniture Maker: Conversations with Wendell Castle, Artist . . . about Selected Works from The Metropolitan Museum of Art* (Rochester, N.Y.: Memorial Art Gallery of the University of Rochester, 1981), p. 102.

3. For an amusing account of the acquisition of this table, see Thomas Hoving, *The Chase, the Capture: Collecting at the Metropolitan* (New York: The Metropolitan Museum of Art, 1975), pp. 226–30.

4. Saint Thérèse of Lisieux (1873–1897), a Carmelite nun, known also as the Little Flower of Jesus, died of tuberculosis at the age of twenty-four. Revered for her devotion and simplicity, she was canonized in 1925.

É.-J. RUHLMANN

1. There is some debate over the correct appellation for Ruhlmann. Christened Jacques-Émile, he went through life as Émile (or Milo to his family and friends). Professionally, however, he referred to himself on his letterhead and business cards as É.-J. Ruhlmann, or simply Ruhlmann. J. Stewart Johnson addresses the issue thoroughly in his "A Note on Ruhlmann's Name: J.-É. or É.-J.," in Bréon and Pepall, *Ruhlmann: Genius of Art Deco*, pp. 146–49 (see note 2 below).

2. Ruhlmann was the subject of a major exhibition held at the Musée des Années Trente in Boulogne-Billancourt (November 15, 2001–March 17, 2002), The Metropolitan Museum of Art (June 10–September 5, 2004), and the Montreal Museum of Fine Arts (September 30–December 12, 2004), which was accompanied by the catalogue: Emmanuel Bréon and Rosalind Pepall, eds., *Ruhlmann: Genius of Art Deco* (Paris: Somogy Éditions d'Art; Montreal: Montreal Museum of Fine Arts, 2004). This biography is adapted from Jared Goss, "Émile Jacques Ruhlmann: Art Deco Designer," *The Magazine Antiques* 166, no. 1 (July 2004), pp. 68–77, and Jared Goss, "The Exposition Internationale des Arts Décoratifs et Industriels Modernes and Ruhlmann's Pavilion du Collectionneur," in Bréon and Pepall, *Ruhlmann: Genius of Art Deco*, pp. 44–53. For additional biographical information, see Florence Camard, *Jacques-Émile Ruhlmann* (New York: Rizzoli, 2011).

3. Ruhlmann was throughout his life an active participant in the annual Salon exhibitions, principally the Salon d'Automne and the Salon of the Société des Artistes Décorateurs.

4. See Jean Badovici, *Harmonies: Interieurs de Ruhlmann* (Paris: Éditions Morancé, [1924]), reprinted in Sarah Schleuning, *Moderne: Fashioning the French Interior* (Miami Beach: Wolfsonian-Florida International University; New York: Princeton Architectural Press, 2008).

5. Furniture by Ruhlmann was shown at international exhibitions in Amsterdam (1922), Rio de Janeiro, Monza, and Barcelona (1923), Madrid and Milan (1927), Athens and Tokyo (1928), and Barcelona (1929). Works were also included in the Inaugural Exposition of French Art at the California Palace of the Legion of Honor in San Francisco (1924–25), the American Association of Museums' traveling exhibition of works from the 1925 Paris Exposition (1926), and in department store exhibitions at B. Altman & Co. and Lord & Taylor in New York and Mandel Bros. in Chicago.

6. For a thorough list of Ruhlmann's clients, see Michèle Lefrançois, "A Made to Measure Clientele," in Bréon and Pepall, *Ruhlmann: Genius of Art Deco*, pp. 54–59.

7. Guillame Janneau, *Technique du décor intérieur moderne* (Paris: Éditions Albert Morancé, [1928]), p. 78. Ruhlmann did not create new furniture models for every commission, but frequently retailored successful models to suit a specific client.

8. Léon Moussinac, *Le Meuble français moderne* (Paris: Librairie Hachette, 1925), p. 67.

9. Pierre Olmer, *Le Mobilier français d'aujourd'hui (1910–1925)* (Paris: G. van Oest, 1926), pp. 36–37.

10. Two particularly noteworthy projects were the François Ducharne residence of 1924–26 in La Muette, in collaboration with architect Pierre Patout, and the Count of Vizela residence of 1930–33 in Porto, Portugal, with architect Charles Siclis.

11. Léon Deshairs, preface to *L'Hôtel du Collectionneur; Groupe Ruhlmann* (Paris: Éditions Albert Lévy, [1926]), p. 2. Deshair's preface is perhaps the most complete description of the pavilion from the period.

12. For a complete listing of Ruhlmann's collaborators, see *Exposition Internationale des Arts Décoratifs et Industriels Modernes: Catalogue générale officiel* (Paris: Imprimerie de Vaugirard, 1925).

13. *Exposition rétrospective E.-J. Ruhlmann*, exh. cat. (Paris: Musée du Louvre, 1934). Ruhlmann was also represented, posthumously, in the exhibition "Le Décor de la vie de 1900 à 1925," held at the Musée des Arts Décoratifs, Paris, in 1937.

14. Marcel Zahar, "Ruhlmann: Œuvres dernières," *Art et décoration* 63 (January 1934), p. 10.

52 | Textile and Wallpaper

1. See Camard, *Jacques Émile Ruhlmann*, pp. 77–79.

2. The pattern is illustrated in Bréon and Pepall, *Ruhlmann: Genius of Art Deco*, p. 294, and in Camard, *Jacques-Émile Ruhlmann*, pp. 71, 75, 78, 79.

3. For the variations, see Emmanuel Bréon, *Jacques-Émile Ruhlmann: The Designer's Archive*, vol. 2, *Interior Design* (Paris: Éditions Flammarion, 2004), pp. 50, 66, 67. Bréon refers to the motif as an *arbuste*, or shrub.

4. This relationship provides the basis for dating the *Sarrazin* pattern. The Metropolitan Museum owns a length of another floral-patterned wallpaper designed by Ruhlmann, printed by Desfossé & Karth around 1918 (acc. no. 2002.171).

5. See Véronique de La Hougue, "Ruhlmann: Wallpapers and Textiles," in Bréon and Pepall, *Ruhlmann: Genius of Art Deco*, pp. 104–9.

53 | *David-Weill* Desk

1. The name Carlton House desk for this form derives from the London residence of the Prince of Wales, later George IV, for whom the first example was designed in the eighteenth century. For an in-depth discussion of this desk, see Jared Goss, "*David-Weill* Desk," in Bréon and Pepall, *Ruhlmann: Genius of Art Deco*, pp. 166–70, from which this text is adapted.

2. Jean Laran, "Notre Enquête sur le mobilier moderne: J.-E. Ruhlmann," *Art et décoration* 37 (January 1920), p. 10.

3. Bibliothèque Nationale de France, sketchbook Hd 939 (5)-4 1913-7.

4. Drawing 90-1-74, Ruhlmann Archive, Musée des Années Trente, Boulogne-Billancourt. It is not known for which Baron Lambert the desk was made.

5. A design for a room setting at the 1921 Salon of the Société des Artistes Décorateurs featuring a version of the desk appears in a sketchbook now in the Musée des Arts Décoratifs (Carnet 33.2 CD 3053). According to Florence Camard, another version of the desk, with macassar ebony veneer and a solid ivory band along the edge of the work surface, was shown at the 1923 Salon; see Florence Camard, *Ruhlmann: Master of Art Deco*, trans. David Macey (New York: Harry N. Abrams, 1984), p. 41.

6. Laran, "Notre Enquête: Ruhlmann," p. 10.

54 | *Tibattant* Desk

1. Both sketchbooks are in the collection of the Musée des Arts Décoratifs, Paris; CD 3037 (1913), p. 47, and CD 3046 (1917), p. 10.

2. Ruhlmann's model numbers are listed in Camard, *Jacques Émile Ruhlmann*, pp. 158, 498.

3. René Chavance, "L'Art décoratif contemporain au Pavillon de Marsan," *Art et décoration* 45 (January–June 1924), pp. 115–16.

4. Ruhlmann probably selected aluminum rather than silver or white-gold leaf for the tooling because it was less prone to tarnish.
5. The "Album of Furniture Records" in the Ruhlmann Archive at the Musée des Années Trente, Boulogne-Billancourt, records one example made with amboyna and ivory veneers and another with amaranth and ivory. Examples in both mahogany and walnut veneer have been sold at auction in the past twenty years.
6. This text is apapted from the author's entry "Lady's Desk," in Bréon and Pepall, *Ruhlmann: Genius of Art Deco*, pp. 80–82.

55 | *État* Cabinet

1. The unsubstantiated date of 1916 for the first corner cabinet was published in the catalogue of the "Exposition rétrospective E.-J. Ruhlmann," presented at the Louvre in 1934 (cat. no. 11). The four known corner cabinets are: Dray collection (1921), sold at Christie's, Paris, June 8, 2006; The Art Institute of Chicago (1922); Brooklyn Museum (1922–23), and Virginia Museum of Fine Arts, Richmond (ca. 1925). The four rectangular cabinets are: Mobilier National, Paris (1922); Musée des Arts Decoratifs, Paris (1922–23); the present example (1925–26); and Hotêl Drouot Richelieu, Paris, June 28, 1989 (lot 258; 1927). At least one further example of this form, though without the floral marquetry, was published in the June 30, 1928, issue of *L'Illustration* and is known to have been made about 1928; see Ghenete Zelleke, "Two Cabinets by Ruhlmann," in Bréon and Pepall, *Ruhlmann: Genius of Art Deco*, pp. 152–57, 196.
2. In "Modern Decorative Arts: Some Recent Purchases," *Bulletin of The Metropolitan Museum of Art* 21, no. 2 (February 1926), p. 38, Breck was obliged to write: "Unfortunately, the furniture by Ruhlmann, who occupies with Süe et Mare a position of leadership among the French exponents of the modern style, has not yet arrived." The next month's *Bulletin* (Joseph Breck, "Furniture by Ruhlmann," p. 88) included a follow-up: "As Ruhlmann is unquestionably one of the most gifted of the French exponents of the modern style and a leader in the field of interior decoration and furniture design, it is fortunate that the three pieces of furniture by him referred to in the February Bulletin arrived in time to be shown in Gallery J8 with other recent purchases. . . . A cabinet in macassar ebony, ornamented on the front with a large vase and flower design inlaid in amaranth wood and two tones of ivory, is perhaps the most striking of the new accessions. The absence of carving is characteristic of modern furniture design. This cabinet is a replica of one bought by the French Government at the recent International Exposition of Decorative and Industrial Art at Paris."
3. Posthumous letter from É.-J. Ruhlmann to the Metropolitan Museum; Archives, the Metropolitan Museum of Art.

56 | Pair of *Duval* Cabinets

1. This date is assigned in the catalogue of the Ruhlmann retrospective exhibition at the Louvre in 1934; see *Exposition rétrospective E.-J. Ruhlmann*, cat. no. 49.
2. Gabriel Henriot, "Le Salon d'Automne: Les Arts décoratifs," *Mobilier et décoration* 6 (1926), p. 122.

3. The Louvre would substitute Ruhlmann's *Meuble au Char* (Chariot Sideboard) for the *Duval* cabinet. According to Florence Camard, Ruhlmann used the cabinet to store hats; see Camard, *Jacques-Émile Ruhlmann*, pp. 217–18.
4. Ibid.

57 | Carpet

1. Period photographs of the boudoir show that two different carpets were used: a square carpet and this round one. It is conceivable that the smaller, ill-fitting square carpet was used before the circular carpet was completed. Gaudissard also designed both the carpet and the tapestry upholstery for Ruhlmann's seating furniture in the pavilion's salon.
2. *Exposition Internationale des Arts Décoratifs et Industriels Modernes: Catalogue générale officiel*, p. 82. There are also two design drawings for the carpet in the Ruhlmann Archives at the Musée des Années Trente, Boulogne-Billancourt, and a gouache design for the carpet with a different colorway in the collection of Florence Camard. Photographs of a carpet of the same design are in the Bibliothèque Nationale, Paris.
3. Two carpets appear in period photographs of this room: this model (no. 3002) and a close variant (no. 3003) with a swirling floral border and a solid-colored central reserve.
4. Illustrated in Bréon and Pepall, *Ruhlmann: Genius of Art Deco*, p. 51.
5. Clément Rousseau to Joseph Breck, July 20, 1925; Archives, The Metropolitan Museum of Art.

58 | Lamp

1. Sketches that incorporate this form can be found in Léon Moussinac, *Croquis de Ruhlmann* (Paris: Éditions Albert Levy, 1924), pls. 42, 44, 46–50. For objects with this form, see Bréon and Pepall, *Ruhlmann: Genius of Art Deco*, p. 293.
2. The monumental lamps, designed for Ruhlmann's interiors on the SS *Île de France* (1926) and in the Chamber of Commerce in Paris (1927), had porcelain shades made at Sèvres. See Bréon and Pepall, *Ruhlmann: Genius of Art Deco*, pp. 115, 117, 292.
3. Illustrated in Camard, *Ruhlmann: Master of Art Deco*, p. 145. Henri Fricotelle was a manufacturer of cigarette paper.

JEAN SERRIÈRE

1. On Serrière, see Dominique Forest and Marie-Cécile Forest, *La Dinanderie française, 1900–1950* (Paris: Les Éditions de l'Amateur, 1995), and Dedo von Kerssenbrock-Krosigk, ed., *Modern Art of Metalwork: Bröhan-Museum, State Museum of Art Nouveau, Art Deco and Functionalism (1889–1939), Berlin* (Berlin: Bröhan-Museum, 2001).
2. Louis-Charles Watelin, "Jean Serrière, peintre et batteur de métal," *L'Art et les artistes* 9 (January–June 1924), pp. 317–18.
3. Serrière in "L'Enseignement rationnel des arts techniques: Une Enquête, III," *Le Bulletin de la vie artistique* 4, no. 17 (September 1, 1923), p. 358.
4. Guillaume Janneau, "Le Mouvement moderne: Recherches et trouvailles," *La Renaissance de l'art français et des industries de luxe* 6, no. 1 (January 1923), p. 102.

5. "Les Expositions," *L'Art et les artistes* 25, no. 110 (October 1930), p. 68.

59 | Chalice

1. Guillaume Janneau, "Le Mouvement moderne: Du Musée Galliera à l'exposition de 1924," *La Renaissance de l'art français et des industries de luxe* 5, no. 1 (January 1922), p. 94.
2. Armand Dayot, "Jean Serrière," *L'Art et les artistes*, n.s., 1, nos. 1–9 (1920), p. 133.

HENRI SIMMEN AND EUGÉNIE JUBIN, KNOWN AS O'KIN

1. The proximity of Montdidier to the Belgian border perhaps explains the common misperception that Simmen was Flemish. For biographical information, see Anne Lajoix, *La Céramique en France* (Paris: Éditions sous le Vent, 1983), pp. 121–22, 177.
2. Quoted in Marcel Valotaire, *La Ceramique française moderne* (Paris: Les Éditions G. van Oest, 1930), pp. 31–32.
3. These include the exhibition of stoneware, faïence, and terracotta at the Musée Galliera, Paris (1911); the American Association of Museums' traveling exhibition of selected works from the 1925 Paris Exposition (1926); the American Federation of Arts' International Exhibition of Ceramic Art (1928–29); and an exhibition of ceramics dating from 1890 to 1930, held at the Musée Nationale de Céramique, Sèvres (1931).
4. "Mme O'Kin . . . counts Japanese among her immediate ancestors"; Ernest Tisserand, "La Céramique française en 1928: Henri Simmen," *L'Art vivant* 4, no. 87 (August 1, 1928), p. 613.
5. O'Kin was referred to variously as Mlle O'Kin, Mme O'Kin, and Mme Simmen-O'Kin (on occasion she is mistakenly referred to as O'Kim and Okim). Alastair Duncan refers to her as Mlle Simmen-Blanche O'Kin; see Alastair Duncan, *The Paris Salons, 1895–1914*, 6 vols. (Woodbridge, Suffolk: Antique Collectors' Club, 1994–2002), vol. 2, *Jewelry: The Designers L–Z*, pp. 139, 140, and vol. 5, *Objets d'art & Metalware*, p. 426.
6. In the early twentieth century, the craft attracted many women, and O'Kin had several accomplished competitors, the best known of whom were Marguerite de Félice and Eve-Marie Le Bourgeois.
7. While both Simmen and O'Kin were active participants in the Salons of the Société des Artistes Décorateurs, neither was represented in 1920 or 1921, suggesting that they were traveling together in Asia.
8. "Les Maîtres du métier à l'Exposition de 1925: Une Enquête; M. Simmen et Mme O'Kin," *Le Bulletin de la vie artistique* 5, no. 13 (July 1, 1924), pp. 289–90.

61 | Lidded Jar

1. Joseph Breck, "Accessions and Notes: Modern Decorative Arts," *Bulletin of The Metropolitan Museum of Art* 24, no. 10 (October 1929), p. 269.

SÉRAPHIN SOUDBININE

1. Very little has been written on Soudbinine. Biographical information can be found in Anne Lajoix, *La Céramique en France, 1925–1947* (Paris: Éditions sous le Vent, 1983), p. 123. A passenger list for

the SS *Paris*, which arrived in New York on April 7, 1926, lists him as "Seraphin Colovastikoff, dit Soudbinine." Ancestry.com, *New York Passenger Lists, 1820–1957*, online database (Provo, Utah: Ancestry.com Operations, 2010).

LOUIS SÜE AND ANDRÉ MARE

1. Jean Gallotti, "M. Louis Süe, architecte et ensemblier," *Art et décoration* 63 (1934), p. 220.
2. On these two designers and their firm, see Florence Camard, *Süe et Mare et La Compagnie des Arts Français* (Paris: Les Éditions de l'Amateur, 1993); Susan Day, *Louis Süe, Architectures* (Brussels: Mardaga, 1986); and Nicole Zapata-Aubé et al., *André Mare: Cubisme et camouflage* (Bernay: Musée Municipale des Beaux-Arts, 1998).
3. André Vera, "Le Nouveau Style," *L'Art décoratif* 27 (January–June 1912), pp. 21–32.
4. In 1913 the group presented "L'Art du Jardin," an exhibition of their work, at the Orangerie de Bagatelle, Paris.
5. A maquette and drawings for the project were included at the famous Armory Show, held in New York in 1913.
6. Members included painters Bernard Boutet de Monvel and Charles Dufresne, painter-decorators Gustave Jaulmes and Paul Vera, decorator Drésa (André Saglio), ironworker Richard Desvallières, glassmaker Maurice Marinot, textile designer Charles Martin, and sculptor Pierre Poisson.
7. Léon Deshairs, "Notre Enquête sur le mobilier modern: La Compagnie des Arts Français," *Art et décoration* 37 (January–June 1920), p. 65. In general, Süe et Mare's work was well received by critics; a notable exception was the architect Le Corbusier.
8. Ibid., pp. 68–69.
9. Ibid., p. 70. Süe and Mare would develop these ideas further in their 1921 publication *Architectures* (Paris: Éditions de la Nouvelle Revue Française, 1921).
10. Gallotti, "M. Louis Süe, architecte et ensemblier," pp. 225–26.

62 | Side Chair

1. André Vera, "Le Nouveau Style," p. 21.
2. The drawing for that chair was published in ibid., p. 29. The design was adapted by Süe for an entire suite, including side chairs, armchairs, and a settee, which were painted yellow with green and red detailing (Musée des Arts Décoratifs, Paris); see Camard, *Süe et Mare et La Compagnie des Arts Français*, pp. 64–65, and Fernand Roches, "Le Salon d'Automne de 1912," *L'Art décoratif* 28 (July–December 1912), p. 313. Süe's competitor André Groult made a plain walnut variant on the Metropolitan's chair (after Süe's design) sometime thereafter; see Félix Marcilhac, *André Groult, décorateur-ensemblier du XXe siècle* (Paris: Éditions de l'Amateur, 1996), pp. 42–43.
3. Leo Randole, "Art Wedded to Industry: A Coterie of French Modernists Who Are Spreading the Gospel of Beauty," *Arts and Decoration* 17, no. 5 (September 1922), pp. 331, 370.

63 | Four Textiles

1. Lamy & Gautier (renamed Prelle & Cie in 1927) first produced *Abondance* in 1918, assigning it the pattern number 7229. In 1924, Lauer was cited as a manufacturer of the pattern in Léon Moussinac, *Étoffes d'ameublement tissées et brochées* (Paris: Éditions Albert Lévy, 1925), pl. 28.
2. For examples of Süe's prewar designs, see *L'Art de la soie Prelle, 1752–2002: Des Ateliers lyonnais aux palais parisiens*, exh. cat. (Paris: Musée Carnavalet, 2002), pp. 196–97.
3. Lamy & Gautier first produced *Bouquets* for Belle France in 1919, assigning it the pattern number 7236. Lauer was cited as a manufacturer of the pattern in 1924 in Moussinac, *Étoffes d'ameublement tissées et brochées*, pl. 28.

64 | Commode and Mirror

1. "Le Carnet d'un curieux," *La Renaissance de l'art français* 1, no. 5 (May 1918), p. 30.
2. Roger Allard, "Reflexions sur quelques meubles modernes," *Feuillets d'art*, no. 1 (1919), p. 47.
3. The Museum's commode has an oak structure, lumber-core plywood is used for the painted surfaces, and the drawers are constructed from oak and chestnut.
4. The motif appears in the section "Les Jardins au soleil," in André Vera, *Les Jardins* (Paris: Émile-Paul Frères, 1919), p. 55.
5. Ibid., pp. 57, 59, 107. A closely related motif was used on the door of a built-in bookcase in the Paris apartment of Marcel Monteux, the son of Gaston Monteux, the financial backer of La Compagnie des Arts Français. Léon Moussinac, *Le Meuble français moderne* (Paris: Librarie Hachette, 1925), pl. 22.
6. There are variations to the carved floral motifs. Süe et Mare made yet another variant of the mirror, with a red-and-gold scheme. Archives, The Metropolitan Museum of Art.
7. Joseph Breck, "Modern Decorative Arts," *Bulletin of The Metropolitan Museum of Art* 18, no. 11 (November 1923), p. 245. The acquisition was also cited in the "Ici et ailleurs" column of *Le Bulletin de la vie artistique* 5, no. 2 (January 15, 1924), p. 47.

65 | Desk and Chair

1. André Mare to Joseph Breck, June 25, 1925; Archives, The Metropolitan Museum of Art.
2. Joseph Breck to Robert W. de Forest, July 4, 1925; Archives, The Metropolitan Museum of Art.
3. Neither the desk nor the chair was without precedent in Süe et Mare's oeuvre. Süe first displayed a similar desk at the 1911 Salon d'Automne, and the two designed several others before 1925. According to Süe et Mare's records, the Metropolitan's chair (model no. 82) is a modification of the design (model no. 59) they submitted for the Concours David-Weill in 1923 (see no. 67); Camard, *Süe et Mare et La Compagnie des Arts Français*, pp. 31, 270, 291.
4. A nearly identical desk, though veneered in palisander and with carved mahogany legs, was sold in Paris by Jean Morelle, Drouot Rive Gauche, December 7, 1977 (lot 89), and was stated to be the prototype for the Metropolitan's example. Süe et Mare would return to the form many times throughout the 1920s, and incorporated the wing-like leg on both desks and pianos.
5. The underside of the desk is fully ebonized as well.
6. Although the manufacturer of the ormolu mounts is not recorded, it is likely they were supplied by Fontaine et Cie, the manufacturer of high-end hardware and locks, whose pavilion at the 1925 Paris Exposition Süe et Mare also designed and furnished.
7. Joseph Breck, "Modern Decorative Arts: Some Recent Purchases," *Bulletin of The Metropolitan Museum of Art* 21, no. 2 (February 1926), pp. 37, 38.
8. "Creative Design in Modern Decorative Arts," *The Christian Science Monitor*, May 7, 1926, p. 9.

66 | Carpet

1. Joseph Breck to Robert W. de Forest, July 4, 1925; Archives, The Metropolitan Museum of Art.
2. A maquette for the Metropolitan's carpet is reproduced in Camard, *Süe et Mare et La Compagnie des Arts Français*, p. 228.
3. André Mare to Joseph Breck, July 17 and July 22, 1925; Archives, The Metropolitan Museum of Art.
4. Joseph Breck to André Mare, August 6, 1925; Archives, The Metropolitan Museum of Art.
5. Joseph Breck to La Compagnie des Arts Français, December 3, 1925; Archives, The Metropolitan Museum of Art.
6. Joseph Breck to La Compagnie des Arts Français, December 30, 1925; Archives, The Metropolitan Museum of Art.
7. Breck, "Modern Decorative Arts: Some Recent Purchases," p. 37.

67 | *David-Weill* Chair

1. The rules were published in *La Revue de l'art ancien et moderne* 45 (January–May 1924), n.p.
2. The Salle Moderne was described in *Vogue* as "designed by Süe et Mare of Paris, in black and subtle Indian-red, with flowered mirrors and paneled ceiling full of lamps like fantastic crystal orchids." Because Süe and Mare had ended their collaboration with La Compagnie des Arts Français by the time this project was completed, it is unclear exactly how involved they were in its realization; see "Bergdorf Goodman Creates a Feeling of the Paris Couture in New York," *Vogue* 71, no. 9 (May 1, 1928), p. 89.
3. Süe et Mare records from 1927 specify upholstery design no. 2513 as "tapisserie pour chaise 45"; see Camard, *Süe et Mare et La Compagnie des Arts Français*, pp. 213, 215.
4. The motif probably has its origins in designs for bookbindings that Mare made before the First World War; Süe et Mare used similar motifs for decorative marquetry (see ibid., pp. 128–29).
5. See Yvonne Brunhammer, *The Art Deco Style*, trans. David Beeson (London: Academy Editions, 1983), p. 45.

RAYMOND TEMPLIER

1. Paul Sentenac, "L'Esprit modern dans les bijoux de Raymond Templier," *La Renaissance de l'art français et des industries de luxe* 15, no. 1 (January 1932), p. 16.
2. On Templier, see Laurence Mouillefarine and Véronique Ristelhueber, *Raymond Templier: Le Bijou moderne* (Paris: Éditions Norma, 2005), and Laurence Mouillefarine and Évelyne Possémé, eds., *Art Deco Jewelry: Modernist Masterworks and Their Makers* (London: Thames and Hudson, 2009).
3. Henri Clouzot, "À l'avant-garde de l'art appliqué," *La Renaissance de l'art français et des industries de luxe* 9, no. 2 (February 1926), p. 224.

4. "Les Bijoux de Raymond Templier," *La Renaissance de l'art français et des industries de luxe* 9, no. 1 (January 1926), n.p. [insert following p. 73].
5. Sentenac, "L'Esprit modern dans les bijoux de Templier," p. 17.
6. "Les Bijoux de Raymond Templier," n.p. [insert following p. 73].

68 | Mirror

1. Émile Sedeyn, "Des Bijoux nouveaux," *Art et décoration* 43 (May 1923), p. 149.
2. The letter, written in English, is dated June 4, 1923; Archives, The Metropolitan Museum of Art.

VAN CLEEF & ARPELS

1. On Van Cleef & Arpels, see Sarah D. Coffin, *Set in Style: The Jewelry of Van Cleef & Arpels* (New York: Cooper-Hewitt, National Design Museum, Smithsonian Institution, 2011).
2. "Van Cleef et Arpels," *La Renaissance de l'art français et des industries de luxe* 6 (May 1923), pp. 364–65.
3. "In affectionate honor of Estelle van Cleef, who was said to have charming social 'minauderies.'" Coffin, *Set in Style*, p. 28.
4. Lipstick and powder refills were supplied by such cosmetics companies as Elizabeth Arden, Guerlain, and, later, Revlon.

5. Because Van Cleef & Arpels retained the patent on the form, the firm's name was included in the marketing of these less expensive versions. A 1934 advertisement for I. Magnin & Co. introduced "La Minaudière"; another from the May Company promoted the "Sophisti-case" the same year. Both advertisements appeared in *The Los Angeles Times*, and stipulated that the design was "originated by Van Cleef and Arpels in Paris." Advertisement for I. Magnin & Co., *The Los Angeles Times*, October 26, 1934, p. 3; advertisement for the May Company, *The Los Angeles Times*, November 8, 1934, p. 10.

69 | Vanity Case

1. A 1928 example by Langlois from the Van Cleef & Arpels Collection has a blue-and-yellow scheme and is set with lapis lazuli; a 1925 example has a blue-and-black scheme set with jade; see Coffin, *Set in Style*, pp. 27, 167.
2. *Vogue* 88, no. 1 (July 1, 1936), p. 82.
3. "'Mr. Backgammon' Has Colorful Career," *The Los Angeles Times*, April 20, 1959, p. B3.

PAUL VERA

1. On Vera, see Agnès Virole, *Paul et André Vera: Tradition et modernité* (Paris: Hazan; Saint-Germain-en-Laye: Ville de Saint-Germain-en-Laye, 2008).
2. Paul Leclère, "Paul Vera, décorateur," *La Demeure française*, no. 1 (Spring 1927), pp. 42, 44.

3. François Fosca, "Paul Vera," *L'Art et les artistes* 10, nos. 50–54 (October 1924–February 1925), p. 34.

70 | *Les Jardins* Folding Screen

1. Joseph Breck, "A Modern Beauvais Tapestry Screen," *Bulletin of The Metropolitan Museum of Art* 27, no. 11 (November 1932), p. 239.
2. Ibid.
3. Ibid., p. 240.
4. At this time, Vera was working for Louis Süe and André Mare's Compagnie des Arts Français. The collaboration with Follot was therefore unusual. The selection of Follot for this screen may have been made by Ajalbert: "That the frames may be in harmony with the tapestries the director [Ajalbert] has sought the coöperation of leading furniture designers." Breck, "Modern Beauvais Tapestry Screen," pp. 239–40.
5. "This [screen] was said to be the first order to be received directly from a foreign buyer by the Manufacture [Beauvais] in more than 100 years"; J. L. G. "A Tapestry Folding Screen," *The Romanic Review* 23, no. 4 (1932), p. 392. It is unclear where the screen was between its display at the 1925 Paris Exposition and its 1932 acquisition by the Metropolitan Museum; presumably it was taken back to the Beauvais factory.
6. Breck, "Modern Beauvais Tapestry Screen," p. 240.
7. Ibid.

MARKS, PROVENANCES, AND REFERENCES

GABRIEL ARGY-ROUSSEAU

1 | *Eurythmics* Vase
1932
Glass
Height 7⅝ in. (19.4 cm), width 5¾ in. (14.6 cm), depth 4½ in. (11.4 cm)
Rogers Fund, 1970 (1970.198.6)

Marks: Impressed on side of vase: G ARGY / ROUSSEAU; impressed on underside of foot: FRANCE

Provenance: [Galerie Sonnabend, Paris, 1970]; sold to The Metropolitan Museum of Art, 1970.

References: Janine Bloch-Dermant, *G. Argy-Rousseau: Glassware as Art: With a Catalogue Raisonné of the Pâtes de Verre* (New York: Thames and Hudson, 1991), pp. 95, 222.

GEORGE BARBIER

2 | Fan
1914
Painted ivory, metal, silk, gilding
Height 8½ in. (21.6 cm), width 15⅝ in. (39.7 cm), length of tasseled cord 10 in. (25.4 cm)
Gift, Mrs. William Randolph Hearst, 1963 (63.90.105)

Marks: Painted on obverse at right edge. G. Barbier / 1914

Provenance: Mrs. William Randolph Hearst, New York, until 1963; gift to The Metropolitan Museum of Art, 1963.

References: *L'Éventail et la fourrure chez Paquin: Dessins de Paul Iribe, Georg Barbier, Georges LePape* (Paris: Marquet, November 12, 1911), design illustrated; *Journal des dames et des modes*, no. 21 (December 20, 1912), p. 42 (design illustrated); Edith A. Standen, "Instruments for Agitating the Air," *The Metropolitan Museum of Art Bulletin*, n.s., 23, no. 7 (March 1965), pp. 256–57; Barbara Martorelli, ed., *George Barbier: The Birth of Art Deco* (Venice: Marsilio Editori, 2008), p. 151 (design illustrated).

VALÉRY BIZOUARD

3 | Flatware
1929–30
Glass, silver gilt
Purchase, Edgar Kaufmann Jr. Gift, 1975 (1975.119.1–.3)

a | Spoon
Length 7⅛ in. (18.1 cm), width 1½ in. (3.8 cm), depth ¾ in. (1.9 cm) (1975.119.1)

Marks: Stamped in bowl of spoon: [head of Minerva within an octagon]; stamped on side of stem: FRANCE

b | Fork
Length 7⅛ in. (18.1 cm), width ⅞ in. (2.22 cm), depth ½ in. (1.27 cm) (1975.119.2)

Marks: Stamped below tines: T FRES

[within a lozenge]; stamped below tines: [head of Minerva within an octagon]; stamped on side of stem: FRANCE

c | Knife
Length 7⅛ in. (18.1 cm), width ¾ in. (1.9 cm), depth ⅞ in. (2.22 cm) (1975.119.3)

Unmarked.

Provenance: [Hinda Kohn, New York, until 1975]; sold to The Metropolitan Museum of Art, 1975.

Previously unpublished.

EDGAR BRANDT

4 | *Perse* Grille
ca. 1923
Iron
Height 81⅜ in. (206.7 cm), width 44⅜ in. (112.7 cm), length of foot 27¾ in. (70.5 cm)
Purchase, Edward C. Moore Jr. Gift, 1924 (24.133)

Unmarked.

Provenance: Edgar Brandt, until 1924; sold to The Metropolitan Museum of Art, 1924.

References: Yvanhoé Rambosson, "Le Salon d'Automne: Les Arts appliqués," *L'Amour de l'art* 4 (1923), p. 753; Société du Salon d'Automne (Paris), *Catalogue des ouvrages* (Paris, 1923), p. 108, no. 227; Guillaume Janneau, *Le Fer* (Paris: F. Contet, 1924), pls. 11, 13; Joseph Breck, "Accessions and Notes: Modern Decorative Arts," *Bulletin of The Metropolitan Museum of Art* 19, no. 11 (November 1924), p. 275; Galerie Edgar Brandt, *Ferrobrandt, Inc.* (New York, [1926]), p. 34; Catherine Arminjon et al., *L'Art de vivre: Decorative Arts and Design in France, 1789–1989* (New York: Vendome Press in conjunction with the Cooper-Hewitt Museum, 1989), p. 35; Joan Kahr, *Edgar Brandt: Master of Art Deco Ironwork* (New York: Harry N. Abrams, 1999), p. 110.

RENÉ BUTHAUD

5 | Three Vases

a | Vase
ca. 1923–24
Glazed stoneware
Height 15 in. (38.2 cm), diameter 7 in. (17.8 cm)
Bequest of James H. Stubblebine, 1987 (1987.473.2)

Marks: Painted on underside of foot: R Buthaud

Provenance: [Lillian Nassau Gallery, New York, until 1968]; James H. Stubblebine, New York, 1968–until d. 1987; bequest to The Metropolitan Museum of Art, 1987.

References: Émile Bayard, *L'Art appliqué français d'aujourd'hui: Meuble, ferronerie, céramique, verrerie, tissus, etc.* (Paris: Ernest Gründ, [1925?]), p. 109; Gaston Quénioux, *Les Arts décoratifs modernes (France)* (Paris: Librarie Larousse, 1925), p. 231; Henri Verne and René Chavance, *Pour comprendre l'art décoratif moderne en France* (Paris: Hachette, 1925), p. 188.

b | Vase
ca. 1923–24
Glazed stoneware
Height 13½ in. (34.3 cm), diameter 7½ in. (19.1 cm)
Purchase, Edward C. Moore Jr. Gift, 1969 (69.289.1)

Marks: Painted on underside of foot: RB [interlaced]. *See no. 6.*

Provenance: René Buthaud, until ca. 1969; [Lillian Nassau Gallery,

New York, ca. 1969]; sold to The Metropolitan Museum of Art, 1969.

References: "Reports of the Departments, 1969–1970: Twentieth Century Art," *The Metropolitan Museum of Art Bulletin*, n.s., 29, no. 2 (October 1970), p. 101; Penelope Hunter-Stiebel, "The Decorative Arts of the Twentieth Century," *The Metropolitan Museum of Art Bulletin*, n.s., 37, no. 3 (Winter 1979–80), p. 18.

c | **Vase**
1929
Glazed stoneware
Height 9¾ in. (24.8 cm), diameter 7 in. (17.8 cm)
Gift of Charles J. Liebman Jr., 1965 (65.151.6)

Marks: Painted on underside of foot: RB [interlaced]. *See no. 6.*

Provenance: [Probably Galerie Georges Rouard, Paris, ca. 1929]; Mr. and Mrs. Charles J. Liebman, New York, ca. 1929; their son Charles J. Liebman Jr., New York, until 1965; gift to The Metropolitan Museum of Art, 1965.

References: Margaret Liebman Berger, *Aline Meyer Liebman: Pioneer Collector and Artist* (New York: W. F. Humphrey Press, 1982), p. 56, no. 21.

6 | **Statuette**
ca. 1935
Glazed earthenware
Height 15 in. (38.1 cm), width 12 in. (30.5 cm), depth 6¼ in. (15.9 cm)
Gift of Cruège-Lorrilliard-Paris, 1993 (1993.237.1)

Marks: Painted on underside of foot: RB [interlaced]

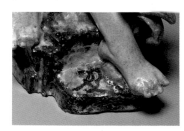

Provenance: René Buthaud, until d. 1986; Buthaud's executor, Pierre Cruège, Neuilly, until 1987; on loan to The Metropolitan Museum of Art, 1987–93; gift to The Metropolitan Museum of Art, 1993.

References: Pierre Cruège, with Anne Lajoix, *René Buthaud, 1886–1986* (Paris: Les Éditions de l'Amateur, 1996), p. 168.

7 | **Study for an Athlete**
ca. 1937
Gouache, charcoal, graphite on paper (backed with fabric)
81 x 39 in. (205.7 x 99.1 cm)
Gift of Michel Fortin, 2011 (2011.97)

Marks: Signed lower left: R. BUTHAUD

Provenance: René Buthaud, until d. 1986; [Michel Fortin, Paris, 1986, until d. 1992]; his estate, 1992–2011; on loan to The Metropolitan Museum of Art, 1989–2011; gift to The Metropolitan Museum of Art, 2011.

References: René Buthaud, *René Buthaud. Collection of the Artist*, exh. cat. (New York: Michel Fortin Gallery, 1981), p. 19.

ÉDOUARD CAZAUX

8 | **Vase**
ca. 1935
Glazed earthenware
Height 17¼ in. (43.8 cm), diameter 8 in. (20.3 cm)
Bequest of James H. Stubblebine, 1987 (1987.473.10)

Marks: Painted on underside of foot: CAZAUX

Provenance: [Alain Lesieutre, Paris]; sold to James H. Stubblebine, New York, 1969, until d. 1987; bequest to The Metropolitan Museum of Art, 1987.

Previously unpublished.

RENÉ CREVEL AND HENRI RAPIN

9 | **Lidded Vase**
1926
Glazed porcelain
Height 28¼ in. (71.8 cm), diameter 11 in. (27.9 cm)
Bequest of James H. Stubblebine, 1987 (1987.473.11ab)

Marks: Painted on body, above stepped waist: A.L d 'ap— / R. Crevel; painted on underside of foot: MADE IN / FRANCE; within a rectangle: S / 1926 / DN;

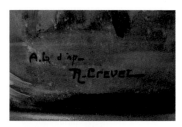

within a cartouche: RF / MANUFACTURE NATIONALE / DÉCORÉ / À / SÈVRES / 1926

Provenance: [Félix Marcilhac, Paris]; sold to James H. Stubblebine, New York, 1971, until d. 1987; bequest to The Metropolitan Museum of Art, 1987.

Previously unpublished.

ÉMILE DECŒUR

10 | **Jar and Two Vases**

a | **Jar**
ca. 1925
Glazed stoneware
Height 6⅝ in. (16.8 cm), diameter 6¾ in. (17.1 cm)
Purchase, Edward C. Moore Jr. Gift, 1929 (29.127.1)

Marks: Impressed on underside of foot: EDecœur [ED conjoined, with reversed E]

Provenance: Purchased by The Metropolitan Museum of Art from Galerie Georges Rouard, Paris, 1929.

References: Joseph Breck, "Accessions and Notes: Modern Decorative Arts," *Bulletin of The Metropolitan Museum of Art* 24, no. 10 (October 1929), p. 270; W. B. Dalton, "Emile Decœur, an Appreciation," *Ceramic Age* 59, no. 5 (May 1952), p. 24.

b | **Vase**
ca. 1920
Glazed stoneware
Height 13¼ in. (33.7 cm), diameter 5½ in. (14 cm)
Purchase, Edward C. Moore Jr. Gift, 1922 (22.184.5)

Marks: Impressed on underside of foot: ED [conjoined, with reversed E]; on circular paper label affixed to underside of foot: A / LA PAIX / 34 / AV. DE L'OPERA

Provenance: [Galerie Georges Rouard, Paris, 1922]; purchased by the Metropolitan Museum of Art, 1922.

Previously unpublished.

c | **Vase**
ca. 1922
Glazed stoneware
Height 9½ in. (24.1 cm), diameter 8¼ in. (21 cm)
Purchase, Edward C. Moore Jr. Gift, 1922 (22.184.6)

Marks: Impressed on underside of foot: EDecœur [ED conjoined, with reversed E]. *See no. 10a.*

Provenance: [Galerie Georges Rouard, Paris, 1922]; purchased by the Metropolitan Museum of Art, 1922.

Previously unpublished.

11 | **Vase**
ca. 1925
Glazed stoneware
Height 8⅝ in. (21.9 cm), diameter 6 in. (15.2 cm)
Gift of Charles J. Liebman Jr., 1965 (65.151.5)

Marks: Impressed on underside of foot: EDecœur [ED conjoined, with reversed E]

Provenance: Mr. and Mrs. Charles J. Liebman, New York, ca. 1925; their son Charles J. Liebman Jr., New York, until 1965; gift to The Metropolitan Museum of Art, 1965.

References: Margaret Liebman Berger, *Aline Meyer Liebman: Pioneer Collector and Artist* (New York: W. F. Humphrey Press, 1982), p. 69.

FRANÇOIS-ÉMILE DÉCORCHEMONT

12 | Bowl
1925
Glass
Height 4½ in. (11.4 cm), width with
handles 11⅝ in. (29.5 cm), depth 7 in.
(17.8 cm)
Purchase, Edward C. Moore Jr. Gift, 1925
(25.211)

Marks: Impressed on side of bowl
near bottom, within a shell shape:
DECORCHEMONT. *See no. 13.*

Provenance: François-Émile Décorchemont, until 1925; purchased by The
Metropolitan Museum of Art, 1925.

References: René Chavance, "Les Pâtes
de verre de Décorchemont," *Art et déco-
ration* 49 (March 1926), p. 76; Penelope
Hunter, "Art Déco, The Last Hurrah," *The
Metropolitan Museum of Art Bulletin*,
n.s., 30, no. 6 (June–July 1972), p. 258;
Véronique Ayroles, *François Décorchemont:
Maître de la pâte de verre, 1880–1971*
(Paris: Éditions Norma, 2006), pp. 6, 118,
122, 123, 129, 265, 316; Jason T. Busch and
Catherine L. Futter, *Inventing the Modern
World: Decorative Arts at the World's Fairs,
1851–1939*, exh. cat. (Pittsburgh: Carnegie
Museum of Art; Kansas City: Nelson-Atkins
Museum of Art; New York: Skira Rizzoli,
2012), pp. 217, 219, 269.

13 | Bowl
1928
Glass
Height 6¼ in. (15.9 cm), diameter 9¾ in.
(24.8 cm)
Gift of Arthur M. Bullowa, 1972
(1972.239)

Marks: Impressed on side of bowl
near bottom, within a shell shape:
DECORCHEMONT

Provenance: Arthur M. Bullowa, New York;
gift to The Metropolitan Museum of Art,
1972.

References: A.-Henri Martinie, "Le XVIIIe
Salon des Artistes Décorateurs," *Art
et décoration* 53 (January–June 1928),
p. 180; Ayroles, *François Décorchemont:
Maître de la pâte de verre* (2006),
pp. 143, 277.

MICHEL DUBOST

14 | *L'Oiseau dans la lumière*
ca. 1925
Manufacturer: Soieries F. Ducharne
Silk and metallic thread brocade
66¾ x 49⅛ in. (169.5 x 124.8 cm)
Gift of Monsieur and Madame Jean
Ducharne, 2004 (2004.84)

Unmarked.

Provenance: François Ducharne, Lyons,
until d. 1975; his son and daughter-
in-law Jean and Marguerite Ducharne,
Lyons; gift to The Metropolitan Museum
of Art, 2004.

References: "Les Soieries de Ducharne,"
in Exposition Internationale des Arts
Décoratifs et Industriels Modernes,
Paris 1925, *Catalogue générale officiel*
(Paris: Les Éditions G. Crès & Cie, 1925),
pp. 174–76; "Winter Fabrics, Collection
Ducharne," *Vogue* 66, no. 5 (September 1,
1925), p. 34; *Encyclopédie des arts
décoratifs et industriels modernes au
XXème siècle* (ca. 1927; repr., New York:
Garland, 1977), vol. 6, pl. XLI; *Les Folles
Années de la soie*, exh. cat. (Lyons:
Musée Historique des Tissus, 1975),
suppl., pp. 70, 79; Jason T. Busch and
Catherine L. Futter, *Inventing the Modern
World: Decorative Arts at the World's
Fairs, 1851–1939*, exh. cat. (Pittsburgh:
Carnegie Museum of Art; Kansas City:
Nelson-Atkins Museum of Art; New York:
Skira Rizzoli, 2012), pp. 132, 134, 269.

RAOUL DUFY

15 | Four Textiles
Manufacturer: Bianchini-Férier

a | *La Chasse*
Designed 1911; manufactured ca. 1920
Printed linen
Length 70½ in. (179.1 cm), width 46½ in.
(118.1 cm)
Purchase, Edward C. Moore Jr. Gift, 1923
(23.14.3)

Unmarked.

Provenance: [Frankl Gallery, New York,
1923]; purchased by The Metropolitan
Museum of Art, 1923.

References: *La Renaissance de l'art fran-
çais et des industries de luxe* (January
1923), p. 46; Léon Moussinac, *Étoffes im-
primées et papiers peints* (Paris: Éditions
Albert Lévy, 1924), pl. 2; *La Renaissance
de l'art français et des industries de luxe*,
April 1924, p. 98; Paul T. Frankl, *Form and
Re-form: A Practical Handbook of Modern
Interiors* (New York: Harper, 1930), p. 102;
Judith Applegate, *Art Deco*, exh. cat.
(New York: Finch College Museum of Art,
1970), cat. no. 448.

b | *L'Afrique*
Designed 1912; manufactured ca. 1920
Printed linen
Length 68½ in. (174 cm), width 47 in.
(119.4 cm)
Purchase, Edward C. Moore Jr. Gift, 1923
(23.14.2)

Unmarked.

Provenance: [Frankl Gallery, New York,
1923]; purchased by The Metropolitan
Museum of Art, 1923.

References: Moussinac, *Étoffes impri-
mées et papiers peints* (1924), pl. 10;
*Catalogue of a Retrospective Exhibition
of Painted and Printed Fabrics*, exh. cat.
(New York: The Metropolitan Museum
of Art, 1927), p. 84, cat. no. 316; Frankl,
Form and Re-form (1930), p. 104;
Applegate, *Art Deco* (1970), cat. no. 445.

c | *Les Fruits*
Designed 1912; manufactured ca. 1920
Printed linen
Length 72 in. (182.9 cm), width 47 in.
(119.4 cm)
Purchase, Edward C. Moore Jr. Gift, 1923
(23.36)

Unmarked.

Provenance: Bianchini-Férier, Lyons,
1923; purchased by The Metropolitan
Museum of Art, 1923.

References: Henri Clouzot, "Les 'Tissus
modernes' de Raoul Dufy," *Art et décoration* 38 (July–December 1920), p. 179;
Moussinac, *Étoffes imprimées et papiers
peints* (1924), pl. 23; Applegate, *Art Deco*
(1970), cat. no. 446; Lesley Jackson,
*Twentieth-Century Pattern Design: Textile
and Wallpaper Pioneers* (New York:
Princeton Architectural Press, 2002),
p. 49.

d | *La Moisson*
Probably designed ca. 1912; manufac-
tured ca. 1920
Printed linen
Length 72 in (182.9 cm), width 47 in.
(119.4 cm)
Purchase, Edward C. Moore Jr. Gift, 1923
(23.116)

Unmarked.

Provenance: Bianchini-Férier, Lyons,
1923; purchased by The Metropolitan
Museum of Art, 1923.

References: Clouzot, "Les 'Tissus modernes' de Dufy" (1920), pp. 181, 182;
Moussinac, *Étoffes imprimées et papiers
peints* (1924), pl. 23; *L'Art décoratif
français, 1918–1925: Recueil de documents parus dans la revue Art et décoration* (Paris: Albert Lévy, 1925), p. 88;
*Retrospective Exhibition of Painted and
Printed Fabrics* (1927), p. 85, cat. no. 317
(titled *The Thrasher*); Applegate, *Art Deco*
(1970), cat. no. 446; *Raoul Dufy créateur
d'étoffes*, exh. cat. (Mulhouse: Musée de

l'Impression sur Étoffes de Mulhouse,
1973), cat. no. 220.

16 | Five Swimmers
   **Raoul Dufy and Josep Llorens
   Artigas**
1926
Earthenware
Height 9⅛ in. (23.2 cm), diameter 7⅜ in.
(18.8 cm)
Bequest of James H. Stubblebine, 1987
(1987.473.1)

Marks: Painted on underside of foot:
Raoul Dufy; LLA [interlaced]; 86 — /
11 Oct 1926

Provenance: Marcel Kapferer, Paris
(dates unknown); [Alain Lesieutre, Paris,
until 1970]; sold to James H. Stubblebine,
New York, 1970–until d. 1987; bequest to
The Metropolitan Museum of Art, 1987.

References: Kenneth E. Silver, *Chaos
and Classicism: Art in France, Italy,
and Germany, 1918–1936*, exh. cat.
(New York: The Solomon R. Guggenheim
Foundation, 2010), p. 174.

JEAN DUNAND

17 | Cobras
ca. 1919
Bronze, gold
.7: Height 15 in. (38.1 cm), width 6 in.
(15.2 cm), depth 9¾ in. (24.8 cm)
.8: Height 12 in. (30.5 cm), width 5¾ in.
(14.6 cm), depth 9 in. (22.9 cm)
Rogers Fund, 1970 (1970.198.7, .8)

Marks: Incised on underside of each
sculpture: JEAN DUNAND

Provenance: [Galerie Sonnabend, Paris,
1970]; purchased by The Metropolitan
Museum of Art, 1970.

References: Émile Sedeyn, "Jean
Dunand," *Art et décoration* 36
(September–October 1919), pp. 118–26;
Katharine Morrison McClinton, "Jean

Dunand, Art Deco Craftsman," *Apollo* 116, no. 247 (September 1982), pp. 177–80; Félix Marcilhac, *Jean Dunand: His Life and Works* (New York: Harry N. Abrams, 1991), p. 273.

18 | Five Vases

a | Vase
ca. 1920
Copper, inlaid silver
Height 7⅞ in. (20 cm), diameter 3¼ in. (8.3 cm)
Purchase, Edward C. Moore Jr. Gift, 1923 (23.39.2)

Marks: Impressed on underside: JEAN DUNAND; on sticker affixed to underside: A / LA PAIX / 34 / AVe DE L'OPERA

Provenance: [Galerie Georges Rouard, Paris, 1923]; purchased by The Metropolitan Museum of Art, 1923.

References: Jean-Louis Gaillemain, "The Dunand Touch," *Connaissance des arts*, no. 551 (June 1998), pp. 102–5.

b | Vase
ca. 1923
Lacquered metal (probably steel), eggshell
Height 6 in. (15.2 cm), diameter 3¼ in. (8.3 cm)
Purchase, Edward C. Moore Jr. Gift, 1923 (23.176.5)

Marks: On paper label affixed to underside: 71

Provenance: [Galerie Georges Rouard, Paris, 1923]; purchased by The Metropolitan Museum of Art, 1923.

References: Joseph Breck, "Modern Decorative Arts," *Bulletin of The Metropolitan Museum of Art* 18, no. 11 (November 1923), p. 246.

c | Vase
ca. 1925
Copper, plated gold
Height 18¼ in. (46.4 cm), diameter 10½ in. (26.7 cm)
Gift of Celia Siegel, in memory of Stanley Siegel, 1975 (1975.72.2)

Marks: Stamped on underside: JEAN DUNAND / 4579. *See no. 18a.*

Provenance: Possibly Stanley Siegel, New York; Celia Siegel, Miami Beach; gift to The Metropolitan Museum of Art, 1975.

References: Penelope Hunter, "Twentieth Century Art," in *The Metropolitan Museum of Art: Notable Acquisitions, 1965–1975* (New York: The Metropolitan Museum of Art, 1975), p. 230.

d | Vase
ca. 1920
Brass, inlaid silver
Height 10¼ in. (26 cm), diameter 6⅛ in. (15.6 cm)
Purchase, Edward C. Moore Jr. Gift, 1923 (23.206)

Marks: Impressed on underside: JEAN DUNAND. *See no. 18a.*

Provenance: [Galerie Georges Rouard, Paris, 1923]; purchased by The Metropolitan Museum of Art, 1923.

References: Penelope Hunter-Stiebel, "The Decorative Arts of the Twentieth Century," *The Metropolitan Museum of Art Bulletin*, n.s., 37, no. 3 (Winter 1979–80), p. 18; Gaillemain, "Dunand Touch" (1998), pp. 102–5.

e | Vase
ca. 1925
Lacquered metal
Height 6⅜ in. (16.2 cm), diameter 8 in. (20.3 cm)
Purchase, Lita Annenberg Hazen Charitable Trust Gift, 1998 (1998.194ab)

Marks: Painted in lacquer on underside: JEAN DUNAND

Provenance: [Rodolphe Perpitch, Paris, until 1986]; [Delorenzo Gallery, New York, 1986–88]; Joseph Bauer, New York, 1988–96; [Delorenzo Gallery, New York, 1996–98]; purchased by The Metropolitan Museum of Art, 1998.

References: Jared D. Goss in "Recent Acquisitions, A Selection: 1997–1998," *The Metropolitan Museum of Art Bulletin*, n.s., 56, no. 2 (Fall 1998), p. 61; Mechthild Baumeister, "Jean Dunand: A Master of Art Déco Lacquer," *Arbeitshefte des Bayerischen Landesamtes für Denkmalpflege* 112 (2000), pp. 207–18.

19 | Three Lacquered Panels

a | *Panther*
Jean Dunand and Paul Jouve
ca. 1924
Lacquered wood, eggshell

Height 23 in. (58.4 cm), width 45¼ in. (114.9 cm), depth 1½ in. (3.8 cm)
Purchase, Edward C. Moore Jr. Gift, 1924 (24.134)

Marks: Painted in lacquer at lower left: PAUL JOUVe; at lower right: JEAN DUNAND / LAQUEUR [within a square]

Provenance: Jean Dunand, until 1924; purchased by The Metropolitan Museum of Art, 1924.

References: Joseph Breck, "Accessions and Notes: Decorative Arts," *Bulletin of The Metropolitan Museum of Art* 19, no. 11 (November 1924), pp. 275, 276; Marcilhac, *Jean Dunand* (1991), p. 235, cat. no. 307; Félix Marcilhac, *Paul Jouve: Peintre, sculpteur, animalier, 1878–1973* (Paris: Les Éditions de l'Amateur, 2005), p. 116.

b | *African Woman*
1928–30
Lacquered wood, oxidized copper
Height 36½ in. (92.7 cm), width 25¼ in. (64.1 cm), depth 1¾ in. (4.5 cm)
Gift of Peter M. Brant, 1974 (1974.373.4)

Marks: Painted in lacquer at lower right: JEAN DUNAND; stamped in ink on reverse: MADE IN FRANCE

Provenance: Templeton Crocker, San Francisco, until 1948; heirs of Templeton Crocker, San Francisco, until 1972; sold to Mr. and Mrs. Peter M. Brant, Greenwich, Conn.; gift to The Metropolitan Museum of Art, 1974.

References: Hunter in "Twentieth Century Art" (1975), p. 230; Marcilhac, *Jean Dunand* (1991), p. 277, cat. no. 239; Gaillemain, "Dunand Touch" (1998), pp. 102–5.

c | *Juliette de Saint Cyr*
ca. 1925
Lacquered wood, eggshell
Height 23¾ in. (60.3 cm), width 35⅛ in. (89.2 cm), depth ⅝ in. (1.59 cm)
Bequest of Marquise Raoul de Saint Cyr, 1988 (1989.176.2)

Marks: Painted in lacquer at lower right: JEAN DUNAND

Provenance: Marquise Raoul de Saint Cyr, New York, until d. 1988; bequest to The Metropolitan Museum of Art, 1988.

References: Marcilhac, *Jean Dunand* (1991), p. 220, cat. no. 165; Baumeister, "Jean Dunand" (2000), pp. 207–18 (illustrated p. 214); Lily Koppel, "An Opulent Home, a Rich Past: A Riverside Mansion That Tobacco Built," *The New York Times*, April 3, 2007, p. B4.

20 | *Fortissimo* and *Pianissimo* Screens
Jean Dunand and Séraphin Soudbinine
1925–26
Lacquered wood, eggshell, mother-of-pearl
Each panel: Height 98 in. (248.9 cm), width 35 in. (88.9 cm), depth 1½ in. (3.8 cm)
Gift of Mrs. Solomon R. Guggenheim, 1950 (50.102.3, .4)

Marks: Lacquered at right edge of each screen: S Soudbinine / Paris 1925–26; at lower right corner of each screen: JEAN / DUNAND / LAQUEUR

Provenance: Mr. and Mrs. Solomon R. Guggenheim, Port Washington, N.Y., until 1950; gift to The Metropolitan Museum of Art, 1950.

References: Judith Applegate, *Art Deco*, exh. cat. (New York: Finch College Museum of Art, 1970), cat. nos. 255, 256; Hunter-Stiebel, "Decorative Arts of the Twentieth Century" (1979–80), pp. 26–27; Michael Komanecky and Virginia Fabbri Butera, *The Folding Image: Screens by Western Artists of the Nineteenth and Twentieth Centuries,* exh. cat. (New Haven: Yale University Art Gallery, 1984), pp. 240–42; Marcilhac, *Jean Dunand* (1991), cat. nos. 1154, 1155; Baumeister, "Jean Dunand" (2000), pp. 207–18.

21 | Bedroom Furniture and Wall Maquette made for Templeton Crocker

ca. 1927–28
Gift of Mr. and Mrs. Peter M. Brant, 1977
(1977.226.1a–d–.7)

a | Bed

Lacquered wood
Height 39⅜ in. (100 cm), width 71⅛ in. (180.7 cm), depth 84¼ in. (214 cm)
(1977.226.1a–d)

Unmarked.

b | Easy Chair

Lacquered wood, goatskin
Height 35¾ in. (90.8 cm), width 24¾ in. (62.9 cm), depth 42 in. (106.7 cm)
(1977.226.2)

Unmarked.

c | Bench

Lacquered wood, goatskin
Height 18 in. (45.7 cm), width 40 in. (101.6 cm), depth 21 in. (53.3 cm)
(1977.226.3)

Unmarked.

d | Commode

Lacquered wood, ivory
Height 31⅞ in. (81 cm), width 55 in. (139.7 cm), depth 21 in. (53.3 cm)
(1977.226.4)

Marks: Branded on back: JEAN DUNAND / 72 RUE HALLÉ / PARIS / MADE IN FRANCE. *See no. 21g.*

e | Side Chair

Lacquered wood, replacement chamois
Height 35 in. (88.9 cm), width 17½ in. (44.5 cm), depth 20½ in. (52.1 cm)
(1977.226.5)

Unmarked.

f | Bedside Table

Lacquered wood, ivory
Height 23⅝ in. (60 cm), width 27½ in. (69.9 cm), depth 13¾ in. (34.9 cm)
(1977.226.6)

Marks: Branded on underside: JEAN DUNAND / 72 RUE HALLÉ / PARIS / MADE IN FRANCE

g | Table

Lacquered wood
Height 23¼ in. (59.1 cm), width 13¾ in. (34.9 cm), depth 13¾ in. (34.9 cm)
(1977.226.7)

Marks: Branded three times on underside: JEAN DUNAND / 72 RUE HALLÉ / PARIS / MADE IN FRANCE

Provenance: Templeton Crocker, San Francisco, 1928–48; heirs of Templeton Crocker, San Francisco, 1948–72; sold to Mr. and Mrs. Peter M. Brant, Greenwich, Conn.; gift to The Metropolitan Museum of Art, 1977.

References: Mary Ashe Miller, "A Twentieth Century Apartment," *Vogue* 74, no. 3 (August 3, 1929), pp. 30–35, 94; Marcilhac, *Jean Dunand* (1991), p. 324, cat. no. 1163; Baumeister, "Jean Dunand" (2000), pp. 207–18.

h | Wall Maquette

Painted plywood
Height 12¼ in. (31.1 cm), width 18½ in. (47 cm), depth ⅜ in. (1 cm)
Purchase, John Stuart Gordon Gift, 2002
(2002.172)

Marks: Inscribed in pencil on reverse, probably at a later date: etude pré-maquette, chambre à coucher de l'apartement Tempelton [*sic*] Crocker 1928, Jean Dunand

Provenance: Jean Dunand, until 1942; his son Bernard Dunand, Paris, until 1998; his daughter and son-in-law Dorothée and Christian Dougoud-Dunand, Villecresnes, until 2002; purchased by The Metropolitan Museum of Art, 2002.

Previously unpublished.

JEAN DUPAS AND CHARLES CHAMPIGNEULLE

22 | *The Chariot of Poseidon*

1934
Glass, paint, gold, silver, palladium leaf
Height 20 ft. 5 in. (6.2 m), width 29 ft. ¾ in. (8.9 m), depth ⅜ in. (.95 cm)
Gift of Dr. and Mrs. Irwin R. Berman, 1976
(1976.414.3a–ggg)

Marks: Reverse painted on panel aaa: Jean Dupas / 1934; reverse painted on panel w: CH. CHAMPIGNEULLE FECIT / PARIS

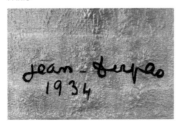

Provenance: Compagnie Générale Transatlantique; SS *Normandie,* until 1942; [Edward G. Collord, United States Appraisers Stores, New York, until 1942]; [Otto Verne, New York, until d. ca. 1975]; Dr. and Mrs. Irwin R. Berman, New York, 1975; gift to The Metropolitan Museum of Art, 1976.

References: Compagnie Générale Transatlantique, *Le Paquebot "Normandie"* (Paris: L'Illustration, 1935), n.p.; Penelope Hunter-Stiebel, "The Decorative Arts of the Twentieth Century," *The Metropolitan Museum of Art Bulletin,* n.s., 37, no. 3 (Winter 1979–80), pp. 32, 33, 35; Bruno Foucart et al., *Normandie: Queen of the Seas* (New York: Vendome Press, 1985), pp. 67, 71; John Maxtone-Graham, *Normandie: France's Legendary Art Deco Ocean Liner* (New York: W. W. Norton, 2007), pp. 93, 206, 245; Frédéric Ollivier, Aymeric Perroy, and Franck Sénant, *À bord des paquebots: 50 Ans d'arts décoratifs* (Paris: Éditions Norma, 2011), p. 194.

GEORGES FOUQUET

23 | Dress Ornament

ca. 1923
Jade, onyx, diamonds, enamel, platinum
Height 9 in. (22.9 cm), width 3¾ in. (9.5 cm), depth ½ in. (1.3 cm)
Gift of Eva and Michael Chow, 2001
(2001.723)

Unmarked.

Provenance: Private collection (Paris?), until 1985; [Champin, Lombrail, Gautier, Enghien-les-Bains, December 15, 1985, lot 112]; sold to Michael and Eva Chow, Los Angeles; gift to The Metropolitan Museum of Art, 2001.

References: Henri Clouzot, "Le Bijou moderne," *L'Illustration,* no. 4422 (December 3, 1927), p. 545; Yvonne Brunhammer, *The Art Deco Style,* trans. David Beeson (London: Academy Editions, 1983), p. 111; Sylvie Raulet, *Art Deco Jewelry* (New York: Rizzoli, 1985), p. 228; Dan Klein, Nancy A. McClelland, and Malcolm Haslam, *In the Deco Style* (New York: Rizzoli, 1986), p. 99; A. Kenneth Snowman, ed., *The Master Jewelers* (New York: Harry N. Abrams, 1990), p. 166; Jason T. Busch and Catherine L. Futter, *Inventing the Modern World: Decorative Arts at the World's Fairs, 1851–1939,* exh. cat. (Pittsburgh: Carnegie Museum of Art; Kansas City: Nelson-Atkins Museum of Art; New York: Skira Rizzoli, 2012), pp. 138, 139, 268.

MARCEL GOUPY

24 | Vase

ca. 1925
Glass, gold
Height 7⅜ in. (18.7 cm), diameter 7¼ in. (18.4 cm)
Bequest of James H. Stubblebine, 1987
(1987.473.6)

Marks: Painted on underside: M. Goupy; printed on partial paper label: ROUARD / Av. de l'Opéra

Provenance: Probably Harvey Feinstein, New York, until 1975; sold to James H. Stubblebine, New York, 1975–87; bequest to The Metropolitan Museum of Art, 1987.

Previously unpublished.

PAUL IRIBE

25 | *Roses*

1914
Silk, metal thread
Length 90 in. (228.6 cm), width 32¼ in. (81.9 cm)
Gift of Mrs. Morris Hawkes, 1926
(26.72.5)

Unmarked.

Provenance: Mrs. Morris Hawkes, New York, until 1926; gift to The Metropolitan Museum of Art, 1926.

References: Henri d'Hennezel, *Musée Historique des Tissus: Catalogue des principales pièces exposées* (Lyons: Société Anonyme de l'Imprimerie A. Rey, 1929), p. 121, pl. XIII; Raymond Bachollet, Daniel Bordet, and Anne-Claude Lelieur, *Paul Iribe* (Paris: Éditions Denoël, 1982), p. 129; Pierre Arizzoli-Clémentel, *The Textile Museum, Lyons* (Paris: Musées et Monuments de France, 1996), p. 107; Lesley Jackson, *Twentieth-Century Pattern Design: Textile and Wallpaper Pioneers* (New York: Princeton Architectural Press, 2002), p. 50.

LÉON-ALBERT JALLOT

26 | Cabinet
ca. 1925
Mahogany, palisander, *Verde di Levanto* marble
Height 51⅝ in. (131.1 cm), width 44¾ in. (113.7 cm), depth 17⅞ in. (45.4 cm)
Purchase, Edward C. Moore Jr. Gift, 1925 (25.212)

Marks: Branded under marble top: LJ [within a circle]; incised: L JAllOT

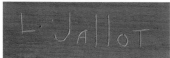

Provenance: Léon-Albert Jallot, until 1925; purchased by The Metropolitan Museum of Art, 1925.

References: "Les Ensembles modernes," *Art et industrie*, November 1925, n.p.; Joseph Breck, "Modern Decorative Arts: Some Recent Purchases," *Bulletin of The Metropolitan Museum of Art* 21, no. 2 (February 1926), p. 38.

RENÉ LALIQUE

27 | *Monnaie du pape* Coffer
Designed 1914
Glass, silver leaf, amaranth, brass
Height 5½ in. (14 cm), width 13 in. (33 cm), depth 7¼ in. (18.4 cm)
Purchase, Edward C. Moore Jr. Gift, 1924 (24.145.1)

Marks: Engraved on lid, lower right corner: R–LALIQUE — FRANCE

Provenance: René Lalique, until 1924; purchased by The Metropolitan Museum of Art, 1924.

References: Félix Marcilhac, *René Lalique, 1860–1945: Maître-verrier; Analyse et catalogue raisonné de l'oeuvre de verre*, 4th ed. (Paris: Les Éditions de l'Amateur, 2011), pp. 55, 286.

28 | *Hagueneau* Wine Glasses
Designed 1924
Glass
Water glass (1978.223.1): Height 8¼ in. (21 cm), diameter 3¾ in. (9.5 cm)
Champagne glass (1978.223.3): Height 7¼ in. (18.4 cm), diameter 4⅝ in. (11.7 cm)
Burgundy glass (1978.223.2): Height 7⅝ in. (19.4 cm), diameter 3⅜ in. (8.6 cm)
Gift of Robert L. Isaacson, 1978 (1978.223.1–.3)

Marks: Etched on underside of each foot: R LALIQUE

Provenance: Robert L. Isaacson, New York, until 1978; gift to The Metropolitan Museum of Art, 1978.

References: *Art et industrie*, November 1925, n.p.; *Encyclopédie des arts décoratifs et industriels modernes au XXème siècle* (ca. 1927; repr., New York: Garland, 1977), vol. 5, pl. LXXVII; Gaston Derys, "L'Exposition de l'oeuvre de René Lalique," *Mobilier et décoration* 13 (March 1933), p. 101; Marcilhac, *René Lalique* (2011), p. 829.

29 | *Tourbillons* Vase
Designed ca. 1925
Glass
Height 7⅞ in. (20 cm), diameter 8 in. (20.3 cm)
Cynthia Hazen Polsky and Leon B. Polsky Fund, 2004 (2004.120)

Marks: Etched on underside of foot: R LALIQUE / FRANCE / N° 973

Provenance: Purchased in Paris, late 1920s; by descent to Sybil Bruel, New York, until 2004; purchased by The Metropolitan Museum of Art, 2004.

References: Ray Grover and Lee Grover, *Carved and Decorated European Art Glass* (Rutland, Vt.: Charles E. Tuttle, 1970), p. 197; Christopher Vane Percy, *The Glass of Lalique: A Collector's Guide* (New York: Charles Scribner's Sons, 1983), p. 38;

Patricia Bayer and Mark Waller, *The Art of René Lalique* ([Edison, N.J.]: Wellfleet, 1996), p. 30; Carolyn Hatch, *Déco Lalique: Creator to Consumer*, exh. cat. (Toronto: Royal Ontario Museum, 2006), pp. 94–95; Marcilhac, *René Lalique* (2011), p. 433.

30 | Vase
1929
Glass
Height 7 in. (17.8 cm), diameter 5 in. (12.7 cm)
Purchase, Edward C. Moore Jr. Gift, 1936 (36.104.3)

Marks: Engraved on underside of foot: R LALIQUE FRANCE / *707-2-29*

Provenance: René Lalique, until 1936; purchased by The Metropolitan Museum of Art, 1936.

References: Marcilhac, *René Lalique* (2011), p. 1054.

31 | Rings and Necklace

a | Rings
ca. 1931
Glass
Each ring: Height ⅞ in. (2.2 cm), width 1¼ in. (3.2 cm)
Purchase, Edward C. Moore Jr. Gift, 1934 (34.99.1–.3)

Marks: Engraved on exterior of each ring: R LALIQUE

Provenance: René Lalique, until 1934; purchased by The Metropolitan Museum of Art, 1934.

References: John Goldsmith Phillips, "New Accessions of Contemporary French and Swedish Decorative Arts," *Bulletin of The Metropolitan Museum of Art* 30, no. 1 (January 1935), p. 5; Marcilhac, *René Lalique* (2011), pp. 526–27.

b | *Perruches* Necklace
ca. 1929
Glass, silver
Overall: length 22 in. (55.9 cm)
Each bead: height 1¾ in. (4.5 cm), width ½ in. (1.3 cm), depth ⅜ in. (.95 cm)
Purchase, Edward C. Moore Jr. Gift, 1934 (34.99.4)

Marks: Stamped on clasp: STERLING

Provenance: René Lalique, until 1934; purchased by The Metropolitan Museum of Art, 1934.

References: Phillips, "New Accessions of Decorative Arts" (1935), p. 5.

ROBERT LALLEMANT

32 | Vase
1927
Porcelain
Height 11¼ in. (28.6 cm), diameter 4⅜ in. (11.1 cm)
Purchase, Lita Annenberg Hazen Charitable Trust Gift, 1986 (1986.33)

Marks: Painted on underside of vase: T R / LALLEMANT / FRANCE

Provenance: [Galerie Jacques De Vos, Paris, until 1986]; purchased by The Metropolitan Museum of Art, 1986.

References: René Chavance, "À propos de quelques céramiques nouvelles de Robert Lallemant," *Mobilier et décoration* 9, no. 7 (July 1929), pp. 130, 133; *Robert Lallemant, ou la céramique méchanisée*, exh. cat. (Paris: Galerie Jacques De Vos, 1984), n.p.; Arlette Barré-Despond, *UAM: Union des Artistes Modernes* (Paris: Éditions du Regard, 1986), p. 330.

JACQUES LE CHEVALLIER AND RENÉ KOECHLIN

33 | Lamp
1926–27
Aluminum, ebonite
Height 11 in. (27.9 cm), diameter 9 in. (22.9 cm)
Purchase, The Horace W. Goldsmith Foundation Gift, 2001 (2001.410ab)

Marks: Stamped on underside of plane with socket: DEPOSE / MADE IN / FRANCE; Type 4 / JLC / N° / R / K [within a rectangle]

Provenance: Private collection, Paris (dates unknown); [Galerie Doria, Paris, until 2001]; purchased by The Metropolitan Museum of Art, 2001.

References: Jean Prouvé, "Le Métal," *L'Art international d'aujourd'hui 9* (Paris: Éditions d'Art Charles Moreau, 1928–29), pl. 8; "Le Luminaire," *Ce temps-ci: Cahiers d'art contemporain*, no. 3 (January 1929), p. 75; Ernest Tisserand, "Esthetique du luminaire," *L'Art vivant* 6, no. 143 (December 1, 1930), p. 942; Sarah Nichols, "Lighting and Le Chevalier," in *Aluminum by Design*, exh. cat. (Pittsburgh: Carnegie Museum of Art; New York: Harry N. Abrams, 2000), pp. 212, 213; Jared D. Goss in "Recent Acquisitions: A Selection, 2000–2001," *The Metropolitan Museum of Art Bulletin*, n.s., 59, no. 2 (Autumn 2001), p. 60; Jean-François Archieri, ed., *Jacques Le Chevallier, 1896–1987: La Lumière moderne, 1896–1987*, exh. cat. (Montreuil: Éditions Gourcuff Gradenigo, 2007), pp. 64–69.

PIERRE LEGRAIN

34 | Stool
ca. 1925
Palisander
Height 13 in. (33 cm), width 29 in. (73.7 cm), depth 10 in. (25.4 cm)
Fletcher Fund, 1972 (1972.283.1)

Unmarked.

Provenance: Jacques Doucet, Paris, until d. 1929; his widow, Jeanne Roger Doucet, Neuilly, until d. 1958; Jacques Doucet's nephew Jean Dubrujeaud, Paris, 1958–68; his son Jean Angladon-Dubrujeaud, Paris, 1968–72; [Hôtel Drouot, Paris, November 8, 1972, lot 28]; sold to The Metropolitan Museum of Art, 1972.

References: Lynne Thornton, "Negro Art and the Furniture of Pierre-Émile Legrain," *The Connoisseur* 181, no. 729 (November 1972), p. 169; Henry Geldzahler, "Creating a New Department," in Thomas Hoving, *The Chase, the Capture: Collecting at the Metropolitan* (New York, The Metropolitan Museum of Art, 1975), p. 229; Penelope Hunter in "Twentieth Century Art," in *The Metropolitan Museum of Art: Notable Acquisitions, 1965–1975* (New York: The Metropolitan Museum of Art, 1975), p. 228; Penelope Hunter-Stiebel, "The Decorative Arts of the Twentieth Century,"

The Metropolitan Museum of Art Bulletin, n.s., 37, no. 3 (Winter 1979–80), pp. 30–31; Penelope Hunter-Stiebel, *The Fine Art of the Furniture Maker* (Rochester, N.Y.: Memorial Art Gallery of the University of Rochester, 1981), pp. 101–5; Lydia Puccinelli, *African Forms in the Furniture of Pierre Legrain*, exh. cat. (Washington, D.C.: National Museum of African Art, 1998), p. 10.

35 | Portfolio and Cigarette Cases

a | Portfolio
ca. 1925
Leather, chrome-plated metal, gold leaf
Height 7⅛ in. (18.1 cm), width 5⅝ in. (14.3 cm), depth ⅜ in. (.95 cm)
Gift of Mrs. Germain Seligman, 1979 (1979.317.1)

Marks: Stamped in gold on interior pocket: PIERRE LEGRAIN

Provenance: Mrs. Germain Seligman, New York; gift to The Metropolitan Museum of Art, 1979.

Previously unpublished.

b | Cigarette Case
ca. 1925
Dyed and tooled leather, gold leaf
Height 3⅛ in. (7.9 cm), width 2½ in. (6.4 cm), depth 1⅛ in. (2.9 cm)
Gift of Mrs. Germain Seligman, 1979 (1979.317.2ab)

Marks: Stamped in gold on inner box: PIERRE LEGRAIN. *See no. 35a.*

Provenance: Mrs. Germain Seligman, New York; gift to The Metropolitan Museum of Art, 1979.

Previously unpublished.

c | Cigarette Case
ca. 1925
Snakeskin, dyed and tooled leather, gold leaf
Height 3⅛ in. (7.9 cm), width 2½ in. (6.4 cm), depth 1⅛ in. (2.9 cm)
Gift of Mrs. Germain Seligman, 1979 (1979.317.3ab)

Marks: Stamped in gold on inner box: PIERRE LEGRAIN. *See no. 35a*

Provenance: Mrs. Germain Seligman, New York, until 1979; gift to The Metropolitan Museum of Art, 1979.

Previously unpublished.

JULES-ÉMILE LELEU

36 | Commode
1925
Amboyna, ivory, *fleur de pêcher* marble, brass, mahogany, birch plywood
Height 35¼ in. (89.5 cm), width 49¼ in. (125.1 cm), depth 18½ in. (47 cm)
Gift of Agnes Miles Carpenter, 1946 (46.93)

Marks: Signed in red crayon on bottom of marble top and in chalk on wood beneath marble: Leleu

Provenance: Agnes Miles Carpenter, New York, presumably ca. 1926 until 1946; gift to The Metropolitan Museum of Art, 1946.

References: Th. Harlor, "L'Exposition des Arts Décoratifs Modernes: L'Aménagement intérieur et le mobilier," *Gazette des beaux-arts*, ser. 5, 12 (July–December 1925), p. 372; Pierre E. Benoit, "Commodes modernes par J. M. Leleu," *Art et Industrie* 3, no. 2 (February 1927), p. 46.

ÉMILE LENOBLE

37 | Three Vases

a | Vase
1925
Glazed stoneware
Height 8⅝ in. (21.9 cm), diameter 9¼ in. (23.5 cm)
Gift of Charles J. Liebman Jr. 1965 (65.151.2)

Marks: Impressed within a circle on underside of foot: L e [conjoined]. *See no. 38.*

Provenance: Mr. and Mrs. Charles J. Liebman, New York, ca. 1925; their son Charles J. Liebman Jr., New York, until 1965; gift to The Metropolitan Museum of Art, 1965.

References: Margaret Liebman Berger, *Aline Meyer Liebman: Pioneer Collector and Artist* (New York: W. F. Humphrey Press, 1982), p. 69.

b | Vase
ca. 1925
Glazed stoneware
Height 11¼ in. (28.6 cm), diameter 8½ in. (21.6 cm)

Gift of Charles J. Liebman Jr., 1965 (65.151.1)

Marks: Impressed within a circle on underside of foot: L e [conjoined]. *See no. 38.*

Provenance: Mr. and Mrs. Charles J. Liebman, New York, ca. 1925; their son Charles J. Liebman Jr., New York, until 1965; gift to The Metropolitan Museum of Art, 1965.

References: Berger, *Aline Meyer Liebman* (1982), p. 69.

c | Vase
ca. 1913
Glazed stoneware
Height 6¾ in. (17.1 cm), diameter 5½ in. (14 cm)
Purchase, Edward C. Moore Jr. Gift, 1922 (22.184.4)

Marks: Painted in blue on underside of foot: EL / A N

Provenance: [Galerie Georges Rouard, Paris, until 1922]; purchased by The Metropolitan Museum of Art, 1922.

References: *Arts and Crafts in Detroit, 1906–1976: The Movement, the Society, the School,* exh. cat. (Detroit: The Detroit Institute of Arts, 1977), p. 125, cat. no. 156.

38 | Vase
1925
Glazed stoneware
Height 12½ in. (31.8 cm), diameter 9½ in. (24.1 cm)
Purchase, Edward C. Moore Jr. Gift, 1925 (25.210)

Marks: Impressed within a circle on underside of foot: L e [conjoined]

Provenance: Émile Lenoble, 1925; purchased by The Metropolitan Museum of Art, 1925.

References: *Encyclopédie des arts décoratifs et industriels modernes au XXème siècle* (ca. 1927; repr., New York: Garland, 1977), vol. 5, pl. LX; Penelope Hunter-Stiebel, "The Decorative Arts of the Twentieth Century," *The Metropolitan Museum of Art Bulletin*, n.s., 37, no. 3 (Winter 1979–80), p. 19.

CLAUDIUS LINOSSIER

39 | Vase
ca. 1923
Copper, silver
Height 9½ in. (24.1 cm), diameter 7 in.
(17.8 cm)
Gift of Mrs. Florence Blumenthal, 1924
(24.157)

Marks: Chased on underside of foot:
CL_LINOSSIER

Provenance: Florence Blumenthal, Paris,
1924; gift to The Metropolitan Museum
of Art, 1924.

Previously unpublished.

MAURICE MARINOT

40 | Three Bottles and Bowl

a | Bottle with Stopper
1922
Glass
Height 4½ (11.4 cm), width 4 in.
(10.2 cm), depth 2⅞ in. (7.3 cm)
Purchase, Edward C. Moore Jr. Gift, 1923
(23.159.1ab)

Marks: Etched on underside of foot:
Marinot. *See no. 40d.*

Provenance: [Galerie Hébrard, Paris,
1923]; purchased by The Metropolitan
Museum of Art, 1923.

Previously unpublished.

b | Bottle with Stopper
1923
Glass
Height 7 in. (17.8 cm), width 4½ in.
(11.4 cm), depth 3¼ in. (8.3 cm)
Purchase, Edward C. Moore Jr. Gift, 1924
(24.131.4ab)

Marks: Etched on underside of foot:
Marinot. *See no. 40d.*

Provenance: [Galerie Hébrard, Paris,
1924]; purchased by The Metropolitan
Museum of Art, 1924.

Previously unpublished.

c | Bottle with Stopper
1924
Glass
Height 4¾ in. (12.1 cm), width 3⅝ in.
(9.2 cm), depth 2⅝ in. (6.7 cm)

Purchase, Edward C. Moore Jr. Gift, 1924
(24.131.6ab)

Marks: Etched on underside of foot:
Marinot. *See no. 40d.*

Provenance: [Galerie Hébrard, Paris,
1924]; purchased by The Metropolitan
Museum of Art, 1924.

References: Penelope Hunter, "Art Déco:
The Last Hurrah," *The Metropolitan
Museum of Art Bulletin*, n.s., 30, no. 6
(June–July 1972), p. 264.

d | Bowl
1923
Glass
Height 5½ in. (14 cm), diameter 6¼ in.
(15.9 cm)
Purchase, Edward C. Moore Jr. Gift, 1924
(24.131.3)

Marks: Etched on underside of foot:
Marinot; in ink on paper sticker on un-
derside: 417 [model number] / [HÉB]
RARD / [. . .] Paris

Provenance: [Galerie Hébrard, Paris,
1924]; purchased by The Metropolitan
Museum of Art, 1924.

References: *L'Amour de l'art* 5 (April 1924),
p. 1; *Le Bulletin de la vie artistique* 5, no. 7
(April 1, 1924), p. 148; The Metropolitan
Museum of Art, *A Special Exhibition
of Glass from the Museum Collections*
(New York, 1936), p. 42.

41 | Four Vessels

a | Lidded Urn
ca. 1925
Glass
Height 11⅝ in. (29.5 cm), width 3⅞ in.
(9.8 cm), depth 3¾ in. (9.5 cm)
Rogers Fund, 1970 (1970.198.1ab)

Marks: Scratched on underside of foot:
Marinot. *See no. 41c.*

Provenance: [Galerie Sonnabend, Paris,
1970]; purchase by The Metropolitan
Museum of Art, 1970.

References: Hunter, "Art Déco: The
Last Hurrah" (1972), p. 264; Penelope
Hunter in "Twentieth Century Art," in
*The Metropolitan Museum of Art: Notable
Acquisitions, 1965–1975* (New York: The
Metropolitan Museum of Art, 1975),
p. 228.

b | Bottle with Stopper
ca. 1925–29
Glass
Height 4⅝ in. (11.7 cm), width 4½ in.
(11.4 cm), depth 2½ in. (6.4 cm)
Rogers Fund, 1970 (1970.198.3ab)

Marks: Scratched on underside of foot:
Marinot. *See no. 41c.*

Provenance: [Galerie Sonnabend, Paris,
1970]; purchased by The Metropolitan
Museum of Art, 1970.

References: Hunter in "Twentieth Cen-
tury Art" (1975), p. 228; Penelope
Hunter-Stiebel, "The Decorative Arts of
the Twentieth Century," *The Metropolitan
Museum of Art Bulletin*, n.s., 37, no. 3
(Winter 1979–80), p. 28.

c | Jar
1927
Glass
Height 9 in. (22.9 cm), diameter 6 in.
(15.2 cm)
Rogers Fund, 1970 (1970.198.2)

Marks: Scratched on underside of foot:
Marinot

Provenance: [Galerie Sonnabend, Paris,
1970]; purchased by The Metropolitan
Museum of Art, 1970.

References: *Decorative Art, 1927: "The
Studio" Yearbook* (London: The Studio,
Ltd., 1927), p. 137; Léon Rosenthal, *La
Verrerie française depuis cinquante ans*
(Paris and Brussels: G. Vanoest, 1927),
pl. XXV, B; Hunter in "Twentieth Century
Art" (1975), p. 228; Hunter-Stiebel,
"Decorative Arts of the Twentieth Century"
(1979–80), pp. 28–29.

d | Lidded Jar
ca. 1925
Glass
Height 9¼ in. (23.5 cm), diameter 5¼ in.
(13.3 cm)
Bequest of Marquise Raoul de Saint Cyr,
1988 (1989.176.1ab)

Marks: Scratched on underside of foot:
Marinot. *See no. 41c.*

Provenance: Marquise Raoul de Saint
Cyr, until d. 1988; bequest to The
Metropolitan Museum of Art, 1988.

Previously unpublished.

JAN AND JOËL MARTEL

42 | Maquette for a Cubist Tree
1925
Painted wood
Height 31½ in. (80 cm), width 15⅛ in.
(38.4 cm), depth 15 in. (38.1 cm)
Purchase, Gifts of Himan Brown and
Adele Simpson, by exchange, 1997
(1997.110)

Marks: Stamped in black ink on underside of base: JM [cipher]

Provenance: Joël Martel, Paris, until
1966; his daughter Florence Langer-
Martel, until ca. 1997; [Galerie Doria,
Paris, 1997]; purchased by The
Metropolitan Museum of Art, 1997.

References: Félix Marcilhac, *Rétrospective
Jan et Joël Martel, sculpteurs*, exh. cat.
(Saint-Jean-de-Monts: Le Musée, 1976),
pp. 11, 37; Dorothée Imbert, *The Modernist
Garden in France* (New Haven: Yale
University Press, 1993), p. 54; *Joël et Jan
Martel: Sculpteurs, 1896–1966*, exh. cat.
(Paris: Gallimard/Electa, 1996), p. 59;
Jared D. Goss, "Twentieth Century: Joel
Martel, Jan Martel," *The Metropolitan
Museum of Art Bulletin*, n.s., 55, no. 2
(Autumn 1997), pp. 74–75.

HENRI ÉDOUARD NAVARRE

43 | Vase
ca. 1928
Glass
Height 6¾ in. (17.1 cm), diameter 4⅞ in.
(12.4 cm)
Purchase, Edward C. Moore Jr. Gift, 1928
(28.158.1)

Marks: Scratched on underside: 359 /
Navarre

Provenance: [Galerie Georges Rouard,
Paris, 1928]; purchased by The
Metropolitan Museum of Art, 1928.

References: *Art et décoration* 4, no. 12 (December 1928), p. 54.

PIERRE PATOUT

44 | Pair of Armchairs
1934
Manufacturer: Établissements Neveu
Mahogany, gilt bronze, wool upholstery
Each: Height 34½ in. (87.6 cm), width 22¼ in. (56.5 cm), depth 20 in. (50.8 cm)
Gift of Dr. and Mrs. Irwin R. Berman, 1976 (1976.414.1–.2)

Unmarked.

Provenance: Compagnie Générale Transatlantique, SS *Normandie*, until 1942; [Edward G. Collord, United States Appraisers Stores, New York, 1942]; [Otto Verne, New York, until d. ca. 1975]; Dr. and Mrs. Irwin R. Berman, New York, ca. 1975; gift to The Metropolitan Museum of Art, 1976.

References: Compagnie Générale Trans-atlantique, *Le Paquebot "Normandie"* (Paris: L'Illustration, 1935), n.p.; Anne Wealleans, *Designing Liners: A History of Interior Design Afloat* (New York: Routledge, 2006), p. 98; John Maxtone-Graham, *Normandie: France's Legendary Art Deco Ocean Liner* (New York: W. W. Norton, 2007), pp. 74, 50, 86, 129; Frédéric Ollivier, Aymeric Perroy, and Franck Sénant, *À bord des paquebots: 50 Ans d'arts décoratifs* (Paris: Éditions Norma, 2011), pp. 208, 210.

PAUL POIRET

45 | Four Textiles
Manufacturer: La Maison Martine

a | Textile
ca. 1919
Printed silk
Length 72 in. (182.9 cm), width 50 in. (127 cm)
Purchase, Edward C. Moore Jr. Gift, 1923 (23.14.8)

Unmarked.

Provenance: [Frankl Galleries, New York, 1923]; purchased by The Metropolitan Museum of Art, 1923.

References: "Hanging Gardens for Autumn Walls," *Vogue* 56, no. 5 (September 1, 1920), p. 78.

b | Textile
ca. 1920
Printed linen
Length 72 in. (182.9 cm), width 52 in. (132.1 cm)
Purchase, Edward C. Moore Jr. Gift, 1923 (23.14.9)

Marks: Printed in selvage: Martine

Provenance: [Frankl Galleries, New York, 1923]; purchased by The Metropolitan Museum of Art, 1923.

References: "Hanging Gardens for Autumn Walls" (1920), p. 78.

c | Textile
ca. 1920
Printed silk
Length 91 in. (231.1 cm), width 33 in. (83.8 cm)
Purchase, Edward C. Moore Jr. Gift, 1923 (23.178.8)

Unmarked.

Provenance: La Maison Martine, Paris, 1923; purchased by The Metropolitan Museum of Art, 1923.

Previously unpublished.

d | Textile
ca. 1920
Printed linen
Length 90 in. (228.6 cm), width 34 in. (86.4 cm)
Purchase, Edward C. Moore Jr. Gift, 1923 (23.178.11)

Unmarked.

Provenance: La Maison Martine, Paris, 1923; purchased by The Metropolitan Museum of Art, 1923.

References: "Hanging Gardens for Autumn Walls" (1920), p. 79.

FRANÇOIS POMPON

46 | Polar Bear
ca. 1923
Marble
Height 11½ in. (29.2 cm), width 19 in. (48.3 cm), depth 6¾ in. (17.1 cm)
Purchase, Edward C. Moore Jr. Gift, 1930 (30.123ab)

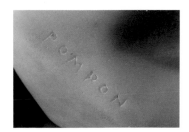

Marks: Incised on left hind paw: POMPON

Provenance: [Galerie Edgar Brandt, Paris, 1930]; purchased by The Metropolitan Museum of Art, 1930.

References: Robert Rey, *François Pompon* (Paris: Les Éditions G. Crès et Cie, 1928), pp. 43–45, pls. 22, 23; *François Pompon: Sculpteur animalier bourguinon*, exh. cat. (Dijon: Musée des Beaux-Arts de Dijon, 1964), pp. 5, 7, 11, 14, pl. I; Catherine Chevillot, Liliane Colas, and Anne Pingeot, *François Pompon, 1855–1933*, exh. cat. (Paris: Gallimard/Electa; Réunion des Musées Nationaux, 1994), pp. 34–38, 79, 85, 86, 92, 94, 211, 212, pl. 3; Peter Barnet and Atsuyuki Nakahara, *Earth, Sea, and Sky: Nature in Western Art; Masterpieces from The Metropolitan Museum of Art*, exh. cat. (Tokyo: Yomiuri Shimbun, 2012), cat. no. 52.

JEAN PUIFORCAT

47 | Tea and Coffee Service
ca. 1922
Silver, lapis lazuli, ivory, gold
Purchase, Edward C. Moore Jr. Gift, 1923 and 1925 (23.177.1ab–3; 25.230.1ab–4)

a | Coffeepot
Silver, lapis lazuli, ivory
Height 5⅞ in. (14.9 cm), width 8 in. (20.3 cm), depth 4¾ in. (12.1 cm) (23.177.1ab)

Marks: Incised on bottom of pot: JeAn e. PUIFORCAt; stamped twice: EP [within a lozenge divided by a spindle]; assay mark stamped three times: [canceled head of Minerva within an octagon]; exportation mark stamped twice: [head of Mercury within an oval]. *See no. 47c.*

b | Sugar Bowl with Lid
Silver, lapis lazuli, gold
Height 3¾ in. (9.5 cm), width 6⅝ in. (16.8 cm), depth 4¼ in. (10.8 cm) (23.177.2ab)

Marks: Incised on bottom: JeAn e. PUIFORCAt; stamped once: EP [within a lozenge divided by a spindle]; assay mark stamped once: [canceled head of Minerva within an octagon]; exportation mark stamped once: [head of Mercury within an oval]. *See no. 47c.*

c | Creamer
Silver, lapis lazuli, gold
Height 3⅛ in. (7.9 cm), width 5 in. (12.7 cm), depth 2¾ in. (7 cm) (23.177.3)

Marks: Incised on bottom: JeAn e. PUIFORCAt; stamped once: EP [within a lozenge divided by a spindle]; assay mark stamped once: [canceled head of Minerva within an octagon]; exportation

mark stamped once: [head of Mercury within an oval]; stamped on bottom: 3

d | Teapot
Silver, lapis lazuli, ivory
Height 4⅜ in. (11 cm), width 8¾ in. (22.2 cm), depth 5⅜ in. (13.7 cm) (25.230.1ab)

Marks: Stamped on bottom: JEAN E. PUIFORCAT; exportation mark stamped once: [head of Mercury within a hexagon]. *See no. 49.*

e | Kettle with Stand and Lamp
Silver, lapis lazuli, ivory
Height 9½ in. (24.1 cm), width 11 in. (27.9 cm), depth 7⅛ in. (18.1 cm) (25.230.2a–e)

Marks: Incised on bottom of stand: JeAn e. PUIFORCAt; stamped four times: EP [within a lozenge divided by a spindle]; assay mark stamped twice: [head of Minerva within an octagon]; exportation mark stamped three times: [head of Mercury within an oval]; canceled assay mark (?) stamped four times: [unidentified cross-hatched hexagonal mark]; stamped on underside of stand: 2609; stamped inside of kettle cover: 7677 / 1970; stamped in bottom of lamp: 2600. *See no. 47c.*

f | Waste Bowl
Silver, gold
Height 2 in. (5.1 cm), diameter 4½ in. (11.4 cm) (25.230.3)

Marks: Incised on bottom: JeAn e. PUIFORCAt; stamped on bottom: EP [within a lozenge divided by a spindle]; assay mark stamped once: [canceled head of Minerva within an octagon]; exportation mark stamped once: [head of Mercury within an oval]; stamped on bottom: 7677 / 185. *See no. 47c.*

g | Tray
Silver, lapis lazuli
Height 2⅛ in. (5.4 cm), width 28 in. (71.1 cm), depth 23¼ in. (59.1 cm) (25.230.4)

Marks: Incised on bottom: JeAn e. PUIFORCAt; stamped on underside of rim: EP [within a lozenge divided by a spindle]; assay mark stamped once: [canceled head of Minerva within an octagon]; exportation mark stamped three times: [head of Mercury within an oval]; stamped on bottom: 7678 / 5155; stamped on underside of rim: 2602. *See no. 47c.*

Provenance: Jean Puiforcat, until 1923 and 1925; purchased by The Metropolitan Museum of Art, 1923 and 1925.

References: Yvanhoé Rambosson, "Le XIIIe Salon des Artistes Décorateurs," *Art et décoration* 41 (March 1922), pp. 97–128; Gaston Varenne, "Jean Puiforcat, orfèvre," *Art et décoration* 47 (January 1925), pp. 1–11; Françoise de Bonneville, *Jean Puiforcat*, trans. Nina Bogin and Vincea McClelland (Paris: Éditions du Regard, 1986), pp. 51 (kettle), 74 (creamer), 76 (service illustrated); Gérard Mabille et al., *Exposition Puiforcat: Puiforcat orfèvre, la maîtrise de l'argent* (Tokyo: N. K. Shimbun, 2002), p. 131; Gail S. Davidson, "Perfection: Jean E. Puiforcat's Designs for Silver," *The Magazine Antiques* 163, no. 1 (January 2003), pp. 174–83.

48 | Bowl

1934
Silver, glass
Height 5½ in. (14 cm), diameter 8¾ in. (22.2 cm)
Purchase, Edward C. Moore Jr. Gift, 1934 (34.105.1)

Marks: Stamped on lower outside edge: JEAN E. PUIFORCAT / PARIS; stamped on bottom: MADE IN FRANCE; stamped on lower outside edge: EP [within a lozenge divided by a spindle]; assay mark stamped on lower outside edge: [canceled head of Minerva within an octagon]; exportation mark stamped on lower outside edge: [head of Mercury within an oval]

Provenance: Jean Puiforcat, until 1934; purchased by The Metropolitan Museum of Art, 1934.

References: John Goldsmith Phillips, "New Accessions of Contemporary French and Swedish Decorative Arts," *Bulletin of The Metropolitan Museum of Art* 30, no. 1 (January 1935), pp. 3–5; Marvin D. Schwartz and Betsy Wade, "Silver," in *The New York Times Book of Antiques* (New York: Quadrangle Books, 1972), p. 234; Bonneville, *Jean Puiforcat* (1986), p. 215.

49 | Soup Tureen

ca. 1937
Silver, gold
Height 10 in. (25.4 cm), diameter 10⅞ in. (27.6 cm)
Purchase, Edgar Kaufmann Jr. Gift, 1972 (1972.5)

Marks: Stamped on bottom: EP [within a lozenge divided by a spindle] MADE IN FRANCE / JEAN E. PUIFORCAT; exportation mark stamped three times: [head of Mercury within a hexagon]

Provenance: [Sonnabend Gallery, New York, 1972]; purchased by The Metropolitan Museum of Art, 1972.

References: René Herbst, *Jean Puiforcat: Orfèvre, sculpteur* (Paris: Flammarion, 1951), p. 38; Penelope Hunter-Stiebel, "The Decorative Arts of the Twentieth Century," *The Metropolitan Museum of Art Bulletin*, n.s., 37, no. 3 (Winter 1979–80), pp. 36–37; Bonneville, *Jean Puiforcat* (1986), p. 93; Annelies Krekel-Aalberse, J. R. ter Molen, and Joost Willink, eds., *Silver of a New Era: International Highlights of Precious Metalware from 1880 to 1940*, exh. cat. (Rotterdam: Museum Boymans-van Beuningen, 1992), p. 69; Dedo von Kerssenbrock-Krosigk, ed., *Modern Art of Metalwork: Bröhan-Museum, State Museum of Art Nouveau, Art Deco and Functionalism (1889–1939), Berlin* (Berlin: Bröhan-Museum, 2001), p. 430.

ARMAND-ALBERT RATEAU

50 | Dressing Table and Hand Mirror

a | Dressing Table

ca. 1925
Bronze, black limestone, Carrara marble, mirror glass
Height 53½ in. (135.9 cm), width 31½ in. (80 cm), depth 15¾ in. (40 cm)
Purchase, Edward C. Moore Jr. Gift, 1925 (25.169)

Marks: Stamped on reverse of mirror frame: A.A.RATEAU / INVR. *See no. 50b.*

Provenance: Armand-Albert Rateau, until 1925; purchased by The Metropolitan Museum of Art, 1925.

References: "The Bathroom of a Palace," *Vogue* 66, no. 10 (November 15, 1925), p. 83; Joseph Breck, "Modern Decorative

Arts: Some Recent Purchases," *Bulletin of The Metropolitan Museum of Art* 21, no. 2 (February 1926), pp. 37–38; Penelope Hunter, "Art Déco: The Last Hurrah," *The Metropolitan Museum of Art Bulletin*, n.s., 30, no. 6 (June–July 1972), p. 263; Marvin D. Schwartz and Betsy Wade, "Morris, Eastlake, and Later," in *The New York Times Book of Antiques* (New York: Quadrangle Books, 1972), p. 81; Alastair Duncan, *A. A. Rateau* (New York: Delorenzo Gallery, 1990), p. 24; Franck Olivier-Vial and François Rateau, *Armand-Albert Rateau: Un Baroque chez les modernes* (Paris: Les Éditions de l'Amateur, 1992), p. 69.

b | Hand Mirror

ca. 1925
Bronze, ivory, mirror glass
Height 12¾ in. (32.4 cm), width 5½ in. (14 cm), depth ¾ in. (1.9 cm)
Gift of the artist, 1925 (25.170)

Marks: Stamped on reverse of frame at top of handle: A.A. RATEAU / INVR

Provenance: Armand-Albert Rateau, until 1925; gift to The Metropolitan Museum of Art, 1925.

References: Breck, "Modern Decorative Arts" (1926), p. 38; Hunter, "Art Déco: The Last Hurrah" (1972), p. 263. Duncan, *A. A. Rateau* (1990), pp. 24, 32.

CLÉMENT ROUSSEAU

51 | Table

1924
Ebony, galuchat, ivory, brass
Height 29½ in. (74.9 cm), width 8½ in. (21.6 cm), depth 18¼ in. (46.4 cm)
Fletcher Fund, 1972 (1972.283.2)

Marks: Scratched into brace joining tabletop to leg and scratched into wood under the same brace: 1924 / Clément Rousseau / JC; medal inserted into frame. Recto: half-length bas-relief portrait of Saint Thérèse of Lisieux. Verso, around outer edge: SŒUR THERESE DE L'ENFANT JESUS / JE VEUX PASSER / MON CIEL / A FAIRE DU BIEN / SUR LA TERRE / [coat of arms of the Carmelite Order]

Provenance: Jacques Doucet, Paris, 1924–29; his widow, Jeanne Roger Doucet, Neuilly, 1929–58; his nephew Jean Dubrujeaud, Paris, 1958–68; his

son Jean Angladon-Dubrujeaud, Paris, 1968–72; [Hôtel Drouot, Paris, November 8, 1972, lot 46]; sold to The Metropolitan Museum of Art, 1972.

References: Thomas Hoving, *The Chase, the Capture: Collecting at the Metropolitan* (New York: The Metropolitan Museum of Art, 1975), pp. 226–31; Penelope Hunter in "Twentieth Century Art," in *The Metropolitan Museum of Art: Notable Acquisitions, 1965–75* (New York: The Metropolitan Museum of Art, 1975), p. 228; Penelope Hunter-Stiebel, "The Decorative Arts of the Twentieth Century," *The Metropolitan Museum of Art Bulletin*, n.s., 37, no. 3 (Winter 1979–80), pp. 30–31; Penelope Hunter-Stiebel, *The Fine Art of the Furniture Maker* (Rochester, N.Y.: Memorial Art Gallery of the University of Rochester, 1981), pp. 101–5.

É.-J. RUHLMANN

52 | Textile and Wallpaper

a | *Sarrazin* Textile

ca. 1917
Manufacturer: Unknown, for Ruhlmann et Laurent
Printed linen
Length 36 in. (91.4 cm), width 44½ in. (113 cm)
Gift of Geoffrey N. Bradfield, 1985 (1985.320.1)

Marks: Written in ink on attached paper label: IR

Provenance: [Phillips, New York, 1985]; sold to Geoffrey N. Bradfield, New York, 1985; gift to The Metropolitan Museum of Art, 1985.

References: Emmanuel Bréon, *Jacques-Émile Ruhlmann: The Designer's Archives*, vol. 2, *Interior Design* (Paris: Éditions Flammarion, 2004), pp. 50, 66, 67; Emmanuel Bréon and Rosalind Pepall, eds., *Ruhlmann: Genius of Art*

Deco, exh. cat. (Paris: Somogy, Montreal: Montreal Museum of Fine Arts, 2004), p. 295.

b | *Sarrazin* Wallpaper
ca. 1917
Manufacturer: Unknown, for Ruhlmann et Laurent
Printed paper
Height 36 in. (91.4 cm), width 22½ in. (57.2 cm)
Gift of Association des Amis de Musée des Années Trente, 2005 (2005.334)

Unmarked.

Provenance: É.-J. Ruhlmann, until 1933; his assistant Jules Deroubaix, Paris, 1933–87; [Sotheby's, Monte-Carlo, 1987]; sold to Sophie and Jérome Seydoux, Paris, 1987–2001; gift to Le Musée des Années Trente, Boulogne-Billancourt, 2001; gift to The Metropolitan Museum of Art, 2005.

References: Bréon, *Ruhlmann: The Designer's Archives,* vol. 2, *Interior Design* (2004), p. 66; Bréon and Pepall, *Ruhlmann: Genius of Art Deco* (2004), p. 295.

53 | *David-Weill* Desk
ca. 1918–19
Amboyna, ivory, galuchat, silk, metal, oak, lumber-core plywood, poplar, walnut, birch, macassar ebony
Height 37½ in. (95.3 cm), width 47½ in. (120.7 cm), depth 29½ in. (74.9 cm)
Purchase, Edgar Kaufmann Jr. Gift, 1973 (1973.154.1)

Marks: Branded on underside of writing surface: Ruhlmann. *See no. 56.*

Provenance: David David-Weill, Paris, probably until d. 1952; [Galerie Luxembourg, Paris, 1973]; purchased by The Metropolitan Museum of Art, 1973.

References: Jean Laran, "Notre Enquête sur le mobilier moderne, J.-E. Ruhlmann," *Art et décoration,* no. 37 (January 1920), pp. 10–11; Penelope Hunter in "Twentieth Century Art," in *The Metropolitan Museum of Art: Notable Acquisitions, 1965–1975* (New York: The Metropolitan Museum of Art, 1975), p. 228; Penelope Hunter-Stiebel, "The Decorative Arts of the Twentieth Century," *The Metropolitan Museum of Art Bulletin,* n.s., 37, no. 3 (Winter 1979–80), pp. 20–21; Jared D. Goss, "*David-Weill* Desk," in Bréon and Pepall, *Ruhlmann: Genius of Art Deco* (2004), pp. 166–70, 288; Florence Camard, *Jacques Émile Ruhlmann* (New York: Rizzoli, 2011), pp. 144, 145, 471, 498.

54 | *Tibattant* Desk
ca. 1923
Macassar ebony, ivory, leather, aluminum leaf, silver, silk, oak, lumber-core plywood, poplar, mahogany

Height 44¼ in. (112.4 cm), width 23¼ in. (59.1 cm), depth 14⅞ in. (37.8 cm)
Purchase, Edward C. Moore Jr. Gift, 1923 (23.174)

Marks: Branded twice on underside: Ruhlmann; stamped on underside behind proper left front leg: A [within a circle]. *See no. 56.*

Provenance: Ruhlmann et Laurent, Paris, 1923; purchased by The Metropolitan Museum of Art, 1923.

References: Joseph Breck, "Modern Decorative Arts," *Bulletin of The Metropolitan Museum of Art* 18, no. 11 (November 1923), pp. 244, 245; Joseph Aronson, *The Encyclopedia of Furniture*, 3rd ed. (New York: Crown Publishers, 1965), p. 169, fig. 500; Penelope Hunter, "Art Deco and The Metropolitan Museum of Art," *The Connoisseur* 179 (April 1972), p. 273; Hunter-Stiebel, "Decorative Arts of the Twentieth Century" (1979–80), p. 24; Jared D. Goss, "Lady's Desk," in Bréon and Pepall, *Ruhlmann: Genius of Art Deco* (2004), pp. 180–83, 290.

55 | *État* Cabinet
Designed 1922; manufactured 1925–26
Macassar ebony, amaranth, ivory, oak, lumber-core plywood, poplar, chestnut, mahogany, silvered brass
Height 50¼ in. (127.6 cm), width 33¼ in. (84.5 cm), depth 14 in. (35.6 cm)
Purchase, Edward C. Moore Jr. Gift, 1925 (25.231.1)

Marks: Branded on back at top of frame: Ruhlmann / O. *See no. 56.*

Provenance: Ruhlmann et Laurent, Paris, 1925; commissioned by The Metropolitan Museum of Art, 1925.

References: Joseph Breck, "Modern Decorative Arts: Some Recent Purchases," *Bulletin of The Metropolitan Museum of Art* 21, no. 2 (February 1926), p. 38; Joseph Breck, "Accessions and Notes: Furniture by Ruhlmann," *Bulletin of The Metropolitan Museum of Art* 21, no. 3, pt. 1 (March 1926), p. 88; Hunter, "Art Deco and The Metropolitan Museum of Art" (1972), p. 273; Penelope Hunter, "Art Déco: The Last Hurrah," *The Metropolitan Museum of Art Bulletin,* n.s., 30, no. 6 (June–July 1972), p. 267; Hunter-Stiebel, "Decorative Arts of the Twentieth Century," (1979–80), p. 25; Penelope Hunter-Stiebel, *The Fine Art of the Furniture Maker* (Rochester, N.Y.: Memorial Art Gallery of the University of Rochester, 1981), pp. 92–98; Ghenete Zelleke, "Two Cabinets by Ruhlmann," in Bréon and Pepall, *Ruhlmann: Genius of Art Deco* (2004), pp. 152–57, 291.

56 | Pair of *Duval* Cabinets
Designed 1924
Brazilian rosewood, ivory, amboyna burl, mahogany, oak, plywood

Each: Height 56 in. (142.2 cm), width 40 in. (101.6 cm), depth 19 in. (48.3 cm)
Gift of Meryl and Robert Meltzer, 2012 (2012.576.1, .2)

Marks: Branded on back of each cabinet: Ruhlmann / A [within a circle]

Provenance: [Christie's or Sotheby's, Monaco, late 1980s]; [French dealer, late 1980s–ca. 1990]; [De Lorenzo Gallery, New York, ca. 1990–93]; sold to Mr. and Mrs. Robert Meltzer, New York, 1993–2012; gift to The Metropolitan Museum of Art, 2012.

References: Gabriel Henriot, "Le Salon d'Automne—Les Arts décoratifs," *Mobilier et décoration* 6, no. 2 (1926), pp. 121–22 (model illustrated); Bernard Champigneulle, "L'Exposition rétrospective de J.-E. Ruhlmann," *Mobilier et décoration* 14 (December 1934), p. 449; *Exposition rétrospective E.-J. Ruhlmann,* exh. cat. (Paris: Musée des Arts Décoratifs, 1934), n.p.; Bréon and Pepall, *Ruhlmann: Genius of Art Deco* (2004), p. 50; Camard, *Jacques Émile Ruhlmann* (2011), pp. 180, 216–18.

57 | Carpet
É.-J. Ruhlmann and Émile Gaudissard
ca. 1925
Manufacturer: Probably Braquenié et Cie
Wool, cotton
Diameter 8 ft. ½ in. (2.45 m)
Purchase, Bequest of Thelma Williams Gill, by exchange, 2002 (2002.365)

Unmarked.

Provenance: [Sotheby's, London, 1998]; [L'Arc en Seine, Paris, ca. 1998–ca. 2002]; [Sotheby's, New York, 2002]; purchased by The Metropolitan Museum of Art, 2002.

References: Maurice Dufrène, *Ensembles mobiliers: Exposition Internationale 1925,* ser. 2 (Paris: Charles Moreau, 1926), pl. 5; Florence Camard, *Ruhlmann: Master of Art Deco* (New York: Harry N. Abrams, 1984), pp. 232–33 ; *Les Ruhlmann de Geneviève et Pierre Hebey,* sale cat. (Paris: Hôtel Drouot, October 28, 1999), pp. 264, 269, 316; Bréon and Pepall, *Ruhlmann: Genius of Art Deco* (2004), pp. 254, 255, 294; Camard, *Jacques Émile Ruhlmann* (2011), p. 122.

58 | Lamp
ca. 1926
Gilt bronze, alabaster
Height 29½ in. (74.9 cm), diameter 13¾ in. (34.9 cm)
Gift of Mr. and Mrs. Michael Chow, 1985 (1985.430.21ab)

Unmarked.

Provenance: [Sotheby's, Monaco, 1983]; Mr. and Mrs. Michael Chow, New York, until 1985; gift to The Metropolitan Museum of Art, 1985.

References: *Exposition rétrospective E.-J. Ruhlmann* (1934), n.p.; Marcel Zahar, "Œuvres dernières de Ruhlmann," *Art et décoration* 63 (January 1934), p. 10; Camard, *Ruhlmann: Master of Art Deco* (1984), pp. 145, 296; Bréon and Pepall, *Ruhlmann: Genius of Art Deco* (2004), p. 292; Camard, *Jacques Émile Ruhlmann* (2011), p. 391.

JEAN SERRIÈRE

59 | Chalice
ca. 1923
Silver
Height 6¼ in. (15.9 cm), diameter 6⅛ in. (15.6 cm)
Purchase, Edward C. Moore Jr. Gift, 1923 (23.159.2)

Marks: Scratched into underside of foot: Jean Serrière; stamped on upper edge of foot: S (?) [within a lozenge]; exportation mark stamped on upper edge of foot and on outer edge of bowl: [head of Mercury within an oval]

Provenance: [Galerie Hébrard, Paris, 1923]; purchased by The Metropolitan Museum of Art, 1923.

References: Armand Dayot, "Jean Serrière," *L'Art et les artistes,* n.s., 1, no. 1 (January 1920), p. 130; Guillaume Janneau, "Le Mouvement moderne," *La Renaissance de l'art français et des industries de luxe* 5, no. 1 (January 1922), p. 92.

HENRI SIMMEN AND EUGÉNIE JUBIN, KNOWN AS O'KIN

60 | Lidded Jar
Henri Simmen
1921–23
Salt-glazed stoneware
Height 3⅛ in. (7.9 cm), diameter 2 in. (5.1 cm)
Purchase, Edward C. Moore Jr. Gift, 1923 (23.176.3ab)

Marks: Painted on underside: H Sim

Provenance: [Galerie Rouard, Paris, 1923]; purchased by The Metropolitan Museum of Art, 1923.

Previously unpublished.

61 | Lidded Jar
ca. 1929
Aventurine-glazed stoneware, wood, ivory, gold leaf
Height 6¼ in. (15.9 cm), diameter 6¾ in. (17.1 cm)
Purchase, Edward C. Moore Jr. Gift, 1929 (29.127.5ab)

Marks: Incised on underside: H Sim / 冋

Provenance: [Galerie Rouard, Paris, 1929]; purchased by The Metropolitan Museum of Art.

References: Joseph Breck, "Accessions and Notes: Modern Decorative Arts," *Bulletin of The Metropolitan Museum of Art* 24, no. 10 (October 1929), p. 269; Penelope Hunter-Stiebel, "The Decorative Arts of the Twentieth Century," *The Metropolitan Museum of Art Bulletin*, n.s., 37, no. 3 (Winter 1979–80), p. 19; Tom Dewey II, *Art Nouveau, Art Déco, and Modernism: A Guide to the Styles, 1890–1940* (Jackson: Mississippi Museum of Art, 1983), p. 52, fig. 85.

LOUIS SÜE AND ANDRÉ MARE

62 | Side Chair
Louis Süe
Designed ca. 1912; manufactured ca. 1920
Manufacturer: La Compagnie des Arts Français
Walnut, silk velvet
Height 35¾ in. (90.8 cm), width 17¼ in. (43.8 cm), depth 19½ in. (49.5 cm)
Purchase, Edward C. Moore Jr. Gift, 1923 (23.175.2)

Marks: Branded under proper left seat rail: [logo of La Compagnie des Arts Français] LOUIS — SUE

Provenance: La Compagnie des Arts Français, Paris, 1923; purchased by The Metropolitan Museum of Art, 1923.

References: Fernand Roches, "L'Horticulture, art décoratif," *L'Art décoratif* 28 (1912), p. 313; André Vera, "Le Nouveau Style," *L'Art décoratif* 27 (January–June 1912), p. 29; Émile Bayard, *L'Art appliqué français d'aujourdhui: Meuble, ferronnerie, céramique, verrerie, tissus, etc.* (Paris: Ernest Gründ, 1925), p. 20; Florence Camard, *Süe et Mare et La Compagnie des Arts Français* (Paris: Les Éditions de l'Amateur, 1993), pp. 270, 271.

63 | Four Textiles

a | Abondance
André Mare
Designed ca. 1911; manufactured after 1918
Manufacturer: Lamy & Gautier or Établissements Lauer for La Compagnie des Arts Français
Silk
Length 100½ in. (257.8 cm), width 49¾ in. (126.4 cm)
Purchase, Edward C. Moore Jr. Gift, 1923 (23.175.9)

Marks: Woven into selvage: Nº 2 'SELECTION' Andre Mare [now concealed by hem]

Provenance: La Compagnie des Arts Français, Paris, 1923; purchased by The Metropolitan Museum of Art, 1923.

References: Léon Moussinac, *Étoffes d'ameublement tissées et brochées* (Paris: Éditions Albert Lévy, 1925), pl. 28; G. Rémon, "Nos Artistes-décorateurs: Süe et Mare," *Mobilier et décoration* 6 (January 1926), p. 16; Camard, *Süe et Mare et La Compagnie des Arts Français* (1993), pp. 135, 233; Nicole Zapata-Aubé et al., *André Mare: Cubisme et camouflage, 1914–1918*, exh. cat. (Bernay: Musée Municipale des Beaux-Arts, 1998), p. 70; *L'Art de la soie Prelle, 1752–2002: Des Ateliers lyonnais aux palais parisiens* (Paris: Musée Carnavalet (2002), pp. 198–99.

b | Draperies
André Mare
ca. 1919
Unknown manufacturer for La Compagnie des Arts Français
Cotton
Length 45 in. (114.3 cm), width 51½ in. (130.8 cm)
Purchase, Edward C. Moore Jr. Gift, 1923 (23.175.12)

Unmarked.

Provenance: La Compagnie des Arts Français, Paris, 1923; purchased by The Metropolitan Museum of Art, 1923.

References: Léandre Vaillat and Louis Süe, *Le Rythme de l'architecture* (Paris: François Bernouard, 1923), p. 63; Henri Verne and René Chavance, *Pour comprendre l'art decoratif moderne en France* (Paris: Hachette, 1925), p. 157; Camard, *Süe et Mare et La Compagnie des Arts Français* (1993), p. 234.

c | Bouquets
Louis Süe
ca. 1919
Manufacturer: Lamy & Gautier or Établissements Lauer for Belle France (later La Compagnie des Arts Français)
Silk
Length 21 in. (53.5 cm), width 26 in. (66 cm)
Purchase, Edward C. Moore Jr. Gift, 1923 (23.175.7)

Marks: Woven into both selvages: — LOUIS SUE — BELLE-FRANCE — 1004 —

63a

64a

Provenance: La Compagnie des Arts Français, Paris, 1923; purchased by The Metropolitan Museum of Art, 1923.

References: Louis Süe and André Mare, *Architectures* (Paris: Éditions de la Nouvelle Revue Française, 1921), pp. 131, 143; Moussinac, *Étoffes d'ameublement tissées et brochées* (1925), pl. 28; Camard, *Süe et Mare et La Compagnie des Arts Français* (1993), p. 234; *L'Art de la soie Prelle* (2002), p. 200.

d | Paris
Louis Süe
ca. 1919
Manufacturer: Établissements Lauer for La Compagnie des Arts Français
Silk
Length 91¼ in. (231.8 cm), width 51½ in. (130.8 cm)
Purchase, Edward C. Moore Jr. Gift, 1923 (23.175.8)

Unmarked.

Provenance: La Compagnie des Arts Français, Paris, 1923; purchased by The Metropolitan Museum of Art, 1923.

References: Moussinac, *Étoffes d'ameublement tissées et brochées* (1925), pl. 30; Camard, *Süe et Mare et la Compagnie des Arts Français* (1993), pp. 171, 232.

64 | Commode and Mirror

a | Commode
Louis Süe, André Mare, and Paul Vera
ca. 1918
Manufacturer: La Compagnie des Arts Français
Oak, lumber-core plywood, chestnut, *Verde di Levanto* marble, paint, gold leaf
Height 35 in. (88.9 cm), width 49½ in. (125.7 cm), depth 22½ in. (57.2 cm)
Purchase, Edward C. Moore Jr. Gift, 1923 (23.175.1)

Marks: Stamped and branded on top surface beneath marble: — LOUIS — SUE [logo of La Compagnie des Arts Français] PAUL - VERA –

Provenance: La Compagnie des Arts Français, Paris, 1923; purchased by The Metropolitan Museum of Art, 1923.

References: "Le Carnet d'un curieux," *La Renaissance de l'art français et des industries de luxe* 1 (May 1918), p. 30 (variant model illustrated); Roger Allard, "Réflexions sur quelques meubles modernes," *Feuillets d'art*, no. 1 (1919),

p. 46 (variant model illustrated); Léon Deshairs, "Notre Enquête sur le mobilier modern: La Compagnie des Arts Français," *Art et décoration* 37 (January–June 1920), p. 71 (variant model illustrated); Émile Sedeyn, *Le Mobilier* (Paris: F. Rieder et Cie, 1921), pl. XVI (variant model illustrated); Joseph Breck, "Modern Decorative Arts," *Bulletin of The Metropolitan Museum of Art* 18, no. 11 (November 1923), cover and p. 245; *Encyclopédie des arts décoratifs et industriels modernes au XXème siècle* (ca. 1927; repr., New York: Garland, 1977), vol. 1, pl. XL (variant model illustrated); Camard, *Süe et Mare et la Compagnie des Arts Français* (1993), p. 78 (variant model illustrated).

b | Mirror
Louis Süe and André Mare
Designed ca. 1919; manufactured 1923
Manufacturer: La Compagnie des Arts Français
Cherry or pearwood, mirror glass, paint, gold leaf
Height 46¼ in. (117.5 cm), width 29¾ in. (75.6 cm), depth 2¼ in. (5.7 cm)
Purchase, Edward C. Moore Jr. Gift, 1923 (23.175.14)

Unmarked.

Provenance: La Compagnie des Arts Français, 1923; purchased by The Metropolitan Museum of Art, 1923.

References: Allard, "Réflexions sur quelques meubles modernes" (1919), p. 46 (variant model illustrated); Deshairs, "Notre Enquête sur le mobilier modern" (1920), p. 71 (variant model illustrated); Sedeyn, *Le Mobilier* (1921), pl. XVI (variant model illustrated); Breck, "Modern Decorative Arts" (1923), cover and p. 245; *Encyclopédie des arts décoratifs et industriels modernes* (ca. 1927), vol. 1, pl. XL (variant model illustrated); Camard, *Süe et Mare et la Compagnie des Arts Français* (1993), p. 78 (variant model illustrated).

65 | Desk and Chair

a | Desk
ca. 1925
Manufacturer: La Compagnie des Arts Français
Ebonized wood (probably beech), oak, zebrawood, gilt bronze, leather
Height 30¼ in. (76.8 cm), width 64½ in. (163.8 cm), depth 33¾ in. (85.7 cm)
Purchase, Edward C. Moore Jr. Gift, 1925 (25.209.1)

Unmarked.

Provenance: La Compagnie des Arts Français, 1925; purchased by The Metropolitan Museum of Art, 1925.

References: Gaston Varenne, "L'Exposition des Arts Décoratifs: Le Mobilier français," *Art et décoration* 48 (July 1925), p. 20; Joseph Breck, "Modern Decorative Arts: Some Recent Purchases," *The Metropolitan Museum of Art Bulletin* 21, no. 2 (February 1926), pp. 36–38; Maurice Dufrène, *Ensembles mobiliers: Exposition Internationale 1925*, ser. 2 (Paris: Charles Moreau, 1926), pl. 28; Rémon, "Nos Artistes-décorateurs: Süe et Mare" (1926), pp. 11, 13; Penelope Hunter-Stiebel, *The Fine Art of the Furniture Maker* (Rochester, N.Y.: Memorial Art Gallery of the University of Rochester, 1981), pp. 85–91; Camard, *Süe et Mare et la Compagnie des Arts Français* (1993), pp. 131, 132, 270, 291.

b | Desk Chair
ca. 1925
Manufacturer: La Compagnie des Arts Français
Ebonized wood (possibly walnut or beech), pigskin
Height 34¼ in. (87 cm), width 23¾ in. (60.3 cm), depth 22¾ in. (57.8 cm)
Purchase, Edward C. Moore Jr. Gift, 1925 (25.209.2)

Unmarked.

Provenance: La Compagnie des Arts Français, 1925; purchased by The Metropolitan Museum of Art, 1925.

References: René Chavance, "L'Art décoratif contemporain au Pavillon de Marsan," *Art et décoration* 45 (January–June 1924), p. 116 (variant model illustrated); Breck, "Modern Decorative Arts" (1926), pp. 36–38; Dufrène, *Ensembles mobiliers: Exposition Internationale 1925*, ser. 2 (1926), pl. 28; Rémon, "Nos Artistes-décorateurs: Süe et Mare" (1926), p. 11; Hunter-Stiebel, *Fine Art of the Furniture Maker* (1981), pp. 85–91; Camard, *Süe et Mare et la Compagnie des Arts Français* (1993), pp. 131, 270, 275.

66 | Carpet
1925
Manufacturer: Établissements Lauer for La Compagnie des Arts Français
Wool
Length: 110 in. (279 cm), width 101 in. (256.5 cm)
Purchase, Edward C. Moore Jr. Gift, 1925 (25.232)

Unmarked.

Provenance: La Compagnie des Arts Français, 1925; commissioned by The Metropolitan Museum of Art, 1925.

References: Camard, *Süe et Mare et la Compagnie des Arts Français* (1993), pp. 226, 228.

67 | *David-Weill* Chair
Designed 1923; manufactured probably late 1920s
Manufacturer: La Compagnie des Arts Français

Palisander, oak, wool
Height 33½ in. (85.1 cm), width 18½ in. (47 cm), depth 17¼ in. (43.8 cm)
Gift of Marilyn F. Friedman, 2013 (2013.45.2)

Unmarked.

Provenance: [Doyle, New York, 2012]; sold to Marilyn F. Friedman, New York, 2012; gift to The Metropolitan Museum of Art, 2013.

References: Jean Badovici, *Intérieurs de Süe et Mare* (Paris: Éditions Albert Morancé, 1924), pl. 11; Fernand David, *L'Art décoratif français, 1918–1925* (Paris: Éditions Albert Lévy, 1925), p. 77; Pierre Olmer, *Le Mobilier français d'aujourd'hui (1910–1925)* (Paris: G. van Oest, 1926), pl. XIII; Alain Lesieutre, *The Spirit and Splendour of Art Deco* (New York and London: Paddington Press, 1974), p. 144; Yvonne Brunhammer, *The Art Deco Style* (London: Academy Editions, 1983), p. 45; Camard, *Süe et Mare et la Compagnie des Arts Français* (1993), pp. 118, 121, 135, 184, 213, 215, 270, 273.

RAYMOND TEMPLIER

68 | Mirror
1921
Silver, gold, carnelian, enamel, pewter
Height with stand 4½ in. (11.4 cm), width 3⅞ in. (9.8 cm), depth 1¼ in. (3.2 cm)
Purchase, Edward C. Moore Jr. Gift, 1923 (23.172ab)

Marks: Inscribed on top of frame: RAYMOND TEMPLIER 1921; stamped within first "E" of inscription above: RT

Provenance: Raymond Templier, Paris, until 1923; purchased by The Metropolitan Museum of Art, 1923.

References: Penelope Hunter-Stiebel, "The Decorative Arts of the Twentieth Century," *The Metropolitan Museum of Art Bulletin*, n.s., 37, no. 3 (Winter 1979–80), p. 17.

VAN CLEEF & ARPELS

69 | Vanity Case
Attributed to Alfred Langlois for Van Cleef & Arpels, Paris
ca. 1928
Gold, enamel, jade, diamonds

Height 3⅜ in. (8.6 cm), width 2⅛ in. (5.4 cm), depth ½ in. (1.3 cm)
Gift of Walter L. Richard, 1957 (57.160a–c)

Marks: Stamped at edge of mirror: VAN CLEEF & ARPELS _ 30589; gold standard mark, stamped four times on inside of box: [falcon's head above the numeral 3, within a hexagon]; engraved on cover of powder compartment: February 8ᵀᴴ 1938; leather case stamped in gold, beneath motif of the Place Vendôme: VAN CLEEF & ARPELS

Provenance: Walter L. Richard, New York, and Bel Air, California, purchased probably 1938 from Van Cleef & Arpels, Paris; gift to The Metropolitan Museum of Art, 1957.

Previously unpublished.

PAUL VERA

70 | *Les Jardins* Folding Screen
Paul Vera and Paul Follot
1923–24
Manufacturer: Manufacture Nationale de Beauvais
Wool, silk, mahogany
Each panel: Height 79 in. (200.7 cm), width 30⅝ in. (77.8 cm), depth 1½ in. (3.8 cm)
Purchase, Edward C. Moore Jr. Gift, 1932 (32.99a–d)

Unmarked.

Provenance: Manufacture Nationale de Beauvais, Paris, 1932; purchased by The Metropolitan Museum of Art, 1932.

References: Jean Ajalbert, "Autour des cartons de Beauvais," *La Renaissance de l'art français et des industries de luxe* 7, no. 11 (November 1924), p. 586; François Fosca, "Paul Vera," *L'Art et les artistes*, n.s., 10, nos. 50–54 (October 1924–February 1925), pp. 215–33; *Encyclopédie des arts décoratifs et industriels modernes au XXème siècle* (ca. 1927; repr., New York: Garland, 1977), vol. 6, pl. XVIII; Joseph Breck, "A Modern Beauvais Tapestry Screen," *Bulletin of The Metropolitan Museum of Art* 27, no. 11 (November 1932), p. 239; Edith A. Standen, *European Post-Medieval Tapestries and Related Hangings in The Metropolitan Museum of Art* (New York: The Metropolitan Museum of Art, 1985), vol. 2, pp. 611–13.

SELECTED BIBLIOGRAPHY

SELECTED EXHIBITIONS

San Francisco 1915. Panama-Pacific International Exposition. Multiple venues in San Francisco, February 20–December 4, 1915. *Official Handbook.* San Francisco: Wahlgreen, 1915.

San Francisco 1923. "Exhibition of Contemporary French Art." Polk Hall, Civic Auditorium, San Francisco, January 4–31, 1923. Catalogue. San Francisco: John Henry Nash, 1923.

Monza 1923. Mostra Internazionale delle Arti Decorative. Villa Reale di Monza, Italy, May–October 1923. Catalogue, *Le arti a Monza nel 1923*, by Roberto Papini. Bergamo: Istituto Italiano d'Arti Grafiche, 1923.

San Francisco 1924–25. "Inaugural Exposition of French Art." The California Palace of the Legion of Honor, San Francisco, 1924–25. Catalogue. San Francisco: James H. Barry, 1924.

Paris 1925. Exposition Internationale des Arts Décoratifs et Industriels Modernes. Multiple venues in Paris, April–October 1925. *Catalogue générale officiel.* Paris: Imprimerie de Vaugirard, 1925. For documentation, see the twelve-volume *Encyclopédie des arts décoratifs et industriels modernes au XXème siècle* below.

Monza 1925. II Mostra Internazionale delle Arti Decorative. Villa Reale di Monza, Italy, May–October 1925. Catalogue, *Opere scelte.* Bergamo: Istituto Italiano d'Arti Grafiche, 1925.

New York and other cities 1926. "A Selected Collection of Objects from the International Exposition of Modern Decorative and Industrial Art at Paris 1925." The Metropolitan Museum of Art, New York, February 1926; traveled to eight other venues. Catalogue. Washington, D.C.: The American Association of Museums, 1926.

Tokyo 1928. Mokuzai Kōgei Gakkai [Japanese Woodwork Association]. "Furansu sōshoku bijutsuka kyōkai tenrankai kagu sōshoku sakuhinshu" [Exhibition of French Decorative Art]. Tokyo Bijutsukan, March 24–May 8, 1928. Catalogue. Tokyo: Mokuzai Kōgei Gakkai, 1928.

American Federation of Arts 1930–31. Third International Exhibition of Contemporary Industrial Art. Museum of Fine Arts, Boston, October 15, 1930–November 10, 1930; The Metropolitan Museum of Art, New York, December 1–28, 1930; Art Institute of Chicago, January 19–February 15, 1931; Cleveland Museum of Art, March 11–April 5, 1931. *Catalogue: Decorative Metalwork and Cotton Textiles.* Introduction by Charles R. Richards. [Portland, Maine]: Douthworth Press, 1930.

Paris 1931. Exposition Coloniale Internationale. Multiple venues in Paris, May–November 1931. Catalogue, *Le Livre d'or.* Paris: H. Champion, 1931.

Paris 1937. "Le Décor de la vie de 1900 à 1925." Musée des Arts Décoratifs, Pavillon de Marsan, Palais du Louvre, Paris, 1937. Catalogue. Paris, 1937.

Paris 1937. Exposition Internationale des Arts et Techniques dans la Vie Moderne. Multiple venues in Paris, May 25–November 25, 1937. See Lemoine and Rivoirard 1987 below.

San Francisco 1939. Golden Gate International Exposition. Treasure Island, San Francisco, February 18–October 29, 1939. Catalogue of the Department of Fine Arts, Division of Decorative Arts, *Decorative Arts: Official Catalog.* San Francisco: San Francisco Bay Exposition Co., 1939.

New York 1939–40. New York World's Fair. Flushing Meadows, Corona Park, Queens, New York, April–October 1939; April–October 1940. *Official Guide Book.* New York: Exposition Publications, 1939.

SELECTED BIBLIOGRAPHY

Alvarez, José. *Histoires de l'art déco.* Paris: Éditions du Regard, 2010.

Archieri, Jean-François, ed. *Jacques Le Chevallier, 1896–1987: La Lumière moderne.* Exh. cat., La Piscine, Musée d'Art et d'Industrie André Diligent, Roubaix; Musée Départemental de l'Oise, Beauvais; and 15, square de Vergennes, Paris, 2007–8. Montreuil: Éditions Gourcuff Gradenigo, 2007.

Arwas, Victor. *Glass: Art Nouveau to Art Deco.* New York: Harry N. Abrams, 1987.

Ayroles, Véronique. *François Décorchemont: Maître de la pâte de verre, 1880–1971.* Paris: Éditions Norma, 2006.

Bachollet, Raymond, Daniel Bordet, and Anne-Claude Lelieur. *Paul Iribe.* Paris: Éditions Denoël, 1982.

Badovici, Jean. *Harmonies: Intérieurs de Ruhlmann.* Paris: Éditions Albert Morancé, 1924. Reprinted in Schleuning and Aynsley 2008.

———. *Intérieurs de Süe et Mare.* Paris: Éditions Albert Morancé, 1924.

Benoist, Luc. *Les Tissus, la tapisserie, les tapis.* L'Art français depuis vingt ans. Paris: F. Rieder et Cie, 1926.

Benton, Charlotte, Tim Benton, and Ghislaine Wood, eds. *Art Deco, 1910–1939.* London: V&A Publications, 2003.

Besnard, Charles Henri. *L'Art décoratif moderne et les industries d'art contemporaines.* Paris: H. Laurens, 1925.

Bizet, René. *La Mode.* L'Art français depuis vingt ans. Paris: F. Rieder et Cie, 1925.

Bloch-Dermant, Janine. *G. Argy-Rousseau: Glassware as Art; with a Catalogue Raisonné of the Pâtes de Verre.* New York: Thames and Hudson, 1991.

Bonneville, Françoise de. *Jean Puiforcat.* Translated by Nina Dogin and Vincea McClelland. Paris: Éditions du Regard, 1986.

Bonney, Thérèse, and Louise Bonney. *Buying Antique and Modern Furniture in Paris.* New York: Robert M. McBride & Company, 1929.

———. *A Shopping Guide to Paris.* New York: Robert M. McBride & Company, 1929.

Breck, Joseph. "Modern Decorative Arts." *Bulletin of The Metropolitan Museum of Art* 18, no. 2 (February 1923), pp. 33–35; 18, no. 11 (November 1923), pp. 241, 244–46.

Bréon, Emmanuel. *Jacques-Émile Ruhlmann: The Designer's Archives.* 2 vols. Paris: Éditions Flammarion, 2004.

Bréon, Emmanuel, and Rosalind Pepall, eds. *Ruhlmann: Genius of Art Deco.* Exh. cat., Musée des Années Trente, Boulogne-Billancourt; The Metropolitan Museum of Art, New York; and Montreal Museum of Fine Arts, 2001–4. Paris: Somogy Éditions d'Art Montreal: Montreal Museum of Fine Arts, 2004.

Brunhammer, Yvonne. *The Art Deco Style.* Translated by David Beeson. London: Academy Editions, 1983.

Brunhammer, Yvonne, and Suzanne Tise. *The Decorative Arts in France: La Société des Artistes Décorateurs, 1900–1942.* New York: Rizzoli, 1990.

Busch, Jason T., and Catherine L. Futter. *Inventing the Modern World: Decorative Arts at the World's Fairs, 1851–1939.* Exh. cat. Pittsburgh: Carnegie Museum of Art; Kansas City: Nelson-Atkins Museum of Art; New York: Skira Rizzoli, 2012.

Camard, Florence. *Ruhlmann: Master of Art Deco.* Translated by David Macey. New York: Harry N. Abrams, 1984.

———. *Süe et Mare et La Compagnie des Arts Français.* Paris: Les Éditions de l'Amateur, 1993.

———. *Jacques-Émile Ruhlmann.* Translated from the 2009 French ed. by Elisabeth Heard. New York: Rizzoli, 2011.

Caunes, Lison de, and Jean Perfettini. *Galuchat.* Paris: Les Éditions de l'Amateur, 1994.

Cazaux-Charon, Mireille. *Édouard Cazaux: Céramiste-sculpteur art déco.* Saint-Rémy-en-l'Eau: Éditions Monelle Hayot, 1994.

Céramiques de Robert Lallemant. Exh. cat., Musée des Arts Décoratifs, Bordeaux; Musée Joseph-Déchelette, Roanne; and Musée des Beaux-Arts, Orléans, 1992–93. Bordeaux: Musée des Arts Décoratifs, 1992.

Chavance, René. *Une Ambassade française; organisée par la Société des Artistes Décorateurs.* Paris: Éditions d'Art Charles Moreau, 1925.

——. *La Céramique et la verrerie*. L'Art français depuis vingt ans. Paris: Les Éditions Rieder, 1928.

Chevillot, Catherine, Liliane Colas, and Anne Pingeot. *François Pompon, 1855–1933*. Exh. cat., Musée des Beaux-Arts de Dijon and three other venues, 1994–95. Paris: Gallimard/Electa; Réunion des Musées Nationaux, 1994.

Clouzot, Henri. *Le Travail du métal*. L'Art français depuis vingt ans. Paris: F. Rieder et Cie, 1921.

Coffin, Sarah D. *Set in Style: The Jewelry of Van Cleef & Arpels*. New York: Cooper-Hewitt, National Design Museum, Smithsonian Institution, 2011.

Day, Susan. *Louis Süe: Architectures*. Brussels: Mardaga, 1986.

Deshairs, Léon. *L'Art décoratif français, 1918–1925: Recueil de documents parus dans la revue Art et décoration*. Paris: Éditions Albert Lévy, 1925.

——. *Intérieurs en couleur: Exposition des Arts Décoratifs, Paris, 1925*. Paris: Éditions Albert Lévy, 1925.

Deslandes, Yvonne. *Paul Poiret, 1879–1944*. Translated by Paula Clifford. New York: Rizzoli, 1987.

Encyclopédie des arts décoratifs et industriels modernes au XXème siècle. 12 vols. Paris: Imprimerie Nationale, Office Central d'Éditions et de Librairie, [ca. 1927]. Reprinted New York: Garland, 1977.

Forest, Dominique, and Marie-Cécile Forest. *La Dinanderie française, 1900–1950*. Paris: Les Éditions de l'Amateur, 1995.

Fouquet, Jean. *Bijoux et orfèvrerie*. Paris: Éditions d'Art Charles Moreau, 1931.

Frankl, Paul T. *Form and Re-form: A Practical Handbook of Modern Interiors*. New York: Harper and Brothers, 1930.

Friedman, Marilyn F. *Selling Good Design: Promoting the Early Modern Interior*. New York: Rizzoli, 2003.

Froment, Roger. *Claudius Linossier, dinandier (1893–1953)*. Exh. cat. Lyons: Musée des Beaux-Arts, 1979.

Giraud, Michel, and Fabienne Fravalo. *Émile Decœur, 1876–1953*. English translations by Michael Taylor. Paris: Galerie Michel Giraud Éditions, 2008.

Guéné, Hélène. *Décoration et haute couture: Armand Albert Rateau pour Jeanne Lanvin, un autre art déco*. Paris: Les Arts Décoratifs, 2006.

Hatch, Carolyn. *Déco Lalique: Creator to Consumer*. Exh. cat. Toronto: Royal Ontario Museum, 2006.

Herbst, René. *Jean Puiforcat: Orfèvre, sculpteur*. Paris: Flammarion, 1951.

Hillier, Bevis. *Art Deco of the 20s and 30s*. London: Studio Vista, 1968.

——. *The World of Art Deco*. Exh. cat., Minneapolis Institute of Arts. New York: Dutton, 1971. Reprinted 1981.

Hunter, Penelope. "Art Déco: The Last Hurrah." *The Metropolitan Museum of Art Bulletin*, n.s., 30, no. 6 (June–July 1972), pp. 257–67.

Hunter-Stiebel, Penelope. "The Decorative Arts of the Twentieth Century." *The Metropolitan Museum of Art Bulletin*, n.s., 37, no. 3 (Winter 1979–80), pp. 2–52.

——. *The Fine Art of the Furniture Maker: Conversations with Wendell Castle, Artist . . . about Selected Works from The Metropolitan Museum of Art*. Rochester, N.Y.: Memorial Art Gallery of the University of Rochester, 1981.

Iribe, Paul. *Choix*. Montrouge: Éditions Iribe, 1930.

Janneau, Guillame. *Technique du décor intérieur moderne*. Paris: Éditions Albert Morancé, [1928].

Joël et Jan Martel: Sculpteurs, 1896–1966. Exh. cat., Hôtel du Département de Vendée, La Roche-sur-Yon, and three other venues, 1996–97. Paris: Gallimard/Electa, 1996.

Jutheau, Viviane. *Jules et André Leleu*. Paris: Éditions Vecteurs, 1989.

Kahle, Katharine Morrison. *Modern French Decoration*. New York: G. P. Putnam's Sons, 1930.

Kahr, Joan. *Edgar Brandt: Master of Art Deco Ironwork*. New York: Harry N. Abrams, 1999.

Kerssenbrock-Krosigk, Dedo von, ed. *Modern Art of Metalwork: Bröhan-Museum, State Museum of Art Nouveau, Art Deco and Functionalism (1889–1939), Berlin*. Berlin: Bröhan-Museum, 2001.

Koda, Harold, and Andrew Bolton, with contributions by Mary E. Davis, Caroline Evans, Jared Goss, Heather Hess, Caroline Rennolds Milbank, Kenneth E. Silver, and Nancy J. Troy. *Poiret*. Exh. cat. New York: The Metropolitan Museum of Art, 2007.

Lajoix, Anne. *La Céramique en France, 1925–1947*. Paris: Éditions sous le Vent, 1983.

Le Bihan, Olivier, et al. *Maurice Marinot, Troyes 1882–Troyes 1960: Penser en verre*. Exh. cat. Paris: Somogy Éditions d'Art; Troyes: Musée d'Art Moderne, 2010.

Leclère, Léon. *La Peinture*. L'Art français depuis vingt ans. Paris: F. Rieder et Cie, 1921.

Lemoine, Bertrand, and Philippe Rivoirard. *Paris 1937: Cinquantenaire de l'Exposition Internationale des Arts et des Techniques dans la Vie Moderne*. Exh. cat., Musée d'Art Moderne de la Ville de Paris. Paris: Institut Français d'Architecture, 1987.

Magne, H.-M. *L'Architecture*. L'Art français depuis vingt ans. Paris: F. Rieder et Cie, 1922.

Marcilhac, Félix. *Jean Dunand: His Life and Works*. New York: Harry N. Abrams, 1991.

——. *Paul Jouve: Peintre, sculpteur, animalier, 1878–1973*. Paris: Les Éditions de l'Amateur, 2005.

——. *René Lalique, 1860–1945: Maître-verrier. Analyse et catalogue raisonné de l'oeuvre de verre*. 4th ed. Paris: Les Éditions de l'Amateur, 2011.

Martinie, A.-H. *La Sculpture*. L'Art français depuis vingt ans. Paris: Éditions Rieder, 1928.

Martorelli, Barbara, ed. *George Barbier: The Birth of Art Deco*. Venice: Marsilio Editori, 2008.

Millot, Jacques, et al. *Pierre Legrain, relieur: Répertoire descriptif et bibliographique de mille deux cent trente-six reliures*. Paris: Librairie Auguste Blaizot, 1965.

Miralles, Francesc. *Llorens Artigas: Catalogue de l'oeuvre personnel et créations avec Dufy, Marquet, Miró*. Barcelona: Fondation Llorens Artigas; Paris: Éditions Cercle d'Art, 1993.

Mouillefarine, Laurence, and Évelyne Possémé, eds. *Art Deco Jewelry: Modernist Masterworks and Their Makers*. London: Thames and Hudson, 2009.

Mouillefarine, Laurence, and Véronique Ristelhueber. *Raymond Templier: Le Bijou moderne*. Paris: Éditions Norma, 2005.

Moussinac, Léon. *La Décoration théâtrale*. L'Art français depuis vingt ans. Paris: F. Rieder et Cie, 1922.

——. *Croquis de Ruhlmann*. Paris: Éditions Albert Lévy, 1924.

——. *Étoffes imprimées et papiers peints*. Paris: Éditions Albert Lévy, 1924.

——. *Le Meuble français moderne*. Paris: Librairie Hachette, 1925.

Musée des Arts Décoratifs, Paris. *Les Années "25": Art Déco/Bauhaus/Stijl/Esprit Nouveau*. 2 vols. Exh. cat. Paris: Union Centrale des Arts Décoratifs, 1966.

Olivier-Vial, Franck, and François Rateau. *Armand-Albert Rateau: Un Baroque chez les modernes*. Paris: Les Éditions de l'Amateur, 1992.

Ollivier, Frédéric, Aymeric Perroy, and Franck Sénant. *À bord des paquebots: 50 Ans d'arts décoratifs*. Paris: Éditions Norma, 2011.

Olmer, Pierre. *Le Mobilier français d'aujourd'hui (1910–1925)*. Paris: G. van Oest, 1926.

du Pasquier, Jacqueline. *René Buthaud*. Bordeaux: Horizon Chimérique, 1987.

Peyré, Yves, and H. George Fletcher. *Art Deco Bookbindings: The Work of Pierre Legrain and Rose Adler*. New York: The Princeton Architectural Press, in association with The New York Public Library, 2004.

Poiret, Paul. *En habillant l'époque*. Paris: B. Grasset, 1930.

——. *King of Fashion: The Autobiography of Paul Poiret*. Translated by Stephen Haden Guest. Philadelphia and London: J. B. Lippincott Company, 1931.

Quénioux, Gaston. *Les Arts décoratifs modernes (France)*. Paris: Librarie Larousse, 1925.

Raoul Dufy. Exh. cat., Hayward Gallery, London, 1983–84. London: The Arts Council of Great Britain, 1983.

Raoul Dufy, créateur d'étoffes. Exh. cat. Mulhouse: Musée de l'Impression sur Étoffes de Mulhouse, 1973.

Raoul Dufy: Le Plaisir. Exh. cat. Paris: Musée d'Art Moderne de la Ville de Paris, 2008.

Raulet, Sylvie. *Art Deco Jewelry*. New York: Rizzoli, 1985.

Répertoire du goût moderne. 5 vols. Paris: Éditions Albert Lévy, 1928–29. Reprinted in Schleuning 2008.

Report of Commission: Appointed by the Secretary of Commerce to Visit and Report upon the International Exposition of Modern Decorative and Industrial Art in Paris, 1925. Washington, D.C.: Department of Commerce, 1926.

Rosenthal, Léon. *La Verrerie française depuis cinquante ans*. Paris and Brussels: G. Vanoest, 1927.

Rudoe, Judy. *Cartier, 1900–1939*. Exh. cat., The Metropolitan Museum of Art, New York, and The British Museum, London, 1997–98. New York: Harry N. Abrams, 1997.

Saunier, Charles. *Les Décorateurs du livre*. L'Art français depuis vingt ans. Paris: F. Rieder et Cie, 1922.

Schleuning, Sarah, with Jeremy Aynsley. *Moderne: Fashioning the French Interior*. Miami Beach: Wolfsonian-Florida International University; New York: Princeton Architectural Press, 2008.

Sedeyn, Émile. *Le Mobilier*. L'Art français depuis vingt ans. Paris: F. Rieder et Cie, 1921.

Siriex, Françoise. *The House of Leleu: Classic French Style for a Modern World, 1920–1973*. Translated by Eric A. Bye. New York: Hudson Hills Press, 2008.

Süe, Louis, and André Mare. *Architectures*. Paris: Éditions de la Nouvelle Revue Française, 1921.

Troy, Nancy J. *Modernism and the Decorative Arts in France*. New Haven: Yale University Press, 1991.

Valotaire, Marcel. *La Céramique française moderne*. Paris: Les Éditions G. van Oest, 1930.

Vera, André. *Le Nouveau Jardin*. Paris: Émile-Paul, 1912.

——. "Le Nouveau Style." *L'Art décoratif* 27 (January–June 1912), pp. 21–32.

——. *Les Jardins*. Illustrations by Paul Vera. Paris: Émile-Paul Frères, 1919.

Verne, Henri, and René Chavance. *Pour comprendre l'art décoratif moderne en France*. Paris: Hachette, 1925.

Virole, Agnès. *Paul et André Vera: Tradition et modernité*. Exh. cat., Espace Paul et André Vera, Saint-Germain-en-Laye, 2008–9. Paris: Hazan; Saint-Germain-en-Laye: Ville de Saint-Germain-en-Laye, 2008.

White, Palmer. *Poiret*. New York: C. N. Potter, 1973.

Zapata-Aubé, Nicole, et al. *André Mare: Cubisme et camouflage, 1914–1918*. Exh. cat., Musée Municipal, Bernay, Arc de Triomphe à l'Étoile, Paris, and Musée Royal de l'Armée, Brussels, 1998. Bernay: Musée Municipale des Beaux-Arts, 1998.

INDEX

PHOTOGRAPH CREDITS

Nos. 1, 4, 8, 12, 13, 15a–d, 16, 17, 18, 19a–c, 20, 21a–h, 23, 17, 28–31a–b, 42, 45, 47–49, 62, 63a–d, 64a–b, 65a–b, 66, 67: © 2014 Artists Rights Society (ARS), New York / ADAGP, Paris

p. 7: Olivier-Vial 1992, p. 118

p. 18, top, bottom: Byron Company, New York, 1921, Courtesy Museum of the City of New York

p. 19, left: Julien Benhamou

p. 19, right: © RMN–Grand Palais/Art Resource, NY, Photo: Michel Urtado

p. 26: Bloch-Dermant 1991, p. 147

p. 28: Martorelli 2008, p. 15

p. 30, bottom: Nimatallah/Art Resource, NY

p. 34: Kahr 1999, p. 45

p. 39: du Pasquier 1987, p. 69

p. 46: Adélaïde Turpain

p. 47: Cazaux-Charon 1994, p. 88

p. 58: Ayroles 2006, p. 78

p. 65: © Archives Fanny Guillon-Laffaille

p. 90: © Maurice-Louis Branger/Roger-Viollet

p. 102: *Mobilier et décoration*, May 1955, p. 49

p. 105: Bachollet, Bordet, Lelieur 1982, p. 163

p. 109: *Mobilier et décoration*, Sept./Oct. 1953, p. 49

pp. 113, 114: Marcilhac 2005, pp. 256, 112

p. 124: *Céramiques de Robert Lallemant*, 1992, p. 6

p. 127: Le Chevallier, Jacques. *Jacques Le Chevallier, la lumière moderne: 1896–1987.* Montreuil: Gourcuff Gradenigo, 2007, pp. 14, 40

p. 136: © CNAC/MNAM/Dist. RMN–Grand Palais/ Art Resource, NY

p. 144: Forest 1995, p. 103

p. 147: © Fondation Llorens Artigas

p. 148: Marinot, Maurice. *Maurice Marinot: Troyes 1882–Troyes 1960, penser en verre.* Paris: Somogy; Troyes: Musée d'Art Moderne, 2010, p. 157

p. 154: *Joël et Jan Martel: Sculpteurs, 1896–1966.* 1996, pp. 84–85

p. 157: *Mobilier et décoration*, Jan. 1954, p. 34

p. 167: Chevillot 1994, p. 86

pp. 176, 197: © Ministère de la Culture/Médiathèque du Patrimoine, Dist. RMN–Grand Palais/Art Resource, NY

p. 177: Olivier-Vial 1992, p. 4

p. 202 right: © RMN–Grand Palais/Art Resource, NY

p. 206: Ayroles 2006, p. 71

p. 210: Choumoff/Roger Viollet/Getty Images

p. 211 top: Camard 1993, p. 26

p. 211 bottom: Zapata-Aubé 1998, p. 65

p. 234: © Saint-Germain-en-Laye, Musée Municipal pour Manufacture Nationale de Sèvres

p. 236: ©CNAC/MNAM/Dist. RMN–Grand Palais/ Art Resource, NY